RADICAL TRADITIONS

THEOLOGY IN A POSTCRITICAL KEY

SERIES EDITORS

Stanley M. Hauerwas, Duke University,
and Peter Ochs, University of Virginia

RADICAL TRADITIONS cuts new lines of inquiry across a confused array of debates concerning the place of theology in modernity and, more generally, the status and role of scriptural faith in contemporary life. Charged with a rejuvenated confidence, spawned in part by the rediscovery of reason as inescapably tradition constituted, a new generation of theologians and religious scholars is returning to scriptural traditions with the hope of retrieving resources long ignored, depreciated, and in many cases ideologically suppressed by modern habits of thought. RADICAL TRADITIONS assembles a promising matrix of strategies, disciplines, and lines of thought that invites Jewish, Christian, and Islamic theologians back to the word, recovering and articulating modes of scriptural reasoning as that which always underlies modernist reasoning and therefore has the capacity — and authority — to correct it.

Far from despairing over modernity's failings, postcritical theologies rediscover resources for renewal and self-correction within the disciplines of academic study themselves. Postcritical theologies open up the possibility of participating once again in the living relationship that binds together God, text, and community of interpretation. RADICAL TRADITIONS thus advocates a 'return to the text,' which means a commitment to displaying the richness and wisdom of traditions that are at once text based, hermeneutical, and oriented to communal practice.

Books in this series offer the opportunity to speak openly with practitioners of other faiths or even with those who profess no (or limited) faith, both academics and nonacademics, about the ways religious traditions address pivotal issues of the day. Unfettered by foundational-ist preoccupations, these books represent a call for new paradigms of reason — a thinking and rationality that are more responsive than originative. By embracing a postcritical posture, they are able to speak unapologetically out of scriptural traditions manifest in the practices of believing communities (Jewish, Christian, and others); articulate those practices through disciplines of philosophic, textual, and cultural criticism; and engage intellectual, social, and political practices that for too long have been insulated from theological evaluation. RADICAL TRADITIONS is radical not only in its confidence in non-apologetic theological speech but also in how the practice of such speech challenges the current social and political arrangements of modernity.

The Church in a Postliberal Age

George A. Lindbeck

Edited by

James J. Buckley

William B. Eerdmans Publishing Company
Grand Rapids, Michigan / Cambridge, U.K.

This collection © 2002 James J. Buckley
Essays © 2002 George A. Lindbeck
All rights reserved

First published 2002 in Great Britain by SCM Press
9-17 St. Albans Place, London N1 0NX

This edition published 2003 in the United States of America by
Wm. B. Eerdmans Publishing Co.
255 Jefferson Ave. S.E., Grand Rapids, Michigan 49503 /
P.O. Box 163, Cambridge CB3 9PU U.K.

Printed in the United States of America

08 07 06 05 04 03   8 7 6 5 4 3 2 1

ISBN 0-8028-3995-9

CONTENTS

PART III

POSTLIBERAL

INTRODUCTION

Radical Traditions: Evangelical, Catholic and Postliberal

James J Buckley

George Lindbeck is a Christian theologian. His books and essays generate debate not only among his fellow Lutherans but also among many other Christians as well as Jews and students of religion in the academy more generally. The goal of this anthology is to collect key samples of his enterprise, especially for readers who may know none or only a few of his books or articles. The samples may, for some, speak for themselves. For others, I have provided a brief introduction to each selection to help educated readers unfamiliar with Lindbeck understand what is at stake.

Why these particular essays? The answer to that question is inseparable from the fact that this is a book in a series on 'radical traditions', the aims of which are described by the editors in a preceding page of this volume. Why these essays in this series? Peter Ochs and Stanley Hauerwas, the editors of the series, could surely answer that question: the idea of this anthology was theirs, with the obvious permission of George Lindbeck. But the selection of essays as well as the commentary are mine alone. The goal of this introduction is not to analyze or assess Lindbeck's theology in some comprehensive way – or to speak about what some would regard as the self-contradictory notion of 'radical traditions' in general terms. The goal is more modest: to suggest how Lindbeck's Christian theology of 'the Church in a postliberal age' can be read as a 'radical tradition'. Lindbeck's Christian theology, I shall here suggest, is at once evangelical, catholic and postliberal. We shall see that this is not the only way to characterize his theology – he once called himself a 'Wittgensteinian Thomistic Lutheran'.[1] But the characterization 'evangelical, catholic and postliberal' does enable us to understand his theology as a 'radical tradition' as well as locate some of his critics.

Evangelical

I began by noting that Lindbeck is a Christian theologian. He is, more specifically, a Lutheran Christian or better, Evangelical Lutheran. He was (as he says in the autobiographical sketch in Chapter One) born of Swedish-American missionary parents in 1923 and educated in 'the possibility of an unambiguous confessional Lutheranism that was devout but not pietistic, and quite unreticent about baptismal regeneration and the real presence'. He received his college education at Gustavus Adolphus College in Minnesota – both the college and the state one of the Lutheran strongholds in the United States. He represented the Lutheran World Federation at the Roman Catholic Second Vatican Council (Vatican II), about which he reminisces in Chapter Two. He has been an Evangelical Lutheran participant in national and international dialogues with other churches (especially, we shall see, the Roman Catholic Church). Through the influence of Lutheran theologians like Kristin Skydsgaard, Peter Brunner, Edmund Schlink and Arthur Carl Piepkorn, he arrived at his theology of Lutheranism as 'a reform movement within the Catholic Church of the West'. The Lutheran movement is thus itself a paradigm – perhaps *the* paradigm – of a 'radical tradition'. It is a radical movement within a larger tradition.

This Evangelical Lutheran heritage pervades each of the essays in this volume. The theology Lindbeck does is 'Lutheran theology in the Lutheran confessional tradition', and he has written on this heritage in a variety of ways.[2] Part I has a selection of essays that address a set of diverse issues relevant to this evangelical heritage: interpretations of the theology of Martin Luther (Chapter Three), the doctrine of justification by faith alone (Chapter Four), the relations between Lutheran and Reformed Christians (Chapter Five) and the Evangelical Lutheran tradition on the salvation of non-believers (Chapter Six). It will become clear in these chapters that 'evangelical' here means centered on 'the three Reformatory "solas"' arising out of the sixteenth century Protestant Reformation: *solus Christus* (Christ alone), *sola fides* (faith alone, including *sola gratia*, grace alone) and *sola Scriptura* (Scripture alone). But these 'solas' can be used in a variety of ways. 'Evangelical' in North America connotes Christians centered on personal conversion experience of Jesus Christ, normed by a Scripture often interpreted as inerrant. Lindbeck worries that this is 'the antiecclesial, the anti- or low-sacramental and the anti- or noncreedal' evangelicalism with which his own theology, in those respects, disagrees.[3]

But we do not have to look to the evangelical tradition as a general phenomenon in North America to find diversity and conflict. The Evangelical Lutheran tradition is and always has been diverse, as the debates internal to

The Book of Concord make clear.[4] Lindbeck once distinguished five groups of Lutherans: those committed to *The Book of Concord* as a whole, like his brothers and sisters in the Missouri Synod; those (like himself) particularly committed to the 'evangelical catholicity' of the Augsburg Confession within *The Book of Concord*; those who gave a priority to Luther's theology over *The Book of Concord*; and those who gave priority to 'experiential' or 'service-oriented' perspectives over any of the previous three.[5] Lindbeck did not intend this as an all-purpose typology. But it does invite readers to keep an ear out for these background debates in the essays below. A radical tradition is not always a peaceful one – although a messianically Jesus-centered radical tradition (a tradition for whom Jesus is Christ or Messiah) will be 'peaceable'.

Catholic

As the previous paragraph suggests, one argument among Evangelical Lutherans is how to relate themselves to the 'one, holy, catholic and apostolic Church' of Christian creeds. The claim that evangelical theology is a reform movement within the Church catholic makes for a theology at once 'evangelical and catholic'. How, then, does a radical tradition navigate its journey with other Christians, including those with whom it disagrees, when it moves within that tradition? The Christian 'ecumenical' movement has provided one answer to this question – the journey is an 'ecumenical' (that is, worldwide) movement toward visible Christian unity. Lindbeck has written a great deal on this movement in general terms.[6] Chapter Seven (Ecumenism and the Future of Belief) is one example. But most of the selections I have chosen for this volume are case studies in particular traditions – cases where an evangelical catholic or radical tradition can contribute to reconciling opposed practices and teachings within that tradition. Chapter Five (on the Lutheran and Reformed traditions) and Chapter Eight (on the Orthodox tradition) are samples of how Lindbeck proceeds in these two cases.

Most of Lindbeck's writing on Christian ecumenism has been on Roman Catholic life and thought. He has long been a student of Roman Catholicism, ever since his graduate days at Yale University. Indeed, he was originally and remains a student of medieval philosophy and theology, writing a dissertation on the late medieval theologian Duns Scotus and teaching courses in medieval philosophy and theology as well as leading seminars in Augustine and Luther. The periodic allusions to Aquinas in the essays included here are the tip of a deeper iceberg.[7] His Lutheran 'evangelicalism', we might say, is a radical movement within this Augustinian-Thomist 'catholicism'.

This (along with his experience at Vatican II and over a quarter of a century's involvement in Lutheran–Catholic dialogues) gives him an entry to the Catholic tradition that few Catholics own – and I speak here as a Roman Catholic. For example, Lindbeck's *The Future of Roman Catholic Theology*, his first book, interpreted Vatican II as a 'radical tradition' of sorts, although this Council does not wear its radical tradition on its sleeves. In fact, Lindbeck notes many places where the Council seems simply to reiterate the old Christian tradition or the new 'western liberal consensus'. Thus, 'like all traditional events it [Vatican II] is an amalgam of the new and the old'. Lindbeck names 'the old' here the 'Christianized classical' view that separates God and our world (supernatural grace and nature) in ways that focus on the salvation of individual souls in unchanging ways. But 'the new' is not – or not always – the modern. Vatican II's new vision is instead called a 'realistically futuristic' eschatology – 'eschatology' because it is centered on the new heaven and new earth God is preparing for the eschaton (God's 'last thing', end or goal for the world); 'futurist' because this eschaton bears on our future personal, social, historical and natural world; 'realist' because it pertains to a God and a world independent of our personal or communal attitudes toward that world or that God. Eschatology and futurology remain essential to Lindbeck's radical tradition, as several of the essays below will testify. But the key point here is that Lindbeck proposes that, under Vatican II's new eschatological vision, 'positions which have been traditionally opposed [between Roman Catholicism and the Reformation] now appear to be complementary aspects of a fuller grasp of Christian truth'. I begin Part II of this anthology with an essay on 'Ecumenism and the Future of Belief' (Chapter Seven) precisely to emphasize the enduring importance of eschatology for Lindbeck's reconsideration of evangelical and catholic disputes.

The Future of Roman Catholic Theology gives many examples of how opposed beliefs might be reconciled – Vatican II's reform of the liturgy, of the structures of the Church and of its way of thinking about the Word of God in Scripture and tradition.[8] But the example I have chosen in Chapter Nine is one often thought, in both Evangelical and Catholic churches, to be an insuperable opposition: the Catholic teaching that papal definitions are, under certain conditions, infallible as opposed to the Evangelical denial of that teaching. Here is a doctrine – further described in the introduction to Chapter Nine – that can be traditionalist at one moment (marking places in the tradition beyond radical transformation) and radical the next (endorsing radical changes that seem to change the tradition into something else). This 'hypertrophied infallibalism' (as Lindbeck calls it in Chapter Nine) hardly seems to be the claim of a coherent 'radical tradition'. Yet Lindbeck's analysis of the post-Vatican II Roman Catholic debate over this issue tries to show how a Church catholic can extract a 'cancer' without destroying the body.

In sum, the Church in all its reconciled diversity is a radical tradition at once evangelical and catholic. It is a reform movement within a comprehensive tradition as it seeks to reconcile the conflicts of that tradition. Chapter Ten makes this climactic point with its 'ecumenically mandated' vision of the Church as 'the messianic pilgrim people of God typologically shaped by Israel's story'.

Postliberal

The Evangelical tradition (I have said) is a radical movement within the Catholic tradition, reconciling its oppositions in the light of God's future. But this radical tradition, evangelical and catholic, lives in a larger world – a world variously friendly and hostile and indifferent to it. How, then, does this church live in this world? Beyond being a theologian of a sort at once evangelical and catholic, Lindbeck practices a theology deeply attentive to the joys and griefs of our world in a way that claims that world for the Church, Jesus Christ and the triune God. Lindbeck's initial autobiography hints at this 'worldly' character of this theology – his birth (1923) and youth in Loyang, China; his education in the United States, including (I would add) a stint teaching for the army at the end of World War II; the time spent in France, Germany, Rome and elsewhere. But this world is far from a single, homogeneous thing. It is a world of particular cultures, languages, religions and people. 'Radical traditions' are themselves always particular – but an evangelical catholic tradition also aspires to think about, describe and interact with other cultural, linguistic and religious traditions in their particularity.

A theology of a particular community with a universal mission (and the label 'postliberal') emerges most clearly in *The Nature of Doctrine: Religion and Theology in a Postliberal Age* (1984). This book was originally written as a contribution to the problem of reconciling conflicting doctrines among Christian churches and an introduction to a larger work in 'comparative dogmatics' (i.e. a proposal of what the Church ought to teach on a range of matters, based on broad and deep comparison of evangelical and catholic churches). But *The Nature of Doctrine* also uses elements of cultural anthropology (Clifford Geertz), social theory (Peter Berger), the linguistic turn in philosophy (Ludwig Wittgenstein) and critical philosophy of religion (William A Christian, Sr) to sum up a view of culture, religion and language Lindbeck calls 'cultural-linguistic'. Pressed to summarize in a sentence what Chapter Eleven describes in more detail, I would say that this cultural-linguistic view is an extended reflection on an analogy – on the way cultures and religions are analogous to languages, and languages are embedded in the forms of life of diverse and particular cultures and religions. Readers will find that the essays in this volume constantly attend to the particularity and singularity of the cultures and religions and languages that shape us at the very core of our being – whether it be the evangelical movement in Part I, the catholic Church of Part II or the essays gathered under the rubric 'postliberal' in Part III.

Lindbeck's ecumenical (evangelical catholic) vision makes use of this cultural-linguistic view to propose what he calls in Chapter Eleven a 'postliberal theology' – a postliberal theology for 'the postliberal age' mentioned in the subtitle of *The Nature of Doctrine*. 'Liberal' here characterizes a very specific position, namely a position that espouses a theory of religion as the bearer of common human experiences and a theory of doctrine as expressions of those experiences. Lindbeck contrasts this 'liberal' position with a 'preliberal' position that treats religions as doctrines and doctrines as sets of true propositions. I say more about these three views – preliberal, liberal and postliberal – in the introduction to Chapter Eleven. But 'postliberal theology' (Lindbeck has said) is less a community of people with a single set of things to be believed and accomplished than a collection of individuals engaged in 'a research program'.[9]

The Nature of Doctrine generated a debate that included theologians and non-theologians. Many were indifferent or even hostile to the quest for visible unity among Christians central to Lindbeck's radical, evangelical catholic tradition.[10] Even further, as Lindbeck notes in the preface to the German translation (Chapter Twelve), the debate that occurred over *The Nature of Doctrine* took place more over the 'cultural-linguistic' theory of religion and doctrine than over the 'ecumenical (evangelical and catholic) theology' in whose service Lindbeck originally conscripted the cultural-linguistic theory. This was ironic, for the theory of religion and doctrine was intended to be (Lindbeck says) 'ad hoc and unsystematic' – as Augustine had used Plato, Aquinas had mined Aristotle, Barth had plundered Kant and Hegel, and as ordinary Christians have often made use of the world in which they live. The misreading of *The Nature of Doctrine* (Lindbeck speculates) was perhaps because the ecumenical movement had turned from the problem of reconciling conflicting evangelical catholic doctrines to what was sometimes called 'the wider ecumenism' of the common struggle for justice, freedom and the conservation of creation. It was also perhaps because the situation among the theologians, philosophers, students of the bible and church history and cultural theorists who debated the cultural linguistic theory was stalemated between those on the right who presumed that a culturally relevant cultural-linguistic theory must be heterodox and those on the left who presumed that claims to ecumenical orthodoxy must be culturally irrelevant.[11]

In any case, Lindbeck's writing since *The Nature of Doctrine* both applies and extends this postliberal theology. Chapter Thirteen on Scripture and the Church describes what the theory and practice of Scripture and Church might look like as well as what blocks their enactment today – a description at once evangelical, catholic and postliberal. But, as Lindbeck says in the autobiographical sketch in Chapter One, his current interest is in developing an Israel-like view of the Church. This is not an abandonment of *The Nature of Doctrine*'s promise of a comparative dogmatics but 'a comparative dogmatics in another form' than originally envisaged. It 'begins with ecclesiology and, included therein, with a christologically developed "Israel-ology" (Rom. 15.8)'[12] – what the autobiographical remarks in Chapter One calls 'an Israel-like view of the church'. Why?

Central to Lindbeck's evangelical catholic tradition is the claim that the particular Jew Jesus is Messiah. This claim, we might say, is the 'radicalization' of the claim that God has freely chosen in steadfast love the particular people, Israel, to be a blessing unto the nations – here, in Jesus, that messianic tradition reaches its promised goal. If Jesus is Israel now faithful to God's covenant, God's Word become flesh for us all, then it is time to form and sustain a community of Jews *and* Gentiles. However, more often than not, Christians have lived and thought as if they were a replacement for Israel rather than an extension of Israel to the Gentiles. A tradition, culture, religion or language that replaces another (rather than, say, 'fulfills' or 'perfects' it) is no longer a 'radical tradition' but something else – something more 'radical' than 'traditional'. Indeed, Lindbeck suggests in Chapter One that the schism between evangelicals and catholics could be rooted in their common misunderstanding and mistreatment of their common Jewish heritage. The first step, then, of a Church in service of a postliberal world is recovering its relationship with the Jewish people. Only this way can we learn to live in the world for the world without becoming that world.

The first two chapters of this book develop the important theme of Lindbeck's theology that the evangelical catholic Church does not exist for its own sake. The final selection in this volume is devoted to expanding it even further. Like Israel, the Church 'is called to serve other religions for the sake of the neighbor, for the sake of humanity, for the sake of God's promise to Abraham that through his seed all nations will be blessed'. *The Church in a Postliberal Age* (the title of this collection of essays) exists *for* that age and thus is the body of the Lord who serves us, each and all. The deep ties of this moment of Lindbeck's theology to the Jewish tradition is one reason for the significant response to Lindbeck's work among Jewish thinkers.[13] This response is evidence for thinking that, while a 'postliberal' radical tradition may not be as ancient a radical tradition as an evangelical catholic one, it may indeed be a promising tradition for Jew and Gentile.

The Church in a postliberal age?

(How) do the elements of this characterization – evangelical, catholic and postliberal – fit together? If I am right, each of them is a radical tradition in its own way, suggesting why these essays belong in a series on radical traditions (in the plural). But (how) do they fit together? This is a question this volume can raise and address but not fully answer.

A reader's answer to this question will partly depend on whether or not he or she addresses it on something like Lindbeck's own terms. On this score, I would emphasize that nothing much hangs on the particular words – evangelical, catholic and postliberal – I have used to characterize Lindbeck's Christian theology. This is partly because the characterization as well as the selection of readings are mine rather than Lindbeck's. While I hope that Lindbeck welcomes this characterization and selection as an interpretation suitable for the purposes I have here, I am (to repeat) not pretending or intending to offer a comprehensive interpretation. As I mentioned earlier, Lindbeck once called himself a 'Wittgensteinian Thomistic Lutheran' – Thomas Aquinas (1225–75) and Martin Luther (1483–1546), the two theologians with whom he is most in conversation and Ludwig Wittgenstein (1889–1951), the Austrian-British philosopher of languages and forms of life. A collection of essays for a more strictly academic audience might devote itself to more essays on Luther and Lutheranism, Aquinas and Thomism, Wittgenstein and post-whatevers than I have done here. Ideally, I think, such an alternative anthology would also include some of the classic texts from the tradition that have shaped his theology, for Lindbeck's is not the theology of the isolated theologian whose writings move outside tradition and traditions but a theology whose writings are always partly glosses and commentaries on his reading of other writings in that tradition and those traditions. In any case, readers who wish to ask about whether these traditions fit together on Lindbeck's own terms are going to have to ask about more than the terms 'evangelical', 'catholic' and 'postliberal'. They are going to have to figure out a way to understand these traditions – evangelical (something like Luther), catholic (something like Aquinas) and postliberal (something like Wittgenstein) – in such a way that they 'know how to go on' from them and how to apply them to their own distinctive circumstances.

Despite such limits on characterizing this radical tradition as evangelical and catholic and postliberal, I do hope that this threefold way of characterizing Lindbeck's theology can help readers not only understand Lindbeck's theology but also locate some of Lindbeck's critics. It will help readers understand his theology if they remembers that each of the three parts – evangelical, catholic and postliberal – are inseparable from the others. The essays below on Evangelical identity are inseparable from the dialogue and debate with (other) Catholics. For example, the essay on justification in Part I (Chapter Four) is inseparable from the theology of the Church in Part II (Chapter Ten). Again, the essays below on postliberal theology in Part III are inseparable from Parts I and II. For example, Chapter Three's reading of Luther is tied closely to the postliberal Christian theology of Israel in Chapter Thirteen; the re-interpretation of infallibility in Part II (Chapter Nine) is inseparable from the cultural-linguistic anthropology used in Part III (Chapter Eleven).

With regard to critics, we might describe them by which of the three strands they share and which they criticize. First, in relation to what I have called the evangelical strand of Lindbeck's theology, we might recall critics within Lindbeck's evangelical movement. There are critics from the Reformed tradition, which Lindbeck writes about in Chapter Five, although these criticisms thus far relate more to the postliberal than evangelical Lutheran strand of Lindbeck's theology.[14] There are also critics within Lindbeck's Lutheran Church. Here I think not of all the various types of evangelical Lutherans I mentioned above (important as they are) but critics within Lindbeck's own argument for Lutheran evangelical catholicity. For example, Robert Jenson, while largely agreeing with Lindbeck's evangelical catholic traditions, disagrees with Lindbeck's theory of doctrine as well as the doctrinal limits Lindbeck places on theologies of the trinity. Reinhard Hütter, again sympathetic to Lindbeck's evangelical catholic project, thinks that Lindbeck's formal, theologically neutral 'cultural-linguistic theory' cannot account for the concrete Church practice Lindbeck rightly seeks to describe, create and encourage. Bruce Marshall has offered a defense of Lindbeck on issues of doctrine, precisely by interpreting him in the light of Thomas – all the while taking Lindbeck's radical traditions into the very trinitarian theology Lindbeck does not develop.[15]

The problems of those who share Lindbeck's evangelical catholicity will be different from those who do not. For example, in relation to the catholic strand of Lindbeck's theology, the Anglo-Catholic John Milbank worries that Lindbeck's 'metanarrative realism' needs to have more ontological depth and political breadth as well as more suspicion of the social sciences than Lindbeck's postliberal (cultural-linguistic) theory or practice can provide. Milbank seems to have many old-fashioned Catholic suspicions of evangelical theology. Lindbeck, we have seen, is often critical of his fellow evangelicals who aim to replace the Catholic tradition rather than reform it. But Milbank is not clear on the role of 'evangelical catholicity' – a post-Constantinian evangelical theology, as we might call it – in his Catholic Church. It is unclear where Milbank stands on many of the elements of an evangelical catholic theology with which Lindbeck is concerned (e.g. the doctrine of justification; ecclesiology). But Milbank's 'radical orthodoxy' is clearly more sympathetic to Lindbeck's radical traditions than are standard 'conservative' or 'liberal' Catholics.[16]

On the third and postliberal strand of of Lindbeck's theology, the 'liberal' Protestant theologian Gordan Kaufman largely agrees with the cultural-linguistic theory of religion and doctrine, but disagrees with putting it 'so exclusively into the service of the theologically conservative enterprise of ecumenical debate'. The liberal Catholic David Tracy charges that the cultural-linguistic theory is something like a guise for 'the voice of Karl Barth'. Here the worry is that 'postliberal' really means 'conservative' (not liberal) or 'evangelical' (not catholic). But Kaufman and Tracy, for all their differences, seem to presume that an evangelical catholic tradition cannot be radical; in other words, they presume that, unless the postliberal strand dominates the other two, we will have simply a new (evangelical catholic) traditionalism.[17] It is precisely this presumption with which Lindbeck disagrees.

My goal is not to sort out the wheat from the chaff in such criticisms. I think that characterizing Lindbeck's theology as evangelical, catholic and postliberal not only provides a way of understanding his theology but also provides a starting point for understanding arguments over it. We can understand such critics as variously criticizing one or two or all three strands of that theology; the more all three strands are taken into account, the greater the chance the criticisms will be on Lindbeck's own terms rather than some other terms.

I have so far proposed that 'evangelical, catholic and postliberal', while not a comprehensive characterization of Lindbeck's theology, is useful for understanding some of the debates over it, including the way some critics only focus on one or two of its strands. But more important than understanding this theology's radical traditions is participating in them. The question of how an evangelical, catholic and postliberal theology fits together is not only or primarily an intellectualist question, even though my citing of an entirely academic tribe of critics in the previous paragraphs might give this impression. It is a question of participating in such traditions – where 'participation' includes being shaped by as well as shaping such traditions. Radical traditions need children and students, parents who work in homes as well as those who go to the marketplace, the voting booth, the corporate board room, the hospital and the court room. A radical tradition is, from this point of view, a matter of practice – here, the practices of those involved in making the preaching and sacramental life, creating and maintaining local as well as more universal communities, ordaining officers to those communities who lead by service and therefore without the insolence of office, equipping a community to recognize and serve the naked and the hungry and the homeless in practical ways, and so forth.

The introductions to each of the following essays were written with an audience of educated readers in mind – readers who seek not only to understand but also to participate in radical traditions. Such readers may not be as interested in the question of whether the three strands cohere as in whether any one of them helps us understand how to be shaped by and shape such radical traditions. From this point of view, there is no need to strain to find some single way in which these radical traditions constitute a single position. This, in turn, means that some of the essays will be easily accessible to educated readers who are not theologians, while others will require more work. I have tried to help such readers in three ways. First, there are shorter or longer introductions to each essay that aim to set a context and suggest interrelations between the chapters. The longer the introduction, the more I thought such readers needed a longer commentary. However, I have tried to resist the temptation to turn these commentaries into an idiosyncratic interpretation. Second, within each essay I have translated the Latin and other foreign words or phrases Lindbeck periodically uses, and also briefly described some of the technical terms he uses or events to which he alludes. But I have not aimed to annotate every historical event to which he alludes or every Christian doctrine or practice he mentions. Different readers will be stretched by different things these essays presume. Third, at the conclusion of most of the essays, I list some of Lindbeck's other essays as possible further reading on that topic. Readers interested in still further reading can consult Bruce Marshall's, Markus Müller's, Reinhard Hütter's and Andreas Eckerstorfer's bibliographies.[18]

Thus far I have proposed that characterizing Lindbeck's theology as a 'radical tradition' at once evangelical, catholic and postliberal can help us understand it as well as the debates over it; that understanding it and these debates is not as important as participating in these radical traditions – figuring out how to use it in particular cultures and local churches as well as in the Christian *internationale* – learning 'how to go on', one step at a time. But understanding and participating in this radical tradition is not enough. As Chapter Eleven makes clear, a postliberal theology must raise questions not only of intelligibility and applicability but also of 'faithfulness' – its own as well as others'. How we can be faithful to a 'radical tradition'? This is a large question, raising philosophical questions about being and becoming as well as practical pastoral and political questions about how to change a church without turning it into something else. But this question is centrally not about us, our philosophies or our pastoral plans. It is centrally a question about God – about a particular God who intends to save us all through a particular messianic people, now Jew and Greek. We might say that this people is God's radical tradition in the world, for the world, whose unsurpassable climax is the Jew Jesus whose spirit is now making us into a new heaven and earth. Faithfulness to this radical tradition is faithfulness to this God, whose patience with our failures is quite beyond human imagining and who shepherds us beyond our wants, from death into life.[19]

1. Confession and Community: An Israel-like View of the Church*

Editor's Introduction

The Christian Century for many years published essays by noteworthy theologians on 'how my mind has changed'. Lindbeck's account of how his mind has changed begins with his birth in China and ends with his current interest in developing 'an Israel-like view of the Church'. In between he discusses his graduate education and teaching at Yale University, his participation as one of the Delegated Observers at the Second Vatican Council, his theology of Lutheranism as a reform movement within the Catholic Church, his conception of modernity as 'just one epoch and culture among others, in some ways better and in some ways worse'. These are each central features of one or more of the subsequent essays in this volume. Readers may wish to keep an eye out for them.

However, it would also be valuable not to exaggerate the importance of this autobiographical sketch for Lindbeck's theology. For example, autobiography as practised here is the way he has been cumulatively shaped by the communities he has been in and around – Protestant, Catholic, Jewish, premodern Chinese and modern American and European. There is (Lindbeck suggests) no autobiographical 'I' unshaped by such particular communities over a course of time – the 'I' who is the cause and effect of what Lindbeck here calls 'individualistic foundational rationalism', or what he will later call 'experiential expressivism' (Chapter Ten). He also suggests that there is a sense that we may never, in this life, fully recover that which 'lies deepest'. Why, readers might ask, can this be accepted

* George A Lindbeck, 'Confession and Community: An Israel-like View of the Church', *The Christian Century* **107** (6 May 1990), pp. 492–6.

without anxiety? The clue to the answer to this question is found in Chapter Four, on justification by faith.

I picture the process of change in my theological thinking in both archaeological and architectural terms: I have dug down into earlier layers of experience, and built on what went before. In my childhood and youth, I encountered cultural and religious groups other than my own; later I would engage them theologically, in reverse order. The Chinese were the first I knew as different, then Jews, Roman Catholics and non-Lutheran Protestants, in that sequence. The latter engaged my theological attention first, and then the Roman Catholics and Jews. The Chinese I have yet to examine theologically, and now that I am in my 60s, perhaps I never will. Their tacit influence on my thinking, however, lies deepest and it is only gradually that I have become aware of how pervasive it has been.

I was born in north central China, far from port cities and displays of western power, and lived there for 17 years until shortly before Pearl Harbor. Because of illness I did not go away to boarding school until I was 12, and my life was very different from the standard accounts of many Americans who grew up in the Far East, such as John Hersey. My parents were Swedish-American Lutheran missionaries who were more Sinicized than they realized. They contributed more than they knew to my childhood sense that the Chinese are the most intelligent, handsome and, at their Confucian best, cultivated of all peoples. To be sure – so my parents thought – they needed Christianity in order to make democracy work and escape communism, as well as for their souls' salvation, but that belief did not make me suppose that westerners are superior. I came to think that apostate Christians were much worse than non-Christian Chinese, as the Nazis were proving. Thus China laid the groundwork for a disenchantment with Christendom that led me 30 years later to hope for the end of cultural Christianity as the enabling condition for the development of a diaspora Christianity. (Some articles I wrote in the 1960s and 1970s seem to me close to Stanley Hauerwas's position, but since then I have had reluctant second thoughts.)

Loyang, the city in which I was born and reared, was without electricity, running water, motorized transportation or even radios. The ways in which our neighbors lived and thought were as unmodern as those of the Han dynasty 2,000 years before. Further, famines, pestilences, brigandage and war (both civil and with the Japanese) engulfed our area repeatedly, and flight to safer places for short or long periods was common. Yet the processes and perceptions of life, I later came to think, were not greatly different from an American suburb, medieval ghetto or first-century Hellenistic household.

As I grew older I concluded that modernity is not unique in either its goodness or badness, but is just one epoch and culture among others, in some ways better and in some ways worse. Those who thought otherwise I found pretentious, including most of the writers of the past 400 years whose works were staple fare in my student days in Minnesota, Connecticut and France. Descartes, Hegel, Nietzsche, Heidegger, Sartre and Bultmann I found unappealing. Instead, I favored an unlikely combination of, on the one hand, medieval thinkers and their contemporary interpreters such as Maritain and Gilson, and, on the other, the Reformers and their neo-Orthodox successors (who were fashionable) and confessional Lutherans (who were not). The only recent theologians I would now add to this list of major influences are Roman Catholics such as Rahner and von Balthasar. On the non-theological side I gained a new dimension in the 1960s from Wittgensteinians, T S Kuhn, Peter Berger, Clifford Geertz and contemporary non-foundationalists. Whatever their differences, they are not bewitched by modern uniqueness: they hold that the basic processes of the linguistic, social and cognitive construction of reality and experience are much the same in all times and places, however varied the outcomes. One need not grow up in China to find such views persuasive, but in my case it helped.

The dichotomy I perceived between Chinese and non-Chinese was soon overlaid by a more salient trichotomy among Christians, non-Christians and Jews. By the time I was six or so, I saw these as the three basic types of human beings. That I would have noticed Jews is odd, for I had never, as far as I knew, met any, and my parents, products of the rural Midwest, probably hadn't either. The Old Testament, however, was as much a part of my upbringing as the New, and I early learned to think of the Jews as Jesus' people. Some of them, furthermore, had once lived in our part of China, and my father was fascinated by the remains of their T'ang dynasty settlements. Now other Jews from other parts of the world were returning to the Holy Land, as the Bible foretold. By 11, I was imaginatively a Darbyite Zionist daydreaming of becoming a kibbutz fighter. The rise of Nazism first made me aware of antisemitism. Some of the German missionaries we knew were at first pro-Hitler. Refugees began arriving in China, and two Jewish boys were members of my high school graduating class of 20.

My premillennialist philo-Semitism did not survive adolescence, but the aftereffects persisted. I was conditioned against Marcionite tendencies – evident in some post-Reformation Lutheranism – to spiritualize and privatize Christianity and neglect the Old Testament. I was also predisposed to welcome, at a much later date, the work of my Yale colleagues Brevard Childs and Hans Frei on canonical reading and on narrative and figural scriptural interpretation, respectively. More and more I have come to think that only the postcritical retrieval of such classic premodern hermeneutical strategies can give due weight to the abiding importance of Israel (including contemporary Judaism) and Israel's scriptures for Christians. This development in my thinking started late, beginning in the 1970s, and first entered my published work in *The Nature of Doctrine* (1984). Now I am writing an ecclesiology that is in large part an 'Israel-ology'.

In contrast to my literary encounter with Jews, I knew Roman Catholics personally before I learned they were different. They were cousins, children of my mother's brother, whom we visited when on furlough in the States. Only gradually did I realize that theirs was the church that had persecuted Luther, slaughtered the innocents of whom I read in Foxe's *Book of Martyrs*, and supposedly taught that salvation was by works, not faith. I hoped that they trusted Jesus and not the Pope's rules and regulations, but believed their chances of salvation would certainly be greater if they were Bible-believing Protestants.

The sad state of the Catholics troubled me in childhood, but not until I was in college did this concern translate into a theological and philosophical interest prompted by reading Gilson and Maritain. That interest led to doctoral work in medieval philosophy and theology as preparation for specialization in contemporary Catholicism. After ten years of teaching medieval thought at Yale (mostly in the philosophy department), I was selected by the Lutheran World Federation to be a delegated observer to the Second Vatican Council (1962–5), and since then have done most of my research and writing in the context of participation in national and international ecumenical dialogue, mostly with Roman Catholics. It is the ecumenical movement even more than my teaching at Yale (since Vatican II, all in the divinity school and the department of religious studies) that has been the context of my thinking.

My ecumenical concerns have been tilted in a Catholic direction. Under the influence of three European Lutherans, Kristin Skydsgaard, Peter Brunner and Edmund Schlink, and one American, Arthur Carl Piepkorn, I came to think that Lutheranism should try to become what it started out to be, a reform movement within the Catholic Church of the West. By such a strategy it can best contribute to the goal of wider Christian unity. This goal and strategy have guided almost all my work since then, though my notions of appropriate and feasible tactics have been changing in the past decade.

My turn away from developments in post-Reformation Protestantism started in midadolescence, years before my tilt toward Rome. In my early years I made no distinction between Lutherans and other Protestants. In order to maintain as much of a common Christian front as possible, American Lutherans in China, including my parents, did not advertise their confessional and sacramental differences from those to whom they were closest,

Protestant conservative evangelicals (or 'evangelicalists', as some Europeans call them). This was easy for them, for they were for the most part pietists of biblicistic and conversionist proclivities, but it confused me. Their pietism, which I confused with Lutheranism, early made me restive, not least because of my precocious reading of *Britannica* articles on evolution and Gibbon's *Decline and Fall* (my father's library was short on comic books). My restiveness was increased by memorizing Luther's *Small Catechism* for confirmation, and by arguments in boarding school with, for example, Southern Baptist classmates about such matters as infant baptism. Obviously Lutherans were different from other Protestants (that was a relief), but I still did not know what they were: I was looking for an identity.

That was provided in my sophomore and junior years by a new headmaster, Pastor Albue, a bright, personable and athletic young missionary, the idol of the high school students. He alerted me to the possibility of an unambiguously confessional Lutheranism that was devout but not pietistic, and quite unreticent about baptismal regeneration and the real presence. Others whom I came to know during the same period pointed in the same direction, most notably the Norwegian missionary scholar K L Reichelt, suspected of heresy by evangelicals because of his immense knowledge of and respect for Buddhism, but remembered by me for his Lutheran preaching.

Through such influences, I began to opt for a Reformation Christianity self-consciously opposed to modern Protestantism in both its conservative and liberal forms. Its starting point is neither biblicistic nor experientialist, and certainly not individualistic, but dogmatic: it commences with the historic Christian communal confession of faith in Christ. For the Reformers, as for the Orthodox and Catholic Churches of East and West, that confession is the one expressed in the ancient trinitarian and christological creeds. The Reformers did not so much try to prove these creeds from Scripture (and certainly not from experience), but rather read Scripture in their light, and then used the Bible thus construed to mold experience and guide thought and action. God's word, in their premodern hermeneutics, was ever applicable, and changed in import with the circumstances. It was not constrained to a single kind of meaning by inerrantist theories of inspiration or liberal ones of revelatory experience. My understanding of the implications of beginning with dogma has developed greatly (see *The Nature of Doctrine*), but not the creedal and confessional starting point. That has remained the integrating center of my later theological work.

Although I early defined myself theologically in opposition to modern Protestantism (rather than in dialogue, as with Roman Catholicism, Judaism and China), I have constantly been preoccupied with Protestants. I have lived with conservative Protestants in my youth, and liberal ones ever since

I arrived at Yale as a student over 40 years ago. I keep hoping that evangelicals will not think my work compromises their emphases on the love of Jesus and on biblical authority, and that liberals will not suppose it is inconsistent with intellectual openness or commitment to peace and justice. The desire to communicate affects theology, and changes I have perceived in the climate of discourse have affected my thinking in recent years.

The most important change for my work in the past 20 years is the increasing polarization between the modern right and left in both Protestantism and Catholicism, and the corresponding decline of a center rooted in premodern communal traditions. That center had been constituted by the Protestant neo-orthodoxy and Catholic *nouvelle théologie*, which were ascending from the 1920s to the 1960s. They had sought renewal in the light of contemporary needs by critically returning to the sources of the faith in Scripture and premodern tradition. They failed, on the whole, to escape the limitations of modern historical criticism and, with partial exceptions, did not retrieve premodern classic hermeneutics. Yet they provided the context for the flourishing in Protestantism and Catholicism of the unitive ecumenism that has been my life's work.

Now, however, interest has shifted more and more to unmediated *aggiornamento*, the updating of faith and practice by direct translation into presumably more intelligible and relevant modern idioms and actions. This is a revival of the liberal strategy, familiar since the Enlightenment, of letting the world set the Church's agenda. What is different is chiefly the agenda and the tactics, for the world has changed. The dechristianization of the public realm proceeds apace, and communal traditions have weakened. The ecumenical focus has shifted from church unity, from reconciling the historic communities, to the service of the world, and therefore away from the kind of ecumenism that has been my chief concern. The new left is more extreme than the old, and is stronger in the historically mainline churches than ever before.

The extremism and the strength of the right is also increasing. Rightists also are unconcerned with church unity and community or with *ressourcement*. They emphasize not the critical retrieval of the sources of the faith but recent traditions formed in earlier modern contexts. Roman Catholic traditionalists cling to a 19th-century version of Tridentism and, judging by Archbishop Marcel Lefebvre and his followers, are more schismatic than the progressives. Protestant evangelicals are also fixated on the 19th century and are systematically antiecumenical. After the interlude between the 1920s and 1960s, the polarization between right and left characteristic of modern mass societies is on the rise and swamping the churches as never before.

Others share this picture of the present situation, but I find it less depressing than most for both non-theological and theological reasons. The four centuries of modernity are coming to an end. Its individualistic foundational rationalism, always wavering between skeptical relativism and totalitarian absolutism, is being replaced, as I earlier mentioned, by an understanding of knowledge and belief as socially and linguistically constituted. Ideologies rooted in Enlightenment rationalism are collapsing. This is unmistakably true of the leftist ones after the *annus mirabilis* 1989, but it is also true of liberal democratic capitalism on the right. Politically pragmatic liberalism may be practically necessary in pluralistic societies, but as an individualistic secular ideology it is no more viable in the long run than its illiberal counterparts. Societies need strong mediating communities through which traditions of personal virtue, common good and ultimate meaning are transmitted to new generations. It is hard to see how such communities can flourish without a religious dimension, and in traditionally Christian lands, that means a Christian one.

I once welcomed the passing of Christendom and found Richard John Neuhaus's demurrers misplaced; but now, as I earlier mentioned, I am having uncomfortable second thoughts. The waning of cultural Christianity might be good for the churches, but what about society? To my chagrin, I find myself thinking that traditionally Christian lands when stripped of their historic faith are worse than others. They become unworkable or demonic. There is no reason to suppose that what happened in Nazi Germany cannot happen in liberal democracies, though the devils will no doubt be disguised very differently. From this point of view, the Christianization of culture can be in some situations the churches' major contribution to feeding the poor, clothing the hungry and liberating the imprisoned. So it was in the past and, given the disintegration of modern ideologies, so it may be at times in the future. Talk of 'Christian America' and John Paul II's vision of a 'Christian Europe' make me uncomfortable, but I have seen a number of totally unexpected improbabilities come to pass in my lifetime, such as Roman Catholic transformations and communism's collapse, and cannot rule these out as impossible.

Whether or not re-Christianization occurs, however, our era is a new one, and the churches are in the midst of a vast transformation. My understanding of what is needed has developed in three interrelated directions in the past decade: hermeneutical, organizational and ecclesiological. Renewal depends, I have come to think, on the spread of proficiency in premodern yet postcritical Bible reading, on restructuring the churches into something like pre-Constantinian organizational patterns, and on the development of an Israel-like understanding of the Church.

These elements belong together. For classic hermeneutics, the Hebrew

Bible is the basic ecclesiological textbook. Christians see themselves within those texts, when read in the light of Christ, as God's people, chosen for service not preferment, and bound together in a historically and sociologically continuous community that God refuses to disown whether it is faithful or unfaithful, united or disunited, in the catacombs or on the throne. It was in some such way as this that the Christians of the first centuries, whom we call catholic, used Israel's story as a template for their own existence. It was they, not the Marcionite or gnostic Christians, who developed a communal life strong enough to become the great majority and win the Empire, despite their lack of social, economic, intellectual, political or military power.

They were also, however, supersessionists who claimed to have replaced Israel, thus denying that the Jews were any longer, except negatively, God's chosen people; and they were triumphalists who believed that the Church could not be unfaithful as Israel had been. The logic of Christian faith thereby became perversely opposed in a variety of ways to the fundamental belief in Jesus as the crucified Messiah. It has taken the disasters of Christian apostasy, often disguised as orthodoxy, in combination with historical-critical work to unmask the problems. We can now see that the early Christian errors resulted from self-serving gentile Christian misappropriations of intra-Jewish polemics over Jesus' messiahship, and that these errors are blatantly opposed to much of the New Testament witness, especially Paul's. But if these errors are rejected, so I have come to think, Christians can now apply Israel's story to themselves without supersessionism or triumphalism. The story's power is undiminished. 'Oneness in Christ' gains a concrete specificity that it otherwise lacks. All Christians, whether Catholics Protestants and Orthodox or African, American and Chinese, belong to a single community of morally imperative responsibility for one another like the members of the early church or contemporary Jews.

These are the issues with which I am now struggling. I think I can show that none of the major Christian traditions is dogmatically opposed to an Israel-like view of the Church, but acceptance of it involves a break with nearly 2,000 years of both modern and premodern Christian self-understandings. Unitive ecumenism, among other things, needs to be reconceived. It can no longer be thought of, as I have done most of my life, as a matter of reconciling relatively intact and structurally still-Constantinian communions from the top down. Rather it must be thought of as reconstituting Christian community and unity from, so to speak, the bottom up. It is here that the structuring of the Church in the first centuries is especially instructive. The ecumenical journey when thus conceived will be longer but also more adventurous: renewal and unification become inseparable.

This focus on building Christian community will seem outrageous to some in view of the world's needs, but it is a strength for those who see the weakening of communal commitments and loyalties as modernity's fundamental disease. Perhaps no greater contribution to peace, justice and the environment is possible than that provided by the existence of intercontinental and interconfessional communal networks such as the churches already are to some extent, and can become more fully, if God wills.

By centering this article on communities, I have not mentioned, for example, those who taught me most about *how* – as distinct from *what* – to think theologically and historically: Robert L Calhoun and H Richard Niebuhr of Yale, and Paul Vignaux of Paris. Nor have I mentioned my daughter, a Christian student of rabbinics, from whom I have learned much about Judaism; nor my wife, a Presbyterian and professor of religious studies, who has in various ways greatly heightened my appreciation of Calvin. Yet the communal focus, though oversimple, is not wrong. As far as my scholarly career is concerned, I have always been primarily interested in how ideas function in communal traditions of language and practice rather than in themselves or in their role in individual lives considered in isolation.

I seem to have come nearly full circle. The ecclesiology on which I am working concerns Chinese, Jews, Roman Catholics and Protestants within the horizon of a crumbling of modernity that brings Christians closer to premodernity than they've been in perhaps 300 years, and closer to the situation of the first centuries than they've been in more than a millennium and a half. We are now better placed than perhaps ever before to retrieve, critically and repentantly, the heritage in the Hebrew scriptures, apostolic writings and early tradition. This retrieval is also more urgent than ever if the churches are to become the kind of global and ecumenical community that the new age needs. Such are the convictions that now inform my thinking, and they are developments rather than departures from my early experiences and youthful theology. Archaeology and architecture almost coincide.

2. Reminiscences of Vatican II*

Editor's Introduction

Lindbeck spent 1962–4 as one of 60 or so Delegated Observers at the Second Vatican Council (1962–5), the meeting of Roman Catholic bishops and theological advisors that 'updated' the Church (*aggiornamento*) by returning to its sources (*ressourcement*).[1] It is clear from the autobiographical sketch in the first chapter as well as in most of the chapters that follow that Vatican II had a major impact on his theology. But it was not only or perhaps even primarily Vatican II's theology and doctrine that was important – a theology that (as I mentioned in the introduction to this volume) often put the old and the new side by side rather than holding a single position on crucial theological issues. What was at least as crucial was the gathering itself of a Christian *internationale* – the Church submitting itself to a reform as massive as any since the Council of Trent (1545–63) and perhaps since the centralization of the Latin Church under the Gregorian Reform of Gregory VII (1033–85). Vatican II's bishops and theologians, lay people and the occasional saint debated the nature and mission of the Church in the world in public sessions and private meetings – and the history of the influence of the public and the private on the outcome of the Council has yet to be written. The following reminiscences are an 'oral history' contributing to that broader story.

It is, I must confess, not the importance of Vatican II for Catholic and Evangelical Theology which makes me choose this topic, but rather the growing interest in oral history. Most of the participants in the Council are

---

* George A Lindbeck, 'Reminiscences of Vatican II', an address delivered at the second annual banquet of the Center for Catholic and Evangelical Theology, Northfield, Minnesota on 23 April 1993 (published as a pamphlet under the same title by the Center for Catholic and Evangelical Theology, n.d.).

already dead – their average age thirty years ago, I would guess, was around sixty, which would put the survivors into their nineties now. This places those of us who were younger – I was a mere child among the graybeards, though I was almost 40 – under pressure to produce. My duty, so I am told, is to spill the beans at length before I lose my memory. Well, that is what I shall try to do.

Unfortunately, beans – i.e. juicy tidbits – are not what I remember well, and the fare I serve you will not be spicy. Furthermore, some of you may have already heard much of what I shall say. If so, forgive me. This time I am speaking for the record, even though, as befits oral history, I haven't checked my facts, and in many cases they are uncheckable. There is no possibility of documenting or otherwise verifying a good many of them. Treat them, therefore, with at least as much caution as you would, for example, Luther's 1545 account of the beginnings of the Reformation. I doubt that my memory is any better than his, and much the same length of time has elapsed in the two cases. Even faulty recollections, however, are grist for the mill of oral historians. As they keep reminding us, it is the remembered past, not von Ranke's *'wie es eigentlich gewesen ist'* which constitutes the reality within which we human beings live.

The 60 or so Delegated Observers, of whom I was one, were a privileged lot. Bishops sometimes complained, and not always humorously, that we outranked them in terms of the Council's protocol. The side door by which we entered St Peter's Cathedral for the daily plenary gatherings during the three months each year the Council was in session was the same one the cardinals used, and like them we sat in ringside seats facing the presiding officers, they on the right, and we on the left of the high altar. The two thousand bishops, in contrast, entered by the distant front portals used by everyone, and were seated in tiers facing each other down the whole length of the central aisle. Often they could not see the speaker or praesidium even by craning their necks. The perhaps equally numerous *periti* (experts and consultants who included some of the world's greatest scholars) were even more disadvantaged. They were tucked away in the awkwardly placed galleries of St Peter's upper reaches. Most of these *periti* were theologians brought along by bishops as advisors and, in some cases, writers of the Latin in which all speeches and other business of the plenary sessions were conducted. There were bishops and even some cardinals whose Latin was not up to following the proceedings, but they were not supplied with transla-tors. We, the delegated observers, in contrast, had learned theologians to sit beside us as translators and informants whenever we wanted them. Cardinal Cushing of Boston offered to equip the aula at his own expense with the electronic equipment needed for simultaneous translation; his offer was rejected, and as a result he stayed home much of the time on the grounds that he could do more good where he understood the language. He claimed with Irish humor at a dinner he held for the North American Observers during the second session that his attendance at the Council would have been better if he had been treated as well as we were. (This, by the way, is one of those possible apocryphal memories about which I warned you. I was at the dinner, and the story fits Cushing's character, but I don't actually remember his saying those words.)

The observers' advantages, furthermore, went beyond protocol to substance. We were regularly briefed and consulted by what was then called the Secretariat for Promoting Christian Unity; we had more opportunities for personal contacts with a wider variety of leading members of different hierarchies and schools of thought than did most bishops. We had, furthermore, the advantage of being oddities. There were only a few of us non-Catholics amidst thousands of Roman Catholics in a Council which had as one of its three main purposes the improvement of ecumenical relations. Furthermore, we had, so to speak, ambassadorial status; the Delegated Observers were official representatives of their respective churches. They had the double task of reporting back what they learned, and of explaining their own communion's probable reactions to what the Council might do. Naturally we were courted, quoted and treated as if we were persons of consequence even when, as in my case, this was not the case.

This is the place to explain, I suppose, how I got to be one of those who hob-nobbed with eminences. Each of the world confessional organizations, such as the Lutheran World Federation was invited by Rome to delegate three observers. The United States in those days was still the major funder of the LWF, and so the powers that be in Geneva were obligated to send at least one American Lutheran who preferably would know Latin, German and French, have worked in the area of Roman Catholic theology, and be able to get leave of absence from his regular job. After scraping the barrel, all that was left at the bottom was an untenured teacher at Yale whose dean and senior faculty, untrammeled by the employment polices now in force, had the flexibility to lend me to the LWF for what amounted to close to three years. The other LWF observers were Vilmos Vajta, a Swede of Hungarian origin who was in charge of the Federation's Studies Department, and Professor Skydsgaard of Copenhagen, perhaps the last generation's major Lutheran scholar and writer on Roman Catholic theology, and founder of the Ecumenical Institute which is now in Strasbourg. Others followed in later sessions when it became clear the Council was of world historic importance. Most notable among these for the American Lutheran situation was Warren Quanbeck of the Luther Seminary. He was the one who brought the American Lutheran Church on board as far as dialogue with Rome is concerned.

As the junior member of the Lutheran delegation and as the only one assigned full-time to Council business even between sessions, I had a job which combined staff work with keeping the LWF and others informed about what was happening in Rome. My base was in Rome itself – I was there with my family from 1962 through 1964 – but I also had to travel: to Helsinki for the LWF Assembly, Montreal for Faith and Order, Scandinavia, Germany, France and all the countries of South America in which there was a Lutheran Church presence. In part the task was to reassure Lutherans that the LWF was not selling out to the 'Whore of Babylon' – and in some places (Norway even more than South America) Lutherans who thought of Rome that way were not lacking. The trip to Brazil was particularly fruitful. Harding Meyer was then at the Seminary in Sao Leopaldo, and I would like to think that his recruitment for the Strasbourg Institute started when I visited there. I became the Protestant observers' liaison with Latin American bishops who spoke French but not English or German. The Hispanic Protestants (and also the Italians such as the Waldensians) lacked channels of communication with the bishops from their countries and thus sometimes used observers like myself from less neuralgic areas as go-betweens. (Incidentally, I have also had experience of Catholics – especially French Dominicans in Oslo – helping me bridge the communication gap between local Lutheran groups which were not talking to each other.)

It was, all things considered, a truly heady experience. The rest of my life has been downhill as far as involvement in publicly notable events is concerned. (Which is just as well. When it comes to a steady diet, I find libraries more congenial than the aula of St Peter's.) But perhaps we need to recall how newsworthy the Council was. It dominated the headlines throughout the world as did no other religion story from its announcement in 1959 until its end in 1965. Indeed, except for relatively temporary episodes such as Kennedy's election, his assassination and the Cuban missile crisis, it was, I suppose, the most important ongoing story of any kind whether religious or secular for half a decade. The crush of reporters from papers, magazines and TV networks at the openings of each of the four sessions was like that at a presidential inauguration, and considerable more international. Even a second stringer like myself was regularly interviewed (and quoted half a dozen times or more) by *Time* and *Newsweek*.

Nor were local newspapers uninterested. Even those in cities as small or smaller than New Haven sometimes sent correspondents to Rome for brief periods. I remember one correspondent from the Midwest (not, by the way, the upper Midwest) who claimed to have a lot of Lutheran readers and asked me whether it was true that some of the delegated observers had knelt to Pope John XXIII during the opening session (remember that what took place inside St Peter's was for the most part closed to the public, including reporters). I saw no harm in admitting the truth of the rumor, but refused to answer when she began asking for names. And then she asked if I was among those who had bowed the knee, and I was trapped. Had I answered and others done the same she could have collected enough denials to establish by elimination who had knelt. For weeks afterwards I had waking nightmares of headlines to the effect that 'Lutheran Observer Refuses to Say whether he Knelt to the Pope'.

Fortunately I could take refuge at home from such trivia. My wife, Vi, and daughter were with me in Rome during those years. In some ways, to be sure, they intensified rather than diffused my involvement in the Council, but in ways that were all to the good. Our small daughter was dandled on the knees of priests and bishops, and my wife had *entrée* into the world of nuns who were vastly more influential behind the scenes than many observers realized. One piece of advise she gave the nuns, however, was largely ignored. She told them to keep their habits, in updated form to be sure, in order to maintain communal bonding and *ésprit de corps*. It was not only women but also male ecclesiasts she entertained without help of servants in our very modest flat in a somewhat dingy apartment building. LWF salaries, to put it circumspectly, were not excessive, but that did not stop her. One of our guests, Cardinal Willibrands, was one of those mentioned as *papabile* at the last conclave, but he was then simply a bishop and second in command to Cardinal Bea at the Secretariat for the Promotion of Christian Unity. One of my favorite memories is that of him and my wife together after dinner smoking his excellent cigars (she had acquired a taste for Dutch brands some years before from a friend from Holland when he was a visiting student at Yale). Let me mention just one further incident from the domestic front. Our daughter grew accustomed to cassock-clad clerics (for cassocks were mandatory in those days in Rome) with the result that when she got back to this country at the age of four, we had to explain to her that ministers are priests who don't wear skirts.

The observers, as you may have guessed from what I have so far said, were not peripheral to the Council. There were at least seven (not, by the way, including yours truly) whose suggestions were credited by Catholic participants with having directly influenced the wording of conciliar documents. Two of these were Lutherans: Skydsgaard and Schlink (who was in a special category representing the EKD). A third person, the NT scholar Oscar Cullmann (who always identified himself in Rome as Lutheran), belonged, together with the Brothers of Taizé, in still another small category, that of special guests of the Holy See. He was widely said to have had more of his proposed emendations accepted than any other single person whether Roman Catholic or non-Roman (but part of this may have been because his Catholic friends would channel suggestions to the drafting committees through him).

This direct influence will be documented once the Acta of the Council are opened, but the indirect influence (which of course affected the non-Romans as much as the Romans) was greater. It was nourished by innumerable conversations at breaks in the daily sessions in St Peter's when everyone crowded to the coffee bars (one of which was dubbed Bar Nun because, until the last session, those admitted to the closed meetings at St Peter's did not include nuns). Then there were the academic and governmental receptions, lectures arranged for and by the bishops for their instruction, and long Italian lunches and dinners. It was scarcely possible to avoid coming to know the already famous or the about-to-be famous: e.g. Küng, Rahner, Congar, Daniélou, Ratzinger, de Lubac and Schillebeeckx. Some of the American heavyweights (Cardinal Wright, Gustav Weigel and John Courtney Murray) I had met before the Council (indeed, I had been Murray's teaching assistant during a semester he spent at Yale), but now my acquaintanceship was extended.

Yet it was not the extensiveness of the contacts but their depth which was pre-eminently important. Conversations sometimes lasted for hours. Themes could be returned to again and again during the four three-month sessions from 1962 to 1965. Trust developed, barriers disappeared, and a sense of common mission for the renewal of the Church, both Roman and non-Roman came to be shared by the observers and most Council members. Solidarity was solidified by the existence of a common enemy, the curia and its Tridentine supporters. At first they were demonized, but once it became clear they could not control the proceedings and the conciliar majority was against them, they turned into fall guys, the butts of jokes. For example, all the progressives were said to be praying that the Lord would open the eyes of Cardinal Ottaviani, the ring-leader of the traditionalists, and if he could not do that, 'please close them gently'. Cardinal Ruffini, the second most notorious conservative, was often linked with Ottaviani. The two of them, it was reported, got into a taxi, asked to be taken to the Council, and fell into deep conversation. Suddenly they realized they were going in the wrong direction: they were outside the old city gate on the Via Popolo heading north. 'But we told you to go to the Council,' Ruffini cries, whereupon the cabbie responds, 'That's where we're going: we're on our way to Trent.'

Such stories, it perhaps needs to be added, were repeated by conservatives as well as by progressives. Change came to seem inevitable. One New England bishop, now dead, told me confidentially during a lunch just the two of us had together that he personally preferred the old ways, including mass in Latin. Yet he had voted for almost all the changes. He had been reading Hans Küng's book on the Church, *The Council Reform and Reunion*, and detested what he read. He would resist the developments Küng urges when he got back to his own diocese. He was too old to change his habits of thought and action. Yet he believed that the Council had no alternative but to give the green light to such developments. In the long run they would dominate the Church.

This dichotomy between policy votes and policy preferences was not uncommon. The bishops as a whole voted for more radical change than they had thought desirable, much less possible, when they arrived for the Council. This willingness to allow developments which were not to their taste is explainable, it seems to me, only in the context of an ecumenical council. It could not have happened in assemblies of the WCC, the LWF, the ELCA or any other denominational legislative body, not to mention Roman Catholic national episcopal conferences or international synods of bishops. None of them are as able to be venturesome or vulnerable to the unexpected as an ecumenical council can be.

The crucial singularity of an ecumenical council is that it runs as long as is needed for the participants to make up their own minds – in the present case, the total time was 12 months spread over 3¼ years. The bishops had the leisure to discuss, to hear extended debate, to attend seminars, to read and think and, in short, to be persuaded. They were persuaded, for example, on the question of biblical criticism. Most of them were deeply suspicious, but the scriptural scholars, not least because of Cardinal Bea, were there in swarms and conducted what were in effect crash remedial Bible courses with remarkable success. During a reception, at the American Embassy of all places, one Californian bishop eagerly told me how his thinking had been transformed by Barnabas Ahern who had impressed him as a saint as well as a scholar. He would like, he said, to get Father Ahern to give a spiritual retreat for his diocesan priests. If someone like Ahern believed in P, J and E and thought there were legendary and midrashic elements in the birth stories, then such views could not be as dangerous as he had supposed. This was not an isolated case. Without many similar alterations of episcopal minds, *Dei Verbum*, the Dogmatic Constitution on Scripture and Tradition, would not have passed. The same is true of the Constitutions on the Liturgy and on the Church, perhaps especially the chapter on Mary. Once these were passed, the other dramatic breakthroughs, the declarations on Ecumenism, Non-Christian Religions and Religious Liberty, followed naturally though not without difficulties.

It needs to be stressed, however, that the bishops were for the most part persuaded by scholarship rather than piety. The renewers argued circles around the traditionalists. They unmasked their opponents as mistaking the post-Tridentine developments, not least the Marian and papal advances of the 19th century, for the total Catholic heritage. It was rather they, the renewers, with their appeal to Scripture and the patristic and to some extent medieval patrimony, who were the true traditionalists. It was they rather than the reactionaries who had tradition on their side.

That is why they won. The attractiveness of *aggiornamento*, updating the Church, and of ecumenism, opening the Church, was greater for the world outside the Council, but what was crucial for the scholastically trained conciliar majority was rather different. The majority were persuaded by reasoned argument, in many cases against their preferences, that the curial conservatives were theologically bankrupt by their own standards. They had been hoist with their own petard, defeated by their own artillery. It was the renewers who had the better knowledge of tradition as a whole and appealed to it more effectively. Yet, though many conservative bishops could no longer vote conscientiously with the curia, their mental habits remained those of 19th-century neo-scholasticism. They had voted for *resourcement*, the return to the sources, without themselves knowing how to put this into effect, with the result that they got kinds of *aggiornamento* and ecumenism that they had not intended.

So far I have generally avoided speaking of the limelight events, so let me conclude with two memories from notable public occasions. First, there was the speech Archbishop Elchinger of Strasbourg gave in St Peter's on how much Catholics owe to non-Catholics even in matters pertaining to the faith. One of his examples was scriptural scholarship. Roman Catholics, he said, owe a great debt to Protestant biblical studies. Second, he spoke of what he called the dogma of justification by faith first defined, as he put it, when the Jerusalem Council referred to in Acts and Galatians exempted Gentile Christians from circumcision and full Torah observance. This central dogma of the Catholic faith, Elchinger continued, has at times been better maintained outside than within Roman Catholicism, and if Catholics are now rediscovering it, it is largely because of the ecclesial communities issuing from the 16th century Reformation.

At these words, to my surprise, I started to cry. Elchinger was in effect saying that Luther was at least in part dogmatically right. I found myself thinking of Abbott Butler's report from the First Vatican Council ninety odd years before of what had happened when the Austro-Hungarian Bishop Strossmeyer had objected (also in St Peter's and from much the same spot) to the view of some previous speakers that all the ills of the modern world, atheism, anarchism, and repudiation of Christian morality, had stemmed from the Reformation. 'We must remember,' Strossmeyer said, 'that there are millions of Protestants who truly love the Lord Jesus.' As he spoke, cries of 'heresy', 'blasphemy', 'come down, come down', grew so loud that he was forced to leave the podium. The contrast between then and now was what made tears of joy roll down my cheeks. It is the only time I have wept in public except at funerals.

The other event I shall mention was a little homily John XXIII gave the observers in a private audience he had with them at the beginning of the second three-month session. That also was a happy occasion. The Council was going the way the Pope, not to mention the observers, welcomed, and none of us knew he was a dying man. He spoke on some favorite words of his from Scripture, 'the mercies of the Lord are new every morning', and said that he had experienced their truth throughout his life. He was one of those who find it hard to decide what to do on any given day, but the Lord was merciful: he always told him every morning. This had happened through his superiors: there were those above him who made the decisions which he carried out. Then, however, he was elected Pope. 'But you know,' he said with his bubbling good humor, 'I needn't have worried. God's mercies continued to be new every morning.' (What we all thought of, of course, was his convoking a Council which nobody, absolutely nobody, it seems, had advised him to call and which had sent the whole Vatican bureaucracy into a tizzy.)

John XXIII would repeat those words if he were with us now. He was basically a traditionalist rather like Mother Teresa, for example, and I suppose he would be appalled at much of the aftermath of the Council. Perhaps he would sometimes even wonder, as Luther did about the Reformation after a comparable lapse of time, whether it was really worth it. Yet the Lord's mercies are new every morning. What stops those words from being Pollyannish is their context: they come from Lamentations (3.22,23). Even in our day, cheerfulness keeps breaking through; and this Center [the Center for Catholic and Evangelical Theology], it seems to me, is an example.

PART I

EVANGELICAL

3. Martin Luther and the Rabbinic Mind*

Editor's Introduction

Lutherans as well as non-Lutherans know of Martin Luther (1483–1546), at least by reputation. But that reputation ranges from views of Luther as radical hero standing against all previous tradition to demonic destroyer of tradition itself. Lindbeck translated Luther, and regularly taught about him in seminars at Yale. In the process he developed a view of Luther as a reformer of the Church catholic rather than the initiator of a Lutheran Church, much less the prototypical modern individual dissenter. This is part of Lindbeck's case for a theology at once 'evangelical and catholic'. Here Luther is read not as a controversialist or an interpreter of Scripture, both of which he surely was. Here Luther is read 'as pastor and catechist', whose catechism (memorized, Lindbeck tell us in Chapter One, by him in his youth) embodies the basic idiom of the gospel in radically traditional ways.

Even further, here Lindbeck's Lutheran tradition relates to his interest in what must be learned from the Jewish people – in this case, from Max Kadushin's interpretation of 'the Rabbinic Mind'. Max Kadushin (1895–1980) was a student of rabbinic biblical interpretation who came to teach at the Jewish Theological Seminary in New York. 'Rabbinic' biblical interpretation is the form that Jewish biblical interpretation began taking (roughly) from the time of the Jewish exiles until modernity. Over against those modern Jews who found such rabbinic biblical interpretation full of contradictions, Kadushin proposed that the rabbis' 'value concepts' (if not their 'statements') were elements of a coherent, organic complex.[1] Kadushin's 'rabbinic mind' is 'the Jewish mind'. This 'mind' is not some sort of thing behind the concrete materialities of Jewish tradition and

---

* George A Lindbeck, 'Martin Luther and the Rabbinic Mind', in *Understanding the Rabbinic Mind. Essays on the Hermeneutic of Max Kadushin*, (ed.) Peter Ochs, Atlanta: Scholars Press 1990.

practice – an all but invisible spirit in an only too visible machine. This 'mind' is organically embodied in various concepts and practices to which Lindbeck alludes throughout this essay.

For example, what Lindbeck here calls *torah* is 'teaching or instruction', but it can also refer to the first five books of the Jewish scriptures or Tanakh as well as to the whole Jewish way of life (e.g. the Way of the Torah). *Shm'a* is the first word of the prayer of Deuteronomy 6.4, 'Hear, O Israel, the Lord is our God, the Lord is one' that is so central to synagogue worship. The *amidah* (literally in Hebrew, the Standing) is the main prayer in Jewish public and private worship, containing nineteen benedictions, modulated for the seasons of the liturgical year. The *seder* (literally in Hebrew, arrangement) is most often used for the home service on the first evening of Passover. These practices are, Lindbeck here proposes, analogous to the organic structure of Luther's catechisms – the Ten Commandments, the Apostle's Creed, the Lord's Prayer, Baptism, and the Lord's Supper.

There are differences between Luther and the rabbinic mind as well as similarities – differences between modes of reform that proceed by 'first order re-interpretations of earlier practice' and those that proceed on 'abstract or second-order principles'. It is interesting to ask whether this difference is simply because of the different circumstances of Luther and the rabbis – the former participant in anti-Jewish Christendom, the latter created by exile from the land. Or is this an abiding difference between Jews and Christians on how their radical traditions set about reforming themselves? That question is related to the even larger questions about 'supersessionism' that Lindbeck addresses in Chapter Fourteen.

When Luther began his reformatory career, his Jewish contemporaries disagreed on whether or not he was returning to Christianity's Jewish roots.[2] Those who thought he was not have largely won the day. Most Jews and non-Jews, including Luther's professed disciples, came to think that his understanding of biblical religion was particularly un-Jewish. That consensus has, if anything, increased in modern times.

The present essay challenges the consensus on two grounds. One is Max Kadushin's portrayal of the rabbinic mind;[3] the other is a picture of Luther as primarily pastor and catechist rather than theological controversialist. According to this depiction, Luther offered his theological ideas only in the context of his recommendations for practice. In this way, he resembled Kadushin's rabbis more than do most other historically important Christian thinkers.[4] Unlike most interpreters, I examine Luther mostly from the parishioners' rather than the usual historical and theological perspectives. Unlike scholars, ordinary folk deeply socialized into the normative versions of Luther's Reformation knew and know him chiefly as pastor and catechist, not theological contro- versialist. I believe that their view comes closer to the original Luther than do most scholarly reconstructions, including Lutheran ones.

After commenting on the importance of Luther as pastor and catechist, I shall deal successively with narrative (*aggadah*) dogma, law (*halakhah*), and reformation, and conclude with an epilogue on lessons for Christians. Whether there are also lessons for Jews in what I shall say will be left to those better versed in Judaism than I. I will mention Luther's anti-Judaism only in passing, for my subject is not Jewish–Christian relations, but rather the similarities between Luther's reformatory portrayal of Christianity and Kadushin's understanding of rabbinic Judaism. I believe that Kadushin would have approved of this investigation. By suggesting that the categories he developed in analyzing Judaism might also be useful in the study of other religions,[5] he showed he was open to the possibility that some Christians understand their religion much as he understands Judaism.

Luther as Pastor and Catechist

Before dealing with the similarities between Luther and Kadushin's rabbis, we need to recall the importance of the pastoral/catechetical side of Luther's work. It overshadows his activity as a theological controversialist, as can be verified by glancing through the tables of contents of the hundred volumes of the critical edition of his writings, the *Weimar Ausgabe* (henceforth *WA*) and noting that the bulk of them are devoted to pastorally oriented sermons, commentaries, table talk, letters and, of course, the catechisms. He was the pastoral writer and controversialist par excellence among the 16th-century Reformers, and his Large and Small Catechisms (1529) were without rival in scope and influence. Only his German Bible – which shaped most other Protestant translations including the King James version – had greater impact outside as well as within the churches which came to bear his name.

Among Lutherans, the Catechisms had semi-canonical status. They were included in *The Book of Concord* (henceforth *BC*), the collection of official confessional statements,[6] and most Lutherans for hundreds of years memor- ized the Small Catechism as part of their confirmation instruction. This was still the practice in the Scandinavian-American Lutheranism in which I was reared, and it often continues in third-world countries (for example, so I have been told, in Namibia, where half the black population is Lutheran). The Large Catechism was written for pastors as a help in explaining the Small. It makes sense to use the two together, as I shall do, as the primary reference work for the comparison of Luther to the rabbis.

The Catechisms provide the most authoritative normative description of Reformation Christianity as a religion of the population at large. This description is to be contrasted with the usual, scholarly ones based primarily on the controversial writings. In the Catechisms, the theological issues of justification by faith alone, of the total corruption of fallen human nature, of double predestination, and of the opposition between law and gospel are never mentioned *expressis verbis*. There is thus little or no hint of that antinomian devaluation of good works, manichaeism and determinism,[7] which Luther's opponents (as well as some of his purported followers) deduced, to his dismay, from systematic construals of his theology. Nor do the Catechisms suggest, as Reformation theology has done to many readers, that Christianity is primarily a matter of belief as contrasted with ethics or of the individual rather than of the community or of subjective attitudes and experience rather than of communal rites and worship. With the hermeneutical help of this or that systematization of Luther's theology, one can find tendencies in these directions, but these tendencies have to be read into the Catechisms, rather than out of them. In short, those presumed features of Luther's thought which are most opposed to rabbinic Judaism are not, at the very least, obtrusively present. In fact, the Catechisms actually display structural similarities between aspects of Christian tradition and aspects of rabbinic Judaism as Kadushin described it.

Luther organized the Catechisms around topics which have their Jewish counterparts. The five major ones, Ten Commandments, Apostle's Creed, Lord's Prayer, Baptism and Lord's Supper, apparently correspond to a catechistic description of the rabbinic concepts of *torah*, the *shm'a*, the *amidah*, circumcision and the Passover *seder*.[8] Furthermore, these elements are, in Kadushin's terms, 'organically related'. Decalogue, creed, prayer and sacraments is each important in its own right, yet no one of them can authentically exist without all the others, and there is no logically deductive or other formally inferential relation of subordination or superordination between them. Like Kadushin's rabbis, then, and unlike medieval Jewish and Christian thinkers such as Maimonides and Aquinas, the Luther of the Catechisms expounds his communal religious tradition in terms of what Kadushin calls an 'organic' complex rather than a 'philosophical' system.[9,10]

There are neither precedents nor imitations, as far as I know, for Luther's remark, recorded in the Table Talk, that the Decalogue is *doctrina doctrinarum*, 'the teaching of teachings', and the Creed is *historia historiarum*, 'the story of stories'. (The *Pater Noster* he went on to say, is *oratio orationum* and baptism and Eucharist, *ceremonia ceremoniarum*, but these are less surprising designations.[11]) Even theologically trained readers may well rub their eyes. Surely 'doctrine' for Christians (even when used, as here, in the general sense of teaching or instruction) has chiefly to do with creedal beliefs, not with directives for behavior? And surely creedal beliefs, in turn, are dogmas in the sense of propositional definitions, not stories interpreted by narrative elaboration, that is, haggadically? It is almost as if Luther deliberately intended, *per impossibile*, to give a rabbinic-like gloss to creed and commandments.

Creed as Narrative

The creed, Luther said, is a summary of the gospel, and the gospel, in turn, is narrative: it proclaims the history of God's gracious dealings with humankind in creation, the coming of Jesus Christ (the climactic part of the story) and the gathering of a people, the Church, through the Holy Spirit. It had been traditional to divide the creed into 12 articles (one for each of the apostles who were supposed to have composed it), but Luther divided it into three articles (Father, Son and Holy Spirit) corresponding to the three major divisions of the biblical narrative in its Christian trinitarian version.[12] The creed mentions only the crucial turning points, and then only with a word or phrase,[13] and Luther's explanations do little to fill in the details. There is no need, because, as he says, 'the proper place to explain all these different points [in the biblical history] is the . . . sermons through-out the year'.[14]

Luther's sermons interpreted scriptural stories in a manner comparable to the haggadic midrash. He quite consciously thought of this as the proper manner to expound the creed.[15] Dogmas, to be sure, are implied by the creedal narratives: God created the world, the Redeemer became man, the dead will be resurrected. These are truth claims, not simply parables designed to shape attitudes and actions (though they are also that). Nevertheless, these dogmas are embedded, first, in stories, which are both epistemologically and affectively or motivationally primary. They are epistemologically prior in biblical religion, though not necessarily elsewhere, because they identify and characterize who and what God is and thus enable human beings to refer to him and rightly talk about him. Further, when they are appropriated by faith *pro me* (to use one of Luther's favorite expressions) and become one's own story, they elicit the fear, love and trust of God above all things which, according to Luther, is the sum and substance of the first commandment[16] and without which we cannot rightly obey any of the others. Thus it is narrative, rather than dogma, which is epistemologically and motivationally of central importance for Luther.

If Kadushin is right, the rabbis thought similarly of *aggadah*. Unlike *halakah* (not to mention any statements of dogma), the *aggadah* 'completely reflects the nature of the value-concepts' which are basic to Judaism.[17] The value concepts, 'not being objective like the cognitive concepts or definite like the defined concepts, had need of Haggadah ... in order to remain vivid'.[18] What I have called the epistemological and motivational priority of the *aggadah* is well expressed by the rabbi who said, 'If you come to know Him who spake and the world came to be, then study *aggadah*, for by that means you come to know the Holy One blessed be He and to cleave to His ways.'[19]

Dogma

If narrative has this priority, what is the place of dogmas? They were certainly important for Luther, but only to guide the interpretation and use of the biblical stories to shape lives. To believe that the Redeemed became human (the catechisms avoid abstract terms such as 'incarnation' and 'trinity') is to accept as one's Lord the Jesus depicted in the gospel stories.[20] In his sermons, Luther stressed the full humanity of Jesus more than had the tradition. He described Jesus as the 'mirror of the Father's heart', in whom its 'profound depth', its 'sheer, unutterable love' is found.[21] Similarly, he interpreted the doctrine of the trinity as a constant reminder that the narrationally distinct agents[22] to whom Christians ascribe the divine deeds of creation, redemption and sanctification in the scriptural stories are most emphatically one God. Luther insisted that such doctrines, truth claims though they be, lose their meaning when abstracted from their narrative and practical settings. That is why he argued so passionately against the medieval scholastics' attempts to construe doctrines as metaphysical propositions. He argued that such attempts change meaning and transmogrify faith.[23]

Kadushin's analysis of the rabbis' use of dogma[24] was similar to my analysis of Luther's use of dogma, with an important exception. He focussed his attention on the differences between rabbinic dogmas and such 'creedal beliefs' as those Maimonides' *Thirteen Articles*.[25] He argued that rabbinic dogmas were 'not pure dogma', because, unlike the latter, they lacked definite terms and therefore represented beliefs ambiguously. Overly concerned to show that the rabbis were uninterested (as was also Luther) in clarifying the propositional status of dogmas, Kadushin ignored the regulative or 'grammatical' functions of rabbinic dogma: such as that of excluding ways of speaking or acting which suggest that, for example, *mattan torah*, Exodus, or resurrection of the dead are not truth claims.[26] I wonder if Kadushin may have thought that the regulative functions of such narratives could be sufficiently displayed by analyzing the value-concepts and 'emphatic trends' embedded in them and that, therefore, dogmas are dispensable.[27] If so, he differed from the rabbis on this point more than Luther did.[28]

Law

The crucial test of Luther's similarity to the rabbis is his attitude towards law. Here, according to long-established standard opinion, the opposition is drastic. More than any other major Christian thinker, he is said to have intensified and generalized the Pauline contrast between law and gospel into a total disjunction. This is the central argument for the uniquely unrabbinic character of his thought. In this section, I shall first outline the argument and then present the very different view found in the Catechisms.

The argument is based on Luther's *Kontrovers theologische* ('contro-versial-theological') writings. His constant refrain in these writings is that the Christian life must be freedom from the law (*lex* or *Gesetz*), because the law is an unmitigated tyrant in both of its aspects: in its *usus civilis*, as heteronomous demand, and in its *usus theologicus*, as terrifying accusation. As heteronomous demand, its role is to coerce wicked human beings (since the Fall, there is no other kind) into an obedience which is individually corrupting though socially necessary. It makes individuals more sinful than they are when ignorant of it because the obedience it extorts is *contre coeur* and thus, consciously or unconsciously, hypocritical.

The second, accusatory *usus theologicus* is no less grim, but drives toward salvation. It pierces the carapace of self-justifying excuses under which human beings hide from God's wrath and thus reveals to them their hopeless sinfulness. The terrified penitent then has no other escape but to trust entirely in the wholly unmerited mercy, grace and forgiveness of God in Christ. Justification is by faith alone.

Apart from the reference to Christ, there is perhaps nothing in this account which a rabbi would not be able to say of the law as it applies to the wicked, but Luther goes on paradoxically to insist that the law coerces and accuses the righteous just as it does the wicked, and yet is also totally abolished for them.[29] This is because they are simultaneously wholly just and wholly sinners, *simul totus justus et totus peccator*. In the Christ with whom they are united by faith, they are freed from the coercive and accus-atory law, but in themselves they remain in bondage: the law continues to be a brutal taskmaster driving them to Christ. They are, so to speak, bilocated,[30] living both in the coming eschatological kingdom and in the present age when the messianic reign has begun but is not yet consummated. It is thus that they are totally under the heteronomous and condemnatory law and yet, at the same time, totally liberated from the law.

One common Lutheran reaction has been to stress the liberation, emphas-izing the gospel at the expense of the law, with the result that Christianity becomes, as such Lutherans as Kierkegaard and Bonhoeffer have com-plained, a religion of 'cheap grace'. Even when the paradoxical dialectic of the *simul* is employed to exclude all tendencies towards permissive anti-nomianism, Luther's account appears thoroughly unrabbinic. There is here no talk of the law as a welcome guide, a light to the feet and a lamp to the path (Ps. 119.105), and there appear to be no Christian analogues to the rabbis' delight in *halakhah*. The law is wholly hateful even to the saints, for as justified, they have nothing to do with it, and as sinners, they are as subject to its demands and condemnations as are those without faith. It seems impossible, therefore, to be a good person in the eyes of God without being guilt-ridden.

It has been said that an uneasy introspectiveness was Luther's major legacy to Protestantism and, by cultural osmosis, to secular movements such as Freudianism.[31] The problem, so the diagnosis goes, is that, however good God's commandments are in and of themselves, human beings *ought* not experience them as such. If they do, they simply prove that they are self-righteous hypocrites who self-protectively refuse to admit that they utterly fail to measure up. The pressure becomes unbearable for those who are not religiously motivated, and antinomianism is the result.[32] It seems that, for Luther and for cultures influenced by him, the law cannot possibly be, as the Psalmist puts it, sweeter than honey and the drippings of the honeycomb (19.10).

When one looks at the Catechisms, Luther's position appears very different. The theological polemic against the law is absent, and Luther meditates on the commandments at length and not without pleasure. They come first, and their exposition in the Large Catechism goes on for 25,000 words:[33] nearly half of the entire Catechism and close to five times as long as his comments on the creed, *historia*. The proportions in the Small Catechism are similar if one adds to the decalogue the appendices on religious practice and household duties.[34] Thus, the Luther of the Catechisms is, at least quantitatively, primarily a halakhist, just as were the rabbis of the Talmud.[35]

This impression of resemblance is strengthened when one considers what Luther said, not simply how much. First, odd as it might seem, he never called the decalogue 'law' (*lex/Gesetz*) in the Catechisms, but, rather, instruction or teaching (*doctrina*) of the type which can variously be termed *praeceptum*, *Gebot* and *mandatum*. In these texts, though not always elsewhere, 'law' never refers to God's commandments, but only to human enactments, especially papal ones which illicitly claim divine sanction.

Second, Luther praised the decalogue as the complete guide for human life. The first commandment, as interpreted briefly by the Small Catechism and at length by the Large, inculcates 'fear, love and trust in God above all things', and thus tells us how all the other commandments are to be obeyed. Each of the prohibitions also has a positive import. 'Thou shalt not kill', for example, does not simply forbid harm to the neighbor, but also requires us to 'help and befriend him in every necessity of life'. Similarly, 'Thou shalt not bear false witness' tells us 'we should apologize for him, speak well of him, and interpret charitably all that he does'.[36] Thus

> anyone who knows the Ten Commandments perfectly knows the entire scriptures. In all affairs and circumstances he can counsel, help, comfort, judge and make decisions in both spiritual and temporal matters. He is qualified to sit in judgment upon all doctrines, estates, persons, laws, and everything else in the world.[37]

Third, Luther praised these precepts as the only reliable way of knowing God's will for human life (as opposed to knowing *who* God is, which knowledge comes only through *historia* or *aggadah*). They are 'inscribed in the hearts of all men'[38] as the abiding structure of human existence as it issued from the Creator's hand. Since they are now obscured by sin, however, reason fails to identify them correctly, and humans must rely on God's proclaiming them outwardly.[39] Luther therefore insisted that the decalogue is 'the true fountain and channel from and in which everything must arise and flow that is to be a good work, so that outside of the Ten Commandments no work or thing can be good or pleasing to God'.[40]

Fourth, Luther treated the denigration of uncommanded works as liberating, rather than limiting. He argued that humans invent laws they can fulfill in order to escape from the impossibility of fulfilling divine commands, but find their own laws oppressive precisely because salvation is made to depend on their fulfillment. The divine law therefore liberates from the expectation of fulfillment. Luther had in mind, specifically, the suffocating medieval panoply of ascetic, monastic, and religious practices which, he argued, were unwarranted by Scripture and turned people away from 'all that God wishes us to do or not to do', namely, the Ten Commandments.[41] These latter deal with 'common, everyday domestic duties of one neighbor toward another, with no show about them'. For when someone

> remains on his knees a whole day in church, this is considered a precious work which cannot be sufficiently extolled. But when a poor girl tends a little child, or faithfully does what she is told, that is regarded as nothing. Otherwise, why should monks and nuns go into cloisters?[42]

Sociologically, Max Weber was right: the Christian freedom which the Reformers proclaimed was a change from other-worldly to inner-worldly asceticism, from an outmoded feudal form of life to an incipiently capitalist and bourgeois one. Yet it was experienced as religiously liberating. It was good to know in the face of medieval religiosity that God asked human beings simply to be what he had created them to be, observers of the Ten Commandments. These are without exception written in the inward parts and therefore observed also in paradise. Even the Sabbath, Luther said, was kept by Adam and Eve before the Fall.[43] Surely the rabbis would have approved.

Fifth, Luther nowhere suggested that humanity's inability at present to fulfill the commandments perfectly is any reason for not trying. Success or failure has nothing to do with eternal salvation, but human beings are much better off on this earth if they make the effort.

> It will be a long time before men produce a doctrine or social order equal to that of the Ten Commandments . . . Just concentrate upon them and test yourself thoroughly, do your very best, and you will surely find yourself with so much to do that you will neither seek nor pay attention to any other kinds of works or other kind of holiness.[44]

Luther had not forgotten the thunder and lightning at Mt Sinai, and he wrote frequently of both the threats against those who disobey and the promises to those who obey.[45] Only toward the end of his exposition on the commandments did he twice note in passing that no one can perfectly fulfill them and that they therefore also accuse even the best, even the most righteous. 'Both the Creed and the Lord's Prayer must help us, as we shall hear.'[46] Nonetheless, they are not a tyrant from which one escapes to the gospel as quickly as possible, but a treasure to be constantly cherished and for whose sake the gospel itself is given:[47]

> Therefore it is not without reason that the Old Testament commands men to write the Ten Commandments on every wall and corner, and even on their garments. Not that we are to have them merely for a display, as the Jews did,[48] but we are to keep them incessantly before our eyes and constantly in our memory.[49]

Luther wrote that he recited the decalogue every morning – together with the creed, the Lord's prayer, and some psalms – and suggested a daily 'hymn on the Ten Commandments' for morning family devotions.[50] We are therefore not surprised to read, in his concluding comment, that the commandments 'are precious and dear above all other teachings, (*omnibus aliis doctrinis*), the greatest treasure given by God'.[51] Elsewhere, Luther applied this language to Jesus Christ and to the gospel which proclaims him, but there is no contradiction. He believed that, by instructing humanity about God's will for all of life, the decalogue provided the scaffolding for a form of life which has the gospel at the center. The first commandment implicitly insists upon that center,[52] for it tells us to 'fear, love and trust

God above all things', and we cannot do this without the gospel, 'which teaches us to know God perfectly ... in order to help us do what the Ten Commandments require'.[53] It is therefore the necessary means to the end of learning to obey the commandments. The stories of God's goodness in creation and redemption are, as I put it earlier, epistemologically and motivationally primary. Justification is unquestionably by faith in the gospel message,[54] but this faith is itself commanded[55] and is for the sake of the commandments. For the pastoral and catechetical Luther, as for the rabbis,[56] the commandments – albeit 10 and not 613 – provide an all-embracing order for human existence. Luther's doctrine of justification by faith, finally, has its counterpart in the rabbinical doctrine that God's goodness towards his people comes before their obedience to him. God's goodness alone makes possible acceptance of his kingship, *malkhut shamayim*, and obedience to his commandments.[57] The reasoning in both cases is that only those whom God makes to trust him through his uncaused love for them will willingly follow his precepts. To the degree that this pattern of thought is basic to the rabbis, Luther's doctrine of justification by faith is actually rabbinic in character, and by no means antinomian.

Reformation

Luther was, however, also unrabbinic, for his method of reform was unlike the rabbis' method, at least as Kadushin describes it. According to Kadushin, the authors of the Talmud offered their reforms through what I would call first-order re-interpretations of earlier practice, without basing those reinterpretations on abstract or second-order principles. Luther, on the other hand, offered his reforms on the basis of abstract reformatory principles, which he derived from second-order reflections on practice. It was for the sake of reform that he drove a wedge between catechesis and theology: for example, between the commandments which are a blessed guide and the law which is a fearsome tyrant. The rabbis did not display this kind of disjunction between first-order teaching and second-order reflection on the concepts involved in the teaching. Kadushin did display such a disjunction, however, in his own attempt to separate value-concepts from the texts which record rabbinic teachings and, thus, to liberate methods of halakhic judgment from the actual talmudic precedents. In this sense, despite the immense rhetorical differences, Luther's method of reform was like Kadushin's own.

If, as I argue, the catechetical Luther were the authoritative one, then Luther was similar to Kadushin in another way as well: both viewed their second-order redescriptions of practice as corrective rather than constitutive. If, on the other hand, the theological Luther were the authoritative one, why did he omit from the Catechisms his redescription of the law as fear-some tyrant? We would have to interpret this omission as a concession to the weak and simple and read the Catechisms as milk for babes not yet mature enough for the strong meat of the full gospel. In this case, despite his professed dislike of philosophy, Luther would have been what Kadushin, derisively, called a philosopher: someone who thinks that second-order redescriptions can communicate the essence of a religion better than its ordinary scriptures, teachings, liturgies and practices.

The only quick way to argue for the corrective thesis is to sketch the story of the Reformation from its perspective. As Luther perceived it, Christian tradition had confused two fundamentally different senses of the concepts of 'precept' (his usual word for 'commandment') and therefore also of 'obedience'. He believed the confusion, in turn, corrupted the tradition's theological reflection as well as its first-order linguistic and behavioral prac-tices. His innovative method of unmasking the confusions was to call pre-cepts 'doctrine' or instruction[58] and confine the term 'law' exclusively to the sphere of legally enacted norms enforced by punishments and rewards.

Luther described God's precepts as instructions in the performance of practices which, when well learned, are intrinsically satisfying. As fallen creatures, to be sure, we do not spontaneously experience the practices in which the commandments instruct us as intrinsically good, but God's good-ness gives us confidence that that is what they are. We thus need not hesitate to train ourselves and others in them, even without faith or desire. The training may be done coercively if necessary,[59] but preferably with 'childish and playful' and 'kind and pleasant methods . . . Then some food may take root, and men may grow up of whom an entire land may be proud.'[60] Luther referred here to what is good in the eyes of human beings, not justification in the eyes of God (*coram hominibus*, not *coram deo*). The practices God commands can to some degree be satisfying in themselves, quite apart from rewards and punishments, even when performance is as inadequate as it always is for human beings, and even when true faith and love of God and neighbor is lacking. In the case of goods which are not simply instrumental, a little is better than nothing at all.[61]

Luther argued that the law, on the other hand, legislates instrumental good. What the law requires cannot be good simply for its own sake: even singing the songs of Zion becomes oppressive when done under compulsion (Ps. 137). To treat the commandments as laws, therefore, is automatically to seek God's favor by good performance, to be self-congratulatory when one delusively supposes one has succeeded, and to be crushed when one realistically realizes one has failed. In either case, one violates the first commandment, engaging in a 'false worship' which is 'unwilling to receive anything as a gift from God', but desires 'by itself to earn or merit everything

. . . just as if God were in our service or debt and we were his liege lords'.[62]

Luther believed that the worst possible form of this legalistic error was to make salvation itself dependent on obedience. As Luther saw it, this was an inveterate human tendency, which the Church of his day made official policy. He believed the policy was strengthened by the influx of superficially Christianized pagans and barbarians as well as by traditions of Roman legalism and Greek teleological thinking (as a modern historian might put it). Even St Augustine's doctrine of salvation by grace alone had been placed in a legalistic framework. Legalists interpreted it to mean that God gave his gift of otherwise unmerited grace to enable believers to live up to the law's high demands of perfect love of God and neighbor and thus to be rewarded with eternal blessedness. They sought to exclude pride – according to the Augustinian adage, 'When God rewards our merits, it is his own gifts which he crowns' – but they did nothing to alleviate anxieties about merit. Those less strenuous than Augustine, moreover, substituted the fulfillable works of human religiosity (ranging from ascetic practices to purchases of indulgences) for God's unfulfillable commands.[63] For the Reformers, this legalism had produced two ills, pandemic in the Christendom of their day: irremediable anxiety and the invention of illusory good works.

To respond to these two ills, Luther offered four conceptual innovations. First, to allay anxiety, he decoupled salvation and obedience. He generalized and radicalized the Pauline principle of 'justification by faith apart from the works of the law' (Rom. 3:28) to the extent of representing Christian existence as one of complete freedom from all norms in their legal (coercive and accusatory) uses.[64] Second, to reduce antinomianism, he 'bilocated' believers as, at once, wholly just and wholly sinners, wholly under the law and wholly freed from the law. Third, he maintained a positive view of the commandments by distinguishing their instructional and legal functions, portraying Christian freedom as freedom from 'legal' rather than 'instructional' obedience. Fourth, through the *sola Scriptura*, he eliminated the imaginary good works of medieval religiosity: accepting only the ten commandments as interpreted by Jesus and supplemented by such apostolically attested ceremonial ordinances as baptism and the Lord's supper.

The fourth innovation may puzzle interpreters, since Luther appealed to 'Scripture alone' at the same time that he offered innovative conceptualizations that go beyond the biblical word and also retained more postbiblical traditions than any of the other Reformers. Luther's own explanations are only partly satisfactory, and it may help to use modern categories. His claim to being biblical as well as traditional becomes intelligible if one thinks of his theological innovations as second-order articulations of rules and concepts implicit in the Bible as this had been traditionally interpreted. Redescribing

Christian faith and practice as a communal tradition of scriptural interpretation, these articulations served as criteria for evaluating given developments
from the tradition as either consistent or inconsistent with the Scriptures'
grammar of faith. For Luther, the essential question was not the content
of a given development, but whether or not it was consistent with the
proper relationship between law and gospel. He therefore had no interest
in purging the Church of pictures, statues, liturgical customs, bishops and
even the papacy, providing they functioned 'in accordance with the gospel'.[65]
He insisted that some postbiblical developments be retained (especially
infant baptism, but also private confession). And he respected one part of
the tradition – the ancient creeds – as much as the rabbis respected the oral
Torah.

In sum, Luther did not treat his reformatory principles as summaries
which substitute for what the Bible or tradition says, nor as premises for
theoretical or practical deductions, nor as formulae to be introduced or
explicated in regular worship, teaching and preaching. He believed that
conceptual redescriptions of the faith were necessary only to correct serious
errors in Church teaching and practice. His dualisms and antitheses were
therefore context-specific, second-order instruments of argumentation, useful, as in the controversial theology, for combatting corrupt religion but
not, as in the Catechisms, for expounding correct practice. If one takes the
pastoral and catechetical level as decisive, then Luther's theology is not
constitutive of his understanding of Christianity.

The contrary view is so pervasive in Luther scholarship, however, that
it is well to conclude this section with a comment on the reasons. Kadushin
blames 'philosophy' for a similar bias in Jewish studies. By this he referred
to a tendency, beginning with the Greeks and climaxing in the Enlightenment, to regard systematically organized defined ideas as the best way of
conveying the constitutive or essential features of any phenomenon whatsoever: rabbinic Judaism, Luther's understanding of Christianity, galaxies or
quarks. In the case of the rabbis, interpreters have to force rabbinic thought
into categories imported from the outside, usually from philosophers such
as Aristotle or Kant. In the case of Luther, the cognate task is easier and
therefore even more tempting. Unlike the rabbis, although like Kadushin,
Luther engaged in second-order reflection. One can without much difficulty
transpose his reformatory redescriptions of Christianity into some more
defined conceptual idiom. There is nothing wrong with this. I have, similarly, used some of Kadushin's *Begrifflichkeit* to speak about Luther, and
have on other occasions for other purposes employed the more existentialist
vocabulary of recent Luther interpreters. Second-order description is fully
compatible with recognizing, as almost every student of Luther does, that
he was a paradoxical, unsystematic and anti-philosophical thinker. Error

arises, however, when one misinterprets the use to which Luther put his own second-order reflections: assuming that, because his reformatory theology is the conceptually most developed and definable part of his work, it must also convey his most authoritative understanding of Christianity.

I hope to have shown that Christianity was for Luther a *halakhically* structured and *aggadically* constituted communal tradition which has no single, describable core meaning or essence any more than does a language or culture. He wrote that the Church 'is the mother which begets and bears every Christian through the word of God',[66] for 'whatever God effects in us he does through the external ordinances' of preaching, sacraments and instruction through which the Church transmits God's word.[67] Theology does not itself transmit that word, but rather performs its function on behalf of that transmission. Theological descriptions can be neither understood nor assessed apart from the practices, worship, story-telling and catechesis by which the community lives. This ecclesiological emphasis is a presupposition rather than an explicit part of Luther's major reformatory themes and can be easily overlooked. Those who overlook it will be unable to interpret his theology as corrective rather than constitutive and unable to perceive his similarities to the rabbis.

Epilogue

What benefits may Christians derive from comparing Luther with the rabbis? It will be well to start with attitudes toward Jews. Interreligious relations are not the subject of this essay, but they cannot be omitted when dealing with the contemporary import of the history we have been surveying. Luther continues to influence many Protestants and a growing number of Roman Catholics. Any change in how these Christians read Luther will affect their understanding of the relationship of Christianity to Judaism.

Luther's anti-Judaism has been widely perceived to be integral to his thought. Once he is interpreted as primarily a pastor and catechist, however, this perception loses its textual warrant. The new interpretation lends support to the historically well-supported view, that the vitriol of Luther's late-life diatribes was a by-product of anti-papal venom. He retrojected papist errors onto the Pharisees as these are pictured in New Testament polemics and then assumed, as Christians were wont to from the beginning, that the Judaism of his own day was this caricatured 1st-century Pharisaism *redivivus*. He said nothing worse about the Jews than he had said at far greater length about the papists. The latter were, however, a clear and present danger and actually guilty of much of what he accused them, while his attacks on Jews were without excuse.[68] It helps to know that, however inexcusable, this anti-Judaism need not be seen as structurally embedded in Luther's thought. Luther's central concerns were largely shared by branches of the Reformation which later became the seed-beds of Protestant philosemitism and, more recently, pro-Zionism. (Neither of these phenomena, to be sure, is free of supersessionism, but on that score, Luther is neither better nor worse than the whole of the tradition from its beginnings down to recent times.)[69]

In sum, the new reading of Luther as catechist should enable Christians to perceive him as closer to the rabbis than they had thought and, thus, to perceive their own religion as closer than they had thought to that of present-day Judaism. The major value of a comparison between Luther and the rabbis, however, is that it increases Christian understanding of Luther, quite apart from its contributions to interreligious understanding. Kadushin's portrait of the rabbis introduces categories of religious thought which are closer to Luther's own than those customarily drawn by modern Luther scholars from studies of the Enlightenment, existentialism, Freudianism or the Holocaust.

Like the rabbis, Luther viewed religious texts as practical guides which shape the total form of life of whole communities in their domestic, economic and political dimensions as well as their specifically religious ones. Like the rabbis, he regarded the decalogue as the preeminent text in this regard, interpreted by the Tanakh and then by subsequent texts (for example, the Talmud for the Jews and the Apostolic writings and tradition for the Christians). Luther shared with his Jewish contemporaries not only many practical precepts, but also precepts which concerned the cosmic setting of human life, as well as the over-arching outline of a narrative stretching from creation to the messianic kingdom. This, to be sure, did not make for irenicism. The very existence of a common framework highlighted points of conflict. Jews and Christians may not be sure how or whether they disagree with Buddhists, for the frameworks seem incommensurable, but they know with painful exactitude where they oppose each other. Nonetheless, these oppositions – most centrally over the identity of the Messiah – do not exclude similarities in patterns of *aggadic* and *halakhic* interpretation. In sum, Luther's Christianity and the Judaism of Kadushin's rabbis have both an epistemological and motivational likeness as well as a similar structure of religious precepts.

The greatest barrier to recognizing these commonalities has been that Judaism was a diaspora religion while Christianity was enmeshed in Christendom. These conditions, however, are changing. Judaism is quasi-established in Israel, and Christians are becoming a minority in their areas of historic dominance. Christians increasingly experience the kinds of sociopolitical marginality which may have contributed to the development of rabbinic Judaism.

In conclusion, it may not be too far-fetched to suggest that, in order to survive, mainstream Christianity will become more concerned about developing distinctive and encompassing forms of minority communal life than it has been since Constantine. If it is to avoid sectarianism, whether old or new (Montanist, Donatist, Mennonite, Quaker, Pentecostal or liberationist), Christianity will need to follow the historic, mainstream practice of seeking guidance, not primarily from the Sermon on the Mount in isolation from the Tanakh, nor from the spirits of the *Zeitgeist*, but from the Decalogue interpreted by the New Testament. Christians may then find models for their practice in both the pastoral/catechetical Luther and contemporary rabbinic reformers. Perhaps Christians may find themselves reading Jewish authors such as Kadushin, as I myself have done, as much to receive help with their intra-Christian problems as to understand the rabbis better.[70]

4. Article IV and Lutheran/Roman Catholic Dialogue: The Limits of Diversity in the Understanding of Justification*

Editor's Introduction

The central dispute of the 16th-century reformations, in the mind of the key theological reformers, was over 'justification' – the meaning and truth of teachings like those of Paul that 'we know a person is justified not by the works of the law but through faith in Jesus Christ' (Gal. 2.16; Rom. 3.28). While Luther's theology of justification was a crucial determinant of later Lutheran theology, even more important was the understanding of justification in Article IV of the Augsburg Confession (1530), and in the Apology of the Augsburg Confession (1531).[1] This Article (along with comparable articles from the Catholic Council of Trent a few years later) has been central to Lutheran–Catholic dialogue since Vatican II – and Lindbeck was involved in writing the documents on justification for both the international and national Lutheran–Catholic dialogues. But Lindbeck's main concern in this essay is with the disagreement among Lutherans themselves about 'the limits of diversity in the understanding of justification' – the doctrine of justification that generated the Reformation's *sola fide* (by faith alone) as an application of Augustine's *sola gratia* (by grace alone).

This is an example of Lindbeck's ecumenical casuistry (i.e. taking up particular cases of disputes among Christians) applied to a crucial issue. Lindbeck identifies the doctrine of justification as the 'metatheological' rule 'that all church teachings and practices should function to promote reliance or trust in the God of Jesus Christ alone for salvation'. In Chapter Ten

---

* George A Lindbeck, 'Article IV and Lutheran/Roman Catholic Dialogue: the Limits of Diversity in the Understanding of Justification', *Lutheran Theological Seminary Bulletin* **61** (1981), pp. 3–16 (including discussion).

Lindbeck will propose that all church doctrines are thus 'metatheological'.

In October 1999, 18 years after the publication of this essay, the Lutheran World Federation and the Roman Catholic Church signed a Joint Declaration on the Doctrine of Justification, arguing that a consensus had been reached on basic truths of justification, warranting the withdrawal of the mutual condemnations of the 16th century. The resulting dispute among Lutherans is not unrelated to the issues Lindbeck discusses in this essay many years earlier.[2]

A Curious Imbalance

Both inside and outside the official dialogues, a curious imbalance has developed in Roman Catholic/Lutheran discussions. On most doctrinal questions, the Catholics, burdened by a long and complex tradition of detailed church pronouncements, seem, at least initially, to have little room to maneuver; but on justification, it appears to be the Lutherans who are boxed in. On this question they often give the impression of being less open to diversity and less ecumenical than their Catholic partners.

More specifically, the Roman Catholic consensus among those who have studied the problem is that justification by faith as interpreted by contemporary Lutherans is not excluded by Catholic teaching.[3] Although the Roman Church has yet officially to affirm justification by faith, it also does not reject it. Thus the Reformation position is a possible option for those in communion with Rome. Lutherans would not have to surrender their traditional affirmations on this point in order to enter into a united church.

Lutherans, in contrast, often sound much more doubtful about the compatibility of their position with traditional Roman Catholic teaching.[4] Justification *sola fide* is for them, as every seminary student learns, the 'article on which the Church stands and falls (*articulis stantis et cadentis ecclesiae*'). It is not simply one option among many. It is, rather, the only proper way of teaching in the Church about salvation. This is the source of the ecumenically awkward situation in which Lutherans seem more intransigent than Roman Catholics.

The underlying issue for Lutherans, obviously, is that of the limits of diversity in the understanding of justification. How much variety is permissible, and what are the criteria for determining when the limits are transgressed? Could we honestly enter into full fellowship with a Roman Catholic Church in which the *sola fide* is viewed as only one possible way among many of teaching about justification?

This Lutheran concern, we need to remind ourselves, seems strange not only to Roman Catholics but to most of our contemporaries. In order to avoid archaism, we must try to state the issue not only in 16th but also in 20th century terms; and here Paul Tillich, although not above criticism, offers some useful as well as familiar suggestions. Many of you will recall his comment in *The Protestant Era* that the doctrine of justification has become unintelligible 'even to Protestant people in the churches; indeed, as I [i.e. Tillich] have over and over again had the opportunity to learn, it is so strange to the modern man that there is scarcely any way of making it intelligible to him. And yet this doctrine . . . has torn asunder . . . Europe . . . has made innumerable martyrs; has kindled the bloodiest and most terrible wars of the past; and has deeply affected European history and with it the history of humanity. This whole complex of ideas which for more than a century – not so very long ago – was discussed in every household and workshop, in every market and country inn . . . is now scarcely understandable even to our most intelligent scholars. We have here a breaking down of tradition which has few parallels.'5

One reason for this unintelligibility, Tillich suggests, is that in the Reformation period the anxiety of sin predominated, whereas now the anxiety of meaninglessness reigns supreme. It is because of this that the Reformers do not speak to our situation. They address the problem of sin, not of meaninglessness. But modern men and women both inside and outside the Church no longer ask Luther's question, 'How do I get a gracious God?' They are not troubled by the divine demand for righteousness nor consumed by the search for divine mercy. They do not live in apprehension of the Last Judgment, purgatorial fires, or the horrors of hell. They may be burdened by what we generally call 'guilt feelings' or a sense of worthlessness, but these are quite different from fear and trembling before God's wrath. It thus makes no sense to tell them – to tell us – that God forgives unconditionally. That is not our problem.

Our problem is meaninglessness. The pluralism of the modern world and the relativization of all religious, moral, political and even scientific absolutes, which has in part resulted from the Protestant critique, has produced a state of pervasive uncertainty and doubt. Most people feel that they do not really believe or know anything, not even their own identity, although they may make vigorous protestations to the contrary. When they are forced to be honest with themselves, the underlying meaninglessness breaks through and they are plunged into despair and hopelessness.

Tillich claims, however, that the contemporary despair over meaninglessness is not fundamentally different from the despair which Luther experienced over sinfulness. Furthermore, not only is the problem basically the same, but so is the solution. Luther's answer may need to be rephrased, but it remains basically valid. We need to recognize, as he did in reference to sinfulness, that we are not damned by the meaninglessness of our lives, nor are we saved by meaningfulness. We need to recognize that we are accepted even though we are unacceptable. God justifies the ungodly. He forgives unconditionally. Our lives are meaningful to him even when they seem utterly meaningless to us; and conversely, their apparent meaningfulness to us is not to be equated with salvation.

What we need to do, therefore, is accept our acceptance. This is what it means to be justified by faith. Justification by faith enables us to live with despair. More precisely, only through justifying faith, only through basic confidence, is it possible honestly and fully to face our deepest anxieties – our anxieties over death, over sin, over meaninglessness. Faith does not abolish these anxieties, but rather enables us to acknowledge them and to bear them. Our existence can be simultaneously both justified and sinful, both meaningful and meaningless.

My reason for summarizing Tillich at such length is not only to remind you of one way of translating justification by faith into contemporary terms, nor is it necessarily to endorse Tillich's translation. It is chiefly to introduce his way of explaining the contrast between standard Reformation and standard Catholic ways of speaking of justification. For the Reformers, God accepts the unacceptable, while for the Catholic tradition, God first makes the unacceptable acceptable and then accepts them.[6] For the Catholic, in other words, God forgives only after first infusing the grace which enables sinners to do the works of love which merit salvation. These good works are, according to such *sola gratia* Catholics as Augustine and Thomas Aquinas, entirely from grace. As Augustine puts it in a passage to which Melanchthon refers in the *Apology*, 'When God rewards our merits, it is his own gifts which he crowns.'[7] Thus the Reformers and those whom Luther and Melanchthon sometimes called the 'better scholastics' can, and sometimes did, basically agree on grace, sin and free will. Both groups could affirm that human beings are by themselves utterly helpless in the face of sin or meaninglessness, and that they are utterly dependent on God for salvation.

Yet, despite this similarity, they are also very different. The Catholic *sola gratia* theology, one might say, assumes the goodness, not of human beings without grace, but of Christians. The task of this theology is to oppose pride by telling believers that they should attribute all their virtues and merits to God. The Reformation position, in contrast, assumes a total absence of inherent goodness even in Christians and tells them, as well as unbelievers, to cling to God alone no matter how terrified, guilty or meaningless their lives may be. In brief, Luther and the Augsburg Confession emphasize faith or trust in opposition to despair, while Augustine and the Catholic councils stress humility and praise of God in opposition to pride.

For the Reformers, as one would expect, the great defect of the Catholic teaching even at its Augustinian best was that it was helpless against despair. It does no good to tell the terrified that they should be humble and praise

God for his transforming grace. The Augustinian *sola gratia* was admirable medicine against fifth century Pelagian confidence, but it was at best innocuous and at worst poisonous when administered to the guilt-ridden penitential consciences of the end of the Middle Ages. The only way to console these consciences is by preaching the acceptance of the totally unacceptable – that is, justification by faith alone.[8]

The question with which we are now confronted is whether this Reformation message remains the right – perhaps the only right – way of proclaiming the gospel in all times and places. Once again we are back at our main theme: the limits of diversity.

A Metatheological Rule

The problem of defining the limits of diversity, it should next be observed, is not properly theological, but rather metatheological. The task, in other words, is not to develop a way of understanding, explaining or picturing justification, but rather that of identifying a rule or criterion in terms of which all theologies of justification – whether Lutheran, Catholic or Tillichian – can be tested. A metatheological norm of justification does not supply a vision or theory of God's justifying action or of the reality of justification in human lives, but rather prescribes conditions which all such theologies of justification must meet. It is comparable to the 'metalinguistic' stipulation of which Gettysburg Seminary's own Professors Robert Jenson and Eric Gritsch, speak;[9] although my own form of the stipulation will be verbally different from theirs. When Lutherans say, as they often do, that the doctrine of justification is not a doctrine among other doctrines, but is rather a criterion of all doctrines, they are in effect suggesting that it is what I have called a metatheological rule.

The 16th-century confessional Lutheran form of this norm is easy to identify. It is the rule that all church teachings and practices should function to promote reliance or trust in the God of Jesus Christ alone for salvation. This rule, taken by itself, does not contain any theories or affirmations about justification. It does not even assert that justification is *sola fide*, but rather 'for Christ's sake alone (*propter Christum solum*)', although it may be hard to see how any theology which adhered to the rule could deny the *sola fide*. As is characteristic of statements in the imperative mood, it does not make affirmations about what is true or false, but simply prescribes: and what it prescribes is a certain form of human behaviour (which includes attitudes and ways of thinking). We should not trust anything for justification except God's unconditional promises in Jesus Christ, not even the faith, virtues and merits, if there be any, which God works in us *sola gratia*.

I shall not try to demonstrate that Luther or the Augsburg Confession applies this rule to the understanding of justification, and to all church teachings, institutions and practices; but given Luther's and the Confession's concern for the consolation of consciences and for *fiducia*, it would not be difficult to make out a plausible case. But the historical question is secondary. It is enough for our purposes simply to stipulate that a theology or practice is tolerable to the extent that it can be used to promote, or at least not hinder, the communication of the reality of justifying faith – that is, faith which clings to God in Christ alone. Further, the more adapted a teaching or practice is to promote, and the less likely it is to hinder such communication, the better it is. These are the limits of diversity. It is now time to consider some consequences of this approach.

Consequences

One consequence is that it becomes easier to understand why we hear so little about justification by faith – about the metatheological rule – in the course of church history. Rules can be followed in practice without any explicit or theoretical knowledge of them. Indeed, explicit knowledge sometimes seems to be a hinderance. Homer was a supreme master of the rules of Greek grammar and rhetoric. He could infallibly avoid turns of phrase which violated the rules. And yet, on another level, he knew no grammar or rhetoric at all because he lived before these disciplines had been invented. Similarly, none of the New Testament writers except St Paul clearly speak of justification by faith, but that does not mean that they failed to follow the rule in practice – though a Lutheran naturally has doubts about James. Much the same can be said, as the Reformers recognized, of early church fathers and medieval saints, not to mention multitudes of ordinary Christians in every generation. In short, justification by faith *propter Christum solum* is the *articulis stantis et cadentis ecclesiae* in the sense in which grammar is essential to intelligible discourse; but this does not mean it needs to be explicitly known.

The converse is also true. Just as skill in following a rule can exist without explicit knowledge of it, so knowledge can exist without skill. We have all had the experience of learning the grammatical rules of a foreign language – and, on one level, learning them very well – and yet not being able to apply them in speaking or writing. Those who are confessional Lutherans are often like such foreigners. They know the rule of justification, but lack the competence to use it to shape their lives or those of their churches. Sometimes, indeed, preoccupation with the rule of justification seems to make it more difficult to practice the reality, just as constant attention to the rules of correct fingering can make it impossible to play a sonata or type 50 words a minute.

Yet in the third place, this does not mean that either textbook grammar or explicit doctrine is unimportant. Formulated rules of language or of faith may not be necessary when the traditioning process is working well, but they are often useful for teaching purposes; and when error is rampant in theory and practice, they become indispensable. It was this latter problem – the problem of theologically defended practices explicitly contrary to the implicit rule of faith – which impelled the development of the doctrine of justification *sola gratia* and *sola fide* in St Paul, St Augustine, and in the Reformers.

This brings us, in the fourth place, to the conflict between Rome and the Reformation. I shall speak of this again later on, and now only make a few comments before we turn to specifically Lutheran treatments of justification. The conflict with Rome has not been directly over the metadoctrinal rule, but rather over theologies of justification. Nowhere does the Tridentine decree, for example, specifically deny the metadoctrine. It does not affirm that trust for salvation should *not* be totally directed to God's premises in Jesus Christ. Indeed, it sometimes uses language that sounds like this rule. Chapter 16, for example, declares '*absit tamen, ut christianus homo in se ipso vel confidat vel glorietur et non in Domino*' ('far be it from a Christian to confide or glory in himself and not in the Lord').[10] To be sure, it goes on to speak of the merit which God works in believers as a condition for the attainment of eternal life (Canon 32), but it also says that this inherent meritorious grace cannot be relied upon (chapter 9). In short, while Trent does not assert reliance for justification on the God and Father of Jesus Christ alone, neither does it assert the contrary.

The Reformation question, however, is whether Trent and Roman Catholic theology in general indirectly contradict the metarule by implying a theological conceptuality which either cannot affirm justification *propter Christum solum* (i.e. *sola fide*) or excludes it. It is often argued that substantialist metaphysics, Aristotelian or Platonic views of man and notions of infused grace necessarily result in pictures of human beings in their relationship to God which are in opposition to the gospel. The theologies which use these pictures generally deny and at best are unable effectively to affirm the unconditional character of God's free gift in Jesus Christ. This is true even of *sola gratia* theologies such as those of Augustine or Thomas Aquinas. For these reasons, Gerhard Ebeling in his recent *Dogmatik* views the Reformation doctrine of justification as unalterably opposed to any substance metaphysics or ontology as well as to the corresponding anthropologies. Robert Jenson seems to adopt a similar position in his sections of *Lutheranism: The Theological Movement and Its Confessional Writings*.[11]

We cannot enter into a full discussion of this problem; but I shall simply observe that those influenced by the Anglo-American analytic movement, as I have been, are in principle suspicious of sweeping *a priori* arguments. One reason for this suspicion is that the meaning of words, concepts and conceptual schemes are largely, even if not wholly, determined by use, Metaphysical notions of substance and infused grace, for example, can be employed for many different purposes; and it is by no means clear that all of these are incompatible with the *sola fide.* In the second place, pre-Reformation theologies are less polemical than post-Reformation ones, and they are much less systematic than has become customary since Schleiermacher. This is true even of the thought of Thomas Aquinas. He was a rigorous, comprehensive and orderly thinker, but he had no 'system' in the Schleiermacherian, Rahnerian or even Barthian sense. This makes it especially hazardous to speculate on what he, or other traditional theologians, could or would have said about problems which they never actually confronted. Scholars such as Stephen Pfürtner may well be right when they suggest that Thomas could have affirmed under the rubric of 'hope' much of what Luther proposes under the heading of 'faith'.[12] In the light of these considerations, it becomes impossible to make universal judgments about the compatibility or incompatibility of past or present Catholic theology with the Reformation norm. It is necessary to discuss the problem case by case. A few comments about specifies will be made later.

Anticipating those comments, however, let us postulate that in the 16th century, Augustinian and Aristotelian conceptual schemes were used to construct theologies which denied or at best made it difficult to affirm that trust for salvation should be directed exclusively to God as known and active in Jesus Christ. Their defect, as we earlier suggested, is that they described justification as a process in which God first makes the unacceptable acceptable, and then accepts. This made it essential for Luther to conceptualize human beings and their relationship to God in radically new ways. Only thus could the *propter Christum solum* be effectively affirmed and its denial effectively opposed in that particular situation.

Yet as a fifth consequence of our approach, it needs to be emphasized that Luther's theology also is relativized by the distinction between the metarule and all theological theories. (St Paul's conceptualization of justification, though not his doctrinal rule, is also relativized – but that will not be discussed in this chapter.) The concepts and models which the Reformers employed are not normative in themselves, but only to the extent that they are necessary and effective to promote the communication of justifying faith. Like any theological ideas, those of the Reformers can be misused. Luther's conceptuality, for example, is often said to be existential – or, in more Anglo-American terminology, 'self-involving' – in contrast to what Otto Pesch has termed the 'sapiential' approach of a thinker such as Thomas Aquinas.[13] If Luther lived in our day, however, he would undoubtedly agree that some existential interpretations of justification are less faithful to the gospel than some sapiential ones. Further, his dialectically dualistic distinctions between law and gospel, between *deus revelatus* and *deus absconditus*, *theologia gloria* and *theologia crucis*, *totus justus et totus peccator*, *coram deo* and *coram hominibus*, and between the two kingdoms, are not immune from abuse. In his hands they were powerful instruments to promote the proclamation of the gospel, but they can also be employed in ways which are heretical or non-Christian.

We need to recall in this connection the secularization of Luther's anthropology. As Wenzel Lohff put it, 'Our "acceptance of being accepted" can be abstracted from "God's acceptance of the sinner in Jesus Christ"'.[14] Albrecht Peters notes[15] that this happened to some extent in Kant, more clearly in Fichte, and most fully in such thinkers as Heidegger and Jaspers. It must be admitted, I suppose, that the existentialist understanding of human authenticity as escape from reliance on the past in surrender to the freedom of the future is an extraordinarily powerful and appealing secularized rendition of Luther's understanding of man's existence in faith. Yet psychological versions of this theological anthropology are probably now more important. At least in the United States, Erik Erikson's theory of the central role of basic confidence in individual development is the currently most widely influential off-shoot of the Reformation doctrine of justification.

It is ironical that just as pagan philosophers such as Plato and Aristotle became fathers of Christian theology, so Luther, the great anti-metaphysician, has become a father of some of the major pagan philosophies of modernity. These philosophies, in turn, have spawned Christian heresies. This happens, for example, when the significance of Jesus Christ *pro nobis* is reduced to that of a particularly effective or redemptive symbol of human authenticity. Tillich can perhaps be criticized on these grounds. In saying this, I do not wish to imply that the secularized philosophical or psychological insights into the human condition inspired by Luther are incapable of genuinely Christian employment. My only intention is to illustrate the thesis that anthropologies or views of human existence inspired by the Reformation may be utilized independently or in opposition to the metadoctrinal rule.

A theologically more important corollary is that even when these concepts are used in accordance with the rule, they may not always be the best way of following the rule. Luther's picture of man standing before God does not make immediately evident the importance, for example, of the communal dimensions of Christian existence or the cosmic dimensions of eschatology. It is even possible for professed followers of Luther to conceptualize justification without reference to the sacraments. Yet for Luther, as we know, the concrete acts of baptism, the Lord's supper and absolution were the supremely unequivocal proclamations of the unconditional character of the promise on which faith depends. That is why in the Smalcald Articles he treats the abuse of the sacrament (or, in his terminology, the abomination of the mass) as the most direct contradiction of justification.[16] He does much the same in opposing the denial of the real presence by the sacramentarians, or the rejection of infant baptism by the Anabaptists. Theological conceptuality was for him secondary. It would seem, then, that if there were a way of understanding human nature which made the centrality of the sacraments for the Christian life more vivid and intelligible than does Luther's own theological anthropology, he might very well have considered it preferable. His own standards would require this whenever a sacramentally oriented theology proved superior as an aid in the communication of the reality of justification (i.e. reliance for salvation *propter Christum solum*). The same principle applies, needless to say, to every aspect of the Reformers' thought. There is nothing sacrosanct about their way of conceptualizing God, or the relation of the two natures in Christ, or the sacraments, or the ministry, or the Church. If in our day there are ways of thinking about these matters which better safeguard and facilitate the transmission of living faith in Jesus Christ, they are to be chosen out of faithfulness to the Reformation itself.

In the sixth place, this relativization of Reformation patterns of thought raises questions regarding much recent Lutheran theology. For many theologians, Luther-interpretation and systematic theology seem to be two sides of a common enterprise. What they see as conceptually basic in Luther is also fundamental for their constructive work. This appears to be true of thinkers as diverse as Paul Althaus and Regin Prenter, Werner Elert and Gerhard Ebeling. They differ in the concepts they emphasize and the purposes for which they employ them, but in each case, a systematization of Luther's ideas is used both to understand him and to construct *Glaubenslehre*.

As will later become clear, I do not deny the value of such contributions, but I question the view that a theology is Lutheran only if it uses a Reformation conceptuality. From the metatheological perspective, a theology might conceivably relegate the law–gospel dialectic to a secondary level, or have an eastern rather than western understanding of sin, or employ a substance metaphysics, and yet be more faithful to the Reformation, more genuinely 'Lutheran', than some systems which are completely dominated by Luther's concepts. In short, the test of Lutheran theological identity is not *what* concepts are used, but *how* they are used. The criterion, so to speak, is a grammatical rule rather than a particular vocabulary.

Yet, in the seventh place, we must add one other consideration in order to distinguish the theology of the Lutheran Reformation from that of the other traditions. Other theologies may follow the metadogmatic rule more or less unconsciously. If so, they are within the limits of acceptable diversity in regard to justification. This makes a difference. To cite a far-fetched example, a Lutheran follower of such an Eastern Orthodox theologian as Gregory Palamas would be different from other Palamites. He would seek to safeguard hesychastic prayer and theology from abuses which others are likely to overlook; and in order to do this, he might profoundly alter their framework of thought, just as Luther altered Augustine's framework. His work might be in some respects better and in others worse than that of non-Lutheran Palamites, but it would in any case be distinctive. The same would be true, needless to say, of genuinely Lutheran Marxists, Aristotelians, existentialists or process thinkers. In all these cases, theologians seek to Christianize conceptual schemes which also have non-Christian employment, but an adherent of Luther and the Lutheran Confessions will Christianize them in a special way. To follow a rule explicitly makes a difference.

This leads to an eighth point, to the effect that the study of Luther and the Reformation tradition becomes more rather than less important in the light of the approach which I have tried to present. Such study, however, also becomes more difficult and demanding. We are called upon, not to repeat Luther, but to do with very different conceptual materials what he did with the ideas available in the 16th century. Some of those ideas may still be important. We therefore need theologians who continue to work with them as do Prenter and Ebeling and others. But more important is how they are used; and here Luther, with his immense skill in applying the metatheological norm, is endlessly instructive. He frees us to follow his example rather than to imitate his thought. He encourages us to use conceptual schemes quite different from his own. He calls us to become more varied, comprehensive and catholic in our theology. He helps us, in short, to become what the Reformation originally professed to be: not a separate confession, but a reform movement within the Church universal.

Conclusions

The time has now come, in conclusion, to ask about the contemporary Roman Catholic situation from the Lutheran perspective I have tried to develop. The first thing to say is that the Reformation problem has not entirely vanished. Denials of the *sola fide* are now apparently of little importance in contemporary Roman Catholic academic theology, but one wonders whether they are not still widespread on the level of piety in the form of habits of thought, preaching and catechesis. This, to be sure, is not a uniquely Catholic problem. Despite all modish talk about the changeability of human nature, the self-justificatory legalistic syndrome appears to be a permanent temptation (whose overt power, to be sure, varies in dependence on personal and cultural circumstances). Denials of justification by faith are also widespread in Lutheranism, not only in practice, but even in explicitly verbalized form, as *inter alia*, M Strommen's *A Study of Generations* has documented. Yet it is of great importance, so Lutherans who have internalized their tradition are likely to believe, that the community of faith make doctrinally explicit that denials of the *sola fide* are illegitimate. It troubles them that this is not the case in Roman Catholicism.

This leads Lutherans to ask a question. Why are Roman Catholics, even when they fail to deny the *sola fide*, so little concerned to emphasize it or to defend it against rejection? Even our partners in dialogue, I think it would be fair to say, manifest no great enthusiasm for the Reformation formulations, although they are unfailingly gracious in trying to understand why we think them important.

Part of the answer, perhaps, is the weight of tradition. As Lutherans see the situation, the Roman Catholic Church tried hard in the 16th century to anathematize the Reformation doctrine. Some of us are inclined to say that the attempt failed. We may even be tempted to suggest, not altogether in jest, that this failure supports belief in the infallibility of the Church: even when it tried, the Holy Spirit prevented it from denying the *articulis stantis et cadentis ecclesiae*. Be that as it may, the attempt to reject the *sola fide* molded four hundred years of Roman Catholic thinking and teaching about justification. The social, psychological, institutional and theological factors which originally prompted the attempt have largely vanished, but it still remains true that to place stress on justification by faith may seem to many Roman Catholics a betrayal of their heritage. This may hold even for many who in theology and practice are in accord with the *sola fide*.

Further, some would argue, there is now little need for explicit attention to the doctrine. In the absence of theologically programmatic and self-conscious legalism and its attendant scrupulosity, the best antidote to self-righteousness and self-dependence is perhaps provided by other themes, such as participation in Christ, which, in contrast to the 16th century, is now dominant in much Roman Catholic theology. Wholehearted trust in anything, including God, is normally not best promoted by constant talk about the need for it. Indeed, the communication of the reality of justifying faith may be hindered in our situation by the kind of massive explicit attention to the doctrine which dogmatization would require.

Yet even if these are valid considerations, Lutherans are likely to suspect that less reputable motives also contribute to the continuing Roman Catholic disinterest in emphasizing the *sola fide*. Some of the original motives may have vanished. Roman Catholics are no longer inclined to defend the abuses in worship and practice criticized by the Augsburg Confession (at least insofar as that critique is derived from concern for justification by faith). There remains a reluctance, however – so many Lutherans think – to admit that ecclesial structures such as episcopacy, papacy and an infallible magisterium must also be judged by the Reformation norm: that is, by their service to the gospel of salvation *propter Christum solum*.

Such things must be said, if at all, without self-righteousness. The criterion accuses everyone. Sometimes Lutherans may resist the Lutheran criterion's applications to church life more than do Catholics. Their widespread indifference to the visible unity of the Church, for example, may be a more serious denial that the structures of the Church should serve the gospel than anything now prevailing on the Roman side. Thus Lutherans may be like the son who said 'I go' and then went not; while Catholics may on occasion follow the rule even while not explicitly articulating or assenting to it. Yet, so a Lutheran is likely to add, the lack of articulation and assent is regrettable. It makes infractions of the rule harder to denounce and easier to legitimize. Not only individual, but also institutional and communal self-interest and self-righteousness can be better opposed, other things being equal, where the *sola fide* is explicitly acknowledged.

A fourth and final comment, however, is that Lutherans cannot by their own principles insist on the Roman Catholic dogmatization of the *sola fide* as a condition for church fellowship. They ask only, in the historic phrase, for 'the freedom of the gospel'. This includes freedom to oppose erroneous or inadequate understandings of justification, and to insist that whatever roles episcopal and papal structures may have must be in the service of God's unconditional promises in Jesus Christ. It does not involve, however, the refusal of communion with churches of East or West who do not take the same strong line on these points as does the Reformation. These churches on their side, to be sure, could not fully join with Reformation bodies unless they acknowledged the *sola fide* as at least a legitimate *proposal* of dogma, but on the Lutheran side, nothing more need or can be asked for. To demand that the proposal be accepted as a prior condition for church fellowship is to betray the Reformation by turning what professed to be a reform movement in the Church universal into a self-inclosed sect.

In short, Lutherans would contradict their own *raison d'etre* if they demanded that others officially affirm the norm of justification *sola fide* as a pre-condition for unity. The reason for this, in brief, is that the *articulis stantis et cadentis ecclesiae* can be adhered to even where it is not articulated (and also, as Lutherans must sorrowfully acknowledge, it can be denied in practice even where it is professedly venerated).

Discussion

Question

The Lutheran World Federation Assembly at Dar-es-salaam in 1977 welcomed the proposal by Lutheran and Catholic theologians to discuss the 'acceptability' of the Augsburg Confession in the Roman Catholic Church. If this search for unity proceeds, what is the role of 'justification by faith' in relation to ecclesiastical authority, which is a thorny issue in ecumenical dialog? Is there a common understanding of justification among Lutherans?

Lindbeck

In responding to this question, there is no need to rehearse what was already said in the lecture about the limits of 'acceptable' understandings of justification. The issue, rather, is that of ecclesiastical authority. Someone will have to speak officially for the churches if their search for unity is to continue to progress; but who can do this for the Lutherans?

The Lutheran World Federation would seem to be the obvious candidate, but this body comes under severe attack whenever efforts are made to increase what in the most recent phase of discussions has come to be called its 'ecclesial density' – that is, its ability to act more nearly as a Church rather than merely as an agency of cooperation and as a forum for discussion.

The critical question arose at Dar-es-salaam when the matter of apartheid in South Africa was declared by the Lutheran World Federation Assembly to be '*status confessionis*'. The Federation asked its member churches, and most specifically, the churches in South Africa, to give their response to this action, but up until now, the 'pro-government' church has not responded. This is one of the problems with the Lutheran World Federation. It cannot even insist that its member churches respond to a question or react to a document. The Assembly can pass resolutions until it is blue in the face; and the member churches can, if they so wish, simply file those resolutions away and forget about them without ever saying either 'Yes' or 'No'. Yet there is hesitation on the part of member churches to increase the power of the Lutheran World Federation in this respect.

Even so apparently modest a step as empowering the Assembly to pass a resolution to which the member churches must then say either 'Yes' or 'No' creates great apprehension on the part of any member churches that their autonomy might be infringed. The Lutheran World Federation happens to be a financially and bureaucratically rather powerful institution, particularly in relationship to weaker and numerically smaller churches in the Third World. There is a fear that the Lutheran World Federation might be able to manipulate votes. Geneva would be able to induce churches out of self-interest to vote the way Geneva wants them to vote, rather than the way they themselves would normally wish to vote. For that reason, the attempt to strengthen the Lutheran World Federation so that it could be the agency through which Lutheran churches could come to act together more effectively looks as if it is going to fail. There are other ways being discussed in which Lutheran churches might learn to act together on these matters, but this is not the place to enter further into this problem.

The point which needs to be stressed is that on any question of major importance in reference to Roman Catholicism, no single Lutheran body will want to act authoritatively or officially by itself. The Lutheran Church in America, for example, will not want to act on the possibility that some form of recognition of the papacy is compatible with the primacy of justification by faith, unless it is pretty sure that this is something that would meet with the approval of most of its sister churches throughout the world. The problem is to find some mechanism for discovering what is the consensus, the solid committed consensus of the organized church bodies.

Gritsch

One is tempted to conclude that Lutherans are better off when they're involved with other Christians. When they wait until the next Lutheran body acts, usually nothing gets done. This is a problem.

Jenson

I have one brief comment on a completely different aspect of that question. When we speak about Roman Catholics acknowledging or recognizing the Augsburg Confession, we must be clear that it is the text that is recognized, not our interpretations of it. That's universally the case; and I think it important to keep it in mind. Lutherans may disagree entirely with one another about how to interpret the text, just as Roman Catholics might disagree on how to interpret the text of the Council of Trent. What is recognized is the text and no particular interpretation of it.

Gritsch

One should note that the text of the Augsburg Confession was intended to be the property of the Church catholic, not the property of the so-called Lutheran churches. That is also something that one should realize when one speaks of 'recognition'.

5. The Reformation Heritage and Christian Unity*

Editor's Introduction

'The Reformation heritage' in the title of this essay is the tradition of the 16th-century Reformation. However, as participants in that tradition usually know and non-participants frequently do not, that Reformation heritage is diverse – diverse to the point that Catholics and others have sometimes argued that this Reformation heritage is a cause of Christian disunity rather than Christian unity. Must not 'radical traditions' ultimately destroy the very traditions they are out to radicalize?

Lindbeck here proposes that this Reformation heritage has a specific contribution to make to Christian unity. He focuses on the differences between Lutherans and Reformed. 'Reformed' came to be the ordinary self-description of churches that arose out of the 16th-century reformations of Calvin and Zwingli rather than out of either Luther or what Lindbeck here calls 'enthusiasts on the left' (Anabaptists and others). The contemporary heirs of these Reformed Christians (Lindbeck points out) include Presbyterians but also a broader range of Christians, including some Anglicans. Indeed, this Reformed tradition rather than Lindbeck's own Lutheran tradition is probably what most English-speaking people think of when they think of 'Protestantism' – and probably rightly so, since (as Lindbeck points out here) it has been the most influential Protestant tradition in modernity

This essay describes the similarities and differences between Lutherans and Reformed and proposes how each (together and apart) can contribute to Christian unity. The similarities center on 'the three Reformatory "solas"': *solus Christus* (Christ alone), *sola fides* (faith alone, including

---

* George A Lindbeck, 'The Reformation Heritage and Christian Unity', *Lutheran Quarterly* **2** (1988), pp. 477–502.

sola gratia, grace alone) and *sola Scriptura* (Scripture alone). Lindbeck emphasizes that the Reformation heritage is not simply 'a liberating force for individuals' but 'a community-building and church-renewing power', aimed at correcting rather than replacing an earlier tradition. The main disagreements between Lutheran and Reformed concern the practice of and teaching about the Eucharist, although one of the interesting features of this essay is the way Lindbeck argues that what are sometimes taken to be crucial disagreements between Lutherans and Reformed (e.g. over church organization and secular politics) do not have to be church-divisive. Why (readers might ask) does Lindbeck have hesitations about 'pulpit and altar fellowship' between Lutherans and Reformed? And what does he think are the distinctive community-building tasks of Reformed and Lutherans in our current circumstances?

Lutherans and Reformed in Dialogue: Divisions Dissolved

Introduction

We shall be dealing with the Lutherans and the Reformed in this section and 'the wider ecumenical context' in the next. Our specific theme in this first section is the successful part of the official church dialogues of recent decades, but we must start by placing them in the wider context of Reformed/Lutheran relations in general.

It may be helpful to compare these relations with, for example, British/American ones. When some of us were young, there was much talk of a union of English-speaking peoples. These peoples, after all, share a common language and culture and have similar democratic traditions. Why not then unite them politically? The argument in favor seemed particularly strong, as I recall, when the United States and the British Commonwealth were the only parts of the free world left to struggle against Hitler and Hirohito, and then again when the United Nations was in the process of formation. In the first case, political union would presumably make the fight easier, and in the second, it would contribute to the unification of all the nations of the world.

There are parallels to Reformed/Lutheran relations in this parable. These two confessional traditions are both rooted in the magisterial Reformation of the 16th century; and it has often been urged in the last 400 years that they should unite against Rome, their common enemy. The proposals for alliance generally embraced the Anglicans (for the Thirty Nine articles, despite John Henry Newman's efforts to argue otherwise, are basically a Reformed document), but it was only reluctantly that left-wing Reformers and free-church Protestants were included for they, like Russians and other communists in our day, were considered subversive.

Yet, as in the case of England and America, similarities did not prevent conflicts between the Lutherans and the Reformed. Lutherans were vehement in their opposition to Zwinglians and, to a lesser extent, Calvinists, and while there was less animus on the side of the Reformed, this was in part, perhaps, because they could afford to be generous. With the exception of the very early period, it is Reformed Protestantism which has been in the ascendent, often at Lutheran expense.

Now, however, we live in a more irenic age. We no longer fight, at least not openly, and alliances against Rome have gone out of fashion (although there is at least one Lutheran/Reformed organization, the *Evangelischer Bund*[1] in Germany, which continues to sound on occasion rather like Ian Paisley in Northern Ireland). The reason for unity now urged upon us is, first of all, that churches should unite whenever possible, and that this should be especially easy for Lutherans and Reformed because of their common Reformation heritage; and second, that they have a special responsibility to share this heritage, the Christian truths emphasized by the Reformers, both with the world and with the Church at large, and they can do this better together than apart.

These two propositions are now part of the standard ecumenical wisdom of the day, but I suspect they need to be questioned, not from an anti-ecumenical perspective, as is usually done, but from an ecumenical one. We should be open at least to the possibility that just as the struggle for democracy in a world we hope will someday be united no longer seems to call for the union of the English-speaking peoples, so also union first between Protestants, between Lutheran and Reformed, may not now be the best way of promoting the Reformation cause. I am not sure that this is so, but we need to understand those who think this way and to ask what, in any case, is the best way of furthering in the Church universal the gospel the Reformers proclaimed.

I am much better prepared to discuss the wider ecumenical context in the second section than the Reformed/Lutheran dialogues in the first. My ecumenical involvement has been chiefly with Roman Catholics rather than with Presbyterians, although my personal relations are with Presbyterians (my wife, as she herself is the first to say, is very much a Calvinist). But there may be advantages in looking at the dialogues from the outside. While it is a handicap not to know them at first hand, it may also be of benefit to compare them with other interconfessional discussions, not least those with Roman Catholics.

I shall start with some descriptive comments designed to identify puzzling features in the dialogues, then discuss these features in terms of non-theological and theological factors. My account will stop half way with those dialogical conclusions on which there is general agreement. Then in the second section, I shall deal with a remaining problem area and turn to ecumenical strategy. We shall ask, in other words, what, if anything, Reformed and Lutherans should do together or separately to share their common heritage with others.

Descriptions

This is not the place for a detailed description of the dialogues. Those who want more information can consult the report of the last American series, *An Invitation to Action*, edited by James Andrews and Joseph Burgess and published by Fortress Press (1984). This book contains the basic documentation of the three American rounds from 1962 to 1983 as well as the text of the European Leuenberg Agreement of 1973.[2] I shall keep my descriptive comments brief because it is on explanation and evaluation that we must concentrate.

The basic pattern of the Lutheran/Reformed dialogues has been similar to that of other bilateral discussions. First, to be sure, they started a bit earlier than most – here in America in 1962 – and unlike other major ones, they are only now beginning to acquire a worldwide component, but in other respects they resemble the majority of dialogues which have developed since the Second Vatican Council both with Rome and between non-Roman churches. Second, the focus of these bilaterals is different from that of multilateral discussions such as those sponsored by the Faith and Order Division of the World Council of Churches. As is illustrated by the Lima report on *Baptism, Eucharist and Ministry*,[3] the multilaterals stay on a rather high level of generality in their effort to develop a consensus among many parties, while the bilaterals look at the specific doctrinal disagreements which have historically divided specific confessional families and ask whether these are now resolvable. Third, most dialogues have hedged their answers. The Lutherans and Catholics, for example, have said that some of their historic disagreements are no longer divisive, others could be removed, while still others continue to seem insurmountable (though the last category keeps on shrinking, at least for those in the dialogue). In contrast to these partial yeas, the Lutherans and Reformed have been wholly affirmative. There are for the discussion participants, no remaining doctrinal barriers to the official establishment of full communion. Fourth, full communion, however, means something different in the Lutheran/Reformed context than when some others are involved, not least Roman Catholics. Protestants generally think of what is technically called 'pulpit and altar fellowship', while for non-Protestants some element of common governance is usually implied even if this be nothing more than the means to convoke a common council when necessary. Not that the Reformed and Lutherans exclude organizational unification, but, as Leuenberg explicitly notes, this depends on circumstances. There is no general rule one way or the other.

On a fifth point, however, all contemporary dialogues are in complete agreement, including the Lutheran/Reformed ones. As Leuenberg puts it, even organizational union should not be 'detrimental to a lively plurality in styles of preaching, ways of worship, church order and diaconal and social action'. Everyone insists these days that the ecumenical church of the future for which we hope should not be a homogenous, centralized monolith.

So much on the dialogues themselves, but something needs also to be said about other factors. First, as I suppose we are all aware, the Reformed/ Lutheran discussions have attracted less attention both inside and outside the churches than have the dialogues with Rome or even the Lutheran conversations with the Anglicans. Perhaps this was partly because their conclusions were expected. After all, most people already believed that the historic Reformed/Lutheran disagreements no longer warrant division. Furthermore, in those places especially in Europe where *de facto* full communion already exists between the Reformation churches, the effect of the dialogues is not to make forays into new territory, but simply to ask for the official ratification of what already exists. Under such circumstances, excitement is likely to be minimal.

But this lack of interest is also related to a second factor: the lack of consequences. In Europe, the practical effects are small. Despite notable exceptions, most Lutherans and Reformed seem content with their present co-existence as non-interacting siblings and are much more enthusiastic about possible *rapprochement* with Rome or (in the case of the Lutherans) also with Canterbury.

Finally, not much energy has gone into the Reformed/Lutheran conversations at least in the United States. The first round from 1962 to 1966 was in many ways excellent. The second, from 1971 to 1974, was by all accounts a disaster largely because of the obstructionist tactics of the conservative Missouri Synod which, with its two and a half million members, constitutes close to a third of American Lutheranism. The third round, from 1981 to 1983, was more successful, but yet cannot be said to have been strongly supported by its sponsoring bodies. Many more working hours have gone into the Lutheran/Roman Catholic conversations, for example, and the documentation is much more impressive in quantity and, so outside observers say, in quality also. In Europe, to be sure, the situation is different: the Leuenberg Agreement is a carefully crafted product of a massive inter-church effort. Yet even the Europeans on both the Lutheran and Reformed sides emphasize other parts of the ecumenical agenda more than their own interrelations, and are more interested in talking to Rome than with each other.

In summary, then, we reach the odd conclusion that although the Lutheran/Reformed dialogues have on paper been more successful than any others, they have evoked little enthusiasm and have had few practical effects. The time has now come to ask why.

Non-theological Factors

In trying to understand this situation, it is not altogether misleading to think of a courtship between two peoples – a courtship far more intense and prolonged than has ever existed between any English-speaking nations. The affair has been on-again, off-again, and as the decades have passed into centuries, both parties have changed. In some respects they have become more similar, in others, dissimilar. One party, the Reformed, has for the most part seen no barriers to union, while the other, the Lutheran, has persisted in finding doctrinal difficulties (although these difficulties have not prevented both sides from a good deal of unofficial cohabitation). Now finally, however, serious discussions – the most important since Marburg, 450 years ago – have led to the conclusion that the ostensible impediments are null and void. Yet in the meantime, the ardor of the Reformed has cooled even if it has not entirely disappeared, and the Lutherans, even when they agree that the doctrinal differences are no longer divisive; tend to remain reluctant. It seems obvious that there are factors at work on both sides other than theological agreements and disagreements: at least some of the divisive differences lie in the so-called non-theological realm. These, then, are the differences which I shall first describe, and then turn in the second place to theological and doctrinal considerations. Actually the two levels are intertwined, as we shall see, but it helps to begin by talking about them separately.

One way of getting at the non-theological factors is to compare a book such as John Leith's *Introduction to the Reformed Tradition* with a similar work on Lutheranism (e.g. Eric Gritsch's and Robert Jenson's book, *Lutheranism*). If we were to do this, we should discover commonalities everywhere, but also major differences. The most visible contrast is in liturgical practice: the Lutherans often retained medieval forms and ceremonies to a degree which shocked even the Anglicans in the days before the 19th century Oxford movement. The difference in polity is not so clearly marked because some Lutheran churches are organized in quasi-presbyterial or synodal patterns, others are episcopal, and still others are almost congregational, but yet the attitudes towards polity have been antagonistic. For Lutherans polity was an *adiaphoron*, a matter of theological indifference, whereas the Reformed, by and large, have taken it with high religious seriousness and have been organizationally far more disciplined and creative. The divergence on polity, in turn, is intertwined with great contrasts in ethos and cultural impact. There has been nothing on the Lutheran side comparable to the Calvinist sense of the Church as an elect, disciplined and holy people dedicated to serve and glorify God by destroying all that is idolatrous and opposed to his will, not only in the community of faith, but in society at large. The Church for Lutherans has been much more a hospital for sick souls than a mighty host. It is not surprising then that a Roman Catholic historian, Christopher Dawson, has said of the Calvinists that in the post-Reformation period they better exemplified than did Catholics or Lutherans the medieval sense of Christian faith as an agent of social and political transformation, and for this reason have been the architects of modernity. Both democracy and free-enterprise capitalism have been described as the products of Calvinism, and while this is to overdo the causal relation, no one would dream of making a similar claim for the other confessional traditions.

These contrasts, to be sure, have sometimes faded in the course of time. In many places, Lutherans came to resemble their Reformed neighbors especially in styles of worship and/or puritanic ethos. In Wuerttenberg, Germany or in parts of Pennsylvania to this day, it is hard to tell the difference. Yet for others, the contrasts are as stark as ever. The ceremonial which surrounds the consecration of a Swedish or Danish bishop, for example, is more medieval than anything which remains in the Church of England or even, as far as that goes, in contemporary Roman Catholicism: the king or queen retains a role on such occasions in Lutheran monarchies which has disappeared in Catholic ones. Although less spectacular, the contrasts can also be acutely felt even in America as I was reminded just the other day when talking to our Yale University chaplain about his boyhood in a small and isolated Lutheran parish in an overwhelmingly Protestant Ohio town. What made life difficult, he said, was that his school mates thought of him as some kind of Catholic. The interior of his church was enough to convince them of that. The other side of this is that many ordinary Lutherans such as those from my home congregation in New Haven do in fact feel more at home attending a Catholic Mass now that it is in English than they do in the Presbyterian church two blocks away. For people in the pew, it seems, the gap between Lutheran and Reformed is sometimes much greater than for most theologians, and this is by no means a new development. Even around 1600 in Europe there was a Lutheran proverb to the effect, 'Better a Jesuit than a Calvinist'. Such sentiments together with their less extreme Reformed counterparts account for much of the indifference with which the dialogues have been treated, and the source of these sentiments is largely, though not entirely, non-theological.

Theology

The time has come to shift from the pew to the seminary classroom, as the dialogues in effect do, and ask how the two confessional families are related theologically. In contrast to the so-called non-theological realm, the commonality is here overwhelming, and it is not surprising that discussions which center on historic theological differences reach the conclusion that none of them are church-dividing. There is one area, as we shall see, where questions persist, but for the remainder of this section we shall deal with agreements, not disagreements.

At the theological center are the three Reformatory 'solas': the *solus Christus, sola fides* (which includes the *sola gratia*) and the *sola Scriptura*. These affirmations were interconnected in a similar even if not wholly identical way for Luther and Calvin and to a lesser extent for Zwingli. For them the heart of the Christian gospel and the Christian life is salvation by grace and faith alone in Christ alone as witnessed to by Scripture alone.

Even today, as much conservative evangelicalism testifies, this tripartite emphasis can be a liberating force for individuals, but the Reformation was much more than a matter of winning individual souls. It was a community-building and church-renewing power. The triad of solas served hermeneutically to produce a basic consensus on how to read the Bible, and because of this agreement, Scripture could function as a truly effective communal authority, as both a judge of the Church and a creator of unity.

The basic hermeneutical principle is this: all Scripture witnesses to Christ and to justification by faith; or, more formally stated, the Bible is supremely authoritative only when read in terms of the *solus Christus* and the *sola gratia-sola fides*. One must immediately add, however, that this hermeneutical rule did not replace but rather corrected the earlier interpretive tradition. That tradition as exemplified by (even) Origen, Augustine and Aquinas, for example, insisted that all available rational means should be employed in interpreting the sacred text, that this must be done with the help and guidance of the Holy Spirit, and that interpretation must take place within the community of faith. The Reformers agreed, and were thereby distinguished from the enthusiasts on the left by the place they gave to reason, from later individualistic Protestantism by their communal emphasis, and from uncommitted scholarship by their stress on the Holy Spirit. Their exegetical method, like so much else of their theology, was fundamentally catholic, but it was a catholicism transformed and purified by a clearer articulation of the three solas than had ever before existed.

Most crucially, the sola triad gave them criteria for identifying the Church, the community of faith within which the Bible should be read. These criteria enabled them to dispense with the institutional marks, such as popes and councils, on which the Catholics relied, and yet they did not dissolve the Church into invisibility. The proper communities of interpretation, they said, are those in which the gospel of justification by faith alone in Christ alone is preached and celebrated (or, in other words, is communicated by word and sacrament). Where this gospel is thus communicated, even if poorly, the Church is visibly present, even if feebly. Calvin was more inclined than Luther to insist on discipline or obedient service as an identifying mark of the Church, but though historically of great importance, this was in its origins more a difference in emphasis and circumstance than in theological principle.

Further, the need for orderly polity, on the one hand, and for doctrinal standards or confessions of faith, on the other, was universally acknowledged. These, to be sure, are not marks of the Church, for the Church can visibly exist without them, but they are normally necessary means of witnessing to the truth and guarding against error.

The Reformation consensus, as you can see, was overwhelming. There is, I suppose, a Lutheran cast to the way I have formulated it. Calvin might want to add a fourth sola – to God alone be glory – but this is not a disagreement. He and Luther had no quarrels on the centrality of the three solas, on the basic hermeneutical method, and on the identification and fundamental structuring of the Church.

Furthermore, because this was a consensus in hermeneutical and church reforming *method*, it allowed for great diversity in conclusions. The mainline Reformers were by no means a homogeneous lot either theologically or practically, but however much they argued with each other, they were held together by a recognizably common interpretive procedure as well as common loyalty to their common Lord. What then were the theological disagreements which split the Reformation movement?

There was really only one, the dispute over the Lord's Supper, but we shall return to that in the next section. The other doctrinal debates were either spin-offs from this or else were ecclesially divisive only in some circumstances and not in others. In the case of predestination, to start with that, Calvin's way of treating it was similar to Luther's, but later Calvinists and Lutherans diverged more and more in both theory and pastoral practice (in part because they were already fighting with each other on other issues) until it became indeed a church-dividing doctrine. The divisiveness of predestination, in other words, was more a product than a cause of the division of the traditions.

Much the same can be said of the quarrels over Calvinist legalism and Lutheran antinomianism. There were differences between Calvin and Luther on church discipline, assurance of salvation, law and gospel, and the third use of the law, but even as late as the Formula of Concord in 1580 these were not thought of as church dividing. By the time of Westminster in 1647, however, both practice and theology had so diverged that Lutherans and the Reformed were in effect anathematizing each other on these issues. There is, for example, the story of a Lutheran pastor who died after vigorously eating, drinking and dancing into the Sabbath morn on the occasion of a Saturday wedding at which he had officiated. Yet after this scarcely edifying end, he was eulogized by the funeral preacher for testifying against Calvinist errors on salvation by grace alone through faith alone, not only in his life, but also in his death.

In reference to the far greater Reformed emphasis on the Church's independence of the state and on its society-shaping influence, there was no general contrast between the two traditions in the early period. It was, after all, a Reformed theologian, Erastus, who gave his name to the doctrine of total church subservience to the civil government, and it was the Magdeberg Lutherans who were the first within the mainstream to teach the permissibility of forceful resistance to tyrannical governments. Calvin did not disagree at all with Luther on the two kingdoms (at least that is what Brian Gerrish says, and he is the best guide I know on the subject[4]). It appears that historical circumstances much more than theology accounts for the different developments in this area. The Reformed were often urban, and thus had a greater chance to influence government than did the Lutherans in their wholly undemocratic and largely agrarian princedoms. Further, the Calvinists had to struggle for their existence in almost all the lands where they were strong, in the Rhineland, Scotland, England, Holland and France, while this was less often necessary for the Lutherans in their parts of Germany, and simply unknown to Scandinavia. Students of the subject are now inclined to think that it was these accidents of history much more than theology which made the Lutherans politically passive and almost medievally conservative in comparison to the world-shaping, capitalistic and democratic Reformed churches. By the 19th century, but not before, some Lutherans were so threatened by the contrast that they began searching in Luther for theological justifications for their political and social backwardness. As it happens, they succeeded, for Luther does sound more conservative than Calvin in those areas, for example on the question of usury. But then his entire working life was spent in a minor university in an agrarian village within the domains of a feudal prince, whereas Calvin's lot was cast in the commercial and intellectual heartland of Europe in a free and independent city. It took three centuries for that non-theological difference to be escalated into a major doctrinal disagreement, but it happened.

On the differences over the Church and its polity, it is helpful to remember that Calvin was a second-generation Reformer who wrote in a situation where all hope of reunion with Rome had vanished and Protestants needed to devise a new constitution for a new Church. Luther never thought in these terms. He acquiesced to prince-dominated church orders as emergency measures designed to provide temporary stability until the Church as a whole was reformed and a purified version of the historic episcopal polity could be re-introduced. If he had lived in Geneva when Calvin did, he might well have produced something comparable to the Fourth Book of the Institutes. Ecclesiology would not then have been the underdeveloped territory in Lutheran theology which it remains to this day. Even now most Lutheran dogmaticians rather neglect the Church, saying little in substance other than it is *creatura verbi*, a creation of the Word, the offspring of the proclamatory and sacramental communication of the gospel. When they venture farther afield, they often borrow either from the Reformed or the Catholics with the result that Lutherans differ from each other on the Church and its ministry almost as much as do Geneva and Rome. Lutheran ecclesiological conflicts have been more within the ranks than with the Reformed.

The christological disputes surrounding the *intra-Lutheranum* and the *extra-Calvinisticum*[5] are a different story, for they began early and were venomously conducted. Yet here again it is hard to imagine that they would have ever been church-dividing if it had not been for their connection with something else – in this case, the Lord's Supper. Beginning with Zwingli, the Reformed argued that if the flesh and blood of the resurrected and ascended Christ are genuinely human, as faith affirms, they are incapable of omnipresence, *non capax infiniti*.[6] They cannot, therefore, be 'in, with and under' the bread and wine as Luther taught. Luther replied in part that Jesus is not now in a spatialized heaven beyond the highest empyrean, but is rather at the right hand of God, and that is everywhere. So far, I suppose, the present-day Reformed no less than Lutherans would agree with him. He then went on to say, however, that the two natures are so united in Christ that his flesh and blood is indeed capable of ubiquity, the finite can receive infinity. In the course of time, this Christological postulate became, so it can be argued, one of the sources of Hegel's philosophy, and it has at times been seen as the root difference between the two traditions; but now, it is perhaps unnecessary to say, no one tries to debate it in its original form. The *extra-Calvinisticum* depended on a Ptolemaic cosmology which has been replaced by Copernican and Einsteinian ones, and the *intra-Lutheranum* insofar as it involves a seemingly physical ubiquity cannot be taken seriously. In any case, given the modern mood and the advent of historical criticism, Lutherans are nowadays no more likely than Calvinists to deny that Jesus was fully human. The problem for both parties in our times is to maintain Christ's divinity.

The disputes of the past we have so far reviewed were not pointless. They patterned behavior in ways which were often as antithetical as those which now divide fundamentalists from non-fundamentalists, pro-life partisans from pro-choice advocates, marxist liberationists from non-marxists. If these current quarrels did not cut across denominational lines, as they in fact do, they would make church fellowship impossible. I, at least, cannot imagine a coalition of fundamentalist, pro-life, anti-marxist Presbyterians (or Lutherans, as the case may be) entering full communion with a group of marxist, liberationist, pro-choice, anti-fundamentalist counterparts. Yet the opposition between Lutherans and Reformed has at times been of almost equal seriousness.

What made the opposition serious, as we have seen, was the intertwining of theology and practice of doctrine and behavior. Thus reconciliation can come about either through changes in theological outlook or in behavioral practice, and most often in both. That in fact is what has happened in the five areas we have reviewed. Ecclesiological disputes have been within rather than between these two confessional families. When it comes to ethos and social impact, Lutherans may still drink and smoke more freely and be less politically engaged than many Presbyterians, but it is much harder now than in the past to draw any general contrasts between the purportedly antinomian and politically passive followers of Brother Martin and the allegedly puritanic, legalistic and politically active heirs of John Calvin. On pre-destination, both doctrine and behavior have altered, especially on the Reformed side, with the result that even the Westminster Confession – that most problematic yet brilliant of doctrinal documents – is now ecumenically innocuous. On Christology, the general theological outlook has shifted so thoroughly that both parties have largely forgotten the original dispute. In reference to all these topics, the dialogues seem wholly convincing when they claim that the remaining differences are a matter of tolerable and potentially enriching theological diversity rather than church-dividing doctrinal disagreement. This is true in both the theological and non-theological domains. When one looks at what has happened to most of the past disputes, it is hard to see why the two traditions do not immediately accept the dialogue recommendations and enthusiastically enter full communion.

The chief, though not the only, reasons for their failure to do this are their differences over the sacraments and especially the Lord's Supper. We shall describe these in the next section and then also deal with what are the truly decisive issues. In what ways if at all is the Reformation heritage – especially the three solas as they identify the hermeneutical method – of continuing importance for you, and for me, and for the unity and renewal of the Church universal? If it is important, what can and should our two confessional families, the Reformed and the Lutheran, do in order to promote it?

Remaining Problems and the Ecumenical Context

The Lord's Supper

The Reformed/Lutheran differences on the sacraments, especially the Lord's Supper, are central. These differences were the cause of the first division at Marburg in 1529, and they are the only historically important ones which remain seriously troubling. They account for most of the hesitation with which the dialogue recommendations have been met, and it is because of them that Lutherans and the Reformed diverge in ecumenical strategy, as we shall see. Treatment in depth would be desirable, but I shall try to be brief.

In brief, then, the Eucharist controversies have three dimensions: theological, liturgical and pastoral or church political. Of these, the theological and liturgical dimensions are no longer in themselves divisive, but the pastoral and church political one is a locus of major difficulties.

The change from the 16th century is not as radical as one might suppose. Theological difficulties are generally thought of as primary, but they did not seem insurmountable to either Calvin or to Luther's closest associate, Phillip Melanchthon. To be sure, Luther's way of conceptualizing the real presence is more medieval, and Calvin's more patristic or Augustinian, but it was possible even then to see them both as high sacramental realists.[7] In our current situation this has become almost self-evident. They both insist that in the eucharistic meal believers genuinely partake of the true body and blood of Christ, and this is enough to make them both acceptable by the standards even of the Catholics with whom Lutherans are in dialogue (and who, it should be remembered, are appointed by Rome). What needs to be affirmed, these Catholics say, is *that* Christ is given and received in his full humanity (which includes his body and blood), but the how of this communication can never be adequately explained and a variety of theological formulations is allowable and necessary. But Calvin no less than Luther agrees on the 'that,' and as far as the 'how' is concerned, if Augustine did not contradict transubstantiation, neither does Calvin. In this contemporary ecumenical context in which Calvin's teaching is seen as compatible with Roman doctrine, reconciliation with Luther seems easy. The problem is to understand why Luther did not agree.

The reasons which can be documented are conceptual and exegetical. Although Luther tried to exclude all philosophical considerations from theology, he was nevertheless a medieval nominalist in his habits of thought, and the platonic elements in Augustine's Eucharist doctrine were much less congenial to him than to Calvin. An even graver difficulty was that he came to depend in his controversy with Zwingli on what for him was uncharacteristically flat-footed and non-contextual proof-texting which, however, also excluded Calvin's later and very different position. Thus Luther and most of his followers came to equate Calvin with Zwingli or as the Formula of Concord puts it, the Calvinists are the more subtle and therefore more dangerous sacramentarians.

We can now see that accusing Calvin of a low sacramentalism (for that is what 'sacramentarianism' refers to) was grossly unfair. Calvin's position was very different from Zwingli's. While he agreed that Christ in his ascended humanity remains, so to speak, in heaven, he insisted against Zwingli that the Holy Spirit genuinely lifts believers up into that heavenly realm to receive the Lord's body and blood. If only Luther had been less stubbornly fixated on his formulations, he would have granted, as did Melanchthon, that this was high sacramentalism. So Calvin thought, and so also do the present dialogue partners whether Lutheran or Reformed.

More than stubbornness was involved, however. This becomes clear once one turns to liturgy, to ways of worship (a dimension which the dialogues unfortunately neglect). The problem here was that the Reformed were *dogmatically* opposed to high church ritual. They were not only low church in their own practice, but they objected theologically to those who were not. Thus they condemned as idolatry and superstition the crucifixes, vestments, bells, and elevation of the host which the Lutherans for the most part retained. They also rejected as unscriptural the practice of private confession in preparation for communion, while Luther defended this as a pastorally useful rite, and regularly went to confession to his dying day. (As a matter of fact, it was not until 200 years later during the Enlightenment that private confession, which by that time had largely declined into catechetical instruction, died out in most Lutheran churches.) Calvin himself was more willing than most of his associates and followers to tolerate such aberrations for the sake of unity as long as doctrine was sound, but even for him, the toleration was a temporary matter: the norm towards which one should always strive was primitive simplicity.

The Lutherans, in contrast, regarded modes of worship as *adiaphora*, just as they did variations in polity. Everything depended on circumstances, on whether high or low church ritual was more effective in a given situation in communicating the gospel of God's saving love and forgiveness in Jesus Christ. Thus when the Reformed insisted on low church ritual as preferable, as more in accordance with God's will, Lutherans resisted. To suppose there are general rules in these matters is, as they usually put it, to confuse law and gospel, to infringe on Christian liberty by legal prescriptions, to turn the Bible into a rubrical textbook. Because for them the freedom of the gospel was at stake, high church ritual often became *status confessionis*:[8]

they professed willingness to abandon it where it was pastorally ineffective, but this willingness disappeared when it was attacked as unscriptural or contrary to divine commands.

The Reformed for the most part found these objections simply bewildering because for them the issue was not Christian freedom but rather idolatry and superstition. For example, as you recall, they applied the Old Testament prohibition of graven images to all pictures and statues in churches including, of course, crucifixes. Further, Reformed Protestantism, in contrast to the Lutheran variety, as we noted already, was shaped chiefly in the second generation of the Reformation when hope for union with Rome had vanished and relations with Catholicism had become wholly polemical. There was a greater need in this situation than any Luther had experienced to make the distinction between Protestants and Catholics dramatically visible, and the success of the Reformed in doing this gave them a competitive advantage over Lutherans in the succeeding anti-Roman centuries. Lastly, as we also noted earlier, the Reformed movement took its rise in the most urbanized, humanistically influenced, and anti-medieval parts of Europe, and there the iconoclastic horror of medieval forms was more intense and widespread than in Lutheran lands.

The main point that concerns us is that iconoclastic fury with its dogmatically low church consequences made Calvinist professions of high sacramentalism incredible to many Lutherans. It seemed impossible to them that anyone who truly believed that Christ's most holy and precious body and blood are truly offered and received in the Eucharist rite could denounce festive flourishes in its celebration as blasphemous idolatry and superstition. If Christ's presence were truly acknowledged, there could be no objections to having both simple meals and celebratory feasts in the church, so the Lutherans maintained.

In our day, ecumenically inclined Reformed Christians are no longer iconoclastically and dogmatically low church, and it is this change in attitude and doctrine which more than anything else, it seems to me, has made the theological differences non-divisive. Opposition to everything Roman has lessened, historical research has taught us that the New Testament is neither high church nor low church (or, perhaps better, it is from our perspective a strange mixture of both), and the Reformed have stopped equating high church ceremonies with idolatry or superstition (the objection nowadays is much more likely to be to unmanly, high-brow aestheticism, but cocktail-drinking Anglicans are more often the butt of this accusation than are beer-swilling Lutherans). Because all this has happened, it is now much easier than in the past for Lutherans to take at face value the sacramental realism of Calvin's eucharistic teaching.

Yet this disappearance of theological and liturgical divisiveness has not eliminated pastoral and church political problems. The difficulty here is that Calvin's high sacramentalism was ineffective against that Protestant disregard of the sacraments (not least the Eucharist) which we usually (and somewhat unfairly) call Zwinglianism. This Zwinglian sacramentarianism, Luther thought, was the greatest internal threat to the Reformation. To suppose that the Lord's Supper is a mere memorial, a sign of the faith of the participants rather than a life-giving source of justifying faith on a par with (though inseparable from) preaching, was to subvert a primary means of grace. Calvin was fatally compromised in Lutheran eyes by his association with the bearers of this plague. Zwinglians were not greatly offended by Calvin's version of sacramental realism (not least because he was liturgically as low church as they were), and he, on his side, remained in communion with them. Thus Calvinist teaching on the sacraments was at best ineffective in repelling sacramentarian influence, and at worst, so Lutherans suspected, it was a camouflage for the spread of the infection.

The intensity of the Lutherans' fears cannot be understood unless one remembers that they were constantly struggling against sacramental minimalism in their own churches. This struggle continues. There is a saying in Bavaria that lay people are Zwinglians, the pastors Calvinists, and only the theologians *echt* ('kosher') *Lutheraner* in their understanding of the real presence. In areas less traditionally orthodox than Bavaria not even the theologians can be counted on. Yet, so the high church party generally believes, as long as the liturgy holds firm or liturgical renewal is taken seriously, the battle is not lost; and in this conviction they are, I suppose, on sound anthropological ground. As anyone who has grown up Lutheran is likely to have experienced, when the sacraments are important in the worship of a church, Zwinglian concepts can coexist with a eucharistic sensibility and piety which is anything but Zwinglian, but they do so uneasily. It is to protect and nurture this sensibility and piety that liturgy and theology are important, and it is the pastorally motivated anxiety that these defenses will be weakened by full communion with the Reformed which is one source of Lutheran reluctance to implement the recommendations of the dialogues.

It is, to be sure, not the only source. Strongly sacramental Lutherans, like many less sacramental ones, generally take confessional subscription seriously. They fear, however, that confessional authority has eroded even more in Reformed churches than in their own. The Reformation heritage itself seems threatened, for where the historic confessions of faith are neglected, there seems little hope for the *solus Christus*, the *sola fides* and the *sola Scriptura* or for the biblical hermeneutics which they undergird. Similar apprehensions are, to be sure, also found among the Reformed, but Lutherans generally suppose, rightly or wrongly, that the defenders of the historic faith are more numerous on their side of the confessional divide. Some of them fear that closer association with the Reformed will further dilute what little adherence to confessional standards still remains.

Not that the Lutherans I am speaking of are opposed to intercommunication of the kind now often called 'eucharistic hospitality'. They approve of the practice of welcoming to the table all baptized Christians who can in good conscience participate in Lutheran communion services and of leaving it to the individual to decide whether or not to partake when attending Reformed or other Christian churches. The closed communion policies of the Missouri Synod are an exception among the world's 70 million Lutherans. Yet many ecumenically open Lutherans who are well aware that they are sacramentally closer to the Reformed Max Thurian and Roger Schütz of Taizé than to most of their fellow church members hesitate for pastoral reasons at full altar and pulpit fellowship.

It is difficult to estimate how numerous these Lutherans are. There are enough of them, however, to give pause to other Lutherans who favor full communion with the Reformed. Those in favor are generally moved by considerations of theological principle, it seems to me, rather than by practical concerns. They believe that full communion should be instituted whenever there are no doctrinal obstacles, and doctrinal obstacles have disappeared now that Lutherans and the Reformed can recognize each other's historic positions as not excluding each other. Yet pulpit and altar fellowship is not for most of them practically urgent, and, given the resistance, they prefer not to push the issue, not to rock the boat. Their reluctance is church political rather than pastoral, but the outcome is the same. The Reformation churches remain apart. They no longer quarrel over their confessions or over eucharistic theology and liturgy as they once did, but it is the sacrament of unity which above all continues to separate them rather than to unite.

The Wider Ecumenical Context

The wider ecumenical consequences of this situation are probably to some extent familiar to most of us. The Reformed, to start with them, are oriented towards their fellow Protestants. They are usually the main movers in Protestant church unions (which sometimes to be sure, as in South India and in the COCU[9] proposals, include Anglicans). The Lutherans, in contrast, generally seem more interested in the Roman Catholics, the Anglicans, or even the Eastern Orthodox. The Reformed picture of the ecumenically united Church of the future includes, needless to say, all confessional families, but the pattern (which tends to be reflected in World Council statements) has a Protestant character. Union should first take place in local situations, and these local and regional churches should be in communion with each other, but the question of whether they should be interconnected by anything more than pulpit and altar fellowship is left open. Organizations such as the World Council are no doubt desirable, yet these are not parts of the structure of the Church, but are rather simply consultative and cooperative agencies. There is little talk of common governance, however minimal, or even of ministries of unity to the wider church such as are provided by the Archbishop of Canterbury in the Anglican communion and the Ecumenical Patriarch in Eastern Orthodoxy, not to mention the Pope in Roman Catholicism. In short, little attention is given to institutionalizing transnational or global unity either in the present or future.

When Lutherans begin talking about ecumenical strategy, the picture is very different. The path to unity does not lead through multilateral unions between all the Christian groups in a given area which then join in larger associations, but rather starts with bilateral unions between different confessions either in local situations or on a worldwide scale. The ultimate hope, to be sure, is that all Christians in a given place will be joined in a fully united local church, but that is a final rather than proximate goal. Most startlingly, Lutherans increasingly understand themselves, just as they did in their sixteenth-century beginnings, not primarily as a church or group of churches, but as a reforming movement within the wider church which was unjustly expelled from the Catholic communion. Thus its mission can be fulfilled and its proper identity regained only by reunion with Rome. Or, to put it another way, the reason for Lutheran existence now, and not only at the time of the Augsburg Confession in 1530, is to bring the Reformation understanding of the gospel first to the Latin church of the West and then to the Church universal. Even the papacy is seen as potentially important for all Christians providing it is re-interpreted and restructured under the gospel (as Lutheran/Catholic dialogues have put it). Thus it seems that their stress on sacraments and historic doctrinal standards makes many Lutherans feel more comfortable about union with Roman Catholics (providing Lutheran teachings and sacraments are acknowledged as legitimate) than with their fellow Reformed heirs of the Reformation legacy.

Both the Reformed and the Lutheran ecumenical agendas are visionary. The type of church unions which the Reformed have favored are not multiplying rapidly, and communion between Rome and Lutherans (or Rome and Anglicans, as far as that goes) is not likely to come closer during the present pontificate according to most observers. Yet goals, however remote, shape present policy. The stress placed by Lutherans on worldwide confessional families, for example, is reflected in the size of the Lutheran World Federation, which is a much more massive operation than the Reformed World Alliance, and by the lesser, though not unimportant, support which they give to the World Council of Churches. It is also manifest in their emphasis on bilateral dialogues with Roman Catholics, Anglicans and Eastern Orthodox, all of whom they talk with on the worldwide level more than with the Reformed (who, on their side, have focussed most of their attention on multi-lateral discussions).

This divergence in ecumenical orientation becomes even more striking when one considers that it is at odds with other and infrastructurally more fundamental developments. The modernizing homogenization of culture and society makes Lutherans and Reformed more and more similar at the grass-roots level both in the United States and elsewhere even while historic forces and ecclesiastical politics tend in some respects to pull them apart. Some think that the homogenizing tendencies will win. They suspect, for example, that the Evangelical Lutheran Church in America will develop into just another mainline American denomination in which the distinctive Lutheran mixture of Jesus-centered evangelical piety and catholic sacramentalism on the one hand, and confessional commitment and anti-fundamentalist biblical criticism on the other, is less and less in evidence. Already in most places in Europe the Lutherans are only marginally more sacramental and confessional than their Reformed counterparts. Zwinglianism cannot be blamed for this as in past centuries, but rather secularizing or other de-Christianizing influences.

Growing similarity of this kind, however, is subversive of all Christian substance, not simply of the specifically Reformation heritage, and it makes the resultant ecumenism problematic. Non-Protestants as well as Protestants are troubled by this development. Among them, for example, is Karl Rahner, perhaps the most influential Roman Catholic theologian of this century as well as a committed ecumenist in favor of immediate union between Rome and the major non-Catholic confessional families of churches including the Reformed and the Lutheran. Yet he has argued that Christian union on the basis of the lowest common denominator – that is, without confessional and sacramental substance – is simply not desirable. There are many in both the Reformed and Lutheran camps who share his reservations. They are in favor of the unification of the churches but see no point to it when what makes it possible is the weakening of all definite commitments and convictions.

The Common Task

What, then, is the ecumenical import of the Reformation heritage, and what, if anything, should the Reformed and the Lutherans do together or separately in order to promote it? These are the questions which I said at the beginning are most important.

It is the Reformation way of reading the authoritative sources of the faith which seems to me of primary ecumenical significance. The Reformation hermeneutics built community then, and something like it is needed to build community now.

This community-building power of Reformation biblical interpretation is perhaps nowhere more evident than in its bridging of the chasm which separated the Lutherans and the Reformed. They were divided at the Lord's table for deep historical, cultural and sociological reasons as well as theological ones, and yet they were so unmistakably similar in their way of reading Scripture that they continued to take each other seriously as fellow Christians who must be listened to even when it would have been less troubling simply to ignore each other. Despite their differences, they constituted a single community of interpretation to an astonishing degree.

Also remarkable is the way in which each confession held together without any overarching organizational structures or even the ability to convoke common councils. (The Synod of Dort was the closest to being a general council on either side, but even it was basically a Dutch gathering with some foreigners in attendance, and it happened only once.) Among the Reformed, to focus on them, the Hungarian, Swiss, Dutch, French, Scots and English churches were utterly independent – they even composed separate confessional documents – but yet their fundamentally common hermeneutics kept them in communion even in the midst of fierce arguments. To be sure, the fact that they had in Rome a common enemy was a unifying factor, but their fellowship had deeper grounds than that. For the first 100 years or so the *sola Scriptura* was unitive, and it was only after the Reformation hermeneutics collapsed that it became divisive.

The collapse, it needs to be emphasized, preceded the advent of biblical criticism. Anti-Romanism intensified, and the later Protestants, unlike Calvin and Luther, read Scripture less and less within the universal catholic community of faith. They abandoned the constant early Reformation consultation of (though not necessarily agreement with) the Greek and Latin fathers of the first centuries, and of medieval theologians such as Bernard of Clairvaux and, to a surprising degree, Thomas Aquinas. Instead they attempted to leap back directly to the Bible. The rise of pietistic individualism made the situation worse: now even the present community which is the contemporary church was ignored, and the insight that the Spirit uses reason (including the best available scholarly tools) was neglected. Protestant Orthodoxy, to be sure, continued to insist on reason in reading the sacred text, but its notion of what is reasonable was increasingly influenced by early modern rationalism and by the literalism of Newtonian science. Rationalistic literalism, however, makes possible all previous Christian ways of reading the Bible, whether Reformation or pre-Reformation. Jesus Christ is no longer the interpretive key to all of Scripture, and the specifically Reformation emphasis on the hermeneutical role of justification by grace alone through faith alone also falls by the wayside. Thus Protestant Orthodoxy gave birth to fundamentalism and to such strange aberrations (from the viewpoint of the historic exegetical mainstream) as Scofield Bible dispensational pre-millenialism. It is chiefly a combination of pietistic revivalism and rationalistic orthodoxy rather than modern biblical scholarship which undermined the older hermeneutics and made the *sola Scriptura* divisive rather than unitive.

On the general cultural scene, however, Enlightenment rationalism and Newtonian literalism are no longer dominant, and historical criticism has undermined fundamentalism among those who agree with the Reformers that God wants Christians to use their minds as well as hearts in construing Holy Writ. Karl Barth on the Protestant side and, among Catholics, those *ressourcement* (that is, back-to-sources) theologians who prepared for Vatican II have shown by their practice that traditional exegesis can accommodate historical-critical conclusions. Yet, on the whole, it is historical-critical methods used independently of historic forms of interpretation which dominate the hermeneutical scene. These methods, however, while indispensable in eliminating ill-founded arguments for past divisions, are by themselves incapable of providing theological guidance of promoting Church unity. If Christians are to be guided towards unity, so the Reformers would say, they need to place themselves within the total community of faith and read the authoritative sources as witnesses in their entirety to Jesus Christ who in his very humanity is Immanuel, God with us, and is alone to be trusted and obeyed in life and death. (If that sounds like Barmen,[10] so much the better, for Barmen is the outstanding ecclesial example of Reformation hermeneutics in recent times.)

This hermeneutics, we must next note, is catholic and ecumenical, not narrowly Reformation Protestant. The contribution of the Reformers, as I suggested earlier, was to clarify and intensify the hermeneutical implications of the pre-Reformation conviction that Scripture is primary and is to be christocentrically interpreted. Even on the question of tradition they had much of the pre-Reformation Church on their side, for what they opposed was the exaltation of tradition over the Bible, and they affirmed rather than denied the importance of listening attentively though critically to the interpretations of the past (that is, tradition). Not only did they admire much earlier exegesis, but their basic emphases are not inconsistent with what the Second Vatican Council says in *Verbum Dei*, the Constitution on Divine Revelation. There also the appeal is fundamentally to Scripture christocentrically interpreted, and tradition is viewed primarily as the Church's understanding down through the ages of the scriptural witness to revelation. The practice of the Reformatory method is not dependent on the specifically Reformation formulations, and it is the practice which counts.

It is hard to see how any Christian unity worth having is possible apart from this practice. There must be some measure of agreement on the way to seek together for what is authentically Christian. If not, one of two things happens. Either ecumenism will be the mindlessly permissive lowest-common-denominator enterprise which Karl Rahner warned against, or else old and new differences will continually breed divisive conflicts rather than being held together in creative tension within the undivided Church of Christ. Clearly popes and councils cannot be the exclusive interpreters (even the Catholic populace now objects to that), nor can prophetic voices be uncritically harkened to (for we must discern the spirits), nor can democratic majorities be trusted, for they are notoriously fickle and arbitrary. What is needed is an intellectually responsible, spiritually fruitful, ecumenically acceptable and communally persuasive process of searching in the authoritative sources for what is authentically Christian for us today. If there is any other candidate besides an up-dated and more catholic version of the Reformation hermeneutical approach, I would be interested in hearing what it is.

It is not enough for such a hermeneutics to be simply scholarly. Academic work is needed – I think here about such colleagues of mine at Yale as Brevard Childs and Hans Frei as well as the last chapter of a book I published on *The Nature of Doctrine* – but pastoral training is no less important and congregational formation absolutely necessary. The reformatory power of the Reformation unfolded only as whole communities became habituated to reading the Bible in the Reformation way, and something similar is necessary for ecumenism. A Dutch pastor once told me that the best parish he had ever had was one in which the people knew their Bibles and the Heidelberg catechism and read one in the light of the other. Over and over again when visiting members he was challenged to relate his liberal and ecumenical sermons to that foundation. He learned to do this, and his congregation responded, but even more important, he said, his liberalism and ecumenism became much more solidly and effectively Christian. What Christian unity needs more than anything else, I suspect, is the multiplication in all the traditions of congregations similarly steeped in the sources, yet reading them not only in Reformed, Lutheran, Pentecostal, Roman Catholic or Eastern Orthodox ways, but also in terms of something like the Lima document on *Baptism, Eucharist and Ministry*. It is only when the Bible is studied assiduously and communally within ecumenical rather than divisive interpretive frameworks that we can expect ecumenism to acquire the force of the Word of God.

From this perspective, the shared ecumenical task both of the Reformed and the Lutherans is to help promote congregational Bible reading of a catholic Reformatory kind in their own ranks and in other confessional families. Yet, as we have seen, there is a difference in orientation. The Reformed responsibility for biblical renewal may be directed chiefly towards low-church Protestantism while that of the Lutherans may point more towards the high-church traditions, Catholic, Orthodox and Anglican. The two Reformation bodies are themselves now so deficient in Bible-reading congregations, however, that they cannot be thought of as philanthropists sharing their rich legacy with others, but rather as themselves in need of the heritage they have squandered. Their journey to regain that inheritance for themselves and for all Christian traditions may take them on divergent paths.

Perhaps, then, their lack of full communion with others is not an ecumenical disadvantage. Perhaps they will thereby be enabled to cooperate more effectively with a wider range of different Christian traditions. At the very beginning, I suggested the analogy of the English-speaking peoples. Just as the way to promote their heritage (the democratic one) in the world at large is not now, it would seem, to unite, so also, perhaps, in the case of the Reformation churches.

This can at most be only temporarily true, however. Churches, though more like the peoples of this world than we ordinarily like to think, are yet subject to divine commands of which other communities know nothing. And one of those commands is unity so that, as John puts it, 'the world may believe'. Lutherans and the Reformed are commanded to unite whenever and wherever this promotes wider Christian unity on the one hand, and strengthens their gospel heritage on the other.

I have no special wisdom on when the time for their unity will arrive, but when it comes, both traditions will benefit. The special Lutheran contribution is that high sacramentalism which Calvin also wanted, while what Lutherans need above all from the Reformed is a sense of the Church as an elect people, continuous with Israel, graciously chosen to testify – corporately and not simply individually – to God's love and glory in all that it is, says and does, constantly erring yet constantly renewed by promises which never fail. When the best of Lutheran sacramentalism is combined with an authentically Reformed sense of the Church, the result, I am prepared to argue, is something like the early Catholic pattern of the first centuries. This early Catholic pattern is also reflected in the Lima document, and it alone seems capable of providing a basis for wider Church unity.

Author's note: In the discussions which followed the delivery of these lectures, I emphasized more than is apparent in the above pages that I personally have hesitations about 'pulpit and altar fellowship' with the Reformed in the United States. Unlike *rapprochement* with Roman Catholics, such fellowship seems to me likely, under present circumstances, to contribute to the further erosion of the confessional and sacramental substance of the Lutheran Reformation.

6. Unbelievers and the *'Sola Christi'**

Editor's Introduction

The topic of the salvation of non-Christians has long been important for Christians. It became even more important in modernity as Christians encountered a globe of diverse religions as well as non-religious ways of life and thought – a world where it became increasingly difficult to live and think as if their neighbors were not saved (that is, damned). On the one hand, God wills the salvation of all humanity (I Timothy 2.4). On the other hand, salvation is through Christ alone (*sola Christi*). If we do not wish to deny God's universal salvific will or the necessity of Christ for salvation, what shall we say about unbelievers? We do not want to say that God aims to save only some – or that some other savior can do what Christ does not. We also do not want to say that God *will* save everyone (a position sometimes called 'universalism'), although we may *hope* for the salvation of all ('quasi-universalism', Lindbeck calls it).

But how? Lindbeck discusses two theories, Karl Rahner's theology of anonymous Christians (where non-Christians are saved now in the deep private depths of their being, whether they know it or not) and his own 'primarily futuristic eschatological theory' (where everyone will be explicitly offered salvation in the future). Lindbeck does not rule out Rahner's theory but argues that his eschatological theory is more plausible. (As the introduction points out, an eschatology is a set of claims about the eschaton – God's end, or ultimate goal for things. In contrast to Christians who claim that God's end is fully present now, Lindbeck calls his eschatology 'futuristic'.)

This essay is a good example of Lindbeck's Lutheran tradition giving central importance to the faith that comes by hearing. It is also a good example of his ecumenical sensibilities, for he disagrees with Rahner but

---

* George A Lindbeck, 'Unbelievers and the "Sola Christi"', *Dialog* **12** (1973), pp. 182–9.

does not rule his position out of the Church. It also embodies a developing philosophical anthropology in which human identity is constituted by ways in which we are shaped 'from outside' rather than autonomously construct ourselves 'from within'. Lindbeck re-iterates this view of unbelievers as a theologically preferable and doctrinally permissible view in *The Nature of Doctrine*. However, the final essay in this volume (Chapter Twelve) will suggest that these 'soteriological' theories (theories having to do with salvation) may help Christians deal with these issues more than they serve non-Christians.

Many church members are troubled by the easy assumption that non-Christians can be saved, and this is not always because they are narrow or self-righteous.[1] They may, indeed, be keenly aware of the immense opportunities for damnation within the Church. What concerns them, rather, is a logical problem, a problem of cognitive dissonance. Scripture affirms, liturgy celebrates and the churches have historically asserted the *sola Christi*, salvation through Christ alone. How then can men and women be saved outside the visible church, that is, apart from explicit faith in God's redemptive action in Jesus Christ?

The fact that the difficulty is one of consistency does not mean, however, that it is purely theoretical. Hearts, minds and whole denominations have been torn asunder by the conflict. The life-work of tens of thousands of missionaries and evangelists, and the expenditure of millions of dollars hangs in the balance. Some say that the identity and viability of Christianity itself depends on the outcome. On the one hand, the *sola Christi* seems indispensable. How can one plausibly claim continuity with Scripture and tradition if one denies that Jesus is the only mediator between God and man, the one who is universal Lord, not only *pro me*, but for everyone? Yet, on the other hand, as the Reformed theologian Heinrich Ott has expressed it, 'Only a sectarian sensibility could manage to consider all men who do not explicitly confess Christ as automatically lost and excluded from the realm of God's saving actions . . . It is precisely out of the spirit of the gospel that this interpretation comes.'[2]

There was a time when the situation was different. Once the whole of the West was professedly Christian and non-Christians were distant or unknown. That made it easy to judge them harshly or unfairly. Now, however, the unbelievers are neighbors, friends and relatives. As Karl Rahner has put it, 'One must rely on their humanity, reliability and decency just as much as on the corresponding qualities in one's fellow believers (in which process one sometimes gets the staggering impression that one can rely much more on the former than the latter).'[3] In short, whatever theology

and logic may say, it has become psychologically and sociologically impossible for most Christians and Christian communities to assign non-Christians
en masse to damnation. Only sectarian groups whose basic attitudes seem
to most church people both inhuman and unchristian succeed in doing this.

The result has been the spread of what might be called 'quasi-universalist'
views. These are not simply the repetition of the universalism historically
associated, rightly or wrongly, with Origen, condemned at Constantinople
in AD 543,[4] and repudiated by most Protestant as well as Catholic traditions
since. This position positively affirmed that all would be restored (*apokatast-
asis*), none would be lost. The advocates of quasi-universalism, in contrast,
do not deny the possibilite of damnation, although they then go on and insist
that Christians are obligated by their confidence in the mercy and power
of God to hope, really hope, that this possibility will never be actualized.
The more exclusive sounding New Testament passages (e.g. Luke 16.16)
must be interpreted in the light of the more universalist ones (e.g. Col. 1.20;
Eph. 1.9, 10; Phil. 2.10, 11; 1 Cor. 15.28; 1 Jn 2.2; Acts 3.21), rather than
vice versa, as most of the post-biblical tradition has done. The exclusivist
statements must be understood, not as predictions, but as warnings of what
the definitive rejection of God in Christ entails. These warnings, furthermore, are directed more to members of the people of God (Israel and the
Church) than to outsiders, for only the former, having met the Messiah,
are in the critical position of being able to decide against him (cf. Heb. 12.25;
2 Pet. 2.21. Such teachings are now in the process of becoming official
doctrine, at least in Roman Catholicism. There are strong hints of these in
the documents of Vatican II,[5] even though these do not go as far as the
bon mot which circulated in the corridors of the Council: 'It is dogma that
there is a hell, but not that there is anyone in it.'

This development, however, still leaves open the question with which we
started. How can non-Christians be saved? How can this be reconciled with
the *sola Christi?* Two basic types of explanation are available. One pictures
God's saving work in Jesus Christ as effective for all men here and now
within the confines of this present life. The other, in contrast, prefers futuristically eschatological imagery. The eternal destiny of human beings is
decided in death or beyond death in the encounter with Jesus, the life of
the world to come.

Two fundamentally different forms of the first approach may be distinguished. The first is associated almost exclusively with Karl Barth. According to this, the way in which God, acting in Christ, saves non-Christians is
thoroughly 'objective'. Their status in the eyes of God has been transformed
quite apart from any 'subjective' changes in themselves. They have become
'potential Christians' or *christiani designati*. When one tries to present this
view in popular 'preachable' terms, it seems to say that explicit faith makes

only a noetic difference, informing non-Christians of what they already are. Yet this Christian reality is not something 'in' the non-Christians. No signs or expressions of it can be discovered by empirical, philosophical or theological examinations of the experiences, religions or ideologies of non-Christians.[6]

According to others, however, the subjecthood, the transcendental heights and depths, of all human beings have been affected by the *gratia Christi* whether they know it or not. This view is dominant, though not universal, among contemporary Roman Catholic theologians, and has been especially fully developed by Karl Rahner.[7] He speaks of an 'anonymous Christianity' produced by the hidden operations of the justifying grace of Christ and manifest, though in distorted and inadequate forms, in the experiences, religions and ideologies of non-Christians. His theory is basically a reworking of classical Thomistic theses regarding infused grace and saving implicit faith in the light of post-Kantian idealistic, romantic and existentialist thought. There are hints of similar ways of viewing the situation of non-Christians in the thinking of Protestant theologians who have been influenced by the same modern philosophical developments. Paul Tillich, for example, speaks of the 'latent church' (which, to be sure, is by no means identical to 'anonymous Christianity',[8] and Wolfhart Pannenberg's interpretation of non-Christian religions in some respects resembles that of Rahner.[9] Yet none of these non-Catholics has thoroughly reconciled the *sola Christi* and the salvation of non-Christians. They lack Rahner's categories of infused grace and implicit faith, and they do not have the incarnational realism with which he, in imitation of some of the early fathers, identifies the universal logos who is 'the real light which enlightens every man' (Jn 1.9 NEB) with, not only the Christ of faith, but the historic Jesus.

Actually it would seem that Protestants should find a primarily futuristic eschatological theory more congenial to their own tradition. The Reformation emphasized the *fides ex auditu*, i.e. the faith which comes through hearing the gospel proclamation (Rom. 10.17). It is only through explicit faith in Christ that men and women are redeemed; and if this does not happen during life, then the beginning of salvation must be thought of as occurring through an encounter with the risen Lord in or after death.

Such was the view of an older group of Lutheran dogmaticians – Häring, Schlatter, R Seeberg and, most recently, Paul Althaus[10] – but it has disappeared at least in what is reputed to be academically respectable theology. One suspects that part of the reason for this is that the very question of personal salvation, of the ultimate destiny of individuals, has become disreputable. Emphasis has shifted to other dimensions of redemption, to its secular, collective or cosmic aspects. Even those who hold to the *fides ex auditu* (as do Bultmann, Ebeling and Käsemann)[11] have generally been so influenced by a certain kind of existentialism that talk of the futuristically eschatological destiny of the individual person tends to be dismissed as dangerously 'objectivizing' or impossibly mythical. Whether for formally existentialist reasons or not, most Protestant theologians systematically refuse to speculate on how it is that non-Christians can be saved. When confronted with this question, as the Catholic theologian Joseph Neuner has observed, 'they will generally answer that we do not know: it is God's concern, not ours; revelation speaks only about salvation in Jesus Christ'.[12]

The result, so it seems, is that Protestants are more inclined than contemporary Catholics to think of the *sola Christi* and the salvation of non-Christians as mutually exclusive. If non-Christians can be saved, then the *sola Christi* must be abandoned. This is the position of the kind of liberalism which feels compelled to surrender the universal Lordship of Christ, the centrality of Jesus for everyone, not simply *pro me*, and which thereby imperils Christian identity. Troeltsch found himself driven to this conclusion towards the end of his life, and so also – to name one of my own fathers in Christ – did H R Niebuhr.[13] If, on the other hand, one grasps the other horn of the dilemma and firmly maintains the *sola Christi*, then it becomes difficult for Protestants, apart from a high degree of theological sophistication or sophistry, to avoid joining the so-called conservative 'evangelicals' in their denial of the possibility of the salvation of non-Christians. This preserves a certain Christian identity at the cost of Christian integrity. It forces the Church into a numbers game which seeks 'to win more and more souls for Christ' without consideration of the overriding need for faithfulness and authenticity. It ignores that the Church is called, not to be large or influential, but to be the sign, the communal sign, of the coming Kingdom in conformity to the one who was the suffering servant of all mankind, including those who did not heed his invitation. In short, the lack of a conceptually and imaginatively consistent reconciliation of the *sola Christi* and the salvation of non-believers is a recipe for disaster.

In what follows, therefore, I propose to compare the two major attempts at reconciliation which we have distinguished: that of 'anonymous Christianity' and the futuristic *fides ex auditu* approach. Both, I shall suggest, can be harmonized with Scripture, and can encourage Christian modesty and openness to dialog with, rather than proselytizing of, other religions. Both also are capable of maintaining the Christian imperative to preach the gospel to all creatures. The major difference between them is that of credibility; and this depends on how one views *fides ex auditu* versus *fides implicita* and the associated, philosophically conditioned, theories of human nature.

First, then, it might seem that Scripture requires a *fides ex auditu* approach, for that is the language which it generally uses, but further consideration suggests that only misguided exegesis would say that it excludes the kind of saving implicit faith or anonymous 'fundamental option' in favor of Christ which Rahner postulates. The acceptability of such a view depends, not on exegesis, but on the systematic and historical framework within which one interprets the biblical data. As contemporary hermeneutics keeps insisting, interpretation is largely dependent on 'pre-understanding' (*Vorverständnis*).

The same indecisive conclusion is reached, it seems to me, if one appeals, not to the letter of Scripture, but to the fundamental spirit or attitude of the early church towards unbelievers. Christians in the first centuries appear to have had an extraordinary combination of relaxation and urgency in their attitude towards those outside the Church. On the one hand, they do not appear to have worried about the ultimate fate of the vast majority of the non-Christians among whom they lived. We hear of no crises of conscience resulting from the necessity they were often under to conceal the fact that they were believers even from close friends or kindred. The ordinary Christian, at any rate, does not seem to have viewed himself as a watchman who would be held guilty of the blood of those he failed to warn (Ezech. 3.18). Yet, on the other hand, missionary proclamation was urgent and faith and baptism were to them life from death, the passage from the old age into the new. From the point of view of most subsequent theologies, the tensions involved in this combination of attitudes seem insupportable; and so it is at least plausible to suppose that the early Christians had certain unrecorded convictions about how God saves unbelievers and how this is related to belief in Christ and membership in the community of faith. One of these convictions, most Protestant and some Catholic exegetes hold,[14] is perhaps reflected in 1 Peter 3.19, and others (about which we shall say a bit more later) can be uncovered by careful exegesis. By and large, however, it would appear that these views never became a problem and so remained unarticulated or unwritten.

Perhaps we could say that, in terms of the basic New Testament eschatological pictures, the 'non-Christians' (Gentiles) are not headed toward either heaven or hell. They as yet have no future. They are still trapped in the past, in the darkness of the old age. Only through the message of the coming Kingdom, of God's Messiah, does the new age, the true future of the world, become real for them, and only then do either redemption or damnation become possible. In any case, whether one accepts this view or not, the scriptural mandate to the theologian in regard to our question is to try to develop an understanding of God's redemptive action outside the Church which helps present-day Christians, like those in the early period, to be both relaxed and urgent in bringing the gospel to others. This, however, is exactly what Rahner and his associates are attempting to do.

Can the same effort be made by those who hold to the *sola fide ex auditu*?

What sense can be made of the possibility of a saving encounter with the risen Lord beyond the confines of this present life? Althaus and the other Lutheran dogmaticians we have mentioned speak in terms of a future state in which unbelievers are given what might be called a 'second chance'. Not least among the problems with this notion is the long tradition (dogmatized on the Catholic side) which holds that the judgment of the unjustified takes place immediately after death. Thus recent Catholic authors, including Karl Rahner,[15] have suggested an alternative which, somewhat surprisingly, can also be utilized from a *fides ex auditu* perspective.

They propose that dying itself be pictured as the point at which every human being is ultimately and expressly confronted by the gospel, i.e. by the crucified and risen Lord. It is only then that the final decision is made for or against Christ, and this is true, not only of unbelievers but also of believers. All previous decisions whether of faith or unfaith are preliminary. The final die is cast beyond our space and time, beyond empirical observation, beyond all idle speculation about 'good' or 'bad' deaths, when a person loses his rootage in this world and passes into the inexpressible transcendence surpassing all words, images and thoughts. We must trust and hope, though not know, that in this dreadful yet wondrous end and climax of life no one will be lost. And here, even if not before, salvation is explicit. Thus it is possible to be hopeful and trusting about the ultimate salvation of non-Christians no less than Christians even if one does not think in terms of infused grace and implicit faith.

Further, this outlook can be developed in such a way as to oppose boasting and a sense of Christian superiority. One must say that the situation of the Christian is in one sense more, not less perilous than that of the non-Christian. Judgment begins in the house of the Lord (1 Pet. 4.19), and many of the first shall be last and the last first (Matt. 19.30). Further, a refusal to accept the Church's invitation to believe is not to be equated with a refusal to accept God's invitation; and even when it is – as the story of Joseph's brothers (Gen. 37.50) and unbelieving Israel (Rom. 9—11) reminds us – God can turn the evil men do into salvation both for themselves and for others (Gen. 50.20).

Perhaps the most important barrier to Christian boasting within this perspective, however, is that the *sola fide ex auditu* suggests, even if it does not demand, an eschatological understanding of salvation which contrasts with the ontological interpretation required by the concept of implicit saving faith. Ontologically interpreted, salvation is primarily an inward grace which is articulated and strengthened by explicit faith. If saving faith comes only through hearing, however, then the process is reversed. Explicit faith in Christ is understood, not as expressing or articulating the existential depths, but rather as producing and forming them.

For the Christian, even the mature Christian, this process has just begun. He has only begun to confess Jesus as Lord, to speak the Christian language, the language of the coming Kingdom. His thoughts, volitions and affections are just beginning to be conformed to the One who is the express image of the Father (Heb. 1.3). The Holy Spirit which is in him is the pledge, not the participation in future glory. He has not yet learned to love God above all things and his neighbor as himself, for this is what comes at the end of the road in the eschatological fulfillment. What distinguishes his love from that of the non-Christian is not its present subjective quality, but rather the fact that it is beginning to be shaped by the message of Jesus' cross and resurrection. Only at the end of the road, only in the eschatological fulfillment, will he have truly learned to love God above all things and his neighbor as himself.

In this perspective, the description Rahner gives of implicit faith is far too glorious even for the *fides ex auditu* and must rather be applied to ultimate completion when faith passes into the beatific vision. Only then, in the murky and untamed depths of his being, will the Christian, as Rahner puts it, experience and accept the abysmal mystery on which he is grounded, 'not as consuming judgment, but as fulfilling nearness'.[16] In short, every aspect of the new life exists in the modality of hope. This is why the believer is *simul justus et peccator*, and why, as Luther put it, 'we do not yet have our goodness *in re*, but *in fide et spe*'.[17] This also is why pride in being a Christian is excluded. He has by grace just begun to learn of the one in whom alone is salvation, but in moral and religious quality he is like other men, worse than some and better than others.

In answer to objections that this makes salvation merely fictive or imaginary, not ontologically real, it can be said, to use a simile, that the man who has changed directions may be only a step removed from his neighbors and yet be living in light rather than darkness, dawn rather than night, the beginning of the new age, not the end of the old. Speaking in more complex terms, the metaphor of a child learning a language is useful. The content of what is said by toddlers is very much the same whether they speak a primitive or a modern tongue. In both cases they express the same elementary needs and reactions in basically the same world of objects to be enjoyed or avoided and of persons to be trusted or feared. But one language may in the long run open up all the riches of human history and of a vastly promising though ominous future, while the other, the better a child learns it, imprisons him more tightly in his little tribe or village. At two years of age, the primitive might still be a potential Plato, Newton or Beethoven; at 20, never.

In terms of this analogy, all human beings are toddlers, whether St Peter, St Paul or the veriest infant in Christ. Eschatologically the decisive question regarding them is whether the language they have begun to learn *ex auditu* is that of Jesus Christ, is that of true humanity, or something else. Is, for example, the love about which they feebly stutter and are just beginning to understand and hope to attain, is this love defined by Jesus' life, death and resurrection, or in some other way? In any case it is ridiculous for Christians to boast. They are, as one American Catholic author has put it,[18] like infants mouthing scraps out of Shakespeare or the *Principia Mathematica*, parrot-like, by rote. Only occasionally do they have inklings of the meanings of the words they utter. Thus, there perhaps is even less reason for such boasting in this perspective than when salvation is *fide explicita et implicita*.

Nor is there any reason to suppose that this position need reduce the possibility of dialogue and cooperation with other religions. To hold that the Christian language is the only one which has the words and concepts which can authentically speak of the ground of being, goal of history and true humanity (for one cannot genuinely speak of these apart from telling and re-telling the story of Jesus Christ), is not at all the same as denying that other religions have resources for speaking truths and realities, even highly important truths and realities, of which Christianity as yet knows nothing and by which it could be greatly enriched. Whatever the faults of Hellenization, it must also be seen as a process by which Christians learned much of value from ancient paganism and the cultures and philosophies which were its offspring. Conversely, one way in which Christians can serve their neighbors may be through helping adherents of other religions to purify and enrich their heritages, to make them better speakers of the languages they have. It can be argued that this is a better basis for dialog than when one seeks to find the grace of Christ at work in non-Christian religions. Then the danger is, not so much that of subverting Christian truth (Rahner certainly does not do that), but rather that of failing to do justice to non-Christian truths. One may guess, for example, that the Buddhist concept of Nirvana is much more instructive if one takes it on its own terms, rather than trying to find in it analogies to heaven.

It would seem that another and apparently opposed imperative, that of evangelization, is also better served by a *sola fide ex auditu* understanding of salvation. To be sure, the alternative view may be able to supply equally good reasons for bringing the gospel to all who are interested in listening, but the way it does this seems pretentious, perhaps imperialistic. There is something arrogant about supposing that one knows what non-Christians are in the depth of their beings better than they know themselves and that therefore one's task is to increase their self-awareness. Evangelism is not ontological psychotherapy, but rather the offer to teach one's own beloved language, the language which speaks of Jesus Christ, to all those who are interested, and then leave it to them and to God as to whether they choose the new language over the old.

As was suggested earlier in this article, perhaps the major difficulty with the approach we are examining is that for many contemporary Protestants and Catholics its futuristic reference seems mythological or unreal. It speaks of the salvation of non-Christians as having no present reality, but as begining (and consummated) in or after death. This violates even Rahner's rules for the 'Hermeneutics of Eschatological Statements'.[19] and is, of course, flatly contradicted by those Protestants whose existentialism leads them to deny a temporally and objectively future Eschaton.

It would be possible to argue in reply that a futuristic eschatology is one of the mythological elements (in the technical, not pejorative sense of the term) which are indispensible to Christianity, and that the arguments against it are functions of the modern mood rather than of modern knowledge. The human sense of what is real or unreal is socially constructed,[20] and what seems credible or incredible to contemporary intellectuals is much more the product of their social-psychological conditioning than of their science.

While I believe this is true, it is more useful for our purposes to reverse the accusations of 'mythology' by mentioning in conclusion the points of view from which the concept of implicit faith and the associated theory of religion seems mythological in the bad sense of the word. This is the case, first of all, from the perspective of many empirically-oriented theories of religion. These regard each religion as a distinctive symbolic system linking motivation and action and providing an ultimate legitimation for basic patterns of thought, feeling and behavior uniquely characteristic of a given community or society and its members.[21] Religions are seen, not as expressions of the depth or transcendental heights of human experience, but as systems of ritual, myth, belief and conduct which constitute, rather than being constituted by, that which is most profound in man, e.g. his existential self-understanding.

As in the case of languages, what religions have in common are formal structures and abstract patterns, not a concrete reality which lies behind their diverse articulations. Religions are thus just as incapable as languages of being understood in those categories of transcendental philosophy which are employed by Rahner, Tillich and others. This means in reference to our particular problem that the concept of implicit faith not only lacks evidence, but also plausibility. From the point of view of much, perhaps most, contemporary history, phenomenology, sociology and psychology of religion, the faiths by which men live, whether Christian or non-Christian, are always acquired *ex auditu*.

The reasons which remain for using the concepts of anonymous grace and implicit faith are philosophical rather than properly theological. If one supposes that what is most fundamentally human in man is pre-conceptual and pre-linguistic and that this can be arrived at by means of transcendental deductions or existentialist analyses, then it makes sense to follow Rahner in using these ideas to account for the salvation of non-Christians. It is doubtful, however, that his theory is persuasive apart from the German philosophical tradition of romanticism, idealism and existentialism (and perhaps then only when combined with a highly reinterpreted and distorted Thomism).

Certainly from the point of view of the currently dominant Anglo-American outlook, this whole construction is more than questionable. Its picture of man is the inversion of the one which Rahner employs.[22] The humanly real, one might say, is not constructed from below upwards or from the inner to the outer, but from the outer to the inner and from above downwards. The acquisition of a language – necessarily from outside – is a 'jump which was the coming into being of man',[23] and all the heights and depths of human knowledge, faith, hope and love are the effects, not the causes, of the manner and the skill with which one uses symbolic systems. Many, though not all, of those who have formulated this approach have been anti-religious and anti-Christian, but this does not destroy the theological usefulness of their insights.[24] We might say that just as a man becomes human by being taught a language, so he begins to be a new creature through hearing, learning and internalizing the language which speaks of Christ.

Now at the end of our discussion, however, we should remind ourselves not to exaggerate its importance. The emphasis on *fides ex auditu* does not depend on a philosophical position, though it may be helped by some and hindered by others. Nor is it impossible to have the right attitude toward non-Christians if one falters at this point. Despite disagreement in theological theory, we can whole-heartedly share Rahner's hope that the Christian of the future 'will not anxiously scan statistics to see whether the Church is really the biggest ideological organization or not, or whether it is growing proportionately quicker or slower than world population. He will indeed go out into the world with missionary zeal and bear witness in the name of Christ. He will wish to give his grace to others, for he possesses a grace which the others still lack ... But he will know that if his zeal is serene and patient it will have a better chance of success. He will know that he can imitate God's forebearance which, according to St Paul, is of positive significance for salvation, not condemnation.'[25]

PART II

CATHOLIC

7. Ecumenism and the Future of Belief*

Editor's Introduction

The 1960s was a decade of theologies of the future unlike any since Karl Barth published his commentary on the epistle to the Romans in the first part of the 20th century. There were debates among biblical scholars over apocalyptic in the Old and New Testament. There were also debates in the culture over where a new generation was headed – not the famous or infamous generation of 1960s college students but the generation duly chastened by the world wars of the first half of the century. The theological form these debates took and still take was as debates over 'eschatology'. The 'eschata' are, in Greek, 'last things' (God's end or goal for things); 'eschatology' is the relatively modern word for studying or making proposals about such things. But, like many such technical words, 'eschatology' is used in different and competing ways. Protestant theologians like Pannenberg, Moltmann and Jenson had proposals for how to center theology on the eschaton – the future. Vatican II, on Lindbeck's reading (as the introduction pointed out), provided a ' "realistically futuristic" eschatology' that transcended the pre-Vatican II divide between 'incarnationalist' and 'eschatologist' Catholics.[1] Some of these many proposals were about an evolving cosmos (Teilhard), some about a speculative universal history (Pannenberg) and some about Christ's entry into the concrete psychological and political dialectics of human history (Moltmann).

Lindbeck's own interest was in the bearing of all this on the concrete (empirical, sociologically visible and describable) Christian community, theologically interpreted. Presuming the world is becoming less Christian, what will the concrete (empirical) future of the Church be?

Later essays will qualify the optimism about historical-criticism here – and his autobiographical sketch in Chapter One notes that he has come

---

* George A Lindbeck, 'Ecumenism and the Future of Belief', *Una Sancta* **25** (1968), pp. 3–17.

to be more concerned with what a de-Christianized world does to that world. But the interest here in ecumenism and eschatology will abide throughout the essays in this volume, all the way through the later chapters on postliberal theology. The motif of Church as servant is also crucial, re-emerging in the final chapter here on the Church and Israel.

This chapter was originally a lecture at Gettysburg Seminary and Mount Holyoke College in the Spring of 1968.

This article is to reflect on the future of the ecumenical movement; but this obviously cannot be done in any effective way without considering the future of religious belief in general and, as it is Christian ecumenism with which we shall deal, Christian belief in particular. I wish this were not so. I would like to limit myself to a nice, manageable topic with which I have some familiarity. It becomes more and more evident, however, that it is only within the context of a projection, however hazardous, regarding the prospects for religion that it is possible to speak meaningfully of the prospects for ecumenism.

The first part is devoted to a sketch of what might be said on at least somewhat empirical grounds about the future of religion. Here my thinking has been nourished by a number of sources, including a theologian like Karl Rahner in his more empirical moods, philosophers such as Cassirer and Suzanne Langer, the recent report in *Daedalus* entitled *Towards the Year 2000* and, most especially, sociologists of knowledge, standing in the tradition of Weber and Durkheim, such as Peter Berger and Thomas Luckmann. I have no professional competence in evaluating these various theories. My only excuse for using them is that I happen to find them, in the way in which I shall combine and modify them, adding up to a more persuasive picture of the future than any other of which I know.

This attempt at an empirical forecast is, however, only the starting point. My chief interest is to reflect as an ecumenist and theologian on this picture of what might be. Thus the overall question is this: if such and such developments are likely to occur for such and such reasons, what should be the reactions and actions of religious communities and individuals who have ecumenical commitments or concerns?

A Perhaps Repulsive Minority

In outline, then, the view of the future with which we shall operate is that of what Rahner calls a 'diaspora' Church, a Church which, as in the early centuries of our era, is once again a small minority, sociologically sectarian, even in traditionally Christian countries. This assumption applies also to other religious communities, to Judaism obviously, but also to Islam and the great religions of the East. If the world really is becoming increasingly secularized, they are all in the process of being reduced to small minorities. However, our concern is with communities of biblical faith, and specifically with Christianity, and we shall say little of other religions.

As befits a sociologically sectarian situation, Christians will presumably tend to assemble in the new world into small groups of men and women who are in close personal interaction. These groups may be expected to be highly 'religious' in character, by which I simply mean that in both belief and behavior they will be sharply differentiated from the surrounding secularized society. They will have convictions about God, about Jesus and about the world and its destiny which will be considered fantastic, perhaps repulsive, by the majority of their fellows; they will engage in peculiar practices like prayer and worship which others find meaningless; and their collective and individual conduct will be viewed as odd or maybe offensive. In short, in some important respects at least, all Christian churches resemble what we now call sects.

The reason for expecting this development is simply that sectarianism would seem to be the only form in which anything like explicitly Christian faith could survive once society becomes thoroughly secularized. Two arguments can be advanced in support of this. In the first place, non-religious motives for belonging to the Church will disappear. Social advantage will vanish, familial and traditional ties will weaken, and psychological and moral therapy will presumably be taken care of by other devices. It will as a consequence, be pointless or absurd to call oneself a Christian unless one believes or wants to believe and act in the strange ways in which those who take their faith seriously are presumably obligated to do. This is the reason for supposing that, once a certain degree of secularization is reached, the remnant who retain their religious adherence will become more, rather than less, committed and devout.

In the second place, from the viewpoint of commonsense, and even more from the perspective of the sociology of knowledge, it is virtually impossible for an individual, when isolated, to maintain patterns of belief and conduct markedly at variance with those of the surrounding culture. Human beings are social animals to the core of their beings. Their sense, their feel for what is real and unreal, good and bad is socially determined, socially constructed. Thus those whose convictions and values are radically different from the majority must huddle together in cohesive groups of the like-minded in order mutually to support each other in maintaining their minority definitions of the real and the good. This, then, is the reason for predicting that religion in the future will become, not only more religious, but more sectarian.

Two Assumptions

You will have noticed that two assumptions underlie this projection: first, our world will become more and more massively and deeply secularized, and second, religion will nevertheless survive. The second assumption seems to me the less debatable of the two, and so I shall say a word about it first. Religions of a certain type have fantastic staying power. The Parasees and the Jews, for example, not to mention Babylonian astrological cultists, have endured thousands of years through incredible vicissitudes, often as minuscule groups. It seems unlikely that Christianity – or Islam or Buddhism, for that matter – would be less persistent. Further, human beings seem to be incorrigibly self-differentiating, incorrigibly resistant to uniformity. It is not only the irrepressible freedom of the human spirit which makes them thus, but also the requirements of society itself. As Kai Erickson has recently argued in a brilliant sociological study, every society needs non-conformists, protestors and marginal groups in order to test and define its own standards of normality. We may expect, therefore, that in the interstices of even the most secularized culture there will be a place for quite extraordinarily deviant enclaves which, by the very nature of the case (for it is against a *secular* society that the deviants will differentiate themselves) are likely often to be highly religious in character. Finally, it seems more than likely that some of these enclaves will be Christian, not only because of the memories with which the history of the west is filled, but also because, with the exception of Judaism, Christianity probably has greater resources in its tradition for a sectarian existence than any other world religion. The Bible does not anticipate that the Church will ever be anything except a little flock until the end of time. From this point of view, majority rather than minority existence is anomalous for Christians.

It is not really, then, the survival of the Church in some form or other which seems empirically doubtful, but rather the other assumption, the assumption that secularization will speed ahead in such a way as to reduce Christianity to sectarian status in the not excessively distant future. In the United States, perhaps even more than in other traditionally Christian countries, there are powerful countervailing forces. Multitudes of people who are basically secularized in outlook still wish to maintain some connection with the Church. In part this is because they continue to feel the need for the ritual celebration with religious coloration of the great events in human existence, of birth, marriage and death. At a deeper level, when confronted by what the existentialists call 'boundary situations', even coolly rational pragmatic secularists often find some help, however fleeting, in the mighty symbols of the ancient faith. Further, as has often been noted, parents, perhaps particularly when they don't know what they themselves believe, continue to feel the need for extra-familial help in instilling some kind of moral standards in their children, and the churches and the synagogues, however poor a job they do, are still the only available agencies specializing in such matters. Finally, as Will Herberg has argued at length, identification as Catholic, Protestant or Jew is highly useful in this country as a support for the frail sense of ego identity, of being a distinct person, amidst the anonymous masses of urban civilization. For all these reasons, it can be argued that there will be no extensive exodus from the churches for a long time to come, and that the turn towards sectarian intensity will be indefinitely postponed.

A Sharp Reversal

It is impossible in the space at our disposal to mount a full-scale counter-argument; and, anyway, there is little empirical data to go on. Let me simply record, therefore, my impressionistic judgment that these countervailing forces are now reaching the end of their effectiveness. In our increasingly secularized world, what was belief for the parents becomes cherished but insubstantial rhetoric for the children and then is repudiated by the grand-children as hypocritical. The grandchildren may recognize that this leaves a vacuum in their lives, as is obviously true of the *Couples* whom Updike describes in his most recent novel, but still Christianity and the Church are dead for them. I am inclined to think, therefore, that also here in the United States, following the European example, the defection from even the external trappings of religion will soon become statistically evident and will proceed with accelerating speed in the next generations. If any churches continue to hold the masses of conventional believers who now fill them, it will be because they have carried the present suburban pattern even further, turning into social clubs whose religious and Christian character is as superficial as that of the Masons.

If this happens, then at some point in the process, perhaps sooner rather than later, we shall witness a sharp reversal of the present dominant religious trends. We are now in the midst of a wave of accommodation to secular thought and culture. This itself is a break from that frantic resistance to modernity which was long characteristic of almost all churches, which began breaking down in main-line Protestant bodies in the 19th century, and which is only now ceasing in Catholicism as part of the aftermath of the Second Vatican Council. The accommodation which we now have is certainly much better than this earlier, and still lingering, conservatism. It has in its various stages, often resulted, for understandable reasons, in great surges of renewed vitality in the various religious communities. If a church wishes to retain its power and numbers and stay in the mainstream of events, it must eventually make concessions. The world is full of partially secularized people with residual religious loyalties who are in varying degrees alienated or uncomfortable when the Church is in sharp opposition to the dominant culture, and whose enthusiasm and support may, as a consequence, dramatically increase when that opposition is reduced. This is an at least partial explanation of the so-called religious revival of the 1950s as well as of the popularity of much that currently passes for renewal in some Catholic circles.

If carried far enough, however, accommodation is self-defeating to the extent that the churches lose genuinely distinctive characteristics and cease to have any convincing reasons for their continued existence. From a sociological perspective, this is presumably the major source of the mounting crisis in much of American Christianity. Its most sensational manifestation is in the death-of-God theologies. After them, there is no place to go. The reaction of genuinely secular men, at least as I encounter them in a secular university, is to shrug and say, 'If that is what Christians believe, why bother?' Only those who are seeking a way to resolve an internal conflict between triumphant secularism and dying religious attachments could possibly take this way of thinking seriously. But the problem, in a less extreme form, is visible in many other ways: in the clergymen who admit, apparently with good conscience, that prayer is personally meaningless to them and that they never engage in it except in connection with their public functions; in the 'suburban captivity of the churches' to the current middle class mores, and also, at the other extreme in the attempts to define the Church as basically an agent of revolutionary change, a kind of gigantic social action movement. It is no wonder that the number of young men and women interested in entering the ministry of the Church declines. If there is nothing really distinctive about that ministry, why not go instead into the Peace Corps or fight for civil rights and peace in Vietnam without the detour represented by the Church?

In saying this, I am not disparaging such causes as those of peace, civil rights and revolutionary change. I am simply pointing out that religion, including Christianity, does not survive when made instrumental to either the society's or the individual's welfare. As Luther would say, works flow from faith, not faith from works; or, to put it in more secular language, the role of religion is to provide and sustain convictions regarding what is ultimately real and good and which legitimate, rather than being legitimated by, certain kinds of conduct.

A Strange Way

As we have already suggested, the sectarian solution would seem to be the only possible one. Any social grouping whose distinctiveness is imperiled by compromise with alien forces must ultimately become sectarian in the sociological sense of the term in order to preserve its identity. This is as true of a political party or an ethnic community as it is of a religious one. Thus as the de-Christianization of the West progresses, the churches will in the long run survive only to the extent that they lose what have classically been considered their churchly characteristics. They must reconcile themselves to the loss of a mass membership. They must strive to become a close-knit fellowship of the genuinely committed who mutually support and encourage each other in the difficult task of maintaining what in the eyes of the society as a whole are increasingly odd and strange ways of thinking and acting.

Creative Minority

If this is right, then the crucial question for the future of Christianity is what kind of sectarian form it will assume. Will it be the kind with which we are chiefly familiar, backward looking, fundamentalist and divisive, or will it be more like the sectarianism characteristic of the early Church which succeeded in embracing a remarkable variety of social classes, races and interests in an ecumenical and catholic unity? Might the Church perhaps even be a creative minority which, despite a sociologically and politically peripheral status, exerts a quite disproportionate influence on the molding of the future?

The answer, I would suppose, is not foreclosed. A hypothetical projection such as ours leaves open many alternatives. Which ones are actualized depend on the spontaneities of history or, in theological language, human freedom and the grace of God.

The particular possibility I want to consider here is that of an ecumenical Christianity which is a creative minority. What are its pre-conditions and the chances that they might be realized? Let us look first at the social context, at the conditions external to the Church and then, in the concluding section at the resources and possibilities internal to the Church which might lead it in the hoped-for direction.

The question regarding secularized society is whether it does not, by its very nature, have deep-seated instabilities which make it difficult to maintain that open, tolerant, rational-pragmatic character which we in western democracies would like to think is its paradigmatic form. Something like counter-revolutionary Nazism or utopian Communism would appear endemic threats to secularism. Nazism and Communism, to be sure, emerged at earlier stages in the process of secularization and so, despite John Birchers on the right and Maoists on the left, anything closely resembling them is not likely again to greet our eyes; but still an open and tolerant kind of pragmatic secularism would appear to have an inherent tendency to fall victim to new tyrannies of the right or left. The bearing of this on the future of religion is simply that in a totalitarian situation, the Church would have little opportunity to be a creative minority; and conversely, in a more open society, it might help decisively to prevent the lapse into the dogmatic repressiveness of either the revolutionary or counter-revolutionary variety.

The Banishing of Religion

The reason for suspecting secularization of radical instability is that, by definition, it undermines those processes of legitimation which, from the viewpoint of the sociology of knowledge, appear to be indispensible to human society. It is platitudinous, but nonetheless persuasive, to say that one of the characteristics of a language-using, symbol-making animal such as man is that he needs to explain and justify his conduct, institutions and very existence by reference to what he considers really real and really good; in terms, that is, of world views and value systems. This can be illustrated in many ways, but perhaps the simplest examples are the familiar ones of moral injunctions.

Every community finds it necessary to curb individual selfishness by recommending concern for the neighbor, even though the nature of that concern and the definition of the neighbor may vary. In doing this, the 19th-century humanist referred to the presumably self-evident rational utilitarian principle, the Marxist appeals to the dialectic of history and the solidarity of the proletariat, the Muslim to the will of Allah as promulgated by the Prophet, and the Christian to the love of God manifest in Jesus Christ. Whatever the form of legitimation, there is always a reference to what is taken to be some final good or reality within man or outside him because otherwise the recommendation of neighborly conduct, the socialization of the untutored savage that is each one of us, lacks shape and force. It turns into a matter of 'Daddy says so', or 'that's what people do'.

Now a secular culture from this point of view is one in which there is a plurality of legitimation systems all of which are undermined and weakened by the fact that they are competing with each other in a unified society in which the various religious and ideological groups are in close interaction. Technologically advanced civilizations of the kind we know are clearly much more prone to secularization than any which have existed in the past, although the later Roman Empire, for example, was fairly far down the road. Modern communications, rapidity of change and social mobility encourage pluralism and make it increasingly difficult for people of diverse religious views to remain segregated from each other.

This results in the weakening of traditional legitimation systems in both the life of the individual and the society at large. In a pluralistic and secular society, religion and ideology are necessarily banished from the public domain. It is impossible to appeal in specific and substantial ways to definite world views and value systems when formulating governmental, business or educational policies because such appeals would be divisive, making it difficult to work with those of opposing convictions. Even such minimal concessions to traditional religiosity as prayers in schools must, therefore, perforce be abolished. More important, questions of high principle and ultimate goals play a smaller and smaller part in the structuring and directing of the society's life. A pluralistic, secular society is by definition one guided in terms of short-range, rational-pragmatic considerations, on the one hand, and whim and emotion on the other.

The effects on the individual are similar. Almost everyone, as we have said, is exposed at close range to a variety of competing legitimation systems which undermine each other's credibility and authority. Thus more and more people grow up with a haphazard collection of beliefs and values lacking depth and integrative power. Anomie, alienation and identity crises reach epidemic proportions. We have, in David Riesman's and Erich Fromm's terms, the multiplication of other-directed, market-oriented personalities guided in their lives by purely personal preferences and by cues provided by neighbors, advertising or the latest fashionable psychological theory. In summary, as the study *Towards the Year 2000* sponsored by the American Academy of Arts and Sciences suggests, our secular culture becomes irresistibly more sensate, sensualistic and hedonistic, increasingly clever in the rational-pragmatic manipulation of means, but utterly confused, and therefore often indifferent, about ultimate meanings, goals or values.

In saying this, I do not intend to deny the virtues of the secular city. Its anonymity, for example, does make possible individual independence and the freedom to develop interpersonal relations on the basis of 'I – Thou' encounters rather than on ties of blood, proximity or property. Further, the rational pragmatism which is its dominant intellectual outlook is obviously indispensible for the functioning of a complex, modern, scientific-technological civilization. It solves practical problems where religion or ideology fail. But what it cannot do is decide about final goals and values. It provides no clues to the nature of true manhood and womanhood, nor can it fill the daily round with a sense of ultimate purpose and meaning. In short, it does not legitimate the human enterprise. Where there is no vision the people perish; and as secularism is the absence of visions, it teeters on the knife-edge between chaos and tyranny.

Ecumenical Sectarianism

What kind of religious minorities would make the greatest contribution in a situation like this? What chance is there that Christianity in particular might respond creatively? This is the third and concluding part of our reflections, and it is here, finally, that we shall say something about 'ecumenical sectarianism'.

In the perhaps unjustifiably odd way in which I am using terms, both 'ecumenical' and 'sectarian', when applied to the Church of the future, do not have many of their current connotations. 'Sectarian' does not necessarily imply a divisiveness internal to the Church, but rather points to the intensity and intimacy of the communal life of a minority sharply differentiated from the larger society. Similarly, the ecumenicity of which we are speaking has little to do with much that passes under that name in present discussions, where it often tends to refer to any blurring of the distinctions and differences, not only between the churches, but also between Christianity and other religions, and between religion and secular culture. Indeed, the contemporary ecumenical movement is largely the product of accommodation to secularization. As the mainstream denominations adapt more and more to an increasingly non-religious society, they come to resemble each other and consequently find union or cooperation easy. The need for unity has also mounted because competition becomes counter-productive as the churches find themselves trying to sell highly similar products to an interchangeable clientele. Thus, as more than one observer has noted, the official ecumenism of the ecclesiastical bureaucracies is in part the product of pressures similar to those which produce price-fixing, mergers and monopolies in the business world.

This process may not in the long-run be unfortunate. It may help rid the various traditions of excess ecclesiastical baggage which has accumulated in the course of centuries of separate existence. Nevertheless, if our analysis is correct, it is a type of ecumenism which has no future once the push towards accommodation is reversed, when religious groups find it necessary for the very sake of survival to reassert their distinctive identities rather than further blur the differences between themselves and the world.

The question regarding the future, therefore, is whether this reassertion of religious identity will transcend the denominational differences of the past, whether its center will be the common Christian heritage, not the

traditional distinctions between East and West, Roman Catholic and Protestant. Is it possible that there might develop an ecumenical sectarianism,
that is, a worldwide network of churches which are sectarian in the flavor
and intimacy of their communal life, but which are ecumenical – or, if you
prefer, 'catholic' – in their inclusion of rich and poor, black and white,
educated and uneducated, alien and native? Something like this once existed
in the early days of the Church, and it is perhaps not wholly unrealistic to
hope that it may re-emerge in new forms during the third millenium of the
Christian era.

Emerging Consensus

It is also possible to hazard some guesses regarding the concrete shape of
Christian thought and life in an ecumenical Church characterized by sectarian intensity. The Bible interpreted by historical-critical methods would
necessarily be of fundamental importance simply because there seems no
other way of achieving any kind of genuine agreement among the diverse
Christian traditions regarding the proper understanding of the faith. Already
we see a surprising consensus among those who read scripture critically
and historically, yet with a devout and unabashed attachment to the full
range of Christian claims however incredible they may seem to modern
man. Barth and Rahner, Metz and Moltmann, Küng and Käsemann, the
Second Vatican Council and the New Presbyterian Confession are in substantial harmony on point after crucial point.

This is not the place to summarize the emerging consensus, but there are
two areas of agreement which are of particular importance for our discussion. One has to do with the this-worldly, not simply transcendent,
character of biblical concerns, another with the suffering servant role of
the Christian and the Church.

The Bible, as is now common knowledge, is a this-worldly book, concerned with the concrete ordering of communal as well as individual life
to a degree quite beyond the comprehension of most Christians through
most of church history. This is apparent not only in the Old Testament
prophets, but also in the Kingdom which Jesus proclaimed. He intended
quite literally, in the words of the New English Bible, 'to announce good
news to the poor, release for prisoners, recovery of sight for the blind; to
let the broken victims go free, to proclaim the year of the Lord's favor'
(Luke 4.18). In Jesus, according to the faith of the New Testament, this
Kingdom has broken with unsurpassable vividness into history, making a
tangible difference in human life until the end of the ages.

The Worldview of Christians

To be sure, the Kingdom is still future; love and liberty have not yet triumphed; the consummation which is also judgment when all things will be united through Christ (Eph. 1.10) with God who will be all in all (1 Cor. 15.28) has not yet come. This futurity is real. Christian faith is not fundamentally retrospective, looking backwards in memory to the incarnation, but is rather prospective, looking forward in hope to an unimaginable and inexpressible fulfillment. As St Paul puts it, 'The created universe waits with eager expectation for . . . the liberty and splendor of the children of God . . . [It] groans in all its parts as if in the pangs of childbirth . . . For we have been saved, though only in hope' (Rom. 8.19–24).

The epoch in which we live, then, is one in which God is preparing mankind for the consummation of that reality, of that good news, which has erupted into our time and space in Jesus Christ. We do not know all the ways in which that preparation is taking place. The Bible is chary of details, but the early Christians believed that everything before Christ – creation itself, the history of Israel, Greek philosophy and Roman peace – was *praeparatio evangelica*, preparation for the gospel. In an analogous way, they interpreted everything which happened after Christ's death and resurrection as things which must needs be in God's will, as developments which are somehow pre-conditions for the consummation, whose necessity account for its delay. This is the way in which they understand the preaching of the gospel to the ends of the earth, the Gentile mission, the destruction of Jerusalem, the persecution of the Church and the fight against the principalities, power and elements of this world of which St Paul speaks. All these were preparation for the end. It seems, then, that if the scriptural authors lived in our day they would still think in the same terms. They would regard the astonishing developments of the last 2000 years, which have been at least partially caused by Messianic hopes and the de-sacralization of nature and state by biblical faith, as things which 'must needs be' before the end comes.

The world and human history, in other words, must not be repudiated by escape into some form of other-worldliness, but must be affirmed, not with short-term optimism, but as the raw material, the baffling mixture of dross and gold, in which God is working out his purposes.

The fundamental role of Christians, individually and collectively, is to witness to this Kingdom in the power of the cross as suffering servants of mankind just as did their Lord. Christians need not worry if they fail to convert large numbers; they can live as a little flock. They can cheerfully leave the question of visible success to God, knowing that he wills to use their witness in apparent defeat as in apparent victory. Faithfulness is all, and faithfulness involves the concern of the Good Samaritan for every kind of human need and suffering. The Church must stand with the poor and the oppressed against the rich and the oppressors, not only here in the United States, but everywhere. It must side with the under-developed nations against the complacency and irresponsibility of the affluent, so-called Christian ones. And it must do so in the power of the cross, as a suffering servant, in the spirit – to cite our greatest contemporary example – of Martin Luther King. It must, in other words, stand for justice and human dignity and reconciling love for all men, including the oppressors, not for hatred or violence. This is the most difficult part of its ministry because the community or person who fights, really fights for true humanity will be met with implacable hostility, and to refuse, absolutely refuse counter-force and counter-hostility under these circumstances leads inevitably to a kind of inner death, and perhaps an outer one as well. Only what we have called a sectarian Church can do it. Only a community of fanatics will battle for reconciliation and true humaneness despite loss of numbers and of social acceptability.

Our final question, then, is to ask what kind of impact such a Church might have in an overwhelmingly secular world. Even if it only very partially resembles what we have described, its influence might well be far greater than one would guess from its small numbers and absence from the centers of public power. I can think of no better way to make this point concretely than to refer once again to Martin Luther King. A secular society, perhaps more than any other kind, depends for its viability on men and women who, like he was, are sacrificially and enduringly committed to resisting the tyrannies and hatreds of right, left and conformist center in the service of universal principles of love, brotherhood and justice. To speak of a sacrificial and enduring commitment to these principles is strictly equivalent, I would suppose, to saying that they must be seen as objective absolutes, rooted in the very nature of ultimate reality – in God's will, if you wish – rather than as a matter of self-expression or rational-pragmatic expediency. They must, to use our previous jargon, be a function of thoroughly internalized legitimation systems which are both comprehensive and humane. And in a world of secular relativism and pluralism such systems of value and world views will, almost by definition, be nourished only in sectarian enclaves.

To have Dr King's loyalties and values – or those of Jesus Christ, for that matter – is not the same as to be a literal imitator. It rarely means being public figures or popular leaders as they were, for very few of us have the necessary gifts. It does not imply any particular degree of education or social standing or political orientation. Although pacifists would disagree, I do not suppose it necessarily involves making an absolute of non-violence, although a self-sacrificial hatred of violence and its embittering self-righteous accompaniments is clearly implied.

A Christian Internationale

The social importance of even a sprinkling of individuals like this is apparent, but their possible impact increases exponentially when one imagines them being assembled in an international underground embracing not only people of different nations, races and classes, but also those divided in their politics. I have sometimes tried to envision in concrete detail the contributions of such an ecumenical movement to the future of mankind, but this is probably a futile exercise. The world changes with accelerating speed, and the circumstances and problems a century from now are beyond calculation. All that can be said with any assurance, it seems to me, is that if this ecumenical sectarian dream is even in some measure actualized, then even a tiny Christian minority might very well play a crucially important stabilizing and humanizing role.

This discussion of the future of religion has been provincially Christian. I do not apologize for this because I fail to see how any of the other traditional religions, with the exception of Judaism and just possibly Islam, could possibly develop an ecumenical sectarianism imbued with the spirit of this worldly suffering service. Failing that, they would simply persist as esoteric cults amidst the secularized, international masses. As such, they might constitute a healthy element of diversification, but it is hard to see how their contribution to world history could be more positive than that.

In the case of the biblical religions, however, it seems to me that, even on empirical grounds, we must take seriously the possibility that the continued progress of secularization may enhance, rather than diminish, their historical impact. Conceivably the destiny of mankind, if mankind has a destiny, may depend on their help in maintaining the fragile fabric of a humane and non-dogmatic secularism which, whatever the faults, does have the virtue of keeping mankind open to the future.

Nothing, to be sure, depends theologically on whether this happens. The faith of the sectarian Christian such as we have described is centered on God, not on the Church's success or failure, or even its faithfulness or unfaithfulness. He believes that there will continue to be a Church until the end of time which God will use in his peculiar ways even if it remains divided and becomes, by any tangible criteria, an utterly impotent and inconsequential sect.

I would like to believe this also, and I suppose in a way I do. Yet, nevertheless, I have to admit that my enthusiasm for the ecumenical movement is largely derived from hoping against hope that individuals and churches can be influenced, even now while we are still in the flood-tide of accommodation, to think those thoughts and make those moves which will encourage the formation of a Christian internationale of sect-like groups passionately committed to the sacrificial service of mankind. I am myself subject to the vice I decry in others of making religion instrumental to social good, of recommending religion on the secular rational pragmatic grounds of its possible utility. I hope, however, that this is a venial fault. As a theological moralist might say, God uses mixed motives to draw men to his truth. The important thing for us to recognize is that, especially in a secular situation, the human usefulness of religion must be rooted in the conviction, nourished by active participation in the community of faith, that God is God and his will is to be done no matter what the outcome. In short, if I may be allowed a pious note, the way to solve our crises of faith or make a specifically religious contribution to the race or peace problems is not to study theology on the one hand, or plunge into secular Christian activism on the other, but to pray, worship and read the scriptures in the company of fellow believers or would-be believers. It is in that context, and that context alone, that theology and activism can find their proper role.

8. Hesychastic Prayer and the Christianizing of Platonism: Some Protestant Reflections*

Editor's Introduction

This lecture, presented at the Ecumenical Institute for Advanced Theological Studies at Tantur/Jerusalem in February 1979, is a good example of theological description and critical assessment of a particular prayer-practice, the 'hesychastic prayer' more commonly known as the 'Jesus Prayer'. This devout practice was developed in the Orthodox tradition, where it raised issues ranging from the place of such prayer in the monastic life to the metaphysics of union with God, which was presumption and product of such prayer.

Here Lindbeck sketches what Protestants can learn from – and teach to – Orthodox on this issue. On the way toward this end, Lindbeck also suggests some of 'the possibilities and limits of the baptism of East Asian forms of prayer' – how the essential task of borrowing such practices and their inseparable beliefs must just as essentially involve transforming them. This essay is a case study, not a general theory of how to appropriate the practices and teachings of other ways of life and thought. But it does suggest how radical traditions can borrow from each other, critically. Even the more general 'cultural linguistic' theory of religion discussed in Chapter Eleven of this volume will insist that the task of discerning the truth and goods in various religions will always be a concrete, *ad hoc* (occasion-specific) affair.

The 'hesychastic prayer' with which this lecture deals is much better known as the 'Jesus Prayer'. Under this name, it enjoys something of a vogue in

---

* George A Lindbeck, 'Hesychastic Prayer and the Christianizing of Platonism: Some Protestant Reflections', in *Prayer in Late Antiquity and in Early Christianity*, Yearbook 1978-9, Tantur/Jerusalem: Ecumenical Institute for Advanced Theological Studies (Franciscan Printing Press), 1981, pp. 71-88.

current devotional literature and has penetrated into the writings of a popular novelist such as JD Salinger, author of *Catcher in the Rye* and *Franny and Zooey*. The Jesus Prayer is brief. It reads in its full form, 'Jesus Christ, Son of God, have mercy on me, a sinner'; but it can be varied and shortened until it becomes, for example, simply 'Jesus have mercy', or even the ejaculation 'Jesus'. Given this familiarity and simplicity, it might seem better to speak of 'Jesus Prayer' than employ the forbidding term 'hesychastic'.

Yet there are reasons for retaining the original word. Hesychasm is a much broader movement than the Jesus Prayer phenomenon which it generated. The name derives from the Greek word meaning 'silence', and it refers to a form of spirituality which became important in 13th- and 14th-century Byzantium. Its roots, to be sure, go back to the 4th-century desert fathers, and it may have come to Greece via the monastic communities at Mt Sinai. Nevertheless, it did not reach the form in which we shall discuss it until it was taken up by the monks of Mt Athos and was given theological formulation by Gregory Palamas (d. 1359), the greatest of the late Byzantine theologians.

The thesis which I shall propose is that in hesychasm the Platonism (or more precisely, the Neo-Platonism) which characterized particularly private or non-liturgical patristic prayer from its beginning was much more successfully Christianized than Protestants have generally supposed. This process of Christianization could have been explored in other forms of prayer which are more familiar to those who, like myself, have worked chiefly with western materials. It is illustrated, for example, by the so-called 'affective'[1] Jesus mysticism of St Bernard; or by the German mysticism of Eckhart or Tauler who – like Bernard – influenced Luther; or even by the Spiritual Exercises of Ignatius Loyola. It may well be asked, therefore, why I have selected hesychasm in order to illustrate the process.

I shall begin, therefore, with a short answer to this question. In a second part, I shall attempt a brief description of hesychasm; then thirdly, look at its relation to Platonism; and finally, conclude with some Protestant reflections.

One reason for dealing with hesychasm has already been mentioned. In the form of the Jesus Prayer, it is a subject of considerable contemporary interest, and – it should be added – of much misunderstanding. The interest started between the two world wars among western Christians with the publication in German (1925) and English (1930) of translations of a 19th-century Russian book called *The Way of the Pilgrim* (3rd edn, 1884), and it has continued to grow. I have already mentioned the novelist Salinger. One more recent promoter is the Lutheran dean of the Gothenburg cathedral in Sweden, who has written a little book on the subject translated into English by an Anglican and introduced by a Roman Catholic priest.[2]

If one asks about the causes of this popularity, part of the answer, it seems, is that the Jesus Prayer has some of the fascination exercised by eastern religions in our day. It utilizes breathing exercises and psychosomatic techniques which are similar, so the comparative religionists tell us, to those of Indian yoga, possibly transmitted in part through Islamic channels. Further, the Jesus Prayer itself functions, so it has been argued by Eliade and others,[3] rather like those Hindu mantras which have recently become familiar in the West through such movements as Transcendental Meditation or Hare Krishna. This may make hesychasm pastorally important. Perhaps we can learn something from it of the possibilities and limits of the baptism of East Asian forms of prayer. I shall say nothing more about this contemporary pastoral dimension, but it does constitute one of the motives which influenced my selection of this topic.

There is a second motive, however, which is closer to the theme of this lecture. Hesychasm is ecumenically important. Timothy Ware in his little book on *The Orthodox Church* (1963) suggests that it is the one major form of prayer which has historically flourished among eastern Christians, particularly in Greece and Russia, but not in the West. It is in some ways the most distinctive and therefore alien form of Byzantine spirituality. It is also immensely important. Olivier Clément[4] holds that hesychasm has at certain key periods played a key role in the extraordinary survival power of Orthodoxy under adverse circumstances. It helped the Church survive the collapse of the Byzantine Empire, to prosper under Mongol overlordship in Slavic lands, and to regain its vitality from time to time both under the Turks in Greece and the Balkans and under the deadening rule of the Tsars in Russia. Perhaps the persistence of Orthodoxy under communism also owes much to hesychasm. Furthermore, the Palamist theology associated with hesychastic prayer is normative for much contemporary Eastern Orthodox theology.[5] In short, what a Protestant thinks of the Christian authenticity of hesychasm will help determine his attitude towards contemporary Orthodoxy especially in its Greek and Slavic forms.

A third reason for choosing hesychasm, as I have already mentioned, is that it is a particularly vivid and helpful illustration of a general thesis about the Christian use of Platonic motifs, but nothing more need be said about this now. One other introductory comment, however, is necessary. It would be less than candid not to admit that my major personal motive for selecting hesychasm is that I knew little about it and wanted to know more. My own special areas of study and teaching are largely confined to the post-Augustinian West, but the encounter with eastern Christianity is inescapable in this ecumenical age. My own interest in hesychastic prayer, therefore, is more contemporary than historical, and is more concerned with theology than with spirituality. Furthermore, what I shall say about the subject is almost entirely confined to secondary sources. I have read only scattered fragments of original texts, and then only in translation from Greek or Russian. The authorities on whom I shall chiefly rely are the Orthodox theologian John Meyendorff,[6] and the Roman Catholic orientalist Irénée Hausherr.[7] The hesychasm to which I shall be reacting is for the most part hesychasm as they present it.

You will notice that I have said nothing about Protestant scholarship in this area. As far as I have been able to discover, there is none of any importance. Protestants have written much, and sometimes well, but they, like myself have relied on secondary sources, and no one has essayed a serious theological assessment. Needless to say, this is a handicap. It would be much easier to attempt a Protestant evaluation if some other Protestant had already undertaken the task. It is much easier to revise, supplement and correct than it is to map unexplored territory. I think the attempt is worth making, but I do hope you will remember that what I shall say is tentative, and that I am much less confident about some of my remarks than I shall perhaps sound.

Let us start, then, with a brief description of hesychastic prayer before we turn to its relation to Platonism and to the problems it raises for Protestants.

Hesychasm, like any form of spirituality, involves both practice and theory, both technique and theology. The two cannot, I think, be separated, although it is no doubt true, as a number of authors have argued, that some aspects of the hesychastic theology of, for example, Gregory Palamas are both logically and practically independent of hesychasm as a spiritual movement. This seems to me to be the case especially of the most controversial and the most discussed aspect of his thought, his doctrine of the divine energies, which has gained a quasi-dogmatic status in much of Orthodoxy, but of which I shall say nothing.

Beginning, then, with practice, I shall simply quote three descriptions, one from *Franny and Zooey*, one from the 19th-century Russian *Way of the Pilgrim* and a third from a classical account probably from the 14th century.

What Salinger has Franny say about the Jesus Prayer is this: 'If you keep saying that prayer over and over again – you only have to just do it with your lips at first – then eventually what happens is that the prayer becomes self-active. Something HAPPENS after a while. I don't know what, but something happens, and the words get synchronized with the person's heartbeats, and then you're actually praying without ceasing . . .' Later on Zooey says, 'The Jesus prayer has one aim, and one aim ONLY. To endow the person who says it with Christ-Consciousness.'[8]

The non-novelistic description in the Russian *Way of the Pilgrim* sounds somewhat similar. The pilgrim says:

And that is how I go about now, and ceaselessly repeat the Prayer of Jesus, which is more precious and sweet to me than anything in the world. At times I do as much as 43 miles a day, and do not feel that I am walking at all. I am aware only of the fact that I am saying my Prayer. When the bitter cold pierces me, I begin to say my prayer more earnestly, and I quickly become warm all over. When hunger begins to overcome me, I call more often on the Name of Jesus, and I forget my wish for food. When I fall ill and get rheumatism in my back and legs, I fix my thoughts on the Prayer, and do not notice the pain. If anyone harms me I have only to think, 'How sweet is the prayer of Jesus' and the injury and the anger alike pass away and I forget it all ... I thank God that I now understand the meaning of those words heard in the Epistle – Pray without ceasing (1 Thess. 5.17).[9]

The extract from the 14th-century text which I shall read is much more complex and technical and much less lyrical. 'True prayer and attention which is without distraction consists in this: at the moment of prayer, the mind [in Greek, *nous*] turning towards the heart, moves constantly around its interior, and thus addresses supplications to the Lord from the very depths of the heart.' I should interrupt at this point and note that 'heart' in this passage is not used symbolically or metaphorically to refer to some psychological function, but applies to the actual physical organ. Hesychasm, in other words, insists that the human being is an indivisible psychosomatic unity which can in its entirety participate in prayer to God. A few pages later, the text continues:

Sit alone in a peaceful cell, in a corner, and do that which I tell you: close the door and raise your mind above any vain and temporal object. Then, letting your beard rest on your chest, turn your bodily eyes with your whole mind concentrating on the middle of the stomach, that is, on the navel. Suppress the breathing of the air which passes through the nose in a way so as not to breathe too often. Explore with the mind inside the entrails to find there the place of the heart where all the powers of the soul naturally gather. In the beginning, you will find a darkness and a dogged heaviness, but in persevering and practising this occupation day and night, you will find, a marvel, a happiness without limit. As soon as in fact mind finds the place of the heart, it perceives suddenly that which it never knew; for it perceives the air as existing at the centre of the heart, and it sees itself all immersed in light and full of discernment. Before, when a worldly thought came from without, the mind was not able to combat it successfully; now through the invocation of Jesus Christ, it drives out and destroys it utterly. It does this before the thought

takes definite form and becomes an object of idolatry . . . You will learn
everything else in watching over your mind and in keeping Jesus in your
heart.[10]

I am not going to analyze the practices advocated in this and similar texts,
but go on immediately to their theological interpretation by Gregory Palamas as presented chiefly by Meyendorff, but with some supplementation
from others.

The Jesus Prayer, according to Palamas, actuates the consciousness and
thus also the effectiveness of the objective presence of Christ at the center
of the mind–body unity which is the human person. It enables the Christian
to experience, to become conscious of, a reality which already exists, viz.
his or her union with Christ. Jesus has already entered in his glorified
humanity into the very center of the self. Here Christ dwells. It is through
this objectively real union or *henōsis*, not simply through faith, love or
knowledge, that the Christian becomes part of the body of Christ. This
union is also, as the eastern tradition has long insisted, properly called
deification. One should not think of Christ's presence according to a model
of one being containing or being contained by another being, rather like an
ikon in a box. Rather, Christ through his presence in his glorified humanity
irradiates believers' bodies and souls so that they also become divinized.

The importance of light imagery in this description needs to be emphasized. The story of the transfiguration was and is of central importance in
the East. As the hesychasts understood it, there on Mount Tabor the divine
energy and radiance which transfused Christ's human nature became visible
for a time to the physical eye. The same light of Mount Tabor now shines
within Christians deifying them in their human bodies as well as souls just
as Christ was deified in his body as well as soul. Thus by turning inwards
through the Jesus Prayer into the self which is body as well as soul, the
Christian can see the transfiguring light which streams from the indwelling
Christ.

Three warnings need to be heeded if this teaching about the Jesus Prayer
is not to be misunderstood. First, deification is not accomplished through
the Jesus Prayer. The union with Christ occurs first. It occurs through the
sacraments, that is, through entering into the Christian community which
is the Church, and through faith, hope, love and the keeping of the commandments. The Jesus Prayer is simply a means for experiencing and inten-
sifying the deification which has already taken place. Indeed, unless one
has already become a Christian, already been united with Christ, the Jesus
Prayer can be dangerous rather than helpful. The non-Christian who enters
into the center of the self through what the comparative religionists term
the 'Jesus mantra' does not find Christ, but something else which may, in

fact, be diabolical. Christians also can go astray in seeking to explore their inner depths. Thus hesychastic literature is full of warnings against the misuse of the Jesus Prayer, and the need for a wise director.

Second, the Jesus Prayer is not an exclusive or indispensable means for experiencing Christ's inner deifying presence. Palamas says of it that it is only one device among many, and that it is simply especially effective for beginners when used under the proper spiritual guidance. It is not a substitute for reading the Bible, or the fathers, or for participating in the communal worship of the church, or for obeying the commandments and cultivating the Christian virtues. These other things are necessary conditions for the vision of the Tabor light, but the Jesus Prayer is simply an optional supplement which, to be sure, can, under certain circumstances, be highly effective.

Third, the Christian's deification through union with Jesus Christ is not yet complete. The process is perfected only in the final resurrection. Then, not only the center of our beings, but every particle of believers' bodies and thought of their minds will be irradiated by that transfiguring glory which shines through Christ's humanity and which is one and the same as the power of the resurrection.

I have already said that this theological interpretation of the Jesus Prayer seems to be inseparable from its practice. I mean by this that its effectiveness as witnessed to by many of its hesychastic practicioners needs to be understood as a joint product of theory and technique. When the ritualized actions represented by the Jesus Prayer are understood in another, a non-hesychastic way, they seem to have either weaker or different results. This, furthermore, seems to be reasonable in terms of contemporary philosophical and anthropological theories of the nature of symbols and rituals and their transforming efficacy in human life. Combining insights from the philosopher Suzanne Langer[11] with certain anthropological and psychological work (such as that of Erik Erikson on ritualization[12]), we might say that the recitation of the Jesus Prayer constitutes a non-discursive symbol which condenses[13] in a particularly powerful way a whole world of meaning which then shapes all aspects of the being, conduct, attitudes and thought of the person who properly employs it. Rituals, like other non-discursive symbolic actions, are by nature, however, inherently ambiguous. They do not themselves determine the meanings which they contain and transmit. The Jesus Prayer can signify many different and even contradictory things, depending on how it is understood. So also, for that matter, can baptism and the Lord's Supper. For example, the yoga-like set of techniques can in one instance result in the interiorization of a Hindu world of meaning, in another instance, of a Christian one. Or, to cite an illustration which has more historical rootage, it seems likely that the Bogomils of the 13th and 14th centuries in Byzantium used techniques very much like those of the Orthodox Jesus Prayer, but the results in the two cases were very different both for communal life and for individual conduct.

Stated theologically, the point is, to be sure, a familiar one: prayer and theology, ritual and instruction, sacraments and word need each other. Without effective patterns of prayer, ritual and sacrament, theology, instruction and the Word itself tend to become lifeless, while without Word, instruction and theology, the prayer practices, ritual and sacraments are blind. They are potentially powerful instruments which can be used for many different purposes both good and bad. This polyvalence is one reason why religions generally refuse to allow their adherents to participate in the sacred rites of other faiths (or vice versa), and why rites of other religions can nevertheless be effectively borrowed and baptized.

After this brief description, let us turn now to the relation of hesychasm to Platonism. This is not the time to trace the historical connections, even if I had the competence. I shall simply say that the work of Hausherr[14] suggests that hesychastic prayer emerges in part from the joining of two types of 4th-century spirituality. One of these, stemming from Evagrius, shows Platonic influence through Origen, while the other, associated with the Pseudo-Macarius, seems to have Messalian connections and is decidedly anti-Platonic. Instead of going into detail on these cloudy questions of historical genesis, I shall simply enumerate some of the Platonic and non-Platonic features of hesychasm. The Platonism of which I shall speak, as I have already mentioned, is more the Neo-Platonism of Plotinus than the original variety. I shall not refer to patristic Platonism as represented, for example, by Origen, the Pseudo-Dionysius and their followers. Only when speaking of the practice of prayer shall I be thinking of Christian as well as pagan Platonism, for what I have called Platonic patterns of prayer were for the most part Christian developments under Platonic influence rather than originating with the Neo-Platonists themselves.

Starting, then, with the practice of prayer, four similarities might be mentioned. Hesychast prayer, like the Platonic variety, can be described as ascetic, contemplative, mystical and, in a sense, other-worldly. First, both types emphasized ascetic self-denial in order to quiet the passions and produce serenity, or what the hesychasts called silence (*hēsychia*) and the Platonists, borrowing from the Stoics, *apatheia*. Second, they both stressed contemplative withdrawal from the external world and the disciplined focussing of attention on non-conceptual and imageless prayer. Third, the aim of these ascetic and contemplative practices was in both cases the mystical experience of the union of the self with the divine. Fourth, all parties believed in withdrawal from the world, not only in contemplation, but in action. Needless to say, Christian monastics carried this withdrawal much farther than did the Neo-Platonic philosophers.

This list of similarities, it should immediately be added, is misleading. The language in which spiritual writers describe and inculcate practice is much more uniform than their actual conduct. Respect for tradition made everyone cling to the same words, even when the actual patterns of ascetic, contemplative, mystical and monastic life varied greatly. In a sense, furthermore, there was no great need to talk about the actual details of practice of prayer because these were transmitted through example and through the teaching of spiritual directors who functioned more like gurus than like modern scholars. Texts were used more to inspire than to instruct in methods, and therefore the same exhortations could be associated with a great variety of concrete experiences and patterns of prayer.

This explains how the hesychasts could continue to use much of the ascetic, contemplative, mystical and other-worldly terminology of their Platonizing predecessors and yet be at one point in complete opposition. Contemplation had become for them somatic rather than intellectual. When the Platonist, whether pagan or Christian, withdrew his attention from the outside world, he also withdrew it from the body. The hesychast, in contrast, became, so to speak, absorbed in his body.

By itself, however, this list of similarities and differences tells us very little about the concrete or experiential relation of hesychastic and Platonizing prayer. For that, as I have already suggested, we have to turn to theology and compare the worlds of meaning associated with the two types of prayer.

Starting with the most general kind of comparison, it is clear that the world of a hesychast theologian such as Gregory Palamas was in form similar to that of the Neo-Platonists, but in content it was very different. By form in this case I refer to the emanationist model of the universe which Palamas inherited from the Greek fathers before him, from Origen, the Pseudo-Dionysius, the Cappadocians and Maximus the Confessor. During a period of over 1000 years, Christians filled this model with new content until, with Palamas, the realities organized within the model became almost totally different. The realities were no longer the intelligible ideas of Plotinus bound together by necessary and impersonal connections, but rather the free God and the free creatures depicted in the biblical stories. Thus we have a peculiar situation in which the content of Palamas' picture of the world is less Neo-Platonic and in some respects more biblical than ever before in the history of the Christian East, even while the structural outlines of that picture of the world continued to follow the Plotinian patterns of emanation and return. In some ways, it seems, the relation of Palamas to Plotinus is rather like that of Marx to Hegel. Marx, you recall, is said to have turned Hegel upside down. In other words, he filled Hegelian forms with new content. What was dialectical idealism in Hegel became dialectical materialism in Marx. Marx, therefore, is in a sense Hegelian, and yet is also the most anti-Hegelian of philosophers. Similarly, Palamas remains in one sense Platonic, and yet he is in other respects the most anti-Platonic of the great Greek theologians.

This double relation to Platonism needs to be illustrated. For our purposes, the best point at which to do this is in reference to the Socratic axiom, 'Know thyself.' Knowledge of the self was for the whole of the Platonic tradition the highest kind of knowledge, and the reason for this is that the real or true self in its deepest and at the same time highest reality is seen as identical to divinity. To turn inwards away from outward things and penetrate to the very essence of the self is therefore at the same time to climb the ladder of being until the mystical experience of deification, of union with God, is achieved.

As we have already seen, Palamas could repeat every one of the Platonic formulas we have just recited. For him also self-knowledge is a matter of turning inwards and away from outward things. For him also it is the best and highest knowledge because it involves deification or union with God. For him also the divine dwells at the very center of the self, and to become united with God is not to lose oneself but to become one's real or true self. Yet for Palamas far more than for some of the earlier Christian theologians, every one of these sentences refers to different realities than for Plato or Plotinus.

1. For the Platonists, the self is not, as it is for Palamas, a psychosomatic unity of mind and body whose center is the heart, but it is rather the intellectual soul whose center or apex is the *nous*, that is, the noetic faculty whereby we contemplate wholly intelligible and immaterial things. Thus the self which one comes to know when one turns inward away from external things is quite different in the two cases.

2. So also is the kind of knowledge which one attains. For the pagan Platonists, it is a highly intellectual knowledge requiring rigorous mathematical, logical and philosophical training, while for Palamas it is a way of understanding oneself in terms of biblical stories and Christian liturgies and doctrines, and it involves an intense, though non-conceptual and imageless awareness of the body. It is a kind of knowledge which is just as accessible to illiterates as to the educated.

3. Lastly, the divinity within for Palamas is not the unutterable One in and beyond the universe of intelligible ideas, but rather Jesus Christ, the second person of the triune God, in the full reality of his glorified humanity. Further, the presence of this divinity is not, as it is for the pagan Platonists, a necessary or natural thing, but rather results from God's

free and gracious action through the third person of the Trinity, the Holy Spirit. Thus the natures of the self and of God, and of their deifying union, and of the self-knowledge which brings consciousness of this union are all radically different in Palamas and the Platonists. The same words in the two cases are used to express contradictory propositions or affirmations.

Yet it would be a mistake to say that these oppositions in content make the formal similarities between Palamas and Platonism unimportant. Orthodox theologians, it seems to me, tend to make this mistake. They forget that it was the Platonism which Palamas inherited from the Greek church fathers which enabled him to give Christian justification and meaning to the practices of hesychastic prayer. The key concept here is the formally Platonic notion of participation in divine reality as deification. This makes it possible to think that Christ's human nature, including his body, is transformed or deified by the hypostatic union with the divine nature, and that this process extends by union with Christ also to believers. At first Christians thought of deification in this life as spiritual and not somatic, but once Platonic mind–body dualism is rejected, as it was by the hesychastic movement, this process of salvation as deification can be understood as involving the body of believers, not only in the future resurrection, but here and now. In this way, as we have already seen, the yoga-like techniques of the Jesus Prayer become both intelligible and legitimate as a means for facilitating awareness of the believers' present union with Christ.

This theological acceptance of the Jesus Prayer, it would seem, could not have happened in the West. Even in the most Platonizing western circles, neither incarnation nor salvation were understood primarily in terms of the strong Platonic notion of participation as deification. Thus when mind–body dualism was rejected, as it was by Aristotelians such as St Thomas Aquinas, the concepts were lacking for understanding or encouraging developments similar to the Jesus Prayer. There was, one might say, no theologically reputable way in the West of picturing Jesus as, so to speak, physically in the heart.

In summary, the relation of heysychastic prayer to the Platonism of the Greek fathers is a paradoxical one. On the one hand, such prayer with its stress on the bodily or somatic dimensions of human life is utterly opposed to the Platonic identification of the self with mind or intellect. Yet, on the other hand, Platonic emphases on deification and self-knowledge provided what may at the time have been the only possible framework within which hesychasm could develop. This form of prayer, however, is now entirely independent of that framework. It must be judged on its own merits.

*   *   *

The time has now come for the Protestant evaluation which was earlier promised. This evaluation is not meant as a definitive judgment on the Jesus Prayer, but simply as a report of what it looks like when viewed in the light of Reformation principles. We shall not go into the question of whether these principles themselves need to be modified.

From the perspective of the Reformers, hesychastic prayer has strengths and weaknesses, and both need to be considered. On the positive side, it is clearly a move in the right direction. On point after point it is, by Reformation standards, an improvement on its Platonizing predecessors. It is, first, eminently Christocentric: its aim is to promote a thoroughly personal relation to Jesus as the one in and through whom alone believers are united to God. Further, hesychasm is at its best thoroughly consistent with the *sola gratia* and the *sola fide*, even though, like the rest of the eastern tradition, it does not make explicit use of these categories. It affirms, however, that the presence of Christ at the core of the self is not dependent on what we are or what we do. Prayer, as we have already noted, does not create that presence, but rather opens believers up to that reality of the indwelling Christ which is wholly the work of God. Thus hesychasm is in principle directly opposed to the works, righteousness and efforts to save oneself which were the main objects of the Reformation protests. This means, in the third place, that hesychasm has room for the Reformers' stress on the continuing sinfulness of the saints, that is, the *simul justus et peccator*. Indeed, it exemplifies this emphasis at least as vividly as the Reformers themselves, for it holds that it is precisely in praying for Jesus' mercy to oneself as a sinner that the Christian becomes aware of that *theōsis*, that 'deification', which is the favorite eastern way of speaking of redemption. Fourth, there is, from the Protestant point of view, something engagingly anti-elitist about the hesychast insistence that the Jesus Prayer can be practised by anyone, not just by monks or priests. It has been in some dimensions a lay movement, and thereby congruent with the Reformation's (and the Second Vatican Council's) emphasis on the priesthood of all believers. Lastly, and closely related to this, the Reformers, especially Luther, agreed with the hesychasts in rejecting the spirtualistic soul–body dualism of Platonism, and the associated tendency to denigrate the body in favor of mind or spirit. Protestants, to be sure, have never learned as did the hesychasts to cultivate the somatic dimensions of prayer, but in principle they should have no difficulty with this. To those who affirm that human beings are psychosomatic unities, it should at least seem possible that mantra-like repetitions and yoga-like breathing exercises can be used by God as means of grace by which to enhance a genuine and fruitful awareness of union with Christ. For all these reasons, Protestants are likely to regard hesychasm as a great advance over earlier forms of patristic spirituality. It is in some respects the eastern equivalent of what the Reformation was in the West.

Yet there are difficulties. Most obvious, although perhaps not most important, is a tendency to react to the Jesus Prayer as unbiblical. Most Protestants are totally unfamiliar with the practice of continuous ejaculatory prayer. They may even regard it as an example of the 'vain repetitions' and 'much speaking' (Matt. 6.7) which Jesus condemned. The hesychasts on their side, however, can appeal to the scriptural injunction to 'pray without ceasing' (1 Thess. 5.17). This kind of issue cannot, however, be settled by proof-texting. The value of a practice depends on the use made of it, on whether it contributes to authentically Christian life, not on whether it is commanded by the Bible or existed in biblical times.

When judged by this standard, the major Protestant problem with the hesychastic movement is likely to be with its failure to emphasize love and service of neighbor and its indifference to social concerns. The aim of the Jesus Prayer seems to be to evoke the sense of union with Christ for its own sake rather than for the sake of others or of society. The hesychastic saint withdraws from the world, not in order to return strengthened for service (as did Jesus after the 40 days, or Paul after his years in Arabia), but because solitude and silence are the proper milieu for life with God. In short, hesychast asceticism is not the inner-worldly kind which Protestants can appreciate and have sometimes practised, but rather seems to be the other-worldly and escapist variety which the Reformers criticized (among other things) in medieval monasticism. It appears to concentrate on a self-centered concern for personal peace, for higher states of consciousness, for the contemplative enjoyment of God. At this point, even if nowhere else, hesychasm apparently remains dangerously Platonic.

It can be argued, however, that this objection applies more to the rhetoric of hesychasm than to its reality. The rhetoric continues to be influenced by the Platonic notion of 'the flight of the alone to the alone', of the individualistic quest for union with the divine, and this has undeniably influenced the spirituality of many enthusiasts of the Jesus Prayer. Yet it is also clear that hesychasm as a whole has not been characterized by an individualism neglectful of others. The historical record, as we have already mentioned, suggests that it has had an important social role in lands such as Greece and Russia in helping to sustain the faith of multitudes in peculiarly difficult circumstances. Further, the hesychastic saint, especially in Russia, seems regularly to have lost the struggle to escape into solitude. Crowds seeking for counsel on matters both spiritual and physical found their way to the hermit's doors. As western readers are most likely to have learned from Dostoevski's picture of Zosimov in *Brothers Karamazov*, these hermits radiated concern for others and on occasion exhausted themselves in serving their needs. Love of neighbor, although not the overt purpose of the Jesus Prayer, was its unintended consequence.

The analogy between this and the relation of faith and good works as described by the Reformers is striking. Trust in God's forgiving mercy in Jesus Christ, so the Reformers emphasized, is not a good work nor is it for the sake of good works, and yet it inevitably produces the works of love even as a good tree bears good fruit. Similarly the Christ-consciousness promoted by the Jesus Prayer flowers into service of others as an overflow, not as an objective. There is no escaping this overflow if the One who gave his life that others might live does in fact become the center of a person's life.

This suggests, in conclusion, not only that the major emphases of hesychasm and the Reformation are compatible, but that they can become mutually corrective and enriching. Perhaps the Reformers' understanding of the relation between faith and works can help to overcome remnants of Platonic other-worldliness in Eastern Orthodox spirituality, while the Eastern Orthodox, in turn, can teach Protestants new ways of cultivating the life of faith, not least by means of the Jesus Prayer. At this point, however, theological analysis must give way to practice. The only way to test this hypothesis is by prayer.

9. Infallibility*

Editor's Introduction

'Infallibility' is one of those topics that most Christians had agreed presented an insuperable obstacle to visible unity among Christians. In fact, among most non-theologians, Evangelical or Catholic, it probably remains the central example of an opposition between Evangelicals and Catholics that blocks developing what the introduction to this volume called an evangelical and catholic theology.

But Lindbeck maintains that what is at stake in the technical discussion of infallibility is, humanly speaking, 'how to extract a tumorous growth from a vital organ without committing suicide' – how to change a tradition radically without destroying it in the process. Lindbeck addresses this question with the help of historians, linguistic philosophers and cultural anthropologists – the same resources Lindbeck will later use to develop his 'postliberal theology' in Chapter Eleven. But what is at stake theologically is God's irrevocable commitment to the covenant people even and particularly in the midst of their sin and error.

Infallibility became a topic of church political debate in the late middle ages, especially during an argument over whether councils or popes had ultimate authority. Those who sided with the councils were called 'conciliarists', and those who sided with popes 'papalists'. But the clearest and most problematic doctrine of infallibility came in the 19th century, well into the times when Catholics and Reformation Christians had ceased speaking with each other after the 16th-century reformations. The First

---

* George A Lindbeck, 'Infallibility', the 1972 Pere Marquette Lecture, Marquette University Press, 1972, plus five theses on infallibility from 'The Reformation and the Infallibility Debate', in *Teaching Authority and Infallibility in the Church. Lutherans and Catholics in Dialogue* VI, (eds), Paul C Empie, T Austin Murphy and Joseph A Burgess, Minneapolis: Augsburg Publishing House, 1980, pp. 314–16 (note 27).

Vatican council, in July of 1870 and in the midst of politically chaotic Italy, issued a 'First Dogmatic Constitution on the Church of Christ' to which Lindbeck often refers here. The first Latin words of this Constitution are *Pastor Aeternus*, eternal pastor or shepherd, referring to Jesus Christ; Lindbeck (like many Catholic theologians) will refer to the Constitution by this Latin title. He presumes an audience familiar with its central teaching: Vatican I's *Pastor Aeternus* teaches that Jesus founded the Church 'linked by the bond of one faith and charity', centered on the episcopal office over which Peter had primacy – a primacy that is now exercised by 'the Roman Pontiff' (the Pope or bishop of Rome). It was this Roman Pontiff who, when he speaks officially (*ex cathedra*, from his cathedral chair), possesses 'that infallibility which the divine Redeemer wills his church to enjoy in defining doctrine concerning faith and morals'. Therefore, the Constitution continued, 'such definitions of the Roman Pontiff are of themselves, and not by the consent of the Church, irreformable'.[1]

The Constitution was controversial among Catholics at the time – and became even more so when Vatican II located the hierarchical structure of the Church (priests, bishops and popes) amidst the entire people of God as the sacrament (the mystery) of God's presence in the world.[2] Both during and after Vatican II, Catholic theologians have debated exactly where the elements of continuity and discontinuity are between the two Vatican Councils. After Vatican II and precipitated by the Pope's re-affirmation of the Catholic Church's traditional teaching on birth control, a dispute broke out among Catholics about the meaning and truth of the doctrine of infallibility – some Catholics arguing that it was dispensable, others that it was indispensable and central, and still others that it was indispensable but not central.

Lindbeck here argues that the debate 'is not parochially Roman'. He brings his re-interpreted Reformation theology to bear on the dispute, suggesting that 'infallible doctrines' are those 'that, at the very least, are not irremediably opposed to the gospel, that they are exempt from ultimately serious error'. In the process he articulates a view of language and culture that will become his later cultural-linguistic theory of religion and doctrine (Chapter Eleven).

This does not mean that Catholic and Reformation Churches now agree on the doctrine of papal infallibility. But a brief appendix to this essay on infallibility, taken from the footnote of an article Lindbeck wrote for the 1978 *Lutherans and Catholics in Dialogue*, suggests why Lindbeck thinks the doctrine may not be church-divisive, even while Catholics and Lutherans do not fully agree.

The folk wisdom of all ages warns the outsider against intervening in domestic disputes. He is likely to misunderstand the problems and becloud the
issues, and runs the additional risk of antagonizing both the quarreling
parties and being forced into ignominious retreat.

In reference to the current controversy over infallibility, however, non-
Catholics have the duty to brave such dangers. The problem is not parochially Roman. It affects all Christians. Whether we like it or not, our
world is increasingly one, and the future of every church will be influenced
by the outcome of this debate.

The aim of this presentation, then, is to record the impressions made by
the discussions now in progress on a Protestant who, while thinking of
himself as ecumenical, is still firmly rooted in the tradition of the Reformers.
After dealing with certain general considerations, we shall in successive
sections examine the historic interconfessional differences over infallibility,
analyze certain features of the current Catholic controversy which are of
particular interest to a Protestant, and conclude with a glance at the future.

One metaphor which could be used in describing the infallibility debate is
that it is concerned with how to extract a tumorous growth from a vital
organ without committing suicide. This is not a condescending comparison.
The Protestant is well aware that his churches lack the vital organ in question. They have no visible center of unity, no institutionalized centripetal
force which holds them together down through the millennia and across
oceans and continents with anywhere near the effectiveness exhibited by
the supreme Roman Catholic magisterium of popes and councils.

Yet, however impressive this teaching office, something has clearly gone
wrong. Magisterial authority hypertrophied into an exercise of infallibility
which, whatever its historical uses or excuses, is now clearly dysfunctional.
Radical surgery appears to be necessary.

We need, however, to keep the problem in perspective. The present difficulties with infallibility are part of a larger pattern which by this time is
thoroughly familiar and has even acquired a standard description. We are,
so it is said, coming to the end of the Constantinian era. Christianity is
ceasing to be chiefly a mass cultural phenomenon, the religion of whole
societies, and is reverting to the minority or diaspora status of the first
centuries.[3] All kinds of developments which were helpful, or at least not
disastrous, during the last 1,600 years are now in urgent need of change.
The churches must return in new ways to the sources of their faith, they must
open themselves to the contemporary world, and they must unite. These calls
for renewal, relevance and reunion, for *Christianitas, modernitas,* and
unitas,[4] are on every lip; and this is diagnostically significant despite the
diverse meanings given to these slogans.

In periods of transition such as this, the center of the battle between old and new shifts constantly. At the moment, the critical point within Roman Catholicism is hypertrophied authority and the theological justification which this has received through a certain theory of magisterial and dogmatic infallibility. As this theory has come to be understood and practised in Roman Catholicism, it is clearly at odds with present needs. It does not conform to what many contemporary Catholics, no less than non-Catholics, think of as the demands of the gospel; the monarchical papalism which is associated with it seems dangerously anachronistic, and it is clearly unecumenical. Pope Paul himself, as we know, has spoken more in sorrow than in anger of the irony that the office with supposedly infallible power which is supposed to be the prime servant of unity has in fact become the chief point of division between the churches.[5]

Hypertrophied infallibilism,[6] however, cannot easily be corrected. It has become so deeply interwoven into the warp and woof of Catholic thought and life that simply to excise it would unravel the whole fabric. It would rupture the continuity and shatter the unity of the Roman communion. Certainly if this were done abruptly, schism would result, and the Catholic Church would become another Protestant denomination or congeries of denominations, all competing for the Roman name but without the substance.

One does not need to be a Catholic or even a Christian to find such a prospect depressing. Some, like Miniver Cheevy, would regret the passing of what they regard as the world's greatest museum of cultural antiquities, while others would bewail the disappearance of yet another threatened species from our ecologically ravished planet. Protestants, however, have more substantial reasons for disquiet. Christianity is a historical religion. It depends for its survival, not on atemporal and universal truths, but on stories of particular times and places such as the Exodus from Egyptian bondage and Jesus' death and resurrection. Without the memories of these stories and the hopes which came into the world with them, Christianity cannot exist. Now, however gravely the Protestant may think that Roman Catholicism has distorted the memories of Jesus and the hopes for his coming Kingdom, he cannot but recognize that it has in concrete historical and sociological terms been the greatest transmitter in the West of the substance of that faith by which Protestantism also lives. Paul Tillich, we recall, has written eloquent pages on the mutual dependence of Catholic substance and Protestant principle,[7] and Martin Luther himself was thoroughly aware that he and his followers had received everything which made them Christians from and through the Catholic Church.[8]

There can, then, be none of the Orangeman's delight in Catholic difficulties, nor joy in the possibility of its shipwreck. It was because they recognized what they had received through the Catholic Church that the first generation of Reformers wished for the renewal, not the disruption of the historic ecclesiastical structures. It was against their will that the visible continuity and unity were broken, and they thought of the separate polities which they established, not as new churches, but as temporary emergency measures.[9] Convergence into a reformed and united Church was their goal, and this once again is the objective of those Protestant ecumenists who are their heirs. From the Reformation point of view also, therefore, the repudiation of infallibility at the cost of Roman Catholic identity would be a doubtful gain. The unity of the churches is not properly attained by surrender, capitulation or loss of identity on any side. This, of course, is in agreement with the emphasis of the Second Vatican Council's Decree on Ecumenism[10] on enriching diversity rather than a sterile homogenization according to any single pattern whether Roman, Eastern Orthodox or, needless to say, Protestant. One might argue with deliberate but perhaps excessive and misleading provocativeness that, for the sake of the non-Catholic as well as the Catholic, *Romanitas* needs to be retained even while infallibilism is profoundly transformed in order to remove its objectionable features.

As has already been said, non-Catholics need to join in the discussions of how this can be done. Catholics are, to be sure, intensely aware of the ecumenical dimension. Many of their proposed reinterpretations of infallibility are in part explicitly designed to remove obstacles to Christian unity. Still it is clearly desirable that Protestants and Eastern Orthodox explain their positions on this matter; and they should do this, not as outsiders, but as in a sense insiders who are also concerned with the internal health and integrity of the Roman communion and are not even indifferent to the need for *Romanitas*.

As this is a Protestant contribution, the focus will be, as we have said, on the requirements of *Romanitas* and the Reformation. We could also, to be sure, look at our subject in terms of Eastern Orthodox views or the preeminent exigencies of *Christianitas* and *modernitas*, but not all approaches can be pursued simultaneously; and in any case, the concentration on our own traditions, on the Catholicism and Protestantism which have dominated the West and shaped our lives, is not unrelated to discovering what both Christianity and contemporaneity demand.

The immediate and pressing relevance of taking our traditional positions seriously becomes evident when one recognizes the neglect of tradition is a major component in the sickness of our age. Without tradition, without shared memories, there is no community: and without community, there is no firm personal identity for the individual.[11] This has been most recently discovered by both blacks and the women's liberation forces. They started with efforts to free the individual, that is, with attempts to give blacks and women new and more fully human identities, a sense of clarity and pride about what it is to be black or about what it is to be a woman. They soon found, however, that in order to do this it is necessary to develop communal consciousness; and communal consciousness, in turn, requires a sense of tradition. The result has been a vast outpouring of historical and pseudo-historical writing about blacks and about women and their struggles for equality in the past.

Similarly, the ability of the Church to foster a sense of community and of personal identity depends on the preservation and enrichment of shared memories of all the communal and individual ways of being Christian which have developed in 2,000 years of history. These traditions need constantly to be reformulated and re-evaluated, but they cannot be abandoned without destroying the resources available for what is, after all, the fundamental Christian mission of providing men and women with the opportunity of being reborn with new personal and communal identities, with Christic identities.

Now, fortunately or unfortunately, the pros and cons of infallibility are an inseparable part of both Catholic and Protestant memories. They cannot be forgotten without impoverishment, nor repressed without festering underground; and consequently they must be consciously and carefully reviewed and, if need be, revised. This is why we are starting with an examination of the past positions of Catholics and Protestants before turning to the present situation. What psycho-analysis is to individuals, history is to communities. It needs to be combined with reality therapy, with concern for contemporary problems; but for certain kinds of difficulties, attention to the past is also indispensable.

On the face of it, however, the historical approach seems counter-productive. Our traditions are not only community-building, they are also divisive. There appears to be no more possibility of reconciling Protestant and Catholic views on infallibility than of squaring the circle. Must we not, therefore, simply forget about the past and, at whatever risk, set about *de novo* the task of forging the new unities and identities which the future needs?

Before yielding to the counsels of despairing relevance, however, it is worth consulting the record to discover whether the traditional Catholic affirmation and Protestant denial of infallibility are in every way incompatible. Logically at least this is by no means self-evident. Contradiction in the strict sense is extraordinarily difficult to demonstrate even from the viewpoint of the Aristotelian laws of thought which our forefathers, Protestant no less than Catholic, generally used in their theological work. The terms of contradictory propositions, we recall, must be taken in precisely the same sense, and this has never been easy to establish even within the context of rationalistic theories of meaning. The difficulties are vastly increased when one is aware, as was St Thomas, of the analogical – that is, as he himself points out, logically equivocal[12] – character of all religiously significant terms. They are further intensified in the light of contemporary linguistic philosophy with its emphasis on meaning as a function of use and context, and these problems are again multiplied by the historians' and cultural anthropologists' insights into the mutability and pluralism of intellectual, religious and psychosocial situations. Father Lonergan in last year's Pere Marquette lecture added a further complication by distinguishing 64 possible differentiations of consciousness[13] each one of which alters meaning. The conclusion to be drawn is that when Catholics affirm and Protestants deny magisterial and dogmatic infallibility, they are almost certainly not speaking of the same things and consequently are not contradicting each other in any precisely specifiable sense. Consequently, although their positions are obviously very different, it is not absurd to ask whether they might be reconcilable within a new hermeneutical setting constituted by changes in theology, piety, institutional forms and the Church's situation in the world.

Even in their original forms, however, they have much more in common than is generally realized. Catholics no less than Protestants affirm that God alone is absolutely infallible.[14] In the past, both of them spoke of the Bible as infallible or inerrant, and both now regard this as a misleading expression unless one explains that, while there are errors in Scripture, these are not of the kind which compromises its witness to revelation.[15] Both parties have also traditionally maintained that the church *in credendo*, that is the Church as the community of believers taken as a whole, is indefectible, meaning by that, in Hans Küng's phrase, that 'it will persist in the truth in spite of all possible errors'.[16] This, in turn, clearly implies a certain degree of infallibility, that is, immunity from at least those incorrigibly dangerous errors which would destroy a fundamental persistence in the truth which is Christ. The Reformers not only recognized the reality of this infallibility of the Church, but they sometimes also used the word,[17] although their successors stopped doing so for much the same reason which Küng mentions, namely, to avoid misleading connotations.[18] At two additional points, however, the Reformers, perhaps because of the still largely medieval character of their assumptions about truth and language, were closer to the traditional Roman position than is Küng. They did not deny that there are infallible dogmas, and they would not have objected to describing these as infallible propositions, that is to say, enunciations which are expressive of infallibly true affirmations, judgments or, in technical scholastic terms, second acts of intellect.[19] The one unmistakably overt disagreement, then, is over the existence of an infallible teaching office within the Church, and even this has its ambiguities.

First, infallibility *in credendo* which, as we noted, the Reformers affirmed, implies a certain infallibility *in docendo*.[20] If the Church as a whole is immune from certain kinds of error, then it will of course refuse to receive the teaching and the teachers which promulgate these errors. To the degree that a magisterium is universally accepted, it is, on these premises, guaranteed against ultimately serious error by the fidelity in faith of the Church which it instructs. This is the logic of the reasoning which Luther uses against the Anabaptists in defending the Catholic teaching on the validity of infant baptism.[21] He argues that if infant baptism were invalid, then, in view of the historic universality of the practice, the Church would have ceased to exist during long centuries. This, however, is impossible in view of the indefectibility and infallibility of the church *in credendo*, and therefore his teaching and the teaching of all the fathers on the validity of infant baptism must be true. Needless to say, this kind of argument from tradition[22] lost popularity in later periods as Protestantism, because of its polemical relations to Rome, became increasingly de-catholicized; and the norm of *sola Scriptura*[23] was used in more and more exclusivist ways.

Second while the Reformers rejected the infallibility of ecumenical councils, they were of course chiefly opposed to the authority of specifically western or Roman ones.[24] Further, the notion of infallibility which they refused to apply to councils was far more massive and sweeping than even conservative Roman Catholics would now hold. It came close to affirming that councils make no mistakes of any kind. It must also be remembered that the first generation of Protestants continued to have an astonishingly high respect for the authority, not only of the early ecumenical councils,[25] but also for possible future ones. They challenged Trent, not on the grounds that councils are incompetent to settle doctrinal disputes in the Church, but because, in their view, it was not representative of the Church as a whole and its freedom was compromised by papal control.[26]

In summary, while the Reformers never affirmed that any council is infallible, they also clearly thought it most unlikely that a fully free and universal one could ever seriously err on any genuinely vital point of doctrine. If one were to add, as do Eastern Orthodox theologians,[27] that a council's decisions are infallible only if they are received by the churches, then the Reformers may well have agreed. They were opposed to what Hans Küng has called '*a priori* infallibility',[28] that is, as Otto Semmelroth has explained,[29] a magisterial infallibility which is automatic, which is guaranteed by the fulfillment of juridical and formal conditions quite apart from considerations of content and reception.

It seems, however, that this *a priori* infallibility has not been clearly and explicitly affirmed in any Roman Catholic dogmatic definition. In *Pastor aeternus*,[30,31] the First Vatican Council laid down some of the necessary conditions for infallible papal pronouncements, and especially by the famous *ex sese, non ex consensu ecclesiae*[32] clause, it gives the impression that they are *a priori* guaranteed, but it nowhere asserts that it has enumerated *all* the necessary conditions. As any lawyer would point out, this leaves a very large loop-hole indeed. What is necessary may fall very far short of what is sufficient. Thus without contradicting anything which the dogma actually says, one could add condition after condition until the requirements for recognizing a papal or conciliar action as infallible are as stringent and limiting as in either the present Eastern Orthodox or a hypothetical Reformation position.

Now while the fathers at Vatican I would no doubt object that they had no intention of leaving room for such a minimalistic interpretation, it is important to observe that they were well aware that they had defined only some of the necessary, rather than the sufficient conditions for the exercise or recognition of infallible teaching. They quite consciously, for example, did not exclude the possibility of a heretical pope who might conceivably attempt in what appeared to be *ex cathedra*[33] pronouncements to mislead the Church.[34] They of course believed that God would prevent him from accomplishing his nefarious designs, perhaps by prompting the Church to resist and depose him as were many medieval popes.[35] In any case, the assent of the Church cannot be compelled by purely formal canonical means, and even when interpreted in historical context, Vatican I, though without mentioning this, leaves open the possibility that reception by the Church is one of the necessary conditions for certifying a teaching of the supreme magisterium as infallible. Further, if this is true of a papal teaching, why not of a conciliar one also?

A second well-known problem is that there is no dogmatic definition and considerable historical obscurity as to what conditions must be fulfilled in order for a conciliar or a papal teaching to qualify as ecumenical, that is, as an exercise of the universal and therefore supreme teaching authority in the Church.[36] This created no difficulty as long as the code of canon law was treated as if it were *de fide*,[37] but now the Second Vatican Council has re-opened the question even on the official level by deliberately refusing to identify the limits of Christ's Church with those of the Roman communion. We recall that instead of saying that the Church of Christ is the Catholic Church, it says with intentional vagueness that it 'subsists' in it. Thus it is dogmatically possible to argue, as some Roman Catholics have done, that a fully dogmatic decision must represent a serious attempt, not simply a formal claim, to speak for and to all churches. From this point of view, obviously, the First Vatican Council was of doubtful ecumenicity.[38] It paid no attention whatever to the views or reactions of large bodies of Christians which now, since Vatican II, are officially recognized as churches or ecclesial communities.

Unexpectedly, therefore, we find that the literal, the propositionally speci-fiable, meaning of the Roman Catholic dogmatic position is not in contradic-tion to a hypothetical Reformation view. Indeed, one can argue that a view which insists that reception by the Church is necessary and not automatic, and requires an ecumenicity which is wider than that of the Roman com-munion, is not only compatible with, but the logical correlate of the Reformers' belief in the infallibility *in credendo* of the Christian community taken as a whole.

Furthermore, interestingly enough, within this perspective papal infalli-bility is no more objectionable than the conciliar variety. The two conditions of reception and full ecumenicity guard equally effectively against the abuses of magisterial authority in both cases. This is perhaps the reason why the Eastern Orthodox,[39] interpreting *Pastor aeternus* within their own frame of reference, have been little disturbed by papal infallibility, but have rather found the main problem in the jurisdictional primacy which it attributes to the Pope.

Yet, while theoretically intriguing, this kind of logical or legalistic rec-onciliation of opposing formulations is not, when taken by itself, of much importance. In order to avoid confusion, one must always, to be sure, start by specifying the propositional meaning of official doctrinal statements. This is the unmistakably clear, undeniable and therefore minimal meaning. Yet one must always remember that the faith affirmations, the real and primary dogmas of a community, are only very partially expressed in official definitions. The fundamental affirmations cannot be captured in isolated propositions because they are functioning parts of the organically unified language systems and correlated forms of life in which the faith of a religious community is basically articulated. Not even the most elaborate network of *de fide* formulae can begin to exhaust the rich complexities of the primary dogmas. As linguists like Chomsky[40] and philosophers like Wittgenstein[41] point out in their different ways, grammatical rules are, in the nature of the case, unable to specify more than a minute portion of the moves which are necessary in order to speak a natural language at all, not to mention use it skilfully. Much the same is true of religious languages. Many state-ments which are logically compatible with the explicitly formulated dog-matic or theological norms are immediately recognized by any competent speaker of the tongue as fundamentally faulty even though neither he nor anyone else is able to devise a rule which successfully excludes them (that is, eliminates the faulty statements without also vetoing acceptable or even necessary ones). In short, the hypothetical Reformation and Roman

Catholic views which I have just outlined may be logically possible in terms of the clumsy grammars of faith which dogmaticians compose and then often think of as more normative than the language of faith itself; but they may still be totally at odds with anything which a skillful native or naturalized speaker of the Roman or Reformation dialects would recognize as authentically Catholic or authentically Protestant.

We need, then, to consider, not only theology and doctrine, but also what traditionally and still today actually functions as dogmatic in the two communions. Here, even though we shall be speaking of realities which the theologian and the philosopher also discuss, it is perhaps more useful to employ the categories of the historian and sociologist of knowledge.[42] Catholic infallibilism and Protestant fallibilism are, not so much matters of propositionally interpretable affirmations, as of emotionally charged and psychosocially powerful images; symbols and myths such as are denoted, for example, by 'eternal Rome'. 'Holy Father' or 'sinless Church', on the one hand or 'Whore of Babylon', 'the Pope is antichrist' or 'sinful Church', on the other. It is in terms of such images that Catholics and Protestants primarily understand both themselves and each other. In addition to this symbolic or mythic superstructure, there is also the concrete infrastructure of individual and communal behavior and institutional forms and procedures. The two levels are dialectically related to each other, with the superstructure providing emotionally and cognitively powerful support to the infrastructural behaviorial and institutional patterns, while these patterns, by their constant and tangible reiteration, clothe the legitimating myths or symbols with a sense of objective reality. Dogmas, from this point of view, are statements which seek to summarize, defend or explicate those portions of the symbol or action systems of the community which are seen as particularly important within a given situation. They may function in many ways, but the doxological and confessional uses were most common in the early church, while more propositional and juridical ones have tended to predominate in later times.[43] The propositional element, however, is not foreign to the levels on which faith is primarily expressed, because affirmations or judgments – that is, convictions about what is objectively true or false – are deeply though confusedly involved in imagistic thinking and, indeed, in behavior itself. The function of specifically theological thought can be described within this perspective as that of providing theoretical rationales or justifications, at least partly in propositional terms, for the dogmas and symbol and action systems of the Church. Because theoretical legitimation raises questions about the consistency of what the Church is now thinking and doing with Scripture, tradition and the needs of the present situation, it can, in the very process of legitimating, become highly critical, and sometimes plays an important, though always accessory, role in reshaping the symbolizations and practices of Christians – unfortunately not always in the right direction.

The interaction of these various factors is complex and often curious. Protestant and Catholic theologians, for example, have been affected by secular political theories in their efforts to buttress their respective positions on infallibility against each other, and have in the process become both symbolically and institutionally further apart than they were originally. Thus 17th-century monarchical absolutism contributed to the development of curial institutional patterns, and through them to that modern papal personality cult which, on the positive side, helped the Roman Church recover quickly from the Napoleonic trauma, but also, less positively, led to the precipitous extremism of Vatican I and to many of the difficulties from which Catholicism is now seeking to extricate itself. Similarly, the ideology of what John Courtney Murray liked to call 'totalitarian democracy'[44] has helped make Protestantism symbolically and institutionally much more thoroughly anti-infallibilist than were the Reformers, yet now the theologians who defend these developments in the name of Christian freedom are generally quite opposed to their theoretical roots in laissez-faire or free-enterprise thinking.

In the midst of these complexities, we need simple labels to refer to the undogmatized but crucially powerful symbolic and institutional components of the Catholic and Protestant traditional positions. We shall call them papalism and anti-papalism, respectively. To be sure, councils were still an important part of the opposing symbolic and institutional complexes in the 16th century, but now the exaggerations of papal authority dominate the whole of the infallibility debate.

It is, then, within these papalist and anti-papalist hermeneutical settings that the dogmas have been interpreted and the theologians have developed their infallibilist and fallibilist arguments. Context, we recall, is a major determinant of meaning, and consequently it is quite right to say that the traditional Roman and Reformation positions were in irreconcilable conflict. The Protestant symbolic, linguistic and action systems taken as organic wholes were in irresolvable collision with the Catholic ones.

From this viewpoint, and contrary to what is often supposed, the question of reconciliation is not basically a matter of changing official doctrines, but rather of altering contexts. Like other types of isolable abstract statements, dogmatic formulations are susceptible to an astonishing variety of divergent interpretations depending on the theological, symbolic and institutional settings in which they are placed. We must now turn, therefore, to the hermeneutical frameworks which are being employed in the current infallibility debate to see whether they lead to interpretations which are reconcilable both with the Reformation and *Romanitas*.

In discussing the current controversy, we must remember that it is only the most recent phase of an ongoing discussion. A great part of the most substantial work on infallibility, while generally done after the pontificate of Pius XII, still antedates Hans Küng's recent book.

This is not the place to present a systematic survey of the literature.[45] We shall simply refer to those items which, whatever their intrinsic merits, typify what are for our purposes especially interesting features of the debate.

Its most important characteristic is that it is almost entirely a quarrel among non-papalists. (They are not, it should be noted, anti-papalist, for that name is better reserved for the Protestant counter-position which thinks of itself as intransigently opposed, unlike the Reformers, not only to the exaggerations of Petrine power, but to the very office itself no matter how it might be restructured and reinterpreted.)[46] While the papalism of the old Roman theology may still dominate the Curia, the *Osservatore Romano*[47] and the Italian hierarchy, it seems to be producing very few theologians these days who are capable of entering the fray and discussing the issues on their own merits. The Second Vatican Council is no doubt responsible for this. Although it did not reject the papalist context for infallibility, as is evidenced by certain passages, especially in the third chapter of *Lumen gentium*, it nevertheless broke the papalist hegemony by introducing fundamentally new perspectives by its treatment of the Church as mystery and as Messianic pilgrim people in the first two chapters, and by the sections on collegiality in the third.[48] This official legitimation of new outlooks, especially when combined with the pressures exerted by biblical and patristic studies and the necessities of *aggiornamento*,[49] marks the demise of papalism among the better theologians, and eventually, one may suppose, though at much longer term, in all parts of the Church.

The controversy, then, is over how to de-papalize magisterial and dogmatic infallibility without de-catholicizing – or, as a Protestant more naturally says, 'de-Romanizing' – the Church.

One extreme, represented by Hans Küng, argues that papalism and infallibility are *de facto* inseparable, and that the overcoming of papalism therefore requires the discarding of infallibility also. The grounds for such a view are strong, and the politician, historian, ordinary language philosopher and sociologist of religion might all be inclined to agree. The major function of infallibility during recent centuries has been to serve as the doctrinal legitimation for papalism, and to the degree that one thinks that meaning is determined by usage, its meaning is papalist. From this point of view, the removal of infallibility from its papalist context obviously and fundamentally alters its meaning. It is nonsensical to argue otherwise, and if the meaning is changed, then it is dishonest to retain the word. There is no doubt that these considerations are also persuasive in common sense terms because common sense, after all, is simply a function of ordinary usage. Thus a thoroughly de-papalized infallibility would mean to most people, whether Catholic or non-Catholic, what they are sure in their guts it does not in fact mean. In terms, then, of the analytic model which we are employing, Küng's fundamental objection is to the word 'infallibility' because of the symbolic and behavioral connotations which it inevitably carries with it, at least in our period of history.

To be sure, he over-extends his case by arguing as if infallible propositions or dogmas are unnecessary or impossible from every point of view and within every conceivable context. If so, then he is not really in opposition to Vatican I because that council 'was blind in regard to the basic problematic',[50] rather than wrongly deciding an issue which it understood. While this is tactically convenient, it confuses and weakens his presentation by making it appear that he is much more relativistic and much less committed to the objective and unsurpassable truth of the Christian gospel than he actually is. His basic objection is to what we earlier called *a priori* infallibility, and he generalizes this into what looks like an attack on all infallible dogmas only because polemical fervor makes him refuse to say anything which might be seen as a concession to the enemy.

This analysis of Küng's position is basically the same as that of his Tübingen colleague, Walter Kasper,[51] who, after Karl Rahner has probably made the most impressive systematic theological contributions to the issues involved in the present debate. If correct, then Küng's substantive views are still much the same as those he earlier expressed when he argued that the concrete associations of the word 'infallibility' have made it unusable, and that it should therefore be replaced by another term.[52] A good many of the participants in the discussion agree. Their basic concern, however, is that any change of terminology or reinterpretation of doctrine be done in such a way as to preserve continuity with the past and thereby still be unmistakably Roman Catholic.

This is the point at which Küng can be faulted. It is not that he has ceased to be a Catholic theologian – even Rahner has retracted on this sensitive point and is willing to concede that operatively he and Küng may not be far apart[53] – but his views lack sufficient visible *Romanitas* to be useful in a community which is committed to maintaining even while reinterpreting its traditions. Or, to put it another way, Küng's book is likely to strike the Protestant as well as the Catholic reader, not as distinctively Roman Catholic, but as the presentation of a kind of Protestant case against infallibility from which, to be sure, elements which are in actual conflict with Roman Catholicism have been removed. Even Catholic writers who are thoroughly sympathetic to the attack on papal infallibility complain that they cannot find in Küng's position any clear answer to the question, 'Why stay in the *Catholic* Church?'[54]

In this quandary, historians in particular are attracted by the possibility of abandoning papal, while retaining conciliar, infallibility. Because their thinking, insofar as they are good at their trade, is highly concrete and in this respect close to that of common sense, they also object to affirmations of papal infallibility which deny the papalism which gave it its original meaning. But the historian's awareness of the commonsensical extends to past epochs,[55] and so he finds nothing odd in returning to a Catholicism which, while thoroughly Roman, knew nothing of papal infallibility. Further, it is now generally agreed among Catholic historians that the conciliarism of the Constance decree *Haec sancta* has as good a historical claim to dogmatic status as *Pastor aeternus* itself.[56] Yet in concrete historical terms, even if not in technical, logical ones, these are in contradiction, and consequently, so Francis Oakly argues,[57] papal infallibility should be abandoned.

Brian Tierney's current work[58] points to an even more profound difficulty. Claims to papal infallibility originated much later than has previously been thought, and were in any case originally designed to limit papal power and resisted by the popes themselves. The original infallibilists argued that because all the acts of past popes are infallible and still binding, present popes can do nothing to change what their predecessors have done. In 600 years a complete reversal has taken place. Instead of 'the Pope can do nothing', papal infallibility now implies for many, so Küng argues, that he can do anything he pleases.[59] Any doctrine with such questionable roots in tradition, so Tierney believes, is of doubtful status within Roman Catholicism, and he apparently assumes that it can therefore be abandoned without threatening the Catholic Church's identity.

It may be doubted, however, that a conciliarist solution is any more acceptable than Hans Küng's denial of all magisterial and dogmatic infallibility. Both are unrealistic. It is hard to imagine how Vatican I could be repudiated without enormous harm to Roman Catholic continuity and unity.

If this is so, then the burden of eliminating papalism while retaining *Romanitas* falls on the systematic theologians after all, despite the impatience which their efforts are likely to arouse in anyone of robust common-sense. The man in the street, Hans Küng and the historians all join in demanding an emphatic answer to the question of whether infallibility is true or false, right or wrong; not noticing that an emphatic answer is also highly ambiguous when the practical and theoretical contexts are not specified. The Protestant Robert McAfee Brown remarked some years ago that 'there is no such thing as being "a little bit infallible"'[60] and Richard

McBrien has recently rebuked Congar for failing to see that infallibility, unlike indefectibility, 'can tolerate no error of any kind, under any circumstances'.[61] The theologian who is concerned with theoretical clarity and refuses to join either side in the church–political struggle cannot, however, respond to such demands for candor. To tell him that 'of course everyone knows what infallibility means' is rather like telling the physicist that everyone knows what weight, matter and movement are, and that therefore the physical science has been a waste of time at least since Aristotle.

Although in a different way, the systematic theologian's interest in theoretical clarity, no less than the physicist's, leads to some odd-sounding definitions. In quotations which will be cited later, both Rahner and Kasper say, in effect, that infallibility is immunity from ultimately serious error. This, it could be argued, is logically equivalent to suggesting that infallible dogmas, however falsely they may have so far been understood, are capable of being given a true or Christian interpretation: they are not irretrievably false, not irreformably in error. There is nothing dishonest about this. Rather, it is a matter of technical precision.

The theologians, then, do not directly attack papalism, but first undermine its theoretical underpinnings in non-historical classical views of dogmatic and magisterial infallibility. After relativizing dogma and unilateral magisterial authority by these means however, they must provide alternative theories of authority in the Church. Here there are two major possibilities which are combined in various ways.

One is suggested, though not developed, by Hans Küng's appeal to scripture as the *norma normans non normata*.[62,63] While this scriptural principle was intrinsically Protestant in its pre-modern forms, it can probably be interpreted in a contemporary historical and communal framework in such a way as to legitimate a quite sufficient degree of *Romanitas* on the symbolic and practical levels; but, as we observed, Küng does not, in the judgment of his Catholic colleagues, sufficiently exploit these potentialities, assuming that they exist.

The alternative is to appeal, against an absolutized teaching office and its dogmas, to the authority of the Church conceived, not in the classical form of a monarchical–hierarchical institution, but as the collegially structured community of faith, of shared religious experience, interpretation and action. The basic theory of this approach has been more fully developed by Karl Rahner than by any other contemporary Catholic theologian,[64] but it has been most consistently used in the current debate by two North Americans, Gregory Baum and Richard McBrien.[65] They employ it to justify a much more Catholic (or, in Protestant terminology, 'Roman') position than Küng offers. Yet, rather surprisingly, they also relativize dogma and its infallibility more thoroughly than he does, and also much more than does Karl Rahner.

The reason is that they emphasize the *fides qua*, the faith by which the Christian believes, at the expense of the *fides quae*, the objective truths which are believed, more than Küng with his stress on the primacy of the scriptural witness to a historically objective gospel is willing or able to do. This radical relativization is consistent with giving primary authority to the Church as a community of shared experience and interpretation. When this is done, a different view of objectivity emerges, and greater emphasis is placed on the non-objectivizable yet immanental depths and heights of religious experience, truth and revelation. Religious communities objectivize revelatory experiences by using whatever appropriate symbolic materials are available to them. If they are Christian, this includes the Bible, and if they are Catholic, also the materials supplied by post-biblical tradition. The religiously significant truth of these objectifications, so Gregory Baum seems to say, is not at all propositional, but simply symbolic.[66]

The radical relativization of dogma which results is evident in Baum's view, not only that 'it may be true that none of the Church's pronouncements taken singly can be called infallible',[67] but also that these doctrines may lose the religiously significant symbolic truth which they once had. Yet there is also *Romanitas* in this position, as becomes clear when he asserts 'There is no reason to suppose . . . that the entire tradition becomes faulty or insecure because of the discovery that one of the doctrinal statements believed to be true turns out to be based on some misconceptions. The actual transmission of truth is so much vaster than doctrine that one does not see how it can be invalidated or harmed by such a discovery.'[68] Hans Küng, so Baum says, overrates Scripture because he 'did not sufficiently appreciate the creative role the Spirit plays in the transmission of the gospel from age to age . . . This overlooks God's ongoing self-communication in the Church, enabling her to discover the focal point of the gospel in new historical circumstances.' There is 'no reason why this special gift should not be called "infallibility" . . . While we separate ourselves from the literal meaning of Vatican I, we preserve and affirm its essential Christian witness.'[69]

Despite what, in the Protestant view, is the *Romanitas* of this confidence in the Spirit's guidance of the Catholic Church, most participants in the discussion are as far removed from it as from Küng's Scripture-centered approach. They occupy a middle ground, stressing Scripture more than do the papalists or Baum, but less than Küng, and the Church as community more than the papalists or Küng, but less than Baum. Further, their emphasis on Scripture and community enables them, they believe, to relativize magisterial dogmatic authority while still retaining a limited, but not empty, notion of propositional infallibility.

It is not easy to maintain this delicate balancing act. Rahner, for example, is inconsistent according to both Küng and Baum, though for different reasons. The first deplores Rahner's failure to draw the logical conclusions from his emphasis on historicity[70] (combined, one might add, with the Rahnerian admission that Scripture is indeed in a sense the *norma normans non normato*), while the second thinks that historicity plus the transcendental philosophy should lead to more emphasis on community and less on dogma.[71] Walter Kasper also criticizes the master, not for maintaining propositional infallibility, but for holding that infallibility 'is related to the truth of the single defined proposition as such' instead of 'understanding the truth of the single proposition only in the context constituted by all dogmatic propositions and their history, and by their relations to scripture and to the contemporary situation within which the gospel is proclaimed'.[72]

These questions of consistency are, however, secondary for our purposes. Given their competence, the mediating theologians can be counted on eventually to develop, if they have not done so already, a reasonably cogent justification for their position.

The substantive issue from the mediating viewpoint is twofold: first, the question of whether Christianity requires propositional infallibility, and second, whether this infallibility can be, in Küng's phrase, *a priori*. On these points, there is an at least apparent division of opinion, with the youthful Kasper maintaining a form of propositional infallibility, but denying that this is *a priori*, while the aged Rahner seems to uphold the need for both.

Kasper piquantly quotes Luther in favor of propositional dogmatic infallibility: '*Tolle assertiones et Christianum tulisti*'[73] – take away assertions and you abolish Christianity. The German bishops' statement on Küng's book makes much the same point in this way: 'the Church's faith . . . includes an unmistakable Yes and an unmistakable No which are not interchangeable. Otherwise the Church cannot remain the faith of Christ.'[74]

This insistence that Christian truth is objective, propositional, not wholly symbolic, can also be phrased in terms of the irreplaceability of the Christian stories. While it is true, as Rahner and, for that matter, Bultmann hold, that the stories are significant for living faith only in so far as they function symbolically as the means of existential self-understanding, still it is of the utmost importance that human beings understand themselves, not in terms of just any religiously evocative stories about the world, but in terms of these particular accounts of a particular man who lived, died and is reported to have risen again. The New Testament writers early designated 'Jesus is Lord' as a statement essential to Christian identity, and they meant it, not only as a profoundly meaningful symbol, but in the emphatically propositional sense of referring to a specific man in a definite time and place. It is systematically impossible to include the statement 'Jesus is not Lord' within an identifiably Christian context. There are also many other propositional affirmations which, while they do not by themselves, in the absence of existentially or symbolically significant appropriation, make men Christian, still cannot be denied without destroying or gravely damaging the identity or integrity of Christian language systems and correlated forms of life. These propositions, then, are intra-systematically infallible. Within a Christian context, they cannot be denied, they cannot be false.

From this point of view, the original Reformation tradition, like historic Christianity in general, is just as deeply committed to infallible dogmatic propositions as is the Catholic. It is likely that Küng would agree if he were not so preoccupied with the excesses of infallibilism that he cannot tolerate the word 'infallibility' in any form.

The problem of *a priori* infallibility, then, is the real sticking point. This is the view that, for example, 'When the Pope declares that he is speaking definitively on a *de fide* question or as the supreme teacher of the Church, then such a declaration, in the standard traditional theory, is *a priori* inerrant . . . it requires no *a posteriori* verifying tests in scripture, tradition or the present faith of the Church.'[75]

Kasper, as we have mentioned, decides with Küng against *a priori* infallibility, while Rahner appears to opt in its favor. The exact scope of Kasper's *a posteriorism* is not clear, however. It is formally similar to the Eastern Orthodox and hypothetical Reformation insistence on the reception of magisterial pronouncements by means of a critical process of examination, but in the absence of any statements regarding the ecumenical scope of the receiving church, it could also be interpreted in a conservative Roman way. If the receiving church is limited to the Roman communion, then one could argue that specifically Roman dogmas, such as the Marian ones or papal infallibility itself, have already won sufficient acceptance to verify their infallible status. Kasper's own position may well be quite different, but he has not yet discussed this problem.

In contrast, Rahner's affirmation of *a priori* infallibility seems at first glance unequivocal, but his reason is curious. A *priori* infallibility is necessary to what he regards as the proper method of practising Catholic theology, a method of which he is a past master. This method consists of assuming the truth of what the magisterium teaches, and then subjecting these teachings to a rigorous and often tediously technical, historical and logical examination in order to distinguish the propositionally specifiable affirmations which they contain from the symbolic and conceptual frameworks in which they are inevitably imbedded in order to determine the range of possible interpretations, including many new ones, to which they are susceptible in new intellectual situations and historical contexts.[76] The procedure is often reminiscent of the lawyer's search for loop-holes in the laws of the land; and in both cases the search always succeeds. The reason is that neither a law nor a dogma can be framed in such a way as to anticipate more than a small fraction of the ever new problems, questions and situations which multiply in the course of time. The Church's dogmas are thus genuinely relativized while yet retaining a propositionally identifiable continuity. They come to resemble a limiting yet open framework which excludes certain options permanently, but still leaves remarkable freedom in searching for new answers to new questions in the light of Scripture and the present experience of the Church.

To be sure, from a Rahnerian point of view, this is not simply a methodological question. The Church itself would suffer if this method were abandoned. The community of theological discourse constituted by the acceptance of a common dogmatic framework is an indispensable, even if far from sufficient, aid in developing and sustaining communication and therefore unity throughout the community of faith. It is thus of great ecclesiological importance that theologians regard the magisterium's dogmas as *a priori* true in a fashion analogous to the way in which lawyers accept legislative acts as binding because they have been legitimately enacted in terms of formal juridical criteria.

Recent investigations of the sociology and methodology of science suggest that Rahner's concerns have considerable weight. Thomas Kuhn points out in his book, *The Structure of Scientific Revolutions*,[77] that in their normal state the exact sciences are the most dogmatic of intellectual disciplines. The neophyte is rigorously drilled in an elaborate set of theories and investigative procedures, and only after he has thoroughly mastered these does he begin devising experiments on his own. Only in the rarest instances, and then only if he is what is called a scientific genius, does he move on to question established positions and formulate new theories. Furthermore, this happens in a fundamental sense only when an older scientific outlook – the Newtonian, for example – begins to prove untenable under the slowly accumulating weight of exceptions and contrary evidence. It is precisely this methodological *a priori* dogmatism of the exact sciences which makes them communal activities par excellence, and which enables them to be cumulative and progressive in a way that humanistic studies are not.

There is, to be sure, a crucial difference between the methodological dogmas of theology and those of either science or law. Theological dogmas have to do with matters of faith which engage the whole man. It would be blasphemous for the Christian to treat as *a priori* true, even in the limited sense just described, what he regards as possibly opposed to Jesus Christ himself. In the theological realm, therefore, *a priori* acceptance of certain premises or starting points requires an assurance that, at the very least, these are not irremediably opposed to the gospel, that they are exempt from ultimately serious error, that they are in this sense *a priori* infallible.

That this is the fundamental meaning of magisterial or dogmatic infallibility for Rahner is clear from his own words. He writes that magisterial
indefectibility or infallibility would be violated 'if the highest teaching and
pastoral office of the Church were to make use of its highest teaching and
pastoral authority over the whole Church ... and in doing so were to
contradict the truth and salvific will of Christ to such an extent that the
acceptance and following of such an act would place the universal Church
as a whole in unambiguous contradiction to Christ, and so into absolute
error as "No" to his truth or as "No" to his unifying and sanctifying
love.'[78] This is a minimal certitude, but it is methodologically sufficient.
The Catholic theologian can continue to take even the most difficult dogmas
seriously because he believes that, however much they may stand in need
of reinterpretation, they ought not and need not be rejected.

If this is the operational meaning of *a priori* infallibility, then it would
appear that there is also a sense in which Walter Kasper accepts it. He writes:
'also the single dogmatic proposition ... participates in the persistence of
the Church in the truth at least in such a manner that its fundamental
tendency does not make impossible access to this truth, but rather –
although sometimes in a very defective way – points towards the truth
which ever transcends it'.[79] This statement indicates that Kasper no less
than Rahner admits that a dogma is to be regarded as exempt from ultimately serious error even when the appearances are against it.

This, however, is a form of *apriorism*, and thus it is apparently only the
automatic or juridically guaranteed kind which Kasper rejects. The *fiat* of
the magisterium is not enough. One should not follow Rahner's recommendation and give the teaching office what he himself calls a 'blank check'.[80]
But when a magisterial definition is received by the Church *in credendo*,
then it apparently does have for Kasper an *a priori* infallibility of the limited
kind we have described. It is not necessary constantly to start *de novo* and
treat all the creeds and confessions of the churches from the Apostolicam
and Niceanum onwards as utterances whose truth and possible relevance
are so uncertain that they are best ignored. Rather, one can trust that God
was at work in their formulation, and thus take them with the kind of critical
seriousness which the living appropriation of tradition always requires.

The disagreement between Kasper and Rahner at this point may not be
decisive. They share with many other contemporary Catholic theologians
a remarkably similar view of the process of reception. It should consist of
a searching interpretation and reinterpretation of magisterial pronouncements in the light of Scripture and the contemporary experience of the
Church. As long as this is in fact done, it perhaps makes little difference
whether or not this process is described as a verification and condition for
recognition of full dogmatic status.

At any rate, within the interpretive framework we have employed, it is moderate infallibilists like Rahner and Kasper who seem to have the best chances of uniting the exigencies of the Reformation and of *Romanitas*. They are at one with the whole of historic Christianity in emphasizing the necessity of affirmations which are infallible within the language and life of faith; they agree with the Reformers on the primacy of Scripture to a degree which we have not had opportunity to emphasize sufficiently; and at the same time they succeed in combining this with methodologically and propositionally serious attention to the dogmas of their church. Common sense may accuse them of dubious compromises, but theologically they are remarkable for comprehensiveness and balance.

To the degree that this analysis is correct, so we must now observe in conclusion, there is no contradiction between dogmatically possible Roman Catholic positions on infallibility and the hypothetical Reformation view which was earlier outlined. If ecumenicity and reception by the Church were added to the conditions for the recognition of a teaching as infallible, then Protestants who stand with the Reformers would have to ask whether they are not simply permitted but required to agree with their Catholic brethren.

To be sure, Catholics more than Protestants would still think of papal approval also as a necessary condition for recognizing a doctrine as infallible, but Protestants could not seriously object to this. Sometimes even popes teach the truth.

Yet before rejoicing at this ecumenical outcome of the discussion, we must remember that the reconciliation is purely theoretical and abstract. It amounts to no more than saying that one can conceive of a new hermeneutical setting, different from past and present ones, in which the doctrinal propositions on infallibility which can be abstracted from the traditional teachings of the two confessions would no longer be incompatible. So far nothing has been said of the concrete possibility of the symbolisms or mythologies, the new institutional forms and the new theologies which would be required.

It seems unlikely that these requirements will be met in the foreseeable future. The major obstacle is not the persistence of the traditional papal and anti-papal mythologies and institutional structures. Their disappearance as effective forces may take a long time, but seems inevitable. The real problem is that the symbol systems which are now gaining the upper hand are radically anti-infallibilist, not only in the sense of being opposed to the excesses of papalism, but to historic Christianity as well. They are relativistic and immanently universalist, quite at odds with an emphasis on the objective particularities which constitute the essence of distinctive Christian identity.

Increasing numbers of Catholics as well as Protestants no longer understand Luther's *Tolle assertiones Christianum tulisti.*

They are inclined to think, for example, that 'Jesus is Lord' is only symbolically true, rather than being also a proposition, formulated within the circle of faith to be sure, but still intending to affirm a genuinely objective truth about the unsurpassable importance of a historically identifiable person for all human beings always and everywhere. To deny this kind of objectivity and the associated propositional infallibility does in one sense reconcile Protestantism and Catholicism, but only at the cost of destroying both.

Looked at in terms of the sociology of knowledge,[81] this anti-infallibilism is a function of the religious accommodationism characteristic of one stage of the the decline of that cultural Christianity which has dominated the West for the last 1,500 years. Most of us harbor the longing, inherited from our Constantinian past, to keep the churches in the mainstream of history. Traditional forms of cultural Christianity have been driven from the centers of power and prestige, and so we strive to create new forms which are better adapted to the de-Christianized sensibilities of the age. This adaptation, however, requires surrendering distinctive Christian claims to unsurpassable and infallible truth. We generally do not notice that we have given up one set of affirmations which explicitly claim infallibility for another set whose equally absolute claims are hidden and disguised. We have surrendered the freedom of consciously confessing our dogmas, and ultimately our God, only to fall into the slavery of unconscious idolatries.

The end of accommodationist anti-infallibilism is not in sight. To be sure, it is logically and sociologically unstable; for once a society is sufficiently de-Christianized, traditional and cultural prestige motives for calling oneself Christian disappear, and there is no reason for claiming the name except committment to the infallible Father of the Lord Jesus Christ indefectibly and infallibly at work in history. It is, however, quite impossible to know whether or when this might happen. The culturally Christian foundations of the West lie deep, and now western civilization is becoming world civilization. As society after society seeks desperately for new myths and symbols to replace those wrecked by modernity, the forms of the Christian heritage without the substance may often be pressed into service. Strange syncretisms in which Christ is worshipped along with Mao or Buddha, Castro or John Birch may still greet our wondering eyes.

Meanwhile, however, awaiting the passing of accommodationist Christianity, chastened infallibilists, whether Protestant or Catholic, can have the satisfaction of knowing that they are closer to each other in their faith in Christ and his Church than to the papalists, anti-papalists and relativizing fallibilists in their own communions.

The Reformation and the Infallibility Debate*

Thesis 1

In an historical perspective, a dogma is a rule of correct usage expressing a 'policy decision' regarding the interpretation in word and action of revelation in a particular situation, rather than a permanently adequate formulation of abiding truth.

Thesis 2

To affirm the 'infallibility' or 'irreformability' of a dogma, therefore, is to say that it was not a false or wrong decision in the circumstances of its time, and the error it rejected is permanently rejected. Thus at least in its negative import, the decision is irreversible.

Thesis 3

All traditions have dogmas which they treat operationally, even if not officially, as irreversible (and in this sense as infallible), but they differ on the criteria:

a) for Roman Catholics, one criterion of dogma is *ex cathedra* promulgation by an ecumenical council or pope
b) the Orthodox also generally insist on conciliar, but not papal action, and often add the requirement of reception by the universal Church
c) for the Reformation, and more specifically the Lutheran tradition, a dogma must be required by Scripture in the sense that it must express a decision that a given position (such as the Arian) is contrary to Scripture's explicit witness to the gospel.

Thesis 4

Given a 'hierarchy' of dogmas (to use the expression of Vatican II), it is possible that the churches could reunite on the basis of agreement on the rightness of a limited number of dogmatic decisions defensible by the Reformation scriptural principle combined with mutual acceptance of the theological

---

* George A Lindbeck, 'The Reformation and the Infallibility Debate', in *Teaching Authority and Infallibility in the Church. Lutherans and Catholics in Dialogue VI*, (eds), Paul C Empie, T Austin Murphy and Joseph A Burgess, Minneapolis: Augsburg Publishing House, 1978/80, pp. 314–16, note 27.

legitimacy (but not imperativeness) of the dogmas peculiar to each of the reuniting groups.

In order to do this, each party would have to interpret their peculiar dogmas (e.g. the Catholic Marian or papal ones or the Reformation *sola scriptura*) in such a way as to enable the others to recognize them, even if not as necessarily true, as not opposed to the gospel of Jesus Christ.

Thesis 5

In reference to magisterial infallibility, this latter condition would be fulfilled if:

a) Catholics understood magisterial infallibility as asserting that God in his mercy will see to it that no dogmatic decisions of the *magisterium* accepted by the Church are irreconciliable with the truth of Christ; and if

b) non-Catholics, while not affirming this as their belief, would hope that it is true – i.e. would not deny the possibility that God has willed to preserve the Church from such errors.

This remaining dogmatic difference between 'believing' and 'hoping' – between 'affirming the reality' and 'granting the possibility' of the immunity of an ecumenical *magisterium* (and of the Church to which it belongs) from doctrinal decisions so faulty that they should be repudiated rather than reinterpreted – is compatible with mutual recognition of the Christian authenticity of each other's positions. It is not a trivial difference, but it need not constitute a barrier to full communion between the churches.

10. The Church*

Editor's Introduction

Lux Mundi was a collection of essays by Anglicans published in 1889 concerned to 'put the Catholic faith into its right relation to modern intellectual and moral problems'.[1] The following essay was written to mark the centenary of that collection. Although Lindbeck notes crucial ways in which this essay is incomplete, it is perhaps the best summary of his ecclesiology – an 'ecumenically mandated' vision of the Church as 'the messianic pilgrim people of God typologically shaped by Israel's story'.

Organizationally, Lindbeck proceeds in what appears to be typical fashion for a theological essay on a topic: he takes the reader through the Church in Scripture and tradition before discussing their applicability to our present-day situation ('the empirical churches'). But the standard organization always threatens to make Scripture and tradition and our own time and place extrinsic to each other – as if we can appeal to Scripture without the lens of tradition or our own time, and vice versa. Lindbeck's argument proceeds differently. His vision of the Church is 'ecumenically mandated' rather than read directly off Scripture or tradition or our own time. The Bible has precedence, but even a tradition with 'monstrous offspring' cannot be 'condemned as simply unfaithful'.

The result of this biblical theology of the Church critically correlated with the tradition is two primary practical lessons for the Church. The primary mission of the Church is to witness to the God who judges and who saves rather than to save souls or improve the social order. And we do this best when our first concern is the mutual responsibility of the witnesses for

---

* George A Lindbeck, 'The Church', in *Keeping the Faith. Essays to Mark the Centenary of Lux Mundi*, (ed.), Geoffrey Wainwright, Philadelphia: Fortress Press and Allison Park: Pickwick Publications, 1988, pp. 179–208.

each other, especially in the concrete ministries by which *diakonia, liturgeiu,* and *unitas* can be fostered (e.g. deacon, priest, bishop).

The State of the Question

The aim of this chapter is to do for our day what Walter Lock did for his in his *Lux Mundi* essay on the Church. He sought to formulate the theological case for Catholic doctrines in a way that fit the situation, and I shall try to do the same. The situation has changed, however, and so also must the means. A different ecclesiological vision is needed to sustain Catholic claims, and the claims themselves need to be reformulated ecumenically. The vision of the Church which we shall explore is that of the messianic pilgrim people of God typologically shaped by Israel's story. Our chief concern is with the contemporary applicability and possible consequences of this ecclesiological outlook. But before turning to these aspects of our theme in the last three sections, we must deal in the first three with its present status, biblical grounding and long eclipse during most of the 2,000 years of Christian history.

Ecclesiology is a dogmatically undeveloped area. As historians remind us, there have been until recently no comprehensive pronouncements on the nature of the Church in any major Christian tradition. Much has been said about it, but not what it is. There are, for example, the four *notae ecclesiae*, spoken of in the ancient creeds: one, holy, catholic and apostolic. The Reformation confessions add to the list. The Church is said to be, among other things, *creatura verbi*, the creation of the word (cf. Confessio Augustana VII), but it is also in its visible form a *corpus mixtum* of the elect and the reprobate (Westminster Confession, 25.5). These, however, are attributes that can also be predicated of other subjects. Authentic preaching and sacraments together with Scripture and pure doctrine can also be described as creations of the word which are one, holy, catholic and apostolic. The same properties have often been attached to what has been conceived as a pure and invisible communion of faith, hope and love. Furthermore, is not Israel also composed of the faithful and the unfaithful, the saved and the unsaved? The traditional attributes neither uniquely identify nor comprehensively describe the Church.

Not only church doctrine but also theological reflection has been lacking in this area. Until 100 years before *Lux Mundi*, a chapter of the kind that Walter Lock wrote would have been a novelty. Specific topics such as ecclesiastical structures and discipline were addressed at length (as, e.g. by John Calvin in Book IV of the *Institutes* or Richard Hooker in his *Laws*), but separate treatises on the Church as a whole are modern phenomena. Among all the major theological loci, ecclesiology has been the last to develop.

Furthermore, even after ecclesiological treatises began to proliferate, it was long before 'people of God' became a central motif. HF Hamilton published a two-volume work on the subject in 1912,[2] but little else appeared for the next two decades. After that, however, there was a spate of studies of the theme even though they have never pre-empted the field. Identifications of the Church as primarily 'sacrament', 'body of Christ' or 'worshiping community', for example, have remained important.[3]

Yet by the time of the Second Vatican Council, the weight of biblical research in particular was such that 'messianic pilgrim people of God' received equal status together with 'sacrament of unity' and (perhaps) 'institution of salvation' as an ecclesiologically fundamental concept.[4] No one of these three characterizations is given precedence, however, and their interrelationships are not defined. The result, in effect, is to accord dogmatic approval to three different ecclesiological options (and perhaps more, for there is no suggestion that the list is exhaustive). People-of-God ecclesiologies are neither more nor less admissible than the other kinds.

From an ecumenical perspective, however, they have a definite advantage. Unlike the two major alternatives in *Lumen gentium*, they are as congenial to evangelical concerns (by which, in this chapter, I mean those of the Reformation) as to Catholic ones,[5] and they are at least as influential in non-Catholic as in Roman Catholic circles. For a discussion, such as the present one, which aims to be ecumenically catholic, they constitute the doctrinally warranted starting point for thinking about the Church.

Yet doctrines, as Karl Rahner in particular has emphasized,[6] are beginnings as well as ends. They lead beyond themselves. Over and over again in church history, magisterially approved formulations have been overshadowed by others which came to seem more adequate. This could happen in the present case. Perhaps some other way of thinking about the Church is preferable in our or in any situation. It is up to the reader to be the judge of that. Yet whatever the ending, there are both doctrinal and ecumenical reasons for beginning with the messianic pilgrim people. This is the way of viewing the Church which currently has the greatest *prima facie* claim to ecumenical catholicity.

Biblical Evidence

In order to sustain such a claim, however, a view of the Church must be biblically warranted. It must, above all, be consistent with the total witness of Scripture as this centers on Jesus Christ. Without this, it can be neither catholic nor ecumenical. In addition, correspondence with scriptural patterns of thought is normally regarded as enhancing biblical backing. There are, to be sure, occasions when a scriptural outlook on a particular topic must be abandoned out of faithfulness to the central message or out of concern for intelligibility and practical effectiveness. The New Testament tolerance for slavery can be cited as an example. Its replication in our post-biblical circumstances would be, for all contemporary churches, directly opposed to Christ Jesus, not to mention unintelligible and practically counterproductive. Conceivably something similar might hold for biblical ways of thinking about the Church. Perhaps they never were fully adequate to the gospel, or perhaps they have become inadequate in the course of time. Yet despite this possibility, it has been the general conviction throughout Christian history that, other things being equal, correspondence to what Scripture says is desirable. Departure from its patterns may be admissible, but only when there are good reasons for it.

This has been recognized even in trinitarian and christological doctrine. The non-biblical formulations of Nicaea and Chalcedon have over and over again been treated by their advocates as unfortunate necessities forced upon the Church by the needs of a new situation (such as, according to Athanasius and his fellows, the heretical misuse of scriptural language). We shall assume that the same rule holds in ecclesiology. Biblical conceptualities may be supplemented or displaced, as at Nicaea and Chalcedon, but only if this is necessary for the sake of greater faithfulness, intelligibility or efficaciousness. The burden of proof is on those whose fundamental categories for thinking about the Church are non-biblical.

In the light of these considerations, it is impossible to avoid the exegetical question of what were the biblical ways of understanding the Church. The answer to this may be decisive and is in any case important for ecclesiology.[7]

Fortunately we need only ask what Scripture meant by the Church when it is conceived primarily as the people of God. On this, something close to a scholarly consensus seems to exist. Problems arise and the consensus dissolves chiefly when one turns to a prior question:

Is the Church of which the Bible tells us primarily the people of God, or is some other designation more fundamental?

Does one get closer to its essence if one calls it, for example, the body of Christ or the community of the Spirit or the worshiping assembly or an event, an institution or a liberation movement?

The scriptural references can be looked at from any one of these or many other angles, and which approach does most justice to the data is exegetically undecidable. We are here inclosed in what has come to be known as a hermeneutical circle, for our pre-understandings help determine what we take to be relevant data.[8] Squaring this circle is out of the question, and we shall therefore proceed on the doctrinally and ecumenically mandated hypothesis that the Church was primarily the people of God in the biblical writings, and ask what that meant.

The historical and exegetical support for this ecumenically catholic hypothesis is strong (whether stronger than for other hypotheses is what we shall not discuss). The early Christians were a Jewish sect. They believed in a crucified and resurrected Messiah who authorized them, some of them believed, to welcome the uncircumcised into their fellowship, but this did not diminish their desire to maintain their legitimacy as Jews. All the categories they possessed for their communal self-understanding were derived from the Hebrew Scriptures (usually, to be sure, in the Greek Septuagint version). These were their only inspired text, and they interpreted it as Jews. It was natural that they should understand their communities as *ekklēsia*, as *qahal*, the assembly of Israel in the new age. (For once philology and etymology cohere with broader historical considerations.)[9] Thus the story of Israel was their story. They were that part of the people of God who lived in the time between the times after the messianic era had begun but before the final coming of the kingdom. Whatever is true of Israel is true of the Church except where the differences are explicit.

Four heuristic guidelines for reading the New Testament references to the Church are suggested by this historical background. First, as befits those who thought of themselves as a people, early Christian communal self-understanding was narrative shaped.[10] The Church, in other words, was fundamentally identified and characterized by its story. Images such as 'body of Christ' or the traditional marks of 'unity, holiness, catholicity and apostolicity' cannot be first defined and then used to specify what was and what was not 'church'. The story was logically prior. It determined the meaning of images, concepts, doctrines and theories of the Church rather than being determined by them. Just as the story of the Quakers is more fundamental than descriptions such as 'church of the poor' or 'church of the wealthy' (for they have been both), and the story of the French is more fundamental than 'monarchy' or 'republic' (for France has been both), so it is also in the case of the Church.

A corollary of this priority of story was that 'church' ordinarily referred to concrete groups of people, not to something transempirical. An invisible Church is as biblically odd as an invisible Israel. Stories of the biblical realistic-narrative type can only be told of agents and communities of agents acting and being acted upon in a space–time world of contingent happenings. Thus to say that it was empirical churches in all their actual or potential messiness of which exalted concepts and images such as 'holy' and 'bride of Christ' were predicated is an analytic implicate of the primacy of narrative.

For the early Christians, in the second place, Israel's history was their only history. They did not yet have the New Testament or later church history as sources. Israel's history, to be sure, was seen through the prism of Christ, and this made a profound difference; but yet, to repeat, the Hebrew Scriptures were the sole ecclesiological textbook. The only inspired stories available to the Church for its self-understanding were the stories of Israel.

A third rule is an extension of this second one. Not only was Israel's story the early Christians' only communal story but it was the whole of that story which they appropriated. It was not only the favorable parts, such as the Old Testament accounts of faithful remnants, which they applied to themselves. All the wickedness of the Israelites in the wilderness could be theirs. They might rebel, as did Korah or perish for fornication, as did three and twenty thousand in the desert (1 Cor. 10.5–10). These happenings, Paul tells his readers, are types (*tupoi*) written for our admonition (v. 11). As of old, judgment continues to begin in the house of the Lord (1 Pet. 4.17), and the unfaithful Church can be severed from the root no less than the unbelieving synagogue (Rom. 11.21). It can, like Eve, yield to the wiles of the serpent and lose its virginal purity (2 Cor. 11.1–4). One can imagine early Christians going on in more extreme situations, such as later developed, to say of the bride of Christ what Ezekiel said of the betrothed of Jahweh (Ezekiel 16.23): she can be a whore worse than the heathen. As was earlier noted, when the New Testament is silent we need to turn to the Hebrew Scriptures, the ecclesiological text par excellence, to discover how the early Christians thought about the Church.

In opposition to most later exegesis, therefore, the relation of Israel's history to that of the Church in the New Testament was not that of shadow to reality or promise to fulfillment or type to antitype.[11] Jesus Christ alone is the antitype or fulfillment. He is depicted as the embodiment of Israel (e.g. 'Out of Egypt have I called my son', Matt. 2.15), and the Church is the body of Christ. Thus Israel's story, transposed into a new key through Christ, becomes prototypical for the history of the Church which is its continuation rather than its fulfillment.

From this it follows, in the fourth place, that Israel and the Church were one people for the early Christians. There was no breach in continuity. A new age had begun, but the story continued and therefore also the people which it identified. The French remain French after the revolution, the Quakers remain Quakers after becoming wealthy, and Israel remains Israel even when transformed by the arrival of the eschaton in Christ. The Church is simply Israel in the time between the times. The continuity of the story and the identity of the people are unbroken.

Discontinuity and nonidentity are problems in the New Testament, not for the Church per se, but for unbelieving Jews on the one hand and gentile Christians on the other. The apostle Paul says of the first group in Romans

11 that they have been cut off, but that this can happen does not differentiate them from Christians. Churches also, as we have already noted, can be severed from the root. They can, in the even more vigorous language of Revelation, be spewed forth, expectorated (Rev. 3.16). Yet when this occurs, it does not alter the identity of the people of the promise. 'The gifts and the call of God are irrevocable' (Rom. 11.29). Unbelieving Jewry will ultimately be restored. Furthermore, post-biblical Judaism which has not heard the gospel (and how can it hear in view of Christian persecution?) lives theologically before Christ and cannot be equated with the unbelieving Jewry of which Paul speaks. Nothing in his account prevents us from saying that the synagogue, like remnants in ancient Israel, is at times more faithful to God's will and purposes than are unfaithful churches. In any case, in the one New Testament writing in which the problem is directly addressed, Judaism after Christ is as inalienably embraced as the Church in the continuous overarching story of the single people, consisting of faithful remnants and unfaithful masses, which stretches from the patriarchal period to the last days.

So strong was this sense of uninterrupted peoplehood that the only available way to think of gentile Christians was, in Krister Stendahl's phrase, as 'honorary Jews'.[12] The uncircumcised, 'alienated from the commonwealth of Israel', have become 'fellow citizens . . . of the household of God', 'fellow heirs, [fellow] members of the same body, and [fellow] partakers of the promise' (Eph. 2.12, 19; 3.6). This inclusion of the Gentiles is represented in Ephesians as the most wondrous aspect of the work of Christ. Where there were two, there is now one, the new man in Christ (Eph. 2.11—3.11), the beginnings of the new humanity, the third race of which the early fathers spoke. Thus has begun the gathering of all humankind into God's people, the promised ascent of the nations to worship in Zion, the crowding of the Gentiles into the heavenly Jerusalem. But Zion does not change identity: the twelve apostles are commemorated on the foundations of the walls of the New Jerusalem, but its gates are marked with the names of the twelve tribes (Rev. 21.12). The inclusion of the uncircumcised in the covenant with Abraham by means of the new covenant in Christ did not, for the earliest Christians, constitute the formation of a different people but rather the enlargement of the old.

From this perspective, not only the enlargement of the people but also its other special features are functions of life in the new age, not changes in identity. Who and what the people is becomes more fully manifest now that the Messiah has come. The bride of Yahweh is the bride and body of Christ. The Spirit is now offered and may be poured out on all flesh as it was not before (Acts 2.17ff.). Thus the *ab initio* trinitarian calling, constituting and empowering of God's people stands revealed. It is a new epoch of unheard-of possibilities and actualities, not a New Israel, which begins at Pentecost.

The early Christian appropriation of the story of Israel, needless to say, differed greatly from situation to situation. Sometimes the differences look like contradictions even in the same author. It is, for example, hard to reconcile what Paul says of unbelieving Jews when encouraging the persecuted Christians of Thessolonica (cf. 1 Thess. 2.14–15) with his later discussion in Romans 9–11. The Church is scarcely ever spoken of as the people of God in the Johannine literature, and in Hebrews, it is sometimes said, it is platonized. Yet there is nothing surprising in this. The use of ancient tales to shape the identity of the nascent church required many twists and turns. If one follows the story line, these intertwine into a single narrative (not systematic) whole but if not, they fragment into distinct and perhaps incompatible ecclesiologies. It is perhaps only in a people-of-God approach that one can speak responsibly of a basically unified New Testament understanding of the Church.[13]

Post-biblical Ecclesiology

This understanding, however, did not persist. It became increasingly unintelligible and inapplicable as circumstances changed. Modifications developed in part to maintain faithfulness to the christological center, but these led at times to unfaithfulness. We cannot assess the present situation in ecclesiology without first noting some of these changes in Christian communal self-understanding.

Modifications of biblical patterns of thought started in the very first generations. The hardening of the opposition between synagogue and church led even Jewish Christians, as such documents as the Letter of Barnabas illustrate, to reject the notion that unbelieving Jews remained part of God's people. Faithfulness became the mark of election, and election, conversely, became conditional on faithfulness. The doctrines of predestination and of salvation *sola gratia*, insofar as they persisted, tended to be applied only to individuals and not to communities. Heretical groups were more and more regarded as not really the Church at all. They were not seen after the fashion of the ancient prophets as the adulterous spouse whom the Lord may cast out for a time but without divorcing.

A second development was that the Church quickly became wholly gentile: it ceased to be sociologically a Jewish sect. It became intellectually and practically impossible for gentile Christians to think of themselves as naturalized citizens in the continuous, uninterrupted commonwealth of Israel. Thus not only was the synagogue excluded but the one people of God was broken into two peoples, the old and the new. This created the problem of how to relate them, and the solution was to read the Scriptures as if Israel were the type, no longer simply of the coming kingdom and of its instantiation in the person of Christ, but also of the Church, which thus became the antitype, the fulfillment. The more unsavory aspects of the history of Israel were no longer genuinely portions of the history of the Church but were projected exclusively on the synagogue.

These modifications, it will be observed, are quite explicitly changes in the scriptural people-of-God pattern rather than simply new applications. Yet despite the monstrous offspring they ultimately engendered, they cannot be flatly condemned as simply unfaithful. They were the historically i.e. contingently necessary conditions for the Church's appropriation of Israel's story. Without that appropriation, so we may plausibly speculate, Gnosticism would have wholly triumphed, the Marcionite rejection of Israel's Scriptures and Israel's God would have become universal among Christians, and the Nazi heresy that Jesus was not a Jew would have become orthodoxy from the second century on. Because the modifications were the only available alternative to utter subversion of the christological center, they can be regarded, despite their magnitude and consequences, as scripturally faithful interpretations of the story of the Church.

Such excuses become increasingly unworkable; however, after the Empire was converted and persecuted Christians became the persecutors. Antisemitism was the paradigmatic problem, but it needs to be seen as an acute manifestation of a more general disease. The dissonance between antitypical claims to fulfillment and empirical reality was the central difficulty. The Church was now a *corpus mixtum* composed overwhelmingly of visible sinners rather than visible saints. The pressure was great to refer its high claims, not to the overall pattern of communal life, but to segregated aspects: to pure (ultimately infallible) doctrines, to individualistically (and, in vulgar understanding, magically) efficacious sacraments, and to divinely established institutions. Even these developments, to be sure, were not in every respect antiscriptural. They might be compared, perhaps, to the Israelite monarchy which God consented to *contre coeur* (1 Samuel 8), and yet also mightily used to preserve his people and prepare for the Messiah (Jesus sprang from the Davidic line). In somewhat similar fashion, so one could argue, the imperial Church preserved the faith amid barbarian chaos, converted Europe, and was the cradle of the first civilization to become worldwide (whether there is anything messianic about western-spawned modernity is another question). Be that as it may, however, the antitypical pretensions of western ecclesiastical establishments (from which Reformation state churches were by no means wholly exempt) could not but evoke sectarian reactions (which, incidentally, have not been so strong in the East where Caesaropapism, whatever its faults, muted churchly arrogance).

The sectarian solutions to the Church's dilemma have on the whole been less biblical but not uniformly less faithful to Scripture than the earlier Catholic ones. They have been less biblical because for the most part they have no longer understood God's people in terms of Israel's story but rather have been modeled after New Testament depictions of fervent first-generation communities especially as found in Acts. Yet however unbiblical one may think the ecclesiology of, for example, the Quakers, it is hard to deny that such groups have at times been faithful remnants amid the faithless masses. Insofar as they were protest movements against Constantinian churches, the sects were in general scripturally justified, but they are also deeply problematic. The intense effort to make the empirical reality of Christian communities conform visibly to images of antitypical fulfillment can have consequences in some ways worse than institutional triumphalism. The arrogant self-righteousness of the company of the visibly holy compares ill with the concern for publicans and sinners sometimes found in churches that conceive of themselves as arks of salvation, as hospitals for sick souls.

The difficulties in traditional ecclesiologies, whether Catholic, Reformation or sectarian, have led in recent centuries to new ways of thinking about the Church which depart even further from biblical patterns but which, once again, can have scriptural authenticity. Not only is Israel's story abandoned but also the referential primacy of empirical communities. Something other than these communities is really the Church, is really the subject of the claims to antitypical fulfillment, with the result that ecclesial arrogance of either the Catholic or the sectarian types is no longer theologically legitimate.

For example, the Church is characterized denotatively (not simply connotatively, or predicatively, or in some promissory or other illocutionary mode)[14] as event or mission or liberating action or the new being in Christ or the fellowship of the Spirit or the communion of Christ's justifying grace which works in anonymous as well as explicitly Christian ways. For the most part, any suggestion that the Church is invisible is stoutly resisted. Rather, it necessarily takes visible form, and in some interpretations referential primacy is accorded to what is empirically or experientially identifiable (e.g. event, mission or liberating action). Nevertheless, however observable or experienceable the main referent may be, it is not first of all a people. It is not empirical churches in all their crass concreteness. These latter are rather imperfect manifestations, realizations, participations or thematizations of the Church's true, eschatological reality.

Thus if our exegetical approach is right, what for the Bible are predicates are in these modern outlooks turned into subject terms. The reference of these terms is not a concrete people of the kind whose identity is rendered by realistic narratives, and it must therefore be described in some other way. Systematic ecclesiology replaces the story of the people of God. This is what happened in recent centuries in almost all major theological outlooks whether Catholic or Protestant.[15]

Yet, we must now recall, there are good reasons for these developments, and unbiblical ways of thinking about the Church are not necessarily unfaithful. They have in some cases eliminated occasions for antisemitism and ecclesial arrogance by making the antitypical church something other than the empirical churches. In this and other respects they may be more genuinely Christian than their predecessors. It would be artificial but not impossible to write a history of ecclesiology in which increasing departures from the Bible were correlated with increasing closeness to Christ.

The question arises, however, whether the progression we have reviewed has reached its end. Perhaps the incipient return to a people-of-God ecclesiology noted at the beginning of this essay can now be carried further. In dealing with this question. I shall first comment briefly on the applicability of this ecclesiology in the present situation and then deal in two concluding sections with some possible applications.

Applicability

There are a number of familiar ways in which the present period is becoming more like the Christian beginnings than the intervening ages. Christendom is passing and Christians are becoming a diaspora. The antagonism of the Church to the synagogue has been unmasked (we hope definitively) for the horror it always was. Ecclesial pretensions to fulfillment have become obnoxious to multitudes of Catholics and Protestants alike. Some of the reasons for distorting and then rejecting the scriptural people-of-God ecclesiology are disappearing, and perhaps its original version is again applicable.

Certainly there are reasons for wanting to apply it. For it, there is no Church except the empirical churches,[16] and this emphasis is badly needed. the empirical churches are losing the loyalty and devotion of their members. Special-interest enclaves are replacing comprehensive communities as the locus of whatever shreds of communal identity the isolated individuals of our society retain. The conviction that the churches even in their crass concreteness have a crucial place in God's plans has weakened. All these considerations call for a return to Israel's story as a template which helps shape Christian communities. These communities need to be understood as witnesses that God has chosen no less irrevocably than he chose Israel to testify to his glory in both their faithfulness and unfaithfulness, in both his mercy and his judgment. Their election needs to be recognized as abiding even though they too may be severed by disobedience from the root (Rom.

11.21). Portions of the chosen people may lose their identity, they may be destroyed as was the Northern Kingdom, but that does not alter the unconditionality of the election of those which remain recognizably Jewish or Christian even when they apostatize. God chastises them when they err – indeed, he does this with special severity – but as his chosen ones, beloved above all nations.

Such convictions have made of Jews the great exception to the sociological and historical generalizations that apply to other nations and have enabled them, despite their dispersion and small numbers, to be a major force in history (not least, it should be recalled, when they were wholly in the diaspora). History shows that Israel's story has unique ability to confer communally significant meaning on whatever happens: it has, one might say, unrivaled power to encode successfully the vicissitudes and contradictions of history. Christianity, it can be argued, has urgent need to make greater use of that same biblical tale if it is to be comparably tenacious and flexible in maintaining its identity as a people irresistibly called (and ineluctably failing) to witness by selfless service of all humankind to the universal yet thoroughly particular God of Abraham, Isaac, Jacob and Jesus.

It must be added, however, that there are as yet few signs that this is happening. On the right, apocalyptic conservatism is on the rise, but this, despite its often ardent support for the Israeli state, not only thinks of Christianity as the replacement of Judaism but restricts the Church to the company of the datably converted. On the political left, liberationists selectively appropriate episodes from Israel's history, especially the exodus, but use these as legitimating precedents for their own campaigns, not as applicable to comprehensive gatherings of sinners and saints, oppressors and oppressed, tyrants and liberators. More generally, despite such dubious phenomena as Jews for Jesus, Christianity continues for the most part to be as gentile in its self-understanding as ever, and few Christians are in the least inclined to think of themselves as even remotely analogous to a Jewish sect or honorary Jews. As long as this is the situation, a biblically Israel-like understanding of the Church will not be intelligible or efficacious, and in a sense not even scripturally appropriate: many Christians would react by becoming even more Marcionite than they already are.

Yet uncertainty about applicability does not preclude discussion of applications. Some of these must be outlined in order to illustrate how the code of Israel's history may be used in our day as, in the first century, to understand who and what the Church is. Attention will focus on the identity of the Church in relation to, first, its mission and unity and, second, its unifying structures. The result is a very partial treatment of the Church. It fails to start, as a full-scale ecclesiology would, with the people of God as worshiping community created by the Father through the Son in the power of the Holy Spirit, constituted by the proclamation of the gospel in word and sacrament, and bearing joyous fruit in works of suffering love. These basal dimensions are discussed, however, elsewhere in this volume, (Keeping the Faith), even if not from a specifically ecclesiological perspective, while questions of the institutionalization of church order are at present the ecumenically most intractable ones. It is, then, the identity and the mission of the messianic pilgrim people in relation to its ordering structures which are the topics of these concluding remarks.

Identity and Mission

The Church's story, understood as continuous with Israel's, tells of God doing in this time between the times what he has done before: choosing and guiding a people to be a sign and witness in all that it is and does, whether obediently or disobediently, to who and what he is. Both God's mercy and God's judgment are manifest in the life of this people as nowhere else.

This is what the narrative is about. By remembering that this is the subject matter, we can identify the Church in the 20th no less than in the 1st century. It is true that the Church looks very different in these two periods, but then so did Israel in the wilderness, under judges and kings, and in exile. The encoded historical data vary, and so do the descriptive results, but the identifying code is the same and therefore also the identified people.

The referential force of this narrative code can be analyzed into distinct aspects. First, the identity and being of the Church rests on God's election, not on its faithfulness. Second, as an implicate of this, the elect communities are stamped by objective marks which are both blessing and curse depending on how they are received. Eating and drinking, Paul reminds us, can be unto judgment (1 Cor. 11.29) and not only life, and the same applies to circumcision and baptism, the *shema* and the *apostolicum*. Even when the sacraments are spiritualized, as by Quakers, the profession that the Christ spoken of in Scripture is the Lord can be a publicly unmistakable brandmark of the group's election. Third, election is communal. Individuals are elect by virtue of visible membership in God's people. Last, the primary mission of this chosen people is to witness to the God who judges and who saves, not to save those who would otherwise be damned (for God has not confined his saving work exclusively to the Church's ministrations). It testifies to this God whether or not it wills to do so, whether it is faithful or unfaithful. The final consummation which has begun in Christ is proleptically present in this people as nowhere else, but so also is the eschatological judgment (1 Pet. 4.17; cf. Amos 3.2 and Jer. 25.29).[17]

The Church thus identified sounds Catholic in its comprehensiveness,

Calvinist in the unconditionality of its chosenness, and Lutheran in its possibilities of unfaithfulness while remaining genuinely the Church; but the total effect, not surprisingly, is more Jewish than anything else. This is true, first, in reference to those who are designated individually and communally as part of the Church. The Church consists of those, whether atheists or believers, reprobate or regenerate, who are stamped with the marks of membership in elect communities.[18] Baptism may be easier to ignore than circumcision (though secular Israelis are adept at doing so), but God remembers. Nor does communal degeneracy erase election. The Amhara and the Falasha in Ethiopia may resemble the animist tribes which surround them, but if one admits they are Christian and Jewish respectively, one is obligated to accept them as fully parts, even if defective parts, of the elect people. Similarly, the apartheid churches of South Africa are no less churches than the black ones they oppress, just as 16th-century Catholics and Protestants were part of the same elect people as the Anabaptists whom they jointly slaughtered, and just as the Gush Emmunim and Peace Now advocates, not to mention the warring sects of whom Josephus tells, are and were fully Jewish. To put this point in the terminology of the social sciences, the people of God consists of cultural-linguistic groupings that can be meaningfully identified by ordinary sociological and historical criteria as Christian or Jewish (even though their chosenness, needless to say, is known only to faith). This is what is meant biblically and, in the present perspective, theologically by a people.[19]

Also Jewish sounding is the Church's mission. It is above all by the character of its communal life that it witnesses, that it proclaims the gospel and serves the world. This revolutionizes one traditional understanding of proclamation of evangelization. While it is crucial that all kinds of human beings – Greek, barbarian, female and slave as well as Jew, male and free – be fully part of the community, sheer numbers are, at most, of tertiary importance. Christians have as much reason as Jews to eschew heedless invitations to outsiders (whether rootless or adherents of other religions) to bear the burdens of election. The possibilities of damnation as well as of salvation are increased within the people of God (think of the story of Ananias and Sapphira in Acts 5 or, as far as that goes, of Judas). The Bible gives us no warrants for saying that all those who do not become Christians are, in any case, excluded from the coming kingdom, although it cannot be said of them as of Christians that salvation, the kingdom, is already present among or in them (Luke 17.21). The purpose of that presence of salvation, furthermore, is witness, and it is up to God to add whom he will to the company (Acts 2.47). Churches should not imitate the Pharisees, whom Jesus condemned for compassing land and sea to make proselytes (Matt. 23.15), but should rather follow the practice that prevailed in the first centuries of prolonged catechesis. The primary Christian mission, in short, is not to save souls but to be a faithfully witnessing people.[20]

It would be a mistake, however, to conclude from this in the currently popular fashion that the Church's mission is therefore primarily *diakonia* in the sense of serving the needs of humanity at large. Christians are responsible first of all for their own communities, not for the wider society. It is by the quality of their communal life that God wills them to be a light to the Gentiles. This does not mean that the chosen people is more important than the world. On the contrary, its role is instrumental: it exists in order to witness to the nations. It does this, however, not primarily by striving to save souls or to improve the social order, but by being the body of Christ, the communal sign of the promised redemption, in the time between the times. When serving the world results in the neglect of the household of faith, the Church becomes not a sign but a countersign, a contributor to that human confusion which is the opposite of God's design. It comes to resemble the philanthropist who loves humankind at a distance but not his neighbors or family in need. Its primary task should be to build up sisters and brothers in the faith, not to liberate the oppressed everywhere; and it is only through performing this task that it becomes a liberating force in world history.[21]

This makes mutual responsibility of all for all crucial to the Church's mission and witness. The need, the shame, the glory and the health or sickness of any one part belong to all. One must aid the distressed communities and seek (by protest from within rather than from without) to correct the wayward ones. This part of the biblical outlook, present in both the Hebrew Scriptures and the apostolic writings, has been better preserved among Jews than Christians. The black Falashas, for example, once they are acknowledged as Jewish, are the special responsibility of Jews everywhere. Contemporary ecumenism moves part of the way in this direction but generally stops short with mutual respect between the churches and invitations to dialogue. Even the ecumenically minded do not generally recognize as their special business the superstition (and now the suffering) of the Ethiopian Copts, the shame of Maronite massacres of Shiites (we are much more concerned about the indirect Israeli responsibility), the apartheid oppressiveness of the Dutch Reformed churches in South Africa, or the electronic vulgarity of television evangelists. Contemporary Christians are concerned about these problems, but no more so (and perhaps less) than about superstition and suffering among non-Christian tribes, massacres in India or Iran or violence and pornography on the screen. Once the traditional understanding of mission as the saving of souls is abandoned, the task of witnessing tends to become indistinguishable from that socially responsible righteousness, that commitment to peace, justice and freedom, to which all human beings are called. The problem is not only practical but theological: it is difficult in most ecclesiological perspectives to legitimate greater concern for Christians than for non-Christians. Perhaps the only way out is a people-of-God perspective in which the mutual concern of all the churches for each other's worship, faith, fellowship and action becomes of paramount importance precisely for the sake of missionary witness to the world.

Ministries of Unity

It is in the context of this mutual responsibility of all for all that we now turn to the question of structures of churchwide unity. These are not fundamental. Mutual care can be exercised in some circumstances without institutionalized ministries of unity (as, e.g. by the collection for the poor of the church in Jerusalem which Paul so energetically promoted). Furthermore, the local ministries of word and sacrament are, by common consent, basic. Disputes over these, however, have not led to schism to the same degree as have those over the wider structures, over the historic episcopacy and the papacy. It is therefore with these that I shall deal.[22]

The use of Israel's story leads to results that are ecumenically catholic, but the way of getting there has resemblances both to Protestant functionalism and traditional Catholic institutionalism. On the functionalist side, it is clear that the leadership structures of the chosen people changed to fit new circumstances. Moses was followed by judges and kings, and the rabbinate developed in the exile and the diaspora. (Prophets, needless to say, were also important, but authentic prophecy is not easily institutionalized, if at all, and is not our present concern.) Further, when the kingdom was divided between north and south, both monarchies were for the most part treated in the canonically edited text (even though the final redaction was southern) as legitimate, and worship at Shiloh as well as at Jerusalem was acknowledged. The functionally sensible rule of international law that effective control in the long run establishes legitimacy has scriptural precedents. If Christians have anything to learn in this respect from Israel's Scriptures (which are also its own), then disputes between the Greek, Roman and Reformation churches over which has the more valid ministerial orders and/ or sacraments are misplaced.

The same scriptural story also has, however, Catholic implications. These implications, to be sure, are not necessarily antifunctional, but they do oppose the widespread Protestant pragmatism which makes of structures a simple adiaphoron, a matter of theological indifference or even dislike. Israel's history, like that of any other sizable and enduring people, makes clear that continuity and tradition are functionally important. Long-surviving institutions, like long-surviving species, can incorporate in their genetic code a wealth of evolutionary wisdom unmatchable by conscious calculation. Or, to make a somewhat similar point less metaphorically, the symbolic weight acquired by durable structures can be incomparably more powerful (for good as well as ill) than anything devised *de novo* to fit contemporary needs. Not only episcopacy and papacy can be cited but also such non-ecclesiastical structures as universities, the American Constitution and the British monarchy. So also it was in Israel. As in all traditional societies, the old was to be preferred unless divinely or historically counter-manded (and, given God's rulership of the universe, the two are not unre-lated). This is not surprising. Whatever else the elect people may be, it is genuinely a people which, by God's will, is not exempt from, even if it is not captive to, the same constraints that influence other human collectivities. In short, a historically embedded functionalism has a Catholic thrust.

Further, however, the structurally Catholic aspects of Israel's narrative are more than functional. It is God who guides his people and orders their common life. The monarchy was established by God even though, as the text explicitly points out, he acted reluctantly in response to what his people thought was historical necessity (1 Samuel 8). Except for the period of the divided kingdom, he always supplied leaders or a single center for the whole people (even if, as during the long diaspora, this was no more than the holy land as an object of longing rather than as an actual possession). Leadership has been recognized as providentially authorized. When one form dis-appeared to be replaced by another, it was rarely because of internal revolt. The prophets mercilessly denounced the abuses and corruptions of the leaders, but they did not doubt that they had been divinely appointed. Even Paul, according to Acts 23.2–3, did not deny that this was true of the high priest of his day whom he called a 'whited wall'. When it came to the Jerusalem leadership of the infant church, his own account of his attitude is poignant. He did not want to go to Jerusalem to consult with James, Peter, John and the others of repute (though 'what they were makes no difference', he adds) about the gospel he had been preaching to the Gentiles, for that could not be challenged. It took, he tells us, a 'revelation' to compel him to go (Gal. 2.2–6). It is almost as if he feared a conflict (which in fact did not take place) between an irresistible force and an immovable object, both divinely authorized. In summary, then, leadership structures are treated in the biblical texts as *de iure divino*, as Catholics would say, and yet also as changeable human law, *ius humanum*, to bring in the Protestant note.[23]

While this narrative way of thinking about church structures may be as nearly Protestant as Catholic, its consequences are Catholic, though without repeating the claims that have been most objectionable to the Reformation churches. The starting point is the conviction that God's providential guidance of his continuously existing people did not stop with biblical times. Only if one believes that the Spirit has guided the Church in the past can one trust God to guide it also in the present and in the future. Tradition counts. Structures that God has used and is using have his authorization and are not to be lightly discarded. Ruptures in continuity are to be avoided except when absolutely necessary, and even then the search for precedents is important.[24]

In the second place, then, the preference is for the reform of past structures, not their replacement. The burden of proof is on those who, for example, reject the historic three-fold ministry as this ministry is recommended in the Lima text, *Baptism, Eucharist and Ministry*. The case for it need not be that it is demonstrably superior to other ministerial orderings, but simply that it can be congruent with the christological center of the faith (which anyone who believes God did not desert his Church from the time of the first centuries is bound to admit), and that it is not irrational or impractical (which in view of its present use by some three-quarters of all Christians seems incontestable). If so, the respect for tradition which trust in God's guidance of the Church involves requires churches that do not have it to adopt (and adapt) the historic policy for the sake of unity whenever this is practically feasible (which in periods of transition such as the present it often is).

This case, however, does not meet the Protestant and Reformation objection that Catholics have in fact claimed far more for their structures than is warranted by their providential origins and use. They have held that the historic episcopate in particular was founded directly by Christ and the apostles, had existed continuously ever since, guarantees the apostolicity of the Church's faith, and is irreversibly indispensable to the *bene esse* (the well-being) or *plene esse* (the full being) or even the *esse* (the very existence) of the Church. Under the pressure of historical evidence, providentially guided development has now generally replaced dominical or apostolic institution, the possibility that apostolic faith may sometimes be more fully present in non-episcopal churches is admitted, and there is no effort to say that bishops are necessary to the being of the Church (if so, how could one account for the non-episcopal churches of the first century?), but the claims to irreversibility and to the necessity for the well-being or the fullness of being of the Church continue to be generally maintained. These are the sticking points for many Protestants who otherwise have no objection to the apostolic succession. Even when their *amour propre* is not wounded by the doubts raised regarding their own orders and sacraments, they view the claim that a specific ordering of the Church is permanently optimal as infringing on God's freedom, confusing law and gospel, and endangering the principle that human beings, including church communities, are justified by faith, not by works. It is *status confessionis*[25] under these circumstances to be non-episcopal.[26]

Even Catholics who are sensitive to the force of this objection, however, are inclined to think that it underestimates the degree to which episcopacy is intertwined with the foundational features of the Church's origins in the immediate post-biblical period. The episcopate emerged early and was, in its original form, much the most successful institutional expression and support in Christian history of that mutual responsibility which we have seen to be at the heart of the Church's mission. Letters to the churches and collections for needy saints in distant places may have sufficed to maintain churchwide mutuality in the New Testament period, but not when the group of apostolic leaders who were personally acquainted with each other passed from the scene. Then the device of requiring each new bishop to be approved and consecrated by neighboring bishops was hit upon, and this developed into an interlocking network covering the Mediterranean world which was both flexible and tenacious enough to contain in a single communion orientations as antithetical as those of Tertullian's Carthage and Origen's Alexandria. (It is misleading to call this a monarchical or monoepiscopal system, for without the requirement of validation from neighboring churches, one bishop in one place does not unify.) Profane historians are as likely as Catholics to conclude that it was chiefly this institutionalization of mutual accountability which explains the astonishing success of the originally Catholic minority (for most Christian groups were at first non-episcopal) in becoming the overwhelming – and therefore catholic – majority. It is to this episcopally unified church, furthermore, that all the major Christian traditions owe their creeds, their liturgies and, above all, their scriptural canon. If these latter are inexpungible, why not also the episcopate? No wonder many Catholics think of it as ineradicable, and they may be right. Yet, on the other hand, the reader of Israel's story cannot but observe that the leadership structure in the comparably decisive period of Jewish history did not survive.[27] The question of irreversibility cannot be settled by appeals to Israel's story. The story provides a framework for reflection, not a formula for automatically settling disputes.

The same holds true for the basically similar problem of papal primacy[28] which divides Orthodox and Anglican Catholics from Rome. Many of these, as well as a not inconsiderable number of Protestants, see no difficulty in admitting the providential origins (and, in that sense, divine institution) of the papacy, and they agree that it has greater potentialities for ministering to the unity of the Church universal than any other existing institution, and yet they resist the contention that Rome must be at the center, and that this is irreversibly true.[29] Although they believe it important for the sake of unity to have at the very least a *primus inter pares* (first among equals) among the bishops, and take it as self-evident that both the weight of tradition and contemporary standing point to the Bishop of Rome, yet it seems to them worse than pretentious to affirm as a matter of faith that God will always will it so. After a time when both were approved, the center in ancient Israel shifted from Shiloh to Jerusalem, and then Jerusalem was destroyed and leadership in various forms was located elsewhere (though Jerusalem in transformed ways has always retained a unifying role). Why may not similar developments occur within the Church? Was not God free to choose Constantinople or Moscow or Canterbury, and might not his choice in the unforeseeable future fall on some as yet unimaginable institutional structure in Africa or the islands of the sea?[30]

Yet this unsolved question of the irreversibility of papal and/or episcopal structures is by itself too marginal, some would say, to justify the division of the churches.[31] The very fact of union, when or if it comes, would make the continuing disagreement practically nugatory. All the churches would, in effect, be acknowledging the historic ministries of unity as God's gifts to be renewed and used in his service, and expressing their thankfulness that these did not disappear at the time of the ruptures in the 11th and 16th centuries. They would at the very least hope that God would not again permit such ruptures or, even worse, the cataclysm of the complete loss of these ministries. The Roman Catholics among them would also believe as a matter of faith that this cataclysm would not occur, but it is hard to see what the operational differences between trustful hope and formal belief would be under these circumstances. This marginality of the issue of irreversibility could be maintained in the context of any historically informed ecclesiology, but it is reinforced by thinking of the Church in terms of its unfolding story as the pilgrim people of God.

Of greater consequence than the difference between hoping and believing is the question of why the Catholic structures are important, and here the answer is clear. The historic episcopacy (with or without the papacy, for the latter is impossible without the former but not vice versa) is the only ministry that exists to promote the unity and mutual responsibility of the worldwide Church. Those churches which lack it have no substitute. To the degree that they are concerned about unity and mutual responsibility, it is to this ministerial ordering of the Church they need to turn.

This, however, is not likely to become clear except to the degree that there is a renewal of the episcopal pattern of the early church. The unifying power of that pattern, it will be recalled, lay in the reciprocal dependence of otherwise independent local churches. None could have leaders except those approved and consecrated by their neighbors. A vertical continuity through time in the laying on of hands was involved in this, but that was not what unified (think of the *episcopi ragantes*). It was, rather, the horizontal mutual responsibility for leadership which was the genius of the arrangement, the chief element in its apostolicity. Only traces of this pattern still remain. Even in the non-papal episcopal churches the emphasis tends to fall on diachronic succession in office rather than the synchronic mutuality of neighboring communities. If something approximating this early Catholic episcopate were restored, the resultant worldwide network of tenaciously interconnected yet organizationally self-reliant churches might well have competitive advantages similar to those of the early Catholics.

The best case for the papacy, perhaps, is that without it there could be no return to this earlier pattern in the Roman half of Christendom, or perhaps anywhere. Other churches also need its help. To the degree that Rome became the nurturer of a worldwide communion of mutually accountable yet largely autonomous churches, it would prove itself even to some of its sternest critics the God-chosen center of the whole.[32] The heirs of the first phase of the Reformation would welcome this development. They could then become what they claimed to be in the Augsburg Confession, a reform movement within the Roman Catholic communion rather than outside.[33]

Other ways of envisioning the Church's Catholic unity are also compatible with this story-shaped understanding of the Church. The Faith and Order organic model as outlined in *In Each Place: Towards a Fellowship of Local Churches Truly United* (Geneva: World Council of Churches, 1977) owes much to Eastern Orthodox insights and could easily be adapted and adopted. One could do the same, though perhaps not so easily, with the model of a communion of communions which underlies the Anglican/Roman Catholic dialogue, and which, in a form that embraces all the major Christian traditions, received eloquent exposition in the last of Karl Rahner's books.[34] There are yet other possible descriptions of the unity for which to strive. The Church's story is incomplete, and how God will lead cannot be known beforehand.

Yet however the goal is described, it must take into account both Catholic and evangelical concerns. The messianic pilgrim people which is the body of Christ in history needs unifying institutional structures. These structures are to be assessed and reformed functionally by the evangelical touchstone of whether they help the churches witness faithfully by all they are, say and do to Christ, in the power of the Spirit, and to the glory of God the Father. These structures, however, as Catholics stress, are also gifts of God to be gratefully received and obediently used to his glory. Episcopacy can be one such gift to the whole Church, and perhaps papacy also. God will lead.

PART III

POSTLIBERAL

11. Toward a Postliberal Theology*

Editor's Introduction

Lindbeck wrote *The Nature of Doctrine* to address problems that had emerged during his long involvement in ecumenical discussions and in teaching at Yale Divinity School about the history and present status of doctrines. Indeed, the book was originally planned as a sort of introduction (prolegomena) to a larger work on the 'comparative dogmatics' of the Christian Church in the service of ecumenical unity. What are doctrines? What are their functions? How do we assess when doctrines divide us and when they do not? How does it happen that a doctrine that divided us in one historical context (e.g. the doctrine of justification in the 16th century) does not divide us in another? Lindbeck had worked on these questions with regard to individual doctrines – like the doctrine of justification (Chapter 4) or infallibility (Chapter 9). But what could be said about them in more general terms?

One problem addressing such questions about doctrine turns out to be that competing answers to these questions seem to depend on competing theories of religion. Lindbeck thus distinguished three distinct theories of religion and doctrine: a 'cognitive-propositionalist' position that emphasizes the cognitive (intellectual) aspect of religion and the way doctrines are truth-claims about objective reality, an 'experiential-expressive' position that emphasizes the inner feelings of religions and the way doctrines express those private experiences and a 'cultural-linguistic' position that emphasizes the way that religions are like languages embedded in forms of life (or like cultures), and the way doctrines are communal, grammatical rules.

Lindbeck advocates this third view – although this third view, I shall later propose, may not so much eliminate as 'absorb' the other two. More

---

* George A Lindbeck, 'Toward a Postliberal Theology', in *The Nature of Doctrine. Religion and Theology in a Postliberal Age*, Philadelphia: The Westminster Press, 1984, chapter 6.

specifically, 'religions are seen as comprehensive interpretive schemes, usually embodied in myths or narratives and heavily ritualized, which structure human experience and understanding of self and world' – all with a view 'to identifying and describing what is taken to be "more important than everything else in the universe", and to organizing all of life, including behavior and beliefs, in relation to this' (pp. 32–3). Doctrines articulate the grammar of such cultural-linguistic schemes. Much of *The Nature of Doctrine* is devoted to further description of each of the three theories and criticism of cognitive propositionalist and experiential-expressivist theories and advocacy of cultural-linguistic theory. He also describes the different views of truth associated with these views of religion, and tests the cultural-linguistic theory on three controversial topics in Christian theology – doctrines about Jesus Christ, about Mary and about infallibility.

There has been more debate about this book than any of Lindbeck's other writings – and, as Lindbeck notes in Chapter 12 below, much of this debate has inverted the primarily theological (ecumenical) intent of the book and its secondarily non-theological (cultural-linguistic) intent. The selection I have chosen is from the final chapter – a chapter which is 'an addendum to the main argument of the book, but a necessary one': an 'addendum' because the main argument of the book deals with the ecumenical application of the theory of religion and doctrine I just sketched; a 'necessary' addendum because, although Christian theology can be no less than such ecumenics, it must also be more. Thus, this chapter is a sort of transition from *The Nature of Doctrine* (which, it will be recalled, was characterized as prolegomena to a larger work) to the actual practise of theology on a range of topics.

As a selection from a larger book, this chapter will require a longer introduction than has been usual here. Lindbeck begins with 'the problem of assessment'. He presumes the problem is deep. Assessing a theology is not primarily assessing whether you or I like it or find it immediately intelligible or practical. It is also not simply counting up the number of other people who find it intelligible or applicable – like assessing a local congregation by the size of its membership or a class by student satisfaction. Indeed, Lindbeck presumes a tradition in which there is no single way to assess a theology – so much so that a division of labor has developed between systematic or dogmatic theology, practical or pastoral theology, and apologetic or foundational theology. What do each of these assess? They assess what Lindbeck calls 'faithfulness' (dogmatic theology), 'applicability' (practical theology) and 'intelligibility' (apologetic theology). This chapter explains what Lindbeck means by each of these three modes of assessment.

One complication of the chapter is that each of these three modes of assessment is understood differently by the three positions on religion and doctrine summarized above – Lindbeck here calls them preliberal propositionalist, liberal experiential-expressivist and postliberal cultural-linguistic. Thus each of the three sections of the chapter not only explains what Lindbeck means by faithfulness or applicability or intelligibility but also contrasts his postliberal cultural-linguistic view with preliberal propositionalists and liberal expressivists. Thus, 'faithfulness' is 'intratextual' in that it depends on attention to specific scriptural texts, subjecting our propositions and experiences outside (*extra*) Scripture to correction by those within (*intra*) Scriptures. Calling a theology 'applicable' (practical) is not assessing it by whether it rightly applies certain propositions or commands or by whether it speaks to my or our present experience. Like the prophets' concern with 'God's future' and futurology more generally, a practical theology aims 'to discern those possibilities in current situations that can and should be cultivated as anticipations or preparations for the hoped-for future, the coming kingdom'. And calling a theology 'intelligible' is not assessing whether all its propositions are correct or shown to be correct. (What Lindbeck here calls 'foundationalism' is a kind of cognitive propositionalism that claims that some propositions provide the indubitable 'foundation' for our knowledge of other ones, although there are many kinds of such foundationalism.) Neither should we dismiss questions of intelligibility, perhaps by labeling them as unfaithful or impractical. Instead, intelligibility or reasonableness in matters theological is a 'skill' communally nurtured and sustained, put into practice in highly occasion-specific ways. For example, there is no *general* response to those who regard Christian theology as unintelligible; there must be a response (an apology, in an old fashioned sense of a word-in-response-to-a-word, an apo-logos) but all such apologetics will be ad hoc (occasion specific).

But perhaps my description of this selection so far emphasizes too much the oppositions between cognitive-propositionalism, experiential-expressivism, and the cultural-linguistic theory. In some ways, the truth of cognitive propositionalism is the claim that Christian faith is intelligible, articulated in doctrines as well as doctrines about doctrines. The truth in experiential-expressivism is that Christian faith is applicable, shaped by our experiences and their expressions. The truth in postliberal or cultural-linguistic theology is that Christian faith is faithfulness to the triune God, creator of the cosmos and incarnate in Jesus Christ and creator of a community of Jews and Gentiles as forerunners of the new heaven and new earth. On this view (and here I go beyond what Lindbeck explicitly says in *The Nature of Doctrine*), the point of postliberal theology is not to eliminate preliberal or liberal theology but to 'absorb' them whenever possible, e.g. whenever they do not contradict that faith. There may not be an irreducible opposition between preliberal, liberal and post-liberal theologies on any single issue as much on whether faithfulness, applicability or intelligibility has priority. For postliberal theology faithfulness must set the context for applicability, even as applicability sets the context for intelligibility. And this contrasts with theologies that have different priorities.

This final chapter of *The Nature of Doctrine* is an addendum to the main argument of the book, but a necessary one. If the theory of religion we have been exploring is useful only for understanding church doctrine and not also in other theological areas, it will ultimately prove unacceptable even to specialists in doctrine. In this chapter, therefore, we shall discuss the implications for theological method of a cultural-linguistic approach to religion, starting with some preliminary observations on the meaning and difficulties of assessing, as we shall afterward do, the faithfulness, applicability and intelligibility of fundamentally different types of theology.

The Problem of Assessment

Systematic or dogmatic theology has generally been thought of in the Christian West as especially concerned with faithfulness, practical theology with applicability, and foundational or apologetic theology with intelligibility; but each of these concerns is present in every theological discipline. When dogmaticians attempt faithfully to describe the normative features of a religion, they are also interested in applicability and intelligibility. Similarly, practical and foundational theologians seek not only to apply and make the religion intelligible but also to be faithful.

Further specification of the meaning of these terms depends on the contexts in which they are employed. Theologies of a given type, whether this be preliberal propositionalist, liberal experiential-expressivist, or postliberal cultural-linguistic, can combine formal similarities with radical material differences in their understanding of faithfulness, applicability and intelligibility. Spanish inquisitors and Enlightenment theologians disagreed radically in creed and practice and yet agreed on the formal point that propositional truth is the decisive test of adequacy. Similarly, Anglo-Catholics such as the authors of *Lux Mundi*, Lutheran confessionalists of the Erlangen school and some 'death of God' theologians shared the liberal commitment to the primacy of experience but differed on the material question of what kind of experiences are religiously crucial. Analogously, a Christian postliberal consensus on the primarily cultural-linguistic character of religions would not by itself overcome substantive disagreements between conservatives and progressives, feminists and antifeminists, Catholics and Protestants. The debates would turn more on conceptual or grammatical considerations than on experiential or propositional ones, but they would also involve disagreements on where proper grammar is to be found, on who are the competent speakers of a religious language. The progressives would appeal to rebels, the conservatives to establishments, and Catholics and Protestants would continue to differ in their understanding of the relation of Scripture and tradition. Nevertheless, the common framework would make possible, though not guarantee, genuine arguments over the relative adequacy of specifiably different positions.

Such arguments are difficult, however, when theologies have formally different views of religion. The problem is that each type of theology is embedded in a conceptual framework so comprehensive that it shapes its own criteria of adequacy. Thus what propositionalists with their stress on unchanging truth and falsity regard as faithful, applicable and intelligible is likely to be dismissed as dead orthodoxy by liberal experiential-expressivists. Conversely, the liberal claim that change and pluralism in religious expression are necessary for intelligibility, applicability and faithfulness is attacked by the propositionally orthodox as an irrationally relativistic and practically self-defeating betrayal of the faith. A postliberal might propose to overcome this polarization between tradition and innovation by a distinction between abiding doctrinal grammar and variable theological vocabulary, but this proposal appears from other perspectives as the worst of two worlds rather than the best of both. In view of this situation, the most that can be done in this chapter is to comment on how faithfulness, applicability and intelligibility might be understood in postliberal theologies,[1] and then leave it to the readers to make their own assessments.

Faithfulness as Intratextuality

The task of descriptive (dogmatic or systematic) theology is to give a normative explication of the meaning a religion has for its adherents. One way of pursuing this task that is compatible with a cultural-linguistic approach is what I shall call 'intratextual', while an 'extratextual' method is natural for those whose understanding of religion is propositional or experiential-expressive. The latter locates religious meaning outside the text or semiotic system either in the objective realities to which it refers or in the experiences it symbolizes, whereas for cultural-linguists the meaning is immanent.

Meaning is constituted by the uses of a specific language rather than being distinguishable from it. Thus the proper way to determine what 'God' signifies, for example, is by examining how the word operates within a religion and thereby shapes reality and experience rather than by first establishing its propositional or experiential meaning and reinterpreting or reformulating its uses accordingly. It is in this sense that theological description in the cultural-linguistic mode is intrasemiotic or intratextual.

In an extended or improper sense, something like intratextuality is characteristic of the descriptions not only of religion but also of other forms of rule-governed human behavior from carpentry and mathematics to languages and cultures. Hammers and saws, ordinals and numerals, winks and signs of the cross, words and sentences are made comprehensible by indicating how they fit into systems of communication or purposeful action, not by reference to outside factors. One does not succeed in identifying the 8:02 to New York by describing the history or manufacture of trains or even by a complete inventory of the cars, passengers and conductors that constituted and traveled on it on a given day. None of the cars, passengers and crew might be the same the next day, and yet the train would be self-identically the 8:02 to New York. Its meaning, its very reality, is its function within a particular transportation system. Much the same can be said of winks and signs of the cross: they are quite distinct from non-meaningful but physically identical eye twitches and hand motions, and their reality as meaningful signs is wholly constituted in any individual occurrence by their intratextuality, by their place, so to speak, in a story.

Meaning is more fully intratextual in semiotic systems (composed, as they entirely are, of interpretive and communicative signs, symbols and actions) than in other forms of ruled human behavior such as carpentry or transportation systems; but among semiotic systems, intratextuality (though still in an extended sense) is greatest in natural languages, cultures and religions which (unlike mathematics, for example) are potentially all-embracing and possess the property of reflexivity. One can speak of all life and reality in French or from an American or a Jewish perspective; and one can also describe French in French, American culture in American terms, and Judaism in Jewish ones. This makes it possible for theology to be intratextual, not simply by explicating religion from within but in the stronger sense of describing everything as inside, as interpreted by the religion, and doing this by means of religiously shaped second-order concepts.

In view of their comprehensiveness, reflexivity and complexity, religions require what Clifford Geertz, borrowing a term from Gilbert Ryle, has called 'thick description',[2] and which he applies to culture, but with the understanding that it also holds for religion. A religion cannot be treated as a formalizable 'symbolic system . . . by isolating its elements, specifying the internal relationships among these elements, and then characterizing the whole system in some general way – according to the core symbols around which it is organized, the underlying structures of which it is the surface expression, or the ideological principles upon which it is based. . . . This hermetic approach to things seems to me to run the danger of locking . . . analysis away from its proper object, the informal logic of actual life.' The theologian, like the ethnographer, should approach 'such broader interpretations and abstract analyses from the direction of exceedingly extended acquaintances with extremely small matters'. 'As interlocked systems of construable signs . . . culture [including religion] is not a power, something to which social events, behaviors, institutions, or processes can be causally attributed; it is a context, something within which they can be intelligibly – that is, thickly – described.' Only by detailed 'familiarity with the imaginative universe in which . . . acts are signs' can one diagnose or specify the meaning of these acts for the adherents of a religion. What the theologian needs to explicate 'is a multiplicity of complex conceptual structures, many of them superimposed or knotted into one another, which are at once strange, irregular and inexplicit, and which he must contrive somehow first to grasp and then to render'. In rendering the salient features, the essential task 'is not to codify abstract regularities but to make thick description possible, not to generalize across cases but to generalize within them'. If this is not done, one may think, for example, that Roman and Confucian *gravitas* are much the same or that atheistic Marxism more nearly resembles atheistic Buddhism than biblical theism. This is as egregious an error as supposing that uninflected English is closer to uninflected Chinese than to German.

Thick description, it should be noted, is not to be confused with Baconian empiricism, with sticking to current facts. It is rather the full range of the interpretive medium which needs to be exhibited, and because this range in the case of religion is potentially all-encompassing, description has a creative aspect. There is, indeed, no more demanding exercise of the inventive and imaginative powers than to explore how a language, culture or religion may be employed to give meaning to new domains of thought, reality and action. Theological description can be a highly constructive enterprise.

Finally, in the instance of religions more than any other type of semiotic system, description is not simply metaphorically but literally intratextual. This is true in some degree of all the world's major faiths. They all have relatively fixed canons of writings that they treat as exemplary or normative instantiations of their semiotic codes. One test of faithfulness for all of them is the degree to which descriptions correspond to the semiotic universe paradigmatically encoded in holy writ.

The importance of texts and of intratextuality for theological faithfulness becomes clearer when we consider the unwritten religions of non-literate societies. Evans-Pritchard[3] tells of a Nuer tribesman who excitedly reported to him that a woman in the village had given birth to twins, both dead, and that one was a hippopotamus and had been placed in a stream, and the other a bird and had been placed in a tree. There are in that society no canonical documents to consult in order to locate these puzzling events within the wider contexts that give them meaning. Is the equation of dead twins with birds and hippopotami central or peripheral to Nuer thought and life? Would the religion and culture be gravely disturbed if this equation were eliminated? Even the wisest of Evans-Pritchard's informants might not have understood these questions, and even if they did, they presumably would have had no idea of how to reach a consensus in answering them. In oral cultures there is no transpersonal authority to which the experts on tradition can refer their disputes. This helps explain why purely customary religions and cultures readily dissolve under the pressure of historical, social and linguistic change, but it also suggests that canonical texts are a condition, not only for the survival of a religion but for the very possibility of normative theological description. In any case, whether or not this is universally true, the intrasemiotic character of descriptive theology is inseparable from intratextuality in the three western monotheisms – Judaism, Christianity and Islam. These are pre-eminently religions of the book.

We need now to speak in more detail of how to interpret a text in terms of its immanent meanings – that is, in terms of the meanings immanent in the religious language of whose use the text is a paradigmatic instance. On the informal level this is not a problem; it becomes so, as we shall see, only when theology becomes alienated from those ways of reading classics,[4] whether religious or non-religious, which seem natural within a given culture or society. Masterpieces such as *Oedipus Rex* and *War and Peace*, for example, evoke their own domains of meaning. They do so by what they themselves say about the events and personages of which they tell. In order to understand them in their own terms, there is no need for extraneous references to, for example, Freud's theories or historical treatments of the Napoleonic wars. Further, such works shape the imagination and perceptions of the attentive reader so that he or she forever views the world to some extent through the lenses they supply. To describe the basic meaning of these books is an intratextual task, a matter of explicating their contents and the perspectives on extratextual reality that they generate.[5]

These same considerations apply even more forcefully to the pre-eminently authoritative texts that are the canonical writings of religious communities. For those who are steeped in them, no world is more real than the ones they create. A scriptural world is thus able to absorb the universe. It supplies the interpretive framework within which believers seek to live their lives and understand reality. This happens quite apart from formal theories. Augustine did not describe his work in the categories we are employing, but the whole of his theological production can be understood as a progressive, even if not always successful, struggle to insert everything from Platonism and the Pelagian problem to the fall of Rome into the world of the Bible. Aquinas tried to do something similar with Aristotelianism, and Schleiermacher with German romantic idealism. The way they described extrascriptural realities and experience, so it can be argued, was shaped by biblical categories much more than was warranted by their formal methodologies.

In the case of Aquinas especially, however, the shaping was in part methodologically legitimated. Traditional exegetical procedures (of which he gives one of the classic descriptions[6]) assume that Scripture creates its own domain of meaning and that the task of interpretation is to extend this over the whole of reality. The particular ways of doing this depend, to be sure, on the character of the religion and its texts. One set of interpretive techniques is appropriate when the Torah is the center of the scripture, another when it is the story of Jesus, and still another when it is the Buddha's enlightenment and teachings. For the most part, we shall limit our observations on this point to the Christian case.

Here there was a special though not exclusive emphasis on typological or figural devices, first to unify the canon, and second to encompass the cosmos. Typology was used to incorporate the Hebrew Scriptures into a canon that focussed on Christ, and then, by extension, to embrace extrabiblical reality. King David, for example, was in some respects a typological foreshadowing of Jesus, but he was also, in Carolingian times, a type for Charlemagne and, in Reformation days, as even Protestants said, for Charles V in his wars against the Turks. Thus an Old Testament type, filtered through the New Testament antitype, became a model for later kings and, in the case of Charlemagne, provided a documentable stimulus to the organization of the educational and parish systems that stand at the institutional origins of western civilization. Unlike allegorizing, typological interpretation did not empty Old Testament or postbiblical personages and events of their own reality,[7] and therefore they constituted a powerful means for imaginatively incorporating all being into a Christ-centered world.

It is important to note the direction of interpretation. Typology does not make scriptural contents into metaphors for extrascriptural realities, but the other way around. It does not suggest, as is often said in our day, that believers find their stories in the Bible, but rather that they make the story of the Bible their story. The cross is not to be viewed as a figurative representation of suffering nor the messianic kingdom as a symbol for hope in the future; rather, suffering should be cruciform, and hopes for the future messianic. More generally stated, it is the religion instantiated in Scripture which defines being, truth, goodness and beauty, and the nonscriptural exemplifications of these realities need to be transformed into figures (or types or antitypes) of the scriptural ones. Intratextual theology redescribes reality within the scriptural framework rather than translating Scripture into extrascriptural categories. It is the text, so to speak, which absorbs the world, rather than the world, the text.

There is always the danger, however, that the extrabiblical materials inserted into the biblical universe will themselves become the basic framework of interpretation. This is what happened, so the Christian mainstream concluded, in the case of Gnosticism. Here Hellenism became the interpreter rather than the interpreted. The Jewish rabbi who is the crucified and resurrected Messiah of the New Testament accounts was transformed into a mythological figure illustrative of thoroughly non-scriptural meanings. Nor did the mainstream wholly escape the danger. It creedally insisted that the Jesus spoken of in Scripture is the Lord, but it often read Scripture in so Hellenistic a way that this Jesus came to resemble a semipagan demigod. The doctrinal consensus on the primacy of Scripture, on the canonical status of the Old as well as the New Testament, and on the full humanity of Christ was not by itself enough to maintain an integrally scriptural framework within which to interpret the classical heritage which the Church sought to Christianize. Better theological and exegetical procedures were needed.

Up through the Reformation, this need was in part filled through the typological methods we have already noted. As one moves in the West from Augustine, through Aquinas, to Luther and Calvin, there is an increasing resistance to indiscriminate allegorizing and an insistence on the primacy of a specifiable literal intratextual sense. Whatever the failures in actual execution, and they were many, the interpretive direction was from the Bible to the world rather than vice versa.

In the Reformers, it should be noted, the resistance to allegorizing and the greater emphasis on intratextuality (*scriptura sui ipsius interpres*) did not diminish but heightened the emphasis on proclamation, on the preached word. Scripture, one might say, was interpreted by its use,[8] by the *viva vox evangelii*. In the intratextual context, this emphasis on the living word involves applying the language, concepts and categories of Scripture to contemporary realities, and is different in its intellectual, practical and homiletical consequences from liberal attempts, of which Ebeling's is the most notable,[9] to understand the Reformation notion of the word of God in terms of an experiential 'word event'.

As the work of Hans Frei shows,[10] the situation has changed radically in recent centuries, and new difficulties have arisen. Typological interpretation collapsed under the combined onslaughts of rationalistic, pietistic and historical-critical developments. Scripture ceased to function as the lens through which theologians viewed the world and instead became primarily an object of study whose religiously significant or literal meaning was located outside itself. The primarily literary approaches of the past with their affinities to informal ways of reading the classics in their own terms were replaced by fundamentalist, historical-critical and expressivist preoccupations with facticity or experience. The intratextual meanings of Scripture continue informally to shape the imagination of the West (even atheistic Marxists think of history as the unfolding of a determinate pattern with an ultimately ineluctable outcome), but theologians do not make these meanings methodologically primary. Instead, if they are existentially inclined, they reinterpret the notion of providential guidance, for example, as a symbolic expression of confidence in the face of the vicissitudes of life; or, if they objectivize, they might, as did Teilhard de Chardin, interpret providence in terms of an optimistic version of evolutionary science. Whether it will be possible to regain a specifically biblical understanding of providence depends in part on the possibility of theologically reading Scripture once again in literary rather than non-literary ways.

The depth of the present crisis is best seen when one considers that even those who doctrinally agree that the story of Jesus is the key to the understanding of reality are often in fundamental theological disagreement over what the story is really about, over its normative or literal sense.[11] Is the literal meaning of the story the history it is on some readings supposed to record, and if so, is this history that of the fundamentalist or of the historical critic? Or is the real meaning, the theologically important meaning, the way of being in the world which the story symbolizes or the liberating actions and attitudes it expresses or the ethical ideals it instantiates or the metaphysical truths about God-manhood it illustrates or the gospel promises it embodies? Each of these ways of construing the story depends on a distinct interpretive framework (historical, phenomenological, existential, ethical, metaphysical, doctrinal) that specifies the questions asked of the text and shapes the pictures of Jesus that emerge. These pictures may all be formally orthodox in the sense that they are reconcilable with Nicaea, but their implications for religious practice and understanding are radically divergent. Nothing better illustrates the point that for most purposes theological issues are more crucial and interesting than doctrinal ones.

The intratextual way of dealing with this problem depends heavily on literary considerations. The normative or literal meaning must be consistent with the kind of text it is taken to be by the community for which it is important. The meaning must not be esoteric: not something behind, beneath or in front of the text; not something that the text reveals, discloses, implies or suggests to those with extraneous metaphysical, historical or experiential interests. It must rather be what the text says in terms of the communal language of which the text is an instantiation. A legal document should not be treated in quasi-kabbalistic fashion as first of all a piece of expressive symbolism (though it may secondarily be that also); nor should the Genesis account of creation be turned fundamentalistically into science; nor should one turn a realistic narrative (which a novel also can be) into history (or, alternatively, as the historical critic is wont to do, into a source of clues for the reconstruction of history). If the literary character of the story of Jesus, for example, is that of utilizing, as realistic narratives do, the interaction of purpose and circumstance to render the identity description of an agent, then it is Jesus' identity as thus rendered, not his historicity, existential significance or metaphysical status, which is the literal and theologically controlling meaning of the tale.[12] The implications of the story for determining the metaphysical status or existential significance or historical career of Jesus Christ may have varying degrees of theological importance, but they are not determinative. The believer, so an intratextual approach would maintain, is not told primarily to be conformed to a reconstructed Jesus of history (as Hans Küng maintains),[13] nor to a metaphysical Christ of faith (as in much of the propositionalist tradition),[14] nor to an abba experience of God (as for Schillebeeckx),[15] nor to an agapeic way of being in the world (as for David Tracy),[16] but he or she is rather to be conformed to the Jesus Christ depicted in the narrative. An intratextual reading tries to derive the interpretive framework that designates the theologically controlling sense from the literary structure of the text itself.[17]

This type of literary approach can be extended to cover, not simply the story of Jesus, but all of Scripture. What is the literary genre of the Bible as a whole in its canonical unity? What holds together the diverse materials it contains: poetic, prophetic, legal, liturgical, sapiential, mythical, legendary and historical? These are all embraced, it would seem, in an overarching story that has the specific literary features of realistic narrative as exemplified in diverse ways, for example, by certain kinds of parables, novels and historical accounts. It is as if the Bible were a 'vast, loosely-structured, non-fictional novel' (to use a phrase David Kelsey applies to Karl Barth's view of Scripture).[18]

Further, it is possible to specify the primary function of the canonical narrative (which is also the function of many of its most important component stories from the Pentateuch to the Gospels). It is 'to render a character ... offer an identity description of an agent',[19] namely God. It does this, not by telling what God is in and of himself, but by accounts of the interaction of his deeds and purposes with those of creatures in their ever-changing circumstances. These accounts reach their climax in what the Gospels say of the risen, ascended and ever-present Jesus Christ whose identity as the divine-human agent is unsubstitutably enacted in the stories of Jesus of Nazareth. The climax, however, is logically inseparable from what proceeds it. The Jesus of the Gospels is the Son of the God of Abraham, Isaac and Jacob in the same strong sense that the Hamlet of Shakespeare's play is Prince of Denmark. In both cases, the title with its reference to the wider context irreplaceably rather than contingently identifies the bearer of the name.

It is easy to see how theological descriptions of a religion may on this view need to be materially diverse even when the formal criterion of faithfulness remains the same. The primary focus is not on God's being in itself, for that is not what the text is about, but on how life is to be lived and reality construed in the light of God's character as an agent as this is depicted in the stories of Israel and of Jesus. Life, however, is not the same in catacombs and space shuttles, and reality is different for, let us say, Platonists and Whiteheadians. Catacomb dwellers and astronauts might rightly emphasize diverse aspects of the biblical accounts of God's character and action in describing their respective situations. Judging by catacomb paintings, the first group often saw themselves as sheep in need of a shepherd, while the second group would perhaps be well advised to stress God's grant to human beings of stewardship over planet Earth. Similarly, Platonic and Whiteheadian differences over the nature of reality lead to sharp disagreements about the proper characterization of God's metaphysical properties, while anti-metaphysicians, in turn, argue that no theory of divine attributes is consistent with the character of the biblical God.

Yet all these theologies could agree that God is appropriately depicted in stories about a being who created the cosmos without any humanly fathomable reason, but – simply for his own good pleasure and the pleasure of his goodness – appointed Homo sapiens stewards of one minuscule part of this cosmos, permitted appalling evils, chose Israel and the Church as witnessing peoples, and sent Jesus as Messiah and Immanuel, God with us. The intention of these theologies, whether successful or unsuccessful, could in every case be to describe life and reality in ways conformable to what these stories indicate about God. They could, to repeat, have a common intratextual norm of faithfulness despite their material disagreements.

Intratextual theologies can also, however, disagree on the norm. They can dispute over whether realistic narrative is the best or only way to identify the distinctive genre and interpretive framework of the Christian canon, and, even if it is, on how to characterize the divine agent at work in the biblical stories. More fundamentally, they could disagree on the extent and unity of the canon. If Revelation and Daniel are the center of

Scripture, as they seem to be for Scofield Bible premillenialists, a very different picture of God's agency and purposes emerges. Further, as current debates over feminism vividly remind us, past tradition or present consensus can serve as extensions of the canon and deeply influence the interpretation of the whole. These extensions can on occasion go beyond the specifically Christian or religious realm. The philosophical tradition from Plato to Heidegger operates as the canonical corpus for much western reflection on God or the human condition; and when this reflection is recognized as operating with a peculiarly western rather than transculturally available idiom, it begins to acquire some of the features of intratextuality.[20] In short, intratextuality may be a condition for the faithful description and development of a religion or tradition, but the material or doctrinal consequences of this self-evidently depend in part on what canon is appealed to.

It must also be noted that intratextuality in a postcritical or postliberal mode is significantly different from traditional precritical varieties. We now can make a distinction (unavailable before the development of modern science and historical studies) between realistic narrative and historical or scientific descriptions. The Bible is often 'history-like' even when it is not 'likely history'. It can therefore be taken seriously in the first respect as a delineator of the character of divine and human agents, even when its history or science is challenged. As parables such as that of the prodigal son remind us, the rendering of God's character is not in every instance logically dependent on the facticity of the story.

Further, historical criticism influences the theological-literary interpretation of texts. A postcritical narrative reading of Scripture such as is found to some extent in von Rad's work on the Old Testament[21] is notably different from a precritical one. Or, to cite a more specific example, if the historical critic is right that the Johannine 'Before Abraham was, I am' (John 8.58) is not a self-description of the preresurrection Jesus but a communal confession of faith, then even those who fully accept the confession will want to modify traditional theological descriptions of what Jesus was in his life on earth. They may agree doctrinally with Chalcedon, but prefer a Pauline *theologia crucis* to the Christological *theologia gloriae* that is often associated with Chalcedon (and that one finds even in great exponents of the theology of the cross such as Luther). Nevertheless, in an intratextual approach, literary considerations are more important than historical-critical ones in determining the canonical sense even in cases such as this. It is because the literary genre of John is clearly not that of veridical history that the statement in question can be readily accepted as a communal confession rather than a self-description.

Finally, and more generally, the postcritical focus on intratextual meanings does involve a change in attitude toward some aspects of the text that were important for premodern interpretation. The physical details of what, if anything, happened on Mt Sinai, for example, are no longer of direct interest for typological or figurative purposes, as they often were for the tradition, but the basic questions remain much the same: what is the nature and function of Torah? It is in the New Testament custodial in Israel and fulfilled in Christ, but what does this imply for later Christianity and its relations to Judaism? Is not Torah by analogical extension both custodial and fulfilled for Christian communities in this age before the end when fulfillment is not yet final; and does this not make Christians much closer to Jews than they have generally thought? What, furthermore, does the Holocaust have to do with Mt Sinai, on the one hand, and another mountain, Calvary, on the other? As these questions indicate, a postliberal intratextuality provides warrants for imaginatively and conceptually incorporating postbiblical worlds into the world of the Bible in much the same fashion as did the tradition. But the consequences inevitably will often be very different because of changes in the extrabiblical realities that are to be typologically interpreted and because of the more rigorous intratextuality made necessary by a critical approach to history.

In concluding this discussion, it needs to be reiterated that the practice of intratextuality is only loosely related to explicit theory. Just as good grammarians or mathematicians may be quite wrongheaded in their understanding of what they in fact actually do, so also with theologians. There is no reason for surprise if an apparent propositionalist, such as Aquinas, or an undoubted experiential-expressivist, such as Schleiermacher, were more intratextual in their actual practice than their theories would seem to allow. Their performance would perhaps have improved if their theories of religion had been different, but this is true only if other conditions remained equal. Native genius and religious commitment are helpful, but in order to convert these into theological competence one also needs a supportive environment, the tutelage of expert practitioners and assiduous practice in a complex set of unformalizable skills that even the best theoretician cannot adequately characterize. Where these conditions are lacking, even good theory cannot greatly enhance performance, and where they are present, poor theory may be relatively harmless.

The implications of these observations do not bode well, however, for the future of postliberal theology. Even if it were to become theoretically popular, the result might chiefly be talk about intratextuality rather than more and better intratextual practice. The conditions for practice seem to be steadily weakening. Disarray in church and society makes the transmission of the necessary skills more and more difficult. Those who share in the intellectual high culture of our day are rarely intensively socialized into coherent religious languages and communal forms of life. This is not necessarily disastrous for the long-range prospects of religion (which is not dependent on elites), but it is for theology as an intellectually and academically creative enterprise capable of making significant contributions to the wider culture and society. Further, theology (in the sense of reflection in the service of religion) is being increasingly replaced in seminaries as well as universities by religious studies. There are fewer and fewer institutional settings favorable to the intratextual interpretation of religion and of extra-scriptural realities.[22] Perhaps the last American theologian who in practice (and to some extent in theory) made extended and effective attempts to redescribe major aspects of the contemporary scene in distinctively Christian terms was Reinhold Niebuhr. After the brief neo-orthodox interlude (which was itself sometimes thoroughly liberal in its theological methodology, as in the case of Paul Tillich), the liberal tendency to redescribe religion in extrascriptural frameworks has once again become dominant. This is under-standable. Religions have become foreign texts that are much easier to translate into currently popular categories than to read in terms of their intrinsic sense. Thus the fundamental obstacles to intratextual theological faithfulness may well derive from the psychosocial situation rather than from scholarly or intellectual considerations.

Applicability as Futurology

We began this chapter by noting that theologies are assessed by their applic-ability as well as their faithfulness. They are judged by how relevant or practical they are in concrete situations as well as by how well they fit the cultural-linguistic systems whose religious uses they seek to describe. In this section we shall deal, first, with the relation of judgments of faithfulness and applicability and, second, with some specific issues that are of special concern today.

All-embracing systems of interpretation possess their own internal criteria of applicability: they can be judged by their own standards. This is evident when we consider how views of present practicality are shaped by visions of reality that encompass more than the present. A Marxist and a non-Marxist, for example, may agree in their factual descriptions of current trends and on the general principle that these trends should be evaluated in terms of long-range consequences, and yet they may differ sharply in their extrapolations. What seems to one the wave of the future will seem to the other a mere eddy in the river of time, and judgments of applicability or practicality will vary accordingly. The difference will be even greater if the non-Marxist is, for example, an Advaita Vedantist for whom the course of history is religiously irrelevant; but this kind of devaluation of the tem-poral future has not generally been characteristic of western faiths.

Concern for the future has traditionally been associated in biblical religions with prophecy. Prophets proclaim what is both faithful and applicable in a given situation, and they oppose proposals that, whatever their apparent practicality, are doomed because of their unfaithfulness to God's future. To be sure, as biblical scholars remind us, prophetic utterances are not predictions in the ordinary sense. Jonah was disappointed by the non-fulfillment of his prophecies against Nineveh, but this did not make him doubt that God had spoken. The repentance that averted the destruction of the city was, so to speak, the point of the prophecy. Similarly, the non-fulfillment of expectations of an imminent Parousia have rarely been taken by those who shared them as evidence that Christ would not return. A similar logic operates in much non-religious forecasting. The failure of Marxist and other secular anticipations of the early demise of religion does not disconfirm secularism, and the predictive inadequacies of contemporary futurology[23] have not discouraged its practitioners. In all these cases, the purpose is not to foretell what is to come, but to shape present action to fit the anticipated and hoped-for future.

Theological forms of this activity are more like contemporary futurology than biblical prophecy. Unlike prophecy, futurology does not depend on first-order inspiration or intuition, but is a second-order enterprise that draws on the full range of empirical studies in an effort to discover 'the signs of the times.'[24] As we have noted, these signs vary greatly from one overall pattern of interpretation to another – from, for example, Marxist to non-Marxist views. In the case of Christian theology, the purpose is to discern those possibilities in current situations that can and should be cultivated as anticipations or preparations for the hoped-for future, the coming kingdom. In brief, a theological proposal is adjudged both faithful and applicable to the degree that it appears practical in terms of an eschatologically and empirically defensible scenario of what is to come.

In the construction of such scenarios, the crucial difference between liberals and postliberals is in the way they correlate their visions of the future and of present situations. Liberals start with experience, with an account of the present, and then adjust their vision of the kingdom of God accordingly, while postliberals are in principle committed to doing the reverse. The first procedure makes it easier to accommodate to present trends, whether from the right or the left: Christian fellow travelers of both Nazism and Stalinism generally used liberal methodology to justify their positions. When, in contrast to this, one looks at the present in the light of an intratextually derived eschatology, one gets a different view of which contemporary developments are likely to be ultimately significant. Similar practical recommendations may at times be advanced, but for dissimilar theological reasons. A postliberal might argue, for example, that traditional sexual norms should be revised because the situation has changed from when they were formulated or because they are not intratextually faithful – but not, as some liberals may be inclined to argue, on the grounds that sexual liberation is an advance toward the eschatological future. Postliberalism is methodologically committed to neither traditionalism nor progressivism, but its resistance to current fashions, to making present experience revelatory, may often result in conservative stances. Yet there are numerous occasions in which the intratextual norm requires the rejection of the old in favor of the new.

These comments on method, however, leave untouched the question of the possible contemporary relevance of postliberalism. Earlier chapters of *The Nature of Doctrine* suggested that a cultural-linguistic approach is supported by intellectual trends in non-theological disciplines, and that it can in its own way accommodate some of the main religious concerns that make experiential-expressivism appealing. Yet we also noted that the present psychosocial situation is more favorable to liberalism than to postliberalism. Sociologists have been telling us for 100 years or more that the rationalization, pluralism and mobility of modern life dissolve the bonds of tradition and community. This produces multitudes of men and women who are impelled, if they have religious yearnings, to embark on their own individual quests for symbols of transcendence. The churches have become purveyors of this commodity rather than communities that socialize their members into coherent and comprehensive religious outlooks and forms of life. Society paradoxically conditions human beings to experience selfhood as somehow prior to social influences, and eastern religions and philosophies are utilized to support what, from a cultural-linguistic perspective, is the myth of the transcendental ego. Selfhood is experienced as a given rather than as either a gift or an achievement, and fulfillment comes from exfoliating or penetrating into the inner depths rather than from communally responsible action in the public world. Thus the cultural climate is on the whole antithetical to postliberalism.

One can argue, furthermore, that there is little likelihood that the cultural trends favoring experiential-expressivism will be reversed in the realistically forseeable future. If the nations are to avoid nuclear or environmental destruction, they will have to become ever more unified. What the world will need is some kind of highly generalized outlook capable of providing a framework for infinitely diversified religious quests. Experiential-expressivism with its openness to the hypothesis of an underlying unity can, it would seem, better fill this need than a cultural-linguistic understanding of religion with its stress on particularity. Western monotheisms especially appear to be disqualified because, on an intratextual reading, these religions cannot without suicide surrender their claims to the universal and unsurpassable validity of very specific identifications of the Ultimate with the

God of Abraham, Isaac and Jacob; of Jesus; or of the Koran. The future belongs, on this view, to liberal interpretations of religion.

In the speculative domain of futurology, however, it is easy to mount counter-arguments. It can be pointed out that the indefinite extrapolation of present trends is a questionable procedure because any given tendency, if carried far enough, destroys the conditions for its own existence. When liberation from constraints produces chaos, the result is new bondage, and law and order are once again experienced as conditions for freedom. Law and order when unchecked, however, create rigidities that harbor the seeds of their own destruction. Similarly, the viability of a unified world of the future may well depend on counteracting the acids of modernity. It may depend on communal enclaves that socialize their members into highly particular outlooks supportive of concern for others rather than for individual rights and entitlements, and of a sense of responsibility for the wider society rather than for personal fulfillment. It is at least an open question whether any religion will have the requisite toughness for this demanding task unless it at some point makes the claim that it is significantly different and unsurpassably true; and it is easier for a religion to advance this claim if it is interpreted in cultural-linguistic rather than experiential-expressive terms. Thus it may well be that postliberal theologies are more applicable than liberal ones to the needs of the future.

These considerations gain in force when one considers what may be necessary for the viability, not of a world order, but of cultural traditions such as the western one. If the Bible has shaped the imagination of the West to anywhere near the degree that Northrop Frye, for example, has argued,[25] then the West's continuing imaginative vitality and creativity may well depend on the existence of groups for whom the Hebrew and Christian Scriptures are not simply classics among others, but the canonical literature par excellence, and who are also in close contact with the wider culture. Much the same argument could be advanced in reference to the Koran and Islamic culture, and perhaps something analogous applies to the religions and cultures of the Far East despite their lack of equally well-defined pre-eminent canons. The general point is that, provided a religion stresses service rather than domination, it is likely to contribute more to the future of humanity if it preserves its own distinctiveness and integrity than if it yields to the homogenizing tendencies associated with liberal experiential-expressivism.

This conclusion is paradoxical: religious communities are likely to be practically relevant in the long run to the degree that they do not first ask what is either practical or relevant, but instead concentrate on their own intratextual outlooks and forms of life. The much-debated problem of the relation of theory and praxis is thus dissolved by the communal analogue of justification by faith. As is true for individuals, so also a religious community's salvation is not by works, nor is its faith for the sake of practical efficacy, and yet good works of unforeseeable kinds flow from faithfulness. It was thus, rather than by intentional effort, that biblical religion helped produce democracy and science, as well as other values westerners treasure; and it is in similarly unimaginable and unplanned ways, if at all, that biblical religion will help save the world (for western civilization is now world civilization) from the demonic corruptions of these same values.

These arguments for the applicability of postliberal approaches cannot be neutrally evaluated. Those who think that religions are more the sources than the products of experience will regard a loss of religious particularity as impoverishing, while others will consider it enriching. Comprehensive frameworks of interpretation provide their own standards of relevance, and thus both liberal and postliberal outlooks have no difficulty in reading the signs of the times in such a way as to justify their own practicality.

Intelligibility as Skill

The case for applicability that has just been outlined is incomplete. It does not discuss whether postliberal theologies would help make religions more intelligible and credible. This is a practical as well as a theoretical question, and it can be formulated in terms of two closely related problems. First, intratextuality seems wholly relativistic: it turns religions, so one can argue, into self-enclosed and incommensurable intellectual ghettoes. Associated with this, in the second place, is the fideistic dilemma: it appears that choice between religions is purely arbitrary, a matter of blind faith.

These may not be mortal weaknesses in other times or places where communal traditions are relatively unbroken and faiths are transmitted from parents to children in successive generations, but they are, so it can be argued, obstacles to the survival of religions in pluralistic situations where religiousness usually involves decisions among competing alternatives. It seems essential in our day to adopt an apologetic approach that seeks to discover a foundational scheme within which religions can be evaluated, and that makes it possible to translate traditional meanings into currently intelligible terms. The postliberal resistance to the foundational enterprise is from this perspective a fatal flaw.

The great strength of theological liberalism, it can be argued, lies in its commitment to making religion experientially intelligible to the cultured and the uncultured among both its despisers and its appreciators. It is in order to clarify the gospel in a world where it has become opaque that liberals typically choose the categories in which to expound their systematic theologies; and it is by their success in communicating to the modern mind that they assess the faithfulness of their endeavors. This same concern accounts for the liberal commitment to the foundational enterprise of uncovering universal principles or structures – if not metaphysical, then existential, phenomenological or hermeneutical. If there are no such universals, then how can one make the faith credible, not only to those outside the Church but to the half-believers within it and, not least, to theologians? The liberal program is in one sense accommodation to culture, but it is often motivated by missionary impulses no less strong than those which send Wycliffe evangelicals overseas to translate the Bible into aboriginal tongues.

Postliberals are bound to be skeptical, not about missions, but about apologetics and foundations. To the degree that religions are like languages and cultures, they can no more be taught by means of translation than can Chinese or French. What is said in one idiom can to some extent be conveyed in a foreign tongue, but no one learns to understand and speak Chinese by simply hearing and reading translations. Resistance to translation does not wholly exclude apologetics, but this must be of an ad hoc and non-foundational variety rather than standing at the center of theology. The grammar of religion, like that of language, cannot be explicated or learned by analysis of experience, but only by practice. Religious and linguistic competence may help greatly in dealing with experience, but experience by itself may be more a hindrance than a help to acquiring competence: children, at least in Jesus' parabolic sense, have an advantage over adults. In short, religions, like languages, can be understood only in their own terms, not by transposing them into an alien speech.

Yet this approach need not confine the theological study of religion to an intellectual ghetto, but can free it for closer contact with other disciplines. The spread of a cultural-linguistic orientation in history, anthropology, sociology and philosophy increases interest in intratextuality, in the description of religions from the inside. Liberal attempts to explain religions by translating them into other conceptualities seem to appeal chiefly to theologians or to other religious people. As modern culture moves ever farther away from its religious roots, these translations become more strained, complex and obscure to the uninitiated. Relativism increases and foundational appeals to universal structures of thought, experience or *Existenz* lose their persuasiveness. Tillich communicated to a wide range of intellectuals a generation ago, but it is doubtful that his numerous liberal successors could now match his record even if they had his talent. Scholarly non-theologians who want to understand religion are concerned with how religions work for their adherents, not with their credibility. Their interest, one might say, is in descriptive rather than apologetic intelligibility. The result, paradoxically, is that a postliberal approach, with its commitment to intratextual description, may well have interdisciplinary advantages, while liberal theology, with its apologetic focus on making religion more widely credible, seems increasingly to be a 19th-century enclave in a 20th-century milieu.

These considerations, however, leave unresolved the problem with which we started this section. The question is whether intratextual descriptive intelligibility is helpful for religious and not simply interdisciplinary purposes; but if intratextuality implies relativism and fideism, the cost for most religious traditions is much too high. If there are no universal or foundational structures and standards of judgment by which one can decide between different religious and non-religious options, the choice of any one of them becomes, it would seem, purely irrational, a matter of arbitrary whim or blind faith; and while this conclusion may fit much of the modern mood, it is antithetical to what most religions, whether interpreted in liberal, preliberal or postliberal fashion, have affirmed.

Antifoundationalism, however, is not to be equated with irrationalism. The issue is not whether there are universal norms of reasonableness, but whether these can be formulated in some neutral, framework-independent language.[26] Increasing awareness of how standards of rationality vary from field to field and age to age makes the discovery of such a language more and more unlikely and the possibility of foundational disciplines doubtful. Yet this does not reduce the choice between different frameworks to whim or chance. As TS Kuhn has argued in reference to science, and Wittgenstein in philosophy, the norms of reasonableness are too rich and subtle to be adequately specified in any general theory of reason or knowledge. These norms, to repeat a point often made in this book [*The Nature of Doctrine*] are like the rules of depth grammar, which linguists search for and may at times approximate but never grasp. Thus reasonableness in religion and theology, as in other domains, has something of that aesthetic character, that quality of unformalizable skill, which we usually associate with the artist or the linguistically competent. If so, basic religious and theological positions, like Kuhn's scientific paradigms, are invulnerable to definitive refutation (as well as confirmation) but can nevertheless be tested and argued about in various ways, and these tests and arguments in the long run make a difference. Reason places constraints on religious as well as on scientific options even though these constraints are too flexible and informal to be spelled out in either foundational theology or a general theory of science. In short, intelligibility comes from skill, not theory, and credibility comes from good performance, not adherence to independently formulated criteria.

In this perspective, the reasonableness of a religion is largely a function of its assimilative powers, of its ability to provide an intelligible interpretation in its own terms of the varied situations and realities adherents encounter.[27] The religions we call primitive regularly fail this test when confronted with major changes, while the world religions have developed greater resources for coping with vicissitude. Thus, although a religion is not susceptible to decisive disproof, it is subject, as Basil Mitchell argues,[28] to rational testing procedures not wholly unlike those which apply to general scientific theories or paradigms (for which, unlike hypotheses, there are no crucial experiments). Confirmation or disconfirmation occurs through an accumulation of successes or failures in making practically and cognitively coherent sense of relevant data, and the process does not conclude, in the case of religions, until the disappearance of the last communities of believers or, if the faith survives, until the end of history. This process certainly does not enable individuals to decide between major alternatives on the basis of reason alone, but it does provide warrants for taking reasonableness in religion seriously, and it helps explain why the intellectual labors of theologians, though vacuous without corresponding practice, do sometimes make significant contributions to the health of religious traditions.

Most premodern theological views of the relation of faith and reason are consistent with this outlook. Even Luther's attacks on 'whore reason' are not fideistic: he affirms the importance of reason (at times including scholastic logic) in expounding Christian truth against both heretics and pagans.[29] On the other end of the spectrum, Aquinas' use of reason does not lead to foundational or natural theology of the modern type. Even when he is most the apologist, as in demonstrating the existence of God, his proofs are, by his own account, 'probable arguments' in support of faith rather than parts of an independent foundational enterprise.[30] Both these thinkers, despite their material differences, can be viewed as holding that revelation dominates all aspects of the theological enterprise, but without excluding a subsidiary use of philosophical and experiential considerations in the explication and defense of the faith. Similarly, a postliberal approach need not exclude an ad hoc apologetics, but only one that is systematically prior and controlling in the fashion of post-Cartesian natural theology and of later liberalism. As Aquinas himself notes, reasoning in support of the faith is not meritorious before faith, but only afterward;[31] or, in the conceptuality employed in this book [*The Nature of Doctrine*] the logic of coming to believe, because it is like that of learning a language, has little room for argument, but once one has learned to speak the language of faith, argument becomes possible.

Yet, though postliberal antifoundationalism need not imply relativism or fideism, the question remains of how to exhibit the intelligibility and possible truth of the religious message to those who no longer understand the traditional words. How, as modern Christians often put it, does one preach the gospel in a de-Christianized world? Those for whom this problem is theologically primary regularly become liberal foundationalists. The first task of the theologian, they argue, is to identify the modern questions that must be addressed, and then to translate the gospel answers into a currently understandable conceptuality. If this is not done, the message will fall on deaf ears inside as well as outside the Church; and unless postliberal theology has some way of meeting this need, it will be adjudged faithless and inapplicable as well as unintelligible by the religious community.

The postliberal method of dealing with this problem is bound to be unpopular among those chiefly concerned to maintain or increase the membership and influence of the Church. This method resembles ancient catechesis more than modern translation.[32] Instead of redescribing the faith in new concepts, it seeks to teach the language and practices of the religion to potential adherents. This has been the primary way of transmitting the faith and winning converts for most religions down through the centuries. In the early days of the Christian church, for example, it was the gnostics, not the catholics, who were most inclined to redescribe the biblical materials in a new interpretive framework. Pagan converts to the catholic mainstream did not, for the most part, first understand the faith and then decide to become Christians; rather, the process was reversed: they first decided and then they understood. More precisely, they were first attracted by the Christian community and form of life. The reasons for attraction ranged from the noble to the ignoble and were as diverse as the individuals involved; but for whatever motives, they submitted themselves to prolonged catechetical instruction in which they practised new modes of behavior and learned the stories of Israel and their fulfillment in Christ. Only after they had acquired proficiency in the alien Christian language and form of life were they deemed able intelligently and responsibly to profess the faith, to be baptized.

Later, when Christianity became socially dominant, this kind of catechesis disappeared, but similar results were obtained, though in diluted form, through the normal processes of maturation. In both cases, whether through catechesis or socialization, an intimate and imaginatively vivid familiarity with the world of biblical narrative was produced that made it possible to experience the whole of life in religious terms. The popular versions of the biblical world may often have been gravely distorted, but they functioned intratextually.

Western culture is now at an intermediate stage, however, where socialization is ineffective, catechesis impossible, and translation a tempting alternative. The biblical heritage continues to be powerfully present in latent and detextualized forms that immunize against catechesis but invite redescription. There is often enough Christian substance remaining to make the redescriptions meaningful. Marxism, as is often noted, is a secularized form of biblical eschatology, and existentialism and depth psychology develop themes from Reformation anthropology divorced from Reformation theology.[33] The experience and self-identity of even the unchurched masses remain deeply influenced by the religious past. They often insist to sociological investigators, for example, that they are just as genuinely Christian as the pious folk who go to church; and they sometimes make this claim, interestingly enough, even when they deny life after death and consider the existence of a creator God unlikely. Jesus Christ is not the Son of God for them, and their picture of him may be drastically unscriptural, but his name is part of their being.[34] They are immunized against catechesis, but are sometimes interested in translations of the gospel into existential, depth-psychological or liberationist language that articulates their latent Christianity.

The impossibility of effective catechesis in the present situation is partly the result of the implicit assumption that knowledge of a few tag ends of religious language is knowledge of the religion (although no one would make this assumption about Latin). More important, however, is the character of churches during times of progressive de-Christianization. In the present situation, unlike periods of missionary expansion, the churches primarily accommodate to the prevailing culture rather than shape it. Presumably they cannot do otherwise. They continue to embrace in one fashion or another the majority of the population and must cater willy-nilly to majority trends. This makes it difficult for them to attract assiduous catechumens even from among their own children, and when they do, they generally prove wholly incapable of providing effective instruction in distinctively Christian language and practice. Those who are looking for alternatives, to, for example, the American way of life turn instead to eastern religions or to deviant offshoots of the Christian mainstream. This situation is not likely to change until de-Christianization has proceeded much further or, less plausibly, is fundamentally reversed.

When or if de-Christianization reduces Christians to a small minority, they will need for the sake of survival to form communities that strive without traditionalist rigidity to cultivate their native tongue and learn to act accordingly. Until that happens, however, catechetical methods of communicating the faith are likely to be unemployable in mainstream Christianity. The by no means illegitimate desire of the churches to maintain membership and of theologians to make the faith credible, not least to themselves, will continue to favor experiential-expressive translations into contemporary idioms.

Conclusion

This chapter ends on an inconclusive note. Postliberal theologies employing a cultural-linguistic understanding of religion can be faithful, applicable and intelligible. There is thus no theological, just as there is no doctrinal, reason for rejecting them. Yet the intratextual intelligibility that postliberalism emphasizes may not fit the needs of religions such as Christianity when they are in the awkwardly intermediate stage of having once been culturally established but are not yet clearly disestablished.

Those of postliberal inclinations will be undeterred. They will argue for intratextuality on both religious and nonreligious grounds: the integrity of the faith demands it, and the vitality of western societies may well depend in the long run on the culture-forming power of the biblical outlook in its intratextual, untranslatable specificity. Theology should therefore resist the clamor of the religiously interested public for what is currently fashionable and immediately intelligible. It should instead prepare for a future when continuing de-Christianization will make greater Christian authenticity communally possible.

Those who hold that religious faithfulness is first of all the presentation of the religious message in currently intelligible forms will, of course, disagree. Their liberal premise, furthermore, can be canonically defended. There is much in Scripture and tradition to suggest that preaching the gospel understandably is a necessary part of faithfulness. In short, as was said at the beginning of this chapter, the case for the theological viability of a cultural-linguistic view of religion can only be presented, not proved. Field-encompassing interpretive frameworks shape their own criteria of adequacy.

The ultimate test in this, as in other areas, is performance. If a postliberal approach in its actual employment proves to be conceptually powerful and practically useful to the relevant communities, it will in time become standard. It was thus that the theological outlooks of Augustine, Aquinas, Luther and Schleiermacher established themselves. There is no way of testing the merits and demerits of a theological method apart from performance.

The present chapter, however, is not a theological performance but at most a fragment of ad hoc apologetics. It discusses theology, but there is, by intratextual standards, scarcely a single properly theological argument in it. Such arguments in defense of its theses can, I think, be found in sources as diverse as Aquinas, the Reformers and Karl Barth, but these have simply been mentioned, not deployed.

Yet, like most programmatic proposals, the present one is not simply an invitation to future work but is also dependent on past performances. The reader will recall that the stimulus for this book comes from the conviction that the doctrinal results of the ecumenical discussions of the last decades make better sense in the context of a cultural-linguistic view of religion and a rule theory of doctrine than in any other framework. Like the subjects of the Postman-Bruner card experiment mentioned in the Forward to *The Nature of Doctrine*, I have repeatedly had the experience of seeing that old categories (such as propositional or symbolic construals of doctrine) simply do not apply to what is now happening, but that light dawns when one uses a new category (church doctrines as instantiations of regulative principles within a cultural-linguistic system). Further, on the specifically theological side, Karl Barth's exegetical emphasis on narrative has been at second hand[35] a chief source of my notion of intratextuality as an appropriate way of doing theology in a fashion consistent with a cultural-linguistic understanding of religion and a regulative view of doctrine.

It remains an open question, however, whether the intratextual path will be pursued. There is much talk at present about typological, figurative and narrative theology, but little actual performance. Only in some younger theologians does one see the beginnings of a desire to renew in a post-traditional and postliberal mode the ancient practice of absorbing the universe into the biblical world. May their tribe increase.

12. Foreword to the German Edition of *The Nature of Doctrine**

Editor's Introduction

As I mention in the introduction to this volume, *The Nature of Doctrine* generated a good deal of debate in English-speaking countries. A German translation appeared a decade after the English. The next selection is the original English of what became the foreword to the German edition. Here Lindbeck offers his own analysis of the reception of *The Nature of Doctrine* as well as a preview of the directions subsequent essays take. (See note 10 in the introduction to this volume for reviews of *The Nature of Doctrine* to some of which Lindbeck here responds.)

This is not the book it was 10 years ago when it was first published. It was captured by unanticipated interest groups who so shaped the public reception that even I, the author, now read it partly through their eyes. The change needs an explanation; and that is the main reason for this foreword.

It does not, however, replace the first one: the original text is basic in any attempt to understand the after effects. Nor does this second foreword substitute for the introduction to the original text. Professors Ulrich and Hütter know, as I do not, what might be of interest to German readers, and their understanding of the book is outstanding – better than that of most American reviewers. Further, the translation needs no comment except commendation. It catches the nuances of Anglo-American thought, and makes a number of corrections which improve on the English-language

---

* This is the original English version of George A Lindbeck's 'Vorwort zu deutschen Ausgabe', *Christliche Lehre als Grammatik des Glaubens. Religion und Theologie in postliberalen Zeitalter*, trans. Markus Müller; introduction Hans G Ulrich and Reinhard Hütter, Gütersloh: Kaiser, 1994, pp. 16–22.

original. Mr Müller, the translator, is to be thanked. The only task remaining for this second foreword is to recount the unexpected transformation wrought by readers' responses.

As is hinted in later sections, the book I thought I had written was simply preliminary to a larger work, a comparative dogmatics which would deal in comprehensive detail with the present status and future possibilities of overcoming the ecclesial divisiveness of historic doctrinal differences between the major Christian traditions, Reformation, Roman Catholic and Eastern Orthodox. I had long collected materials for this project while teaching (since 1951) in a university theological faculty with committed and articulate students and teachers from all these confessions. Further, I began participating even before Vatican II in international as well as national ecumenical dialogues, was a Delegated Observer at the Council, and served in the 1970s and 1980s as Lutheran co-chair of the Lutheran World Federation/Vatican Joint Study Commission. Increasingly, however (to anticipate points dealt with in the body of the book at greater length), I found myself puzzled by the views of doctrine current both in church pronouncements and in theological and non-theological scholarly treatments of the subject. They did not adequately reflect the tacit understandings embedded in operative practices either in the ecumenical present or the non-ecumenical past. When I employed the usual concepts, as I did in various drafts of the projected comparative dogmatics, the results were incoherent. It seemed necessary to develop and justify an understanding of church doctrine better suited to my purposes before I could proceed. The result was the present slim volume conceived as a prolegomenon to a more substantial study of the ecumenical situation.

In the meanwhile, however, my intended audience had largely vanished. By 1984, ecumenical interests had shifted from overcoming the doctrinal barriers which block Christian unity to co-operating in common struggles for, to use the World Council of Churches formula, Justice, Peace and the Integrity of Creation (commonly known by the acronym, JPIC). Ecumenists of this new type are not much interested in doctrine, and instead it is systematic and historical theologians, philosophers and sociologists of religion, and even, though to a lesser extent, scriptural scholars who have been the most engaged and frequent participants in discussions of this book.

This surprised me. The only fresh aspect of the book, I had supposed, was its ecumenical focus. The ingredients were borrowed. My Yale colleagues, Hans Frei and David Kelsey, supplied the narrative hermeneutic (admittedly different in character from what usually passes under that name) which the book favors, while its grammatical or regulative understanding of doctrine has patristic roots retrieved with the help of such authors as, among theologians, the German Lutheran, Edmund Schlink, and the

Canadian Jesuit, Bernard Lonergan, and, among philosophers, Ludwig Wittgenstein. (They are not responsible, to repeat the usual disclaimer, for the use I have made of their work.) Similarly, the 'cultural-linguistic' theory of religion is, except for its name, adapted from Clifford Geertz, and amounts, the way I use it, to little more than a semiotic version of that mélange of ideas from Weber, Durkeim, Hegel and Marx used by everyone who talks about religion in our day (and which I know chiefly at second hand, not least as transmitted through Peter Berger).[1]

Not only were my ideas mostly borrowed, they were also used in what I thought of as a pretheological and thus, wherever possible, theologically neutral way. The theories of doctrine and religion, for example, can be turned either to the right or the left and employed for non-Christian as well as Christian purposes (just as has been done with Platonic, Aristotelian, Schleiermacherian and Hegelian conceptualities down through the centuries). My use of them is meant to be ad hoc and unsystematic, thus conforming both to Karl Barth's recommendations for the employment of non-scriptural concepts in theology and to contemporary anti-foundational trends in Anglo-American philosophy. The purpose is not to legislate doctrinally, but to explore the mutual immanence of the changeability and unchangeability of Christian doctrine in order to make it conceptually easier to combine commitment to the search for Church unity with faithfulness to historic creeds and confessions. Those who do not share this goal can also become postliberal, if they wish, by borrowing, as I have done, similar understandings of religion and doctrine from non-theological sources and using them for their different theological purposes. The book, to repeat, is pretheological, and I naïvely supposed it would be interesting chiefly to doctrinally committed ecumenists.

Why, then, did the discussion come to be dominated by non-ecumenists who, on the left, cared little about the visible unity of the Church and less about creedal and confessional integrity, and on the right, were not only indifferent to uniting the churches, but often opposed? The reason, it would seem, is that the book's combination of avant garde conceptualities and commitment to historic doctrine was perceived as a direct attack on liberalism, on the one hand, and as seductively dangerous to conservatism, on the other. The desire to be both intellectually up-to-date and creedally orthodox is not uncommon on the right, but it is in tension with fear of the new: preliberalism seems safer than postliberalism. Reactions on the left are often a mirror image of those on the right: there is agreement with the right that the avant garde is by definition heterdox, except that this is viewed as desirable. Whatever is perceived as orthodox is retrograde. A position of which it can be said that 'the hands may be hands of Wittgenstein and Geertz but the voice is the voice of Karl Barth' is obviously self-contradictory.[2] If this is not so, if orthodoxy can no longer be accused of ineluctable opposition to new intellectual developments, then the case for liberalism in most of its North American varieties collapses. Fortunately for me, there are also many readers who are enthusiastically in agreement with the book, but even for them it is generally a work in genres I had not intended such as dogmatics, philosophy or theology of culture.

In summarizing these responses, one can say that the book has not functioned as an ecumenical prolegomenon, but as a contribution to the wider discussion of whether or how modernity (and its parasitic negation in postmodernity) is being replaced by a new cultural, religious, intellectual and theological situation. From this perspective, it is not an isolated work but part of a growing stream of theological, ethical and religious studies. It was not even novel when it first appeared: Alasdair MacIntyre and Stanley Hauerwas were already producing philosophical and theological works with affinities to this one.[3] Looked at in the context of this larger discussion, there is much that is lacking in the present book: MacIntyre's treatment of what he calls 'traditions of inquiry' would have been helpful in specifying the relations of doctrine, theology, practice and religious communities, and there is a need for fuller discussions of such philosophical topics as antifoundationalism and the relation of truth and justified belief, of literary theory (not least deconstruction), of communalism in contemporary sociology and political science, of narrative hermeneutics and its relation to both premodern and historical-critical exegesis, and of the relation of my project to the two theologians with whom I have been most in conversation over the years, Thomas Aquinas and Martin Luther. The inclusion of this additional material would have resulted in a longer and different book, but one closer to the one it was assumed I had intended to write.

What are the prospects for the postliberal cultural-linguistic approaches which this book recommends? Their future seems bright in non-theological disciplines, but not theological ones, and their chances of influence are even dimmer on the North American scene at large. This is to be expected. Where communal bonds are weak and social structures favor individualism, as on this continent, the self is thought of and experienced with special intensity as an isolated ego. On the intellectual level and even more the emotional one, it is hard to acknowledge that selfhood is a socially and interpersonally constructed reality. Religious people in particular seem to find it hard to admit that humans are to the core of their beings social animals. Pietistic revivalists, old-style liberals and new age spiritualists differ on many points but not, for the most part, in their individualism and experientialism. It is for them sacrilegious to think of the most intimately inward of religious experiences as socially shaped, to accord primacy to cultural-linguistic factors over experiential ones or, speaking theologically in Luther's terminology, to grant the superiority of the external over the internal word. More of the younger than of the older generation of theologians is affected by what this book calls postliberalism – it is hard not to be in view of the strength of cultural-linguistic approaches in other disciplines – but they are unlikely to have much influence on the general course of theology in the churches for the forseeable future. In the absence of further social disintegration resulting in major social crises, both conservative and liberal resistance to postliberal outlooks seems likely to prevail.

As far as my own work is concerned, it has become clear to me in the last decade, not least because of the discussions prompted by this book, that a comparative dogmatics needs to take a different form than I originally envisioned. It should start with ecclesiology and, included in that, with what might be called 'Israel-ology'. The two cannot be separated in a scriptural narrative approach: Israel and the Church are one elect people, and rethinking their relation is fundamental to ecumenism. This rethinking must be theological, i.e. based on Scripture as it functions in communities for which the scriptural witness to the God of Israel and of Jesus is authoritative. It makes use of analyses such are found in the present work, but is not based on them. As this foreword has emphasized, the theories of religion and doctrine I have proposed are intended to be pretheological rather than theologically foundational. They are dispensable when the situation changes or when better intellectual tools are devised for thinking ecumenically in the present post-Christendom and postliberal state of the Church. In the meantime, my hope is that what I have written will be helpful to those concerned about the *causal Christi* on both sides of the Atlantic.

13. Scripture, Consensus and Community*

Editor's Introduction

In this essay we find Lindbeck's position on Scripture and community stated as clearly as anywhere. He aims, as his first sentence says, to bring 'classic hermeneutics' to bear on our 'postcritical context'. What does he mean? Although there is no single, standard definition of 'hermeneutics' in contemporary theology, we might say that hermeneutics is the set of theories and practices it takes to read, interpret and use Scriptures. 'Classic hermeneutics' is the way Christians traditionally practised such hermeneutics. Lindbeck offers a lengthy description of such classic hermeneutics by offering a condensed narrative of the origin and development of the scriptural canon, the deformations of the use of Scripture and their attempted reformations by the 16th-century Protestants and Catholics, up through the replacement of the classic hermeneutics with Christian fundamentalist or secular historical, philosophical or other more 'critical' hermeneutics. What Lindbeck's first sentence calls our 'postcritical context' is a context in which no single one of these hermeneutics has a monopoly except among small groups, and even then often for only a brief time.

Lindbeck aims to 'retrieve' classic hermeneutics, overcoming the losses of competing modern hermeneutics without losing sight of their gains. The essay presumes readers who know (or are willing to find out about) heterodox historical groups such as Marcionites and Gnostics and Donatists. What Lindbeck calls the *sensus fidelium* is 'the sense of the faithful' – in Augustine's expression, the consent of all the faithful 'from the bishops to the last of the faithful laity' (*On the Predestination of the Saints* 14, 27). On what Lindbeck calls 'typology' and 'allegory', recall that Romans 5.15 speaks of Adam as a 'type' of Christ, and 1 Corinthians

* George A Lindbeck, 'Scripture, Consensus and Community', in *Biblical Interpretation in Crisis. The Ratzinger Conference on Bible and Church*, (ed.), Richard John Neuhaus, Grand Rapids: William B Eerdmans, 1989, pp. 74–101.

speaks of Israel's exodus and journey in the desert as a 'type' of the messianic age; Galatians 4.24 describes the story of Abraham, Hagar, Sarah and their children as an 'allegory' of Paul's contemporaries, who are children of Hagar and Sarah. 'Typological (or allegorical) interpretation' is an extension of Paul's hermeneutics to all of Scripture – a way of showing the unity of the biblical narrative from Adam to the Church. There are debates about such typological and allegorical reading strategies – some take the distinction between the two as quite firm, others quite fluid. As he suggests in a note on the text, Lindbeck makes a quite firm distinction between the two here – but his argument does not depend on such a firm distinction. In any case, the pragmatic proof of any heremeneutics will not be theoretical but practical – that is, the gathering and upbuilding of communities of 'pastors, biblical scholars, theologians and laity together [who] seek God's guidance in the written word for their communal as well as individual lives'.

Introduction

This essay is concerned with the consensus-and-community-building potential of the 'classic' pattern of biblical interpretation. The basic outlines of that pattern prevailed from the earliest days of the Church well into the 17th century, and it often played a unitive role which has been sadly lacking in recent times. It produced interpretations which are different but not necessarily opposed to those of modern scholarship. The rationalist and empiricist literalism of modernity was its chief enemy; its demise antedates the beginnings of historical criticism in the 18th century; and it has for the last 200 years been mostly misunderstood rather than rejected. Perhaps, then, its reappropriation is possible in our postmodern era; and, in any case, its consensus-and-community-forming potential is needed.

The need is particularly evident when one considers the present state of the *sensus fidelium* in most major Christian communions. There seems to be less and less communal sense of what is or is not Christian. The Eastern Orthodox are perhaps a partial exception, but their sense of community is also being eroded by modern developments. As ethnic, cultural and religious traditions weaken, consensus dissolves and communal authority declines. Public opinion must be manipulated in order to gain agreement; but public opinion, in the Church as elsewhere, is pluralized or polarized. ('Public opinion', as I am using the phrase, is measured by such things as Gallup polls. The *sensus fidelium*, in contrast, consists ultimately of what 'nuclear' Christians – to use Joseph Fichter's terminology – discover they believe in times of crisis and are willing to die for.) Even in single congregations it becomes difficult or impossible to discover or develop a common mind on what is or is not essential. Knowledge of the Bible (which is transmitted through general culture, folklore, proverbs, catechesis and liturgy, as well as direct Bible-reading and preaching) is in decline. The use of Scripture is not part of people's lives, and thus reading and hearing it (when they do read and hear it) has little impact. Perhaps this is why the change to the vernacular and the renewed emphasis on Scripture at Vatican II seem to have done little to make the Roman Catholic *sensus fidelium* more biblically informed. Most serious, there is a lack of a generally intelligible and distinctively Christian language within which disagreements can be expressed and issues debated. Thus the *sensus fidelium* becomes less dependable even when, as in democratic societies, more depends on it. The crisis, if what follows is correct, is related to the loss of the once universal classic hermeneutical framework.

However one diagnoses its causes, the need for more and better knowledge of the Bible is not likely to be denied. I will say more later about the need, but my main focus will be on the past and possible present usefulness of the classic hermeneutics. Stated compactly and technically, the issue which concerns us is the extent to which the Bible can be profitably read in our day as a canonically and narrationally unified and internally glossed (that is, self-referential and self-interpreting) whole centered on Jesus Christ, and telling the story of the dealings of the Triune God with his people and his world in ways which are typologically (though not, so at least the Reformers would say, allegorically) applicable to the present.[1] I shall speak at length of the past because an understanding of the historic role of this way of interpreting and using Scripture is the best argument for present need and possibility.[2] We shall look first, in the next section, at the origins of the classic hermeneutical pattern and at the conditions under which it best promoted a biblically informed and communally unitive *sensus fidelium*. The last three sections deal successively with the disintegration of this pattern, the present situation, and the possibilities for the future.

The historical analysis in this paper is for the most part, I hope, relatively free of confessional bias, but its emphasis on the importance for the health of the Church of a biblically instructed laity bears the marks of the Reformation heritage. Perhaps, however, Catholics can now also agree with this emphasis; and if not, they are still, from a Reformation perspective, in need of reform. This, however, is no reason for boasting: contemporary Protestants, not least Lutherans, need reform in this and many other respects no less than Roman Catholics.

The Classic Hermeneutic: Premodern Bible Reading

In the early days, to rehearse familiar facts, it was not a different canon but a distinctive method of reading which differentiated the church from the synagogue. Christians read the Bible they shared with the Jews in the light of their at first orally transmitted stories of the crucified and resurrected Messiah in whose name they prayed and into whom they were incorporated in baptism and Eucharist. Jesus was for them the climax and summation of Israel's history. When joined to him, even Gentiles became members of the enlarged people of God, citizens of the commonwealth of Israel (Eph. 2.12). Its history became their history, and its Bible their Bible. It was not simply a source of precepts and truths, but the interpretive framework for all reality. They used typological and, less fundamentally, allegorical techniques derived from their Jewish and Greek milieux to apply the canonically fixed words to their ever-changing situations.

As time went on, an explicit rule of faith and an enlarged canon came into existence. The two developments were synchronically interrelated. The rule of faith, in its various versions, articulated the liturgically embedded Christological and Trinitarian reading of the Hebrew Scriptures; the selection of certain writings out of the many then circulating which claimed apostolic status depended on their usefulness within the context of the *sensus fidelium* formed by this implicit or explicit rule of faith. (The use, and therefore meaning, of the text, be it noted, was the one it had in the canon-forming situation, not in some putative historically reconstructed original one.) Thus a certain way of reading Scripture (viz. as a Christ-centered narrationally and typologically unified whole in conformity to a Trinitarian rule of faith) was constitutive of the Christian canon and has, it would seem, an authority inseparable from that of the Bible itself. To read the Bible otherwise is not to read it as Scripture but as some other book, just as to read Homer's *Odyssey* for philological or historical purposes, for example, is to turn it into something other than an epic poem.

In the light of this interrelation of canon, hermeneutics and the *sensus fidelium*, the Catholic/Protestant arguments about whether Scripture or the Church are prior seem futile. Israel's Scriptures, read in the fashion we have noted, were constitutive of the communities which produced an enlarged canon in order to reinforce their identities against Gnostic, Marcionite and other groups which called themselves Christian. Looked at in terms of historical development, what we now call the Catholic Church of the first centuries was constituted by those Christian groups (in some times and places perhaps a small minority) for which the Hebrew Bible read Christologically was of special importance. (The 4th-century Donatists were perhaps the first major schismatic movement to retain the catholic reverence for the

Old Testament.) Even though these Old Testament-oriented churches soon became overwhelmingly Gentile in membership, they developed a Christian analogue of the Jewish sense of being a single people. Their widely separated communities were bound together by ties of mutual helpfulness, responsibility and openness to each other's correction. Because of this, they were able to cooperate in developing, not only congruent versions of a single rule of faith and a common enlarged canon, but also unified, though not uniform, ministerial, liturgical and disciplinary patterns and structures. A far-flung, flexible and yet tenacious network of mutual aid societies came to span the Mediterranean world.

Not surprisingly, it was these communities which out-distanced all other claimants to the Catholic name (for Marcionites and others also claimed to be the one and only Catholic Church). It was their Scriptures, not some other canon, which became the basic Christian Bible; and in this sense the Church is prior to the Bible. Yet, on the other hand, it was Scripture – initially Hebrew Scripture read Christologically – which had the consensus, community and institution-building power to make of these communities the overwhelmingly dominant and therefore Catholic Church. It does not even seem far-fetched to say that it was the Bible which conquered the empire in defiance of the normal laws of sociological gravity: non-violently, despite persecution, and without special economic, social, cultural or ethnic support. Other texts in other contexts – the Koran and Buddhist scriptures, for example – have also formed and sustained major trans-ethnic communities, but never in comparable independence of external assistance. Thus the priority of the Bible seems at least as plausible as the priority of the Church. No choice is necessary, however: it is best to think of the co-inherence of Bible and Church, of their mutually constitutive reciprocity. It was, furthermore, the Church as *sensus fidelium*, not as separately institutionalized magisterial authority, which was decisive in this process. Those writings which proved profitable in actual use among the people were the ones which were included in the canon.

The canon is now closed for all those who believe in the finality, the eschatological decisiveness, of Jesus Christ. The balance, one might say, has shifted. The Church, whether as institutionalized magisterium or as the sense of the faithful, no longer forms scripture, but is rather formed by it. Yet the Bible's community-forming role, needless to say, is not independent of community. It helps constitute the *ecclesia* only when interpreted communally in accordance with a community-constituting hermeneutics. That hermeneutics remained for long centuries the classic one.

As the Middle Ages manifest, the Bible classically interpreted can shape communal and personal identities even when (in contrast to the early church) almost all lay folk are illiterate. The laity learned the fundamental outline and episodes of the scriptural drama through liturgy, catechesis and occasional preaching. That drama defined for them the truly real world, and within it they inscribed their own reality (as the products of the popular imagination from paintings, sculpture and mystery plays to oaths and proverbs make evident). Nor was this absorption of ordinary life by the Bible simply an imaginative matter. Charlemagne's typological identification of himself as a Christian King David set over God's people, for example, was not an empty metaphor but a history-transforming trope. The extraordinary unity of western culture in the Middle Ages – far greater than it is at present – would not have been possible without such institutional developments as the papacy and the Holy Roman Empire, but it was above all the result of the reality-defining power of a single pre-eminent text, the Bible, classically interpreted.

This is not to deny that the Bible was also grossly misinterpreted: classical hermeneutics is no guarantee of Christian faithfulness. Deviations of piety, theology and church structure can be treated as immemorial Christian tradition and retrojected into the Bible or the early church (e.g. The Donation of Constantine). Persecutions and inquisitions were biblically legitimated. Nor were those whose personal motives were selflessly Christian, even cruciform, exempt from these distortions: it was St Bernard who preached the Second Crusade which, to his horror, unleashed the second great anti-semitic pogroms. (Nor, it must be hastily added, are such corruptions confined to the Middle Ages: it was Luther who wrote some of the most painfully anti-Jewish diatribes in history.) Yet the Bible within the classical framework resists definitive capture by even communally self-interested misreadings. The centrality of the stories of Jesus and the typological application to the present Church (in accordance with 1 Cor. 10) of the Old Testament tales of God's wrath, as well as mercy, against his ceaselessly unfaithful people confer self-correcting potential on communal interpretation. Those who denounce communally authorized misreadings, furthermore, are admonished by the example of the prophets, of Jesus and of the apostles to remain loyal to the community and, according to Paul as reported in Acts, respectful of its leaders even if they are unbelieving high priests (23.5). A more effective strategy for maintaining unity despite disagreement cannot easily be imagined.

The strategy failed at the time of the Reformation. As early Jewish Christians were cast out of synagogues despite their desire to stay, so Luther and his associates were excommunicated by Rome. The parallel has difficulties, not least the fact that Luther's language regarding the pope does not follow Paul's example as recorded in Acts 23.5; but our purpose here is not to explore the shared responsibilities for the schism but to look at the unifying role of Scripture during the Reformation period. This role, needless to say, is chiefly evident on the Protestant side: the Catholic reform, great though it was, built more on purified tradition than directly on the sacred page.

It is the Reformed more than the Lutherans who in the 16th and early 17th centuries best exhibit the consensus-and-community-building power of a biblically informed *sensus fidelium*. They were led by the best-educated ministry in Christendom and appealed especially to the literate artisan and rising middle classes, and yet they also constituted an inclusive popular movement which was able in an impoverished rural country such as Scotland, for example, to sweep also the peasantry and the aristocracy into the fold. Their churches were scattered from Hungary to New England in highly diverse situations, and yet they constituted a self-consciously united communion held together by nothing except a common approach to Scripture. They had no overarching organizational structures, nor Book of Common Prayer, as did the Anglicans, nor unified body of confessional writings, as did the Lutherans. Yet they formed a single community of interpretation which was diverse yet tenaciously united.

Their reading of the Bible largely conformed to the classic pattern: they read it as the all-embracing story of the present as well as past dealings of the Triune God with God's people and God's world. While they carried further the medieval Aristotelian minimization of allegory, already well-advanced in Aquinas, they were not modern literalists, for typology and typological applications were crucial. Through endless sermons and continual reading, the laity in many congregations came to know the Bible from Genesis to Revelation with a thoroughness never equaled before or since. Under the guidance of their preachers – for their reading was communal, not individualistic – they searched the Bible with close attention both to its details and encompassing patterns in order to shape their lives and thoughts in obedience to God's Word. Calvin's commentaries and *Institutes* guided but did not control their interpretations: for several generations, their theology, church organization and practice developed within a broad consensus along similar lines.

Some of the developments were dreadfully misguided, as the Reformed themselves now almost universally acknowledge. One major difficulty was that they yielded even more than others to the then prevailing passion to find a single, all-embracing and unchanging system of doctrine in the Bible. Given their Augustinian premises (once again largely shared with Lutherans and at least Jansenist Catholics), the result was the fatal hyper-Augustinian flaw of individualistic, supralapsarian, double predestination. The dreadful decrees obscured God's mercy and, as Lutherans complained, unwittingly undermined the Reformation *sola gratia* and *sola fide*. Further, despite Calvin's theological sacramental realism, the Reformed tended to become more and more ritually impoverished, not only in comparison to the

Catholics of their day but also to the Lutherans and to the early church. Yet they compensated for the lack of liturgical guidance (not only through rites but pericopes) in the reading of Scripture by their conceptually disciplined and thorough knowledge of its contents and skill in its use. From this they derived the dynamism which made them (as a Roman Catholic historian, Christopher Dawson, has remarked) the shapers of modernity much more than Catholics, Lutherans or Anglicans. Post-Constantinian history offers no equally impressive example of the unity and community-building power of a biblically informed *sensus fidelium*.

Yet the success of the Reformed was limited in scope and duration. They did not unite the Reformation churches. Their rationalistic (though also biblicistic) antitraditional penchant for doctrinal systems ran counter to the ecclesial traditionalism of the Anglicans and the sacramental traditionalism of the Lutherans. As time went on, furthermore, debates over what was supposed to be the one and only system of biblical doctrine (most fully elaborated in the Westminster Confession and the Helvetic Consensus) replaced the more flexible hermeneutic of the 16th century (not to mention the early church). Most of the Protestant divisions after the 16th century originated among the Reformed, and the loss of the classic interpretive pattern is largely responsible. This loss, however, was not confined to them, and it is to some remarks on its disappearance throughout western Christendom that we must now turn.

Modernity: Losses Though Not Without Gains

Recent work in the history of exegesis[3] suggests that the crucial change in the modern period has been the neglect of the narrative meaning of Scripture. In realistic narratives of the biblical type, the identity and character of the personal agents with whom they are chiefly concerned (viz. God and human beings) is enacted by the plotted interaction of intention and circumstance. This is the Bible's chief device for telling its readers about themselves, their world, and their God. Definitions of essence and attributes and descriptions of inner experience, of states of consciousness, can perhaps sometimes be inferred from the biblical materials, but if these inferences are primarily relied upon, much of what the Bible communicates about God and human beings is lost. Further, loss of narrative meaning weakens the glue which holds the canon together and makes difficult the typological use of the biblical stories to shape the present communal and personal identity of Christians. Lastly, Trinitarian and Christological doctrine lose their function as directives for Scripture reading (e.g. Christ is to be understood in the light of the whole Bible and the whole Bible in the light of Christ) and, especially for *sola Scriptura* Protestants, become fragile and hermeneutically

inoperative deductions from the text. Thus when narrative meaning is neglected, the entire classic interpretive pattern crumbles.

It appears that narrative meaning was neglected because it was misunderstood: it was turned into another kind of meaning. Instead of asking what
the biblical narratives tell about God and human beings and how they are
to be used in shaping life and understanding reality, the primary question
became whether they are accurate reports of the events of which they tell.
The narrative meaning of the stories was confused with their factual (scientific and historical) meaning, and was thereby lost.

Not everyone remained interested in factual meaning, as we shall note
in a moment, but those who did divided into two camps: inerrantists and
historical critics. Both tended to think that facts (defined by the prevailing
rational and empirical standards of the day) are what are important in
any document, and most notably in the book of books, the Bible. Their
disagreement was over the factual veracity of the text or, more broadly,
over how to go about determining the factual meaning. The inerrantist
tendency was to insist that everything which could by any stretch of the
imagination be supposed to be a factual assertion must be so interpreted
and accepted as accurate; while historical critics used the text as a source
of data for reconstructing what could (by the general, and never entirely
stable, standards of the day) be plausibly taken to be the originating events,
personalities or situations (e.g. The historical Jesus). There were many gra-
dations between the extremes, but for all the participants in the debate
from fundamentalist rigorists to hyperskeptical liberals, the narrative meaning had collapsed into the factual and disappeared.

One consequence was that the Bible tended to become uninteresting:
facts, even miraculous ones, are not self-involving. When inerrantists said,
as some of them did, that miracles had ceased after the New Testament
period, they made the miracle stories inapplicable to the present. Not surprisingly, the significance of Scripture was sought in other meanings. Its
importance was thought to lie in what it had to say about religious experience or general truths about humanity and divinity or morality or in its
symbolic or mythological import. Pietists (followed by romantic idealists
such as Schleiermacher and modern existentialists such as Bultmann)
stressed religious experience; rationalists, whether orthodox or unorthodox,
general truths; Enlightenment thinkers such as Kant, morality; and those
errantists who lost interest in historical reconstructions, mythology and
symbolism. Until our own lifetimes, however, virtually no one on either the
right or the left gave much attention to biblical narrative as a genre in its
own right. The classic hermeneutics became effectively dead.

The basic causes of its demise, as I have already suggested, antedate the
rise of historical criticism. Confessional rivalries culminating in wars of

religion, on the one hand, and the mentality associated with the development of modern science, on the other, each played a part. The two phenomena are interconnected.[4] Communal certainties were undermined by Christian fratricide (much more unsettling than ever before in the West because it was between established churches), and many turned for firm foundations to individual reason and experience. Rationalists, beginning with Descartes, sought incorrigible self-evidence in the consciousness of innate truths of reason, while empiricists, such as Locke, looked for it in conscious sensory perception. Thus the focus on individual consciousness stands at the beginning of the modern era and became, in Kant and his successors, the turn to the transcendental autonomous subject. The disregard of the communal and non-conscious dimensions of cognition which this focus implied would have seemed naïve to Aristotle, not to mention a modern sociologist of knowledge, but with the collapse of the unity of western Christendom, the terror of anarchy, intellectual as well as political, was rampant. There was, it seemed, nowhere to turn but to the individual's reason and experience (or, in the case of Roman Catholicism, to an official magisterium increasingly independent of Scripture and even of tradition). In the case of Protestantism, the search for certainty led to such notions as the right and duty of private interpretation, factualistic inerrancy and plenary verbal inspiration. Interpretation was no longer seen as a communal enterprise, the individual was supposed to need no hermeneutical guidance, and true Christianity was construed as a creedless religion: 'The Bible and the Bible alone is the religion of Protestants.' All of these ideas originated in the 17th century, favored the later development of biblical criticism (even if in reaction against the extremes of inerrancy and plenary inspiration), and were antithetical to the classical hermeneutic. In a world obsessed with the kind of certainty which comes from factuality, from immediate experience, and, especially on the Catholic side, from rational, institutional and juridical clarity, there was no interest in the narrative meaning of the biblical stories.

Yet there were gains as well as losses from these developments, especially from historical criticism. Concentrating on factuality has, in the long run, made possible the realization that the factual and narrative meanings of the biblical stories are distinct and to some degree (though by no means totally) independent of each other.[5] It has also cleared the way for the recovery of the biblical message by unmasking misuses of Scripture which go back, in some cases, to the first centuries. Think, for example, of the supersessionist understanding of the relation of Israel and the Church which developed almost immediately in the conflict with the synagogue. It was projected backward onto Scripture (some would say into Scripture) with increasingly ghastly consequences as the Church became persecutor rather than persecuted. Not only were Jewish/Christian relations poisoned, but the fundamental structure of faith was in some respects distorted. Under the pressure of anti-Jewish reading, the plain meaning of Rom. 9—11, for example, was denied and eventually transformed, beginning with Augustine, into an individualistic doctrine of predestination which has burdened the West ever since. Similarly, the anti-Jewish (as distinct from anti-Judaizing) understanding of Paul's distinction between law and gospel has contributed to a fatal oscillation between legalism and antinomian 'cheap grace' (to use Bonhoeffer's phrase). Supersessionism, furthermore, has increased ecclesial triumphalism. Despite such passages as 2 Cor. 11.1–4 and 1 Cor. 10.5–11, both Catholics and Protestants have, in their very different ways, denied that the Church, while remaining genuinely the Church, can be the *sponsa meretrix* susceptible to gross unfaithfulness comparable to Israel's. This is only the beginning of a long catalogue of deeply embedded distortions of Scripture from which historical-critical scholarship can help free us.

Yet this is a basically negative contribution. Modern scholarship can tell us much about what texts did not mean in the past and, with rather less certainty, reconstruct what they did mean; but, insofar as it remains critically historical, it provides no guidance for what they should mean in our present very different situations. It tells us at best what God said, not what God says now. There seems to be no exegetical bridge between past and present. This gap, much more than questions about inerrancy or inspiration, is the heart of the current crisis of scriptural authority and the source of the conflict of interpretations.

The Present Situation

When exegesis fails to span the distance between past and present, theology takes up the task. This has always been true, but historically theologians were also *doctores sacrae paginae* rather than a separate guild. More important, their task was structurally different. Narrative and typological interpretation enabled the Bible to speak with its own voice in new situations. Scripture, in Calvin's phrase, could serve as the spectacles, the lens, through which faith views all reality; and, to change the figure, the world of the reader could be absorbed into the biblical world. Platonism and Aristotelianism, for example, were assimilated into the scriptural framework and thus Christianized. (The inescapability of this task of putting non-Christian thought to Christian uses needs to be emphasized. Even theologians who want to be entirely biblical cannot avoid it. Luther, despite his detestation of Aristotle, continued to employ, often quite consciously, the ockhamist Aristotelianism in which he had been trained, and there is not a little Platonism in Calvin's thought.)

Now, however, the interpretive direction is reversed: the biblical message

is translated into contemporary conceptualities. This always happens unconsciously in varying degrees (subtly in Luther and Calvin, and more blatantly
in much Christian Platonism), but from Schleiermacher through Karl
Rahner and to liberation theologies, translation into non-biblical idioms has
been done deliberately and systematically. In terms of creedal orthodoxy, the
results have not necessarily been un-Christian. Further, they have often
made easier the continued commitment to the faith of would-be believers
(as Paul Tillich did for many of my generation), although their value in
converting the culturally de-Christianized is doubtful. Yet in reference to
the concern of this chapter for the biblical formation of the *sensus fidelium*,
their influence has been small and perhaps negative.

The main difficulty is that their interpretations tend to replace Scripture
rather than lead to it. In reading the Fathers and the Reformers – or even
a medieval Scholastic such as Thomas Aquinas – one's understanding of
what they are saying is enriched when one studies their numerous scriptural
references (although, admittedly, the enrichment is small when the references are to standard *dicta probantia*). This is not true in the case of most
modern theologians. In Karl Rahner – to cite someone from whom I have
greatly profited – the biblical references are few, are almost always to
scholarly interpretations rather than the text, function rather like *dicta
probantia*, and when one investigates them, they do little to increase understanding of his thought. He may have developed an authentically Christian
idealist-existentialist-evolutionary *Weltanschauung*, but this, as is characteristic of good translations, seems at times only externally related to its originating text. One can learn to think well in his categories while remaining
biblically illiterate. This is impossible in the case of Augustine, Luther (*pace*
Ebeling) or Aquinas (*pace* the neo-Thomists or even Gilson). The difficulty
cannot be removed by admonitions to study the Bible, or reminders that
one should not mistake theological commentary for that on which one
comments. Nor is it much alleviated by the fact that theologies for which
a contemporary framework is controlling may enlarge and correct our
awareness of the biblical witness (as has been done, for example, to cite a
couple of items among many, by the liberationist emphasis on the 'preferen-
tial option for the poor', and the feminist reminder that the first witnesses
to the Resurrection were women). Rather, the problem is one of conceptual
structure: the more a theology translates the scriptural message into an alien
idiom (rather than vice versa) the more easily it can be construed as having
captured the essence of the gospel, just as, to make an outrageous comparison, Freud's psychoanalytic interpretation is often treated by Freudians
as having captured the essence of *Oedipus Rex*. Those well-versed in
Sophocles' play may have their understanding of it enriched, but those who
are not are tempted to think that the interpretation presents what is impor-

tant about the text better than the text itself and therefore never consult the original. This is one reason for doubting that translating the faith into contemporary thought patterns will contribute to a biblically informed *sensus fidelium*.

A further difficulty is that 'translation theology' is doubly pluralistic and thus doubly unlikely to contribute to the formation of a coherent 'sense of the faithful' whether biblical or non-biblical. The only major source of theological diversity in premodern theology is the historical situation. The biblical message as classically interpreted is relatively stable: what chiefly changes are the philosophies and other culturally conditioned outlooks which are interpreted within the framework. In the modern exegetical context, in contrast, there are two major sources of diversity. Theologians start with historical reconstructions of the biblical message which are inescapably diverse, tentative and changing; and then seek to translate these reconstructions into contemporary conceptualities which are also diverse and variable. Not surprisingly, the results are often mutually unintelligible. There is no single overarching universe of biblical discourse within which differences can be discussed. When, in contrast, the Bible is read as a unified whole telling the story of the dealings of the Triune God with his people and world, theologies as structurally different as those of Jonathan Edwards, Aquinas and Irenaeus (Irenaeus, as is often noted, has a structural resemblance to modern evolutionism) share the same conceptual language.

From this perspective, contemporary non-theological pluralism intensifies but does not fundamentally alter the problem. It is true that we live in an age of transition, of expanded horizons, and of vastly accelerated change in which theology is properly pluralized by the need to relate the faith to new situations and non-western cultures. Yet if the classic hermeneutic were retrieved, one might hope that this multiplicity would not lapse into the mutual unintelligibility which now seems inescapable. The pluralistic cacophony is in part the product of theology itself rather than the non-theological situation, and its influence on the sense of the faithful, insofar as it has any influence at all, cannot help but be disintegrating.

Fortunately the *sensus fidelium* persists in relative independence of professional theologians. It is nourished by Scripture as transmitted through liturgy, preaching, catechesis, personal reading and the general culture; and it is sustained by communal bonds which are sociological and ethnic as well as specifically ecclesial. If this were not so, no church could survive the *furor theologicum*.

Yet there is no room for complacency. To return to our starting point, the sources of nourishment and support just mentioned are growing weaker. Even the Roman Catholic scriptural renewal anticipated as a result of the liturgical reforms of Vatican II and its emphasis on preaching and Bible study seems moribund on the popular level. My experience is that the Roman Catholic undergraduates who take religion courses in the university at which I teach are now less scripturally literate than 20 odd years ago when they had been drilled on pre-Vatican II catechisms. The Bible is increasingly a closed book even for those Protestants and Catholics who make an effort to know it better. To the degree that instruction is guided by historical criticism, as it is for most educated laity, the lesson is that interpretation is a technical enterprise which requires prolonged specialized training. If their biblical interests survive this discouragement, educated lay people (indeed, the clergy also) turn by preference to popularized commentaries by those presumed competent to read the text, the professional exegetes and theologians. In those circles where the text itself is widely and assiduously studied – conservative Protestant, charismatic, base communities and groups interested in spirituality – the reading is often so remote from the classic hermeneutics, so divisive and/or individualistic, that the kind of historical reconstructions which stay within the Christian mainstream seem preferable. It is now the scholarly rather than the hierarchical clerical elite which holds the Bible captive and makes it inaccessible to ordinary folk. The original forgers of its scholarly chains, ironically, were mostly Protestants, but now keeping it fettered is an interconfessional enterprise (though, again ironically, the Reformers would perhaps be less displeased with the Roman Catholic participants: their reconstructions of the message are probably on the whole closer to the *regula fidei* the Reformers treasured than are the Protestant ones). The *sensus fidelium* survives, but with difficulty, and the conflict of interpretations compounds the problem.

A third factor must be added, however. Churches can survive conflicts of interpretation and the weakening of communal bonds with relative ease as long as there is a continued demand for their services (though they may have to alter the services they offer), and providing they can avoid basic structural transformations. The ecclesiastical establishments of England and the Scandinavian and, to a lesser extent, some American Protestant denominations have until recently well illustrated this principle. Ours, however, is a watershed age in which the principle no longer holds for any communion. Tradition, even where it is strongest, in Eastern Orthodoxy, can no longer simply be reiterated. Roman Catholicism has already begun major restructuring at Vatican II, and the historic Protestant patterns no longer suffice. Constantinian Christendom seems to be definitively ending, and reshapings of ecclesial thought and practice greater than those of the Reformation and comparable, perhaps, to the 4th century may well be unavoidable. In the face of such challenges, the paralysis created by the conflict of interpretations and the enfeeblement of the *sensus fidelium* is traumatic. Unless there is some measure of consensus on how to change and what to retain, community and communal authority are immobilized.

This places the interpretation of Scripture at the center of the crisis because communal authority, in the Christian sphere, depends on consonance with the Bible. There is agreement on this among all the major traditions despite their differences on the interrelations of Bible, tradition and magisterium. The primacy of Scripture is fundamental for the patristic tradition the Orthodox follow, the *sola Scriptura* for the Reformers, and, on the Roman Catholic side, the servant role of the magisterium in reference to Scripture was clearly asserted in *Verbum dei* at Vatican II (as was also, though less explicitly, the interpretive rather than independent authority of tradition).[6] Thus if the decisions of a Christian community are perceived as disagreeing with the Bible (or, in matters of major importance, as unsupported by Scripture), they will be regarded as illegitimate. The problem is compounded when not even the leaders are clear on the hermeneutical standards relevant to determining whether teachings and policies are biblical or unbiblical. Then any decision is likely to be viewed as arbitrary, and attempts to enforce it may well be seen as tyrannical.

Providing the *sensus fidelium* is strong, communal authority survives hermeneutical conflict among the teachers of the Church (who de facto in our day, whatever the juridical situation, include the exegetes and theologians). The interpretation best adapted to the instinct of faith will then ultimately triumph even if it is initially a minority one. This, it will be recalled, is why the Athanasians won over the Arians after Nicaea. The converse also holds: if the sense of the faithful is enfeebled but the teachers relatively united, no crisis develops. Those whose religious reflexes are weak or confused are not likely to challenge majority expert opinion on what is authentically Christian (or Roman Catholic, or Lutheran, etc.) even if personally they would like it to be otherwise. It is the combination of the two problems – conflict of interpretation and a feeble sense of the faith – which dissolves the legitimacy of authority in times of major change.

Democracy does not rescue legitimacy in such a situation. In the absence of perceived scriptural backing (and this is what the conflict of interpretations makes impossible), the votes and policies of conventions of elected representatives seem to Protestants no less arbitrary than the dictates of Rome. Indeed, Rome may have an advantage: it regularly consults exegetes and theologians (even if a narrow sample) more seriously than do Protestant denominations; and when its bishops meet in council, they deliberate for months at a time over a period of years in order to reach their own conclusions rather than assemble for a week to rubber stamp (or, very rarely, reject) staff prepared documents. Bureaucratic control (the Protestant equivalent of curial domination) is not constitutionally mandated in any church and is therefore experienced as illegitimate. Improving the staff (which is often well qualified already) does not help, for the fault is systemic and ultimately hermeneutical: there is little effort to relate what the churches officially do to what on paper are their supremely authoritative documents, the Bible and the confessions of faith which, as 'a pure interpretation' of Scripture, are supposed to provide guidelines for biblical interpretation.

Thus the situation, to use a secular comparison, is similar to what would exist if Americans were to ignore their constitution. Nationwide discussions of constitutional hermeneutics were occasioned this past year by the nomination of Judge Bork to the Supreme Court, but comparably serious popular debates over biblical and confessional interpretation in mainline Protestantism, not least Lutheranism, seem inconceivable. Such issues are assiduously avoided because of their divisiveness, but with the result that ecclesiastical authority is delegitimatized just as a civil authority is when it disregards its constitutional basis.

This secular comparison suggests a further point: the problem of authority is in part a matter of playing by the rules of the game, and is to this extent independent of the intrinsic value of the rules. One does not need to accord divine status to constitutions or rule books in order to be outraged when they are ignored by those who are supposed to act in accordance with them. The present difficulty is deeper than willful disregard. Because the official rules are uninterpretable, the game is changed in mid-course and principles such as majority rule (which is really that of the articulate minority) are arbitrarily introduced. It is perhaps childish to be outraged; adult members, unless they are church employees or belong to special interest groups, lose interest and confine their attention to the local church. Denominational loyalty, as the statistics on transfers of membership indicate, has largely disappeared, and what the official churches do even in regard to ecumenical church-to-church relations is of less and less concern. In short, as long as there is no underlying agreement on how Scripture is to be interpreted, democracy does not contribute to institutional legitimacy in Protestantism.

Yet there are ways in which the crisis of authority is graver in organizationally non-democratic churches. In their case, the appearance of illegitimacy (whether it is only apparent or also real is another question) creates special problems. This is so because the official leaders count for more, and more depends on them, and their actual power is greater.

Because they count for more, they are held accountable. Protestant leaders are partly shielded from blame by the (unbiblical and anti-Reformation) supposition that their role is to enact majority opinion, but in the Roman Catholic Church this is not possible. The authorities are held responsible by both right and left for whatever are perceived as constitutional deviations: departing from tradition, not following the progressive spirit of Vatican II, disregarding gospel imperatives, etc. Their loss of legitimacy is more serious than in Protestantism because more depends on them: when their directives are disregarded, the chaos is greater than in communions where long experience of weak leadership has produced habits of local responsibility and/or laissez-faire tolerance (Anglican civility is a prime example).

Lastly, their power to speak and to act forcefully creates special dangers. Efforts to restore order by action from above are seen as tyrannical (in the Protestant case, in the rare instances they occur – e.g. very recently, in a Lutheran imbroglio in Pittsburgh – they look like comically non-authoritative managerial bungling). Bishops' statements and papal encyclicals alike are attacked with unprecedented vigor by those who disagree. Thus the more loudly authorities speak through episcopal conferences or Vatican utterances, the less they are listened to. Reasserting hierarchical power in the absence of a legitimating consensus among experts and the faithful is counterproductive, as the exemplary instance of *Unum sanctum* indicates (it was shortly after its promulgation that Philip le Bel had Boniface VIII arrested). It may conceivably lead to institutional paralysis such as existed at the end of the Middle Ages (though this time schism between rival claimants to the papal throne is not part of the danger).

Thus for both Catholics and Protestants, though in different ways, the institutional viability of the churches, especially in this age of transition, seems to depend on the recovery of a consensus-and-community-building hermeneutics. It is to some remarks on this possibility that we shall now turn.

Retrieval

In a contribution to a recent Festschrift for Professor Frei, Ronald Thiemann, Dean of Harvard Divinity School, speaks of the biblical stories as 'followable', as constituting a 'followable' world.[7] This is a convenient tag for what Scripture becomes when the classic hermeneutics is employed. The question in this section is the extent to which the Bible can again become followable, not only for individuals (it has never ceased to be that), but also for communities, and in ways which are unitive rather than divisive. I shall suggest, first, that the postmodern situation is favorable, and second, that there are some beginnings in biblical scholarship and theology. I shall then comment on the ways in which the *sensus fidelium* might be affected.

With the loss of Enlightenment confidence in reason and progress, the worlds within which human beings live are increasingly thought of as socially, linguistically and even textually constructed. Sociology, anthropology, history, philosophy and literary studies have all contributed to this development. We are aware as never before of the degree to which human beings and their perceptions of reality are socially and culturally determined. Nothing is exempt from this conditioning, not even the natural sciences. Within our own lifetime, historians of science such as TS Kuhn and philosophers such as Wittgenstein, Quine and Rorty (to mention examples only from the anglophone sphere) have undermined the 19th-century distinction between *Natur-u.-Geisteswissenschaften*. Physics and poetry are not differentiated ontologically or epistemologically: it is not that they refer to distinct types of reality or arise from distinct ways of knowing which makes them different. Rather they are seen as products of social practices which, though diverse in structure and purpose, have overlapping features. This explains the remark I made in the discussion that one hears rigorous scholars say, as if it were a commonplace, that the epistemological grounding of quarks and Homeric gods is basically the same. It is rhetorical force rooted in communal practice which gives them their cognitive status, and when rhetoric and practice change, so does that status. Homeric gods were real and quarks non-existent for ancient Greeks; their status is reversed for us, and there are no definitively formulatable context-free criteria for determining who is right and who is wrong (though there may be unformulated implicit ones).[8]

The recent literary emphasis on textuality becomes understandable against this background. Texts, understood as fixed communicative patterns embedded in rites, myths and other oral and representational traditions, are already basic in preliterate societies. They can be used in different contexts, for different purposes, and with different meanings, and thereby provide frameworks in which individual utterances ('speech acts') are socially significant and effective. This power is enhanced when they take written form, for they can then have a comprehensiveness, complexity and stability which is unattainable in other media (not even modern electronic and cinematographic ones). In short, texts project worlds in which entire cultures can and have lived.[9]

Furthermore, without such texts, it is difficult, perhaps impossible, for large-scale communities of discourse to develop. Sinic civilization as it spread from China into Korea, Japan and Vietnam depended on the Confucian corpus; the various types of Buddhism on interlocking Buddhist canons; and Judaism, Christianity and Islam, needless to say, on their respective sacred scriptures. Without a central core of privileged and familiar texts, social cohesion becomes more difficult to sustain and depends more on bureaucratic management, the manipulation of public opinion, and ultimately, perhaps, totalitarian force. Reason in the form of science or philosophy is too restricted in scope (it neglects imagination, for example), and too contradictory and changing in its pictures of the cosmic setting of human life to provide a satisfactory substitute. What is needed are texts projecting imaginatively and practically habitable worlds.

A habitable text need not have a primarily narrative structure (with the exception of the Bible, none of the canons earlier mentioned do), but it must in some fashion be construable as a guide to thought and action in the encounter with changing circumstances. It must supply followable directions for coherent patterns of life in new situations. If it does this, it can be considered rational to dwell within it: no other foundations are necessary or, in the contemporary climate of opinion, possible.

Much contemporary intellectual life can be understood as a search for such texts. Contemporary Marxists and Freudians, for example, now rarely seek to ground their favorite authors' writings scientifically or philosophically. They simply ask that they be followable, that they be construable in such a way as to provide guidance for society, in the one case, and for individual life, in the other. Thus it is that Enlightenment systems which once claimed rational foundations have now turned into foundationless hermeneutical enterprises.

Classic biblical hermeneutics was born in a similar foundationless era when followable texts were in short supply. The Jews had a great advantage: not only did the monotheistic character of their sacred book give it universal scope and unity, and not only did the long history and diversity of the writings it contained give it extraordinarily wide applicability in varying circumstances, but it had directive force and community-building power far superior to the philosophical systems which were its only real rivals. Once Scripture was made applicable to non-Jews by the Christian movement, it proved widely appealing. It was a pre-eminently habitable text in a world needing habitations, and the nations flocked into it.

Ours is again an age when old foundations and legitimating structures have crumbled. Even the defenders of reason think it unreasonable to ask anything more than that they be followable of philosophies and religions or of the texts which give them richness, comprehensiveness and stability. There are fewer and fewer intellectual objections to the legitimacy or possibility of treating a classic, whether religious or non-religious, as a perspicuous guide to life and thought. The only question is whether one is interested and can make it work.

There are, in the second place, some developments which suggest that it can be made to work. Biblical scholars are increasingly interested in the literary features, social and communal functioning and canonical unity of the scriptural text. It is, however, for others better qualified than I to comment on these beginnings. Instead, I shall simply mention the names of Karl Barth and Hans Urs von Balthasar. Here are 20th-century theologians whose use of the Bible is more nearly classical than anything in several centuries and who yet are distinctively modern (e.g. they do not reject historical criticism). Both are wary of translating the Bible into alien conceptualities;

both seek, rather, to redescribe the world or worlds in which they live in biblical terms;[10] both treat Scripture as a narrationally (or, for von Balthasar, 'dramatically') and typologically unified whole; and in both the reader is referred back to the biblical text itself by exegetical work which is an integral part of the theological program. In short, these two theologians inhabit the same universe of theological discourse as the fathers, medievals and Reformers to a greater degree than do most modern theologians. Discussions between them are possible – perhaps even decidable – by reference to the text because they approach Scripture in basically similar ways; whereas in the case of most other theologians, major differences arise from the extrabiblical conceptualities (idealist, Marxist, etc.) by means of which they interpret Scripture and are therefore undecidable: sometimes there is not even a common language in which they can be discussed.

Yet their approaches to Scripture have not been widely adopted. Even Barth's followers (I do not know about von Balthasar's) are for the most part influenced by his theology, not his exegesis. This is understandable, for his exegesis is at times deeply flawed (even if corrigible).[11] What we have in these two authors is only a first, even if important, stage in the work of making the Bible followable in our day, of making it readable classically, and yet not anticritically. The analogous task in the Greco-Roman world took hundreds of years, and although it reached a kind of climax in Augustine and the Cappadocians, it could never, given the mutability of that and every world, be definitively completed. We are perhaps at the beginnings of retrieval in theology and biblical scholarship, but no more than that.

The third and most difficult question, however, is whether the Bible read classically but not anticritically can come to inform the *sensus fidelium*. The condition for this happening is that communities of interpretation come into existence in which pastors, biblical scholars, theologians and laity together seek God's guidance in the written word for their communal as well as individual lives. Their reading of Scripture will be within the context of a worship life which, in its basic eucharistic, baptismal and kerygmatic patterns, accords with that of the first centuries. They may differ in their views of the *de iure divino* status of the threefold pattern of ministry and of the papal institutionalization of the Petrine function, but not on the legitimacy of these forms of ministry as servants of word, sacrament and unity, nor on the fundamental character of the ministerial office as divinely instituted to feed and lead God's flock. There will be in these communities a renewed sense that Christians constitute a single people chosen to witness among the nations in all they are, say, and do to the salvation that was, that is, and that is to come, and guided by God in his mercy and judgment and in their faithfulness and unfaithfulness, toward the promised consummation. They will care for their own members and will also be deeply concerned about Christians everywhere. Openness to receive and responsibility to give help and correction from and to other churches will be embedded in their institutional and organizational fabrics.

This is a dream, a cloud no larger than a hand on the horizon, and yet if it began to be actualized, even if in only a few and scattered places, it would be living proof that Scripture is a unifying and followable text. The news would travel quickly (it always does in our day), and its influence would mushroom. Public opinion might be widely affected, perhaps even quickly, in all communions, and the transformation of the *sensus fidelium* (which takes longer) might follow in due course.

Not all the problems of how to reshape the Church in this age of transition would be solved by such a development. Christians will continue to differ, not only on political questions of peace and justice and of socialism and capitalism but also on matters of direct ecclesial import such as the ordination of women. Is the tradition against women's ordination basically cultural and thus similar to the Church's long accommodation to slavery? Retrieval of the classic hermeneutics even in combination with historical criticism does not decide this issue. Yet it changes the context of the debate. Attention focuses, not on entitlements, privileges and gender, but on the pastoral office itself as God's instrument for the nurturing of his people with word and sacrament. What builds up the Church is what counts. Sociologically and historically speaking, it is ultimately the *sensus fidelium* which decides in such matters in any case but to the degree the instinct of the faithful (their connatural knowledge, as Aquinas would say) is scripturally shaped, it not only does but *should* decide.

There is much in the more theologically oriented ecumenical discussions which points in the direction of these remarks. The life of worship and ministry which is the necessary (not sufficient) context for unifying communal Bible interpretation is basically that described in the Faith and Order Lima document, *Baptism, Eucharist and Ministry*. Similarly, to cite just one other item, the most recent report of the Lutheran/Roman Catholic International Study Commission, *Facing Unity*, marks the beginnings of cooperative thinking on how interconfessional communities of interpretation (though it does not call them that) might develop which would contribute to the reshaping and renewal rather than disruption of present church orders.

Yet it must be admitted that, even more than Church unity, the hope for the actualization of the consensus-and-community-building potential of the classic pattern of biblical interpretation in a postmodern setting seems impossibly visionary. It is not even being talked about, much less put into practice. Those circles in which serious Bible reading is most widespread –

conservative Protestant, charismatic, Cursillo, base communities – are often fundamentalist and almost always precritical in their hermeneutics. They also need to recover the classic pattern.

On the other hand, there is no reason for discouragement. Scripture permits and perhaps urges us to dream dreams and see visions. Barriers have been erased, retrieval has begun, and we can begin to imagine far more than was possible a mere generation ago that Roman Catholics, Eastern Orthodox and heirs of the Reformation will learn to read the Bible together as the Christ-centered guide for themselves and their communities. God's guidance of world and church history has sown the seeds for the rebirth of the written word, and it is for believers to pray, work and hope against hope that God will bring these seeds to fruition through the power of the Holy Spirit.[12]

14. The Gospel's Uniqueness: Election and Untranslatability*

Editor's Introduction

The formidable title of this essay brings together three of Lindbeck's deepest concerns: the unique gospel, the election of the Jewish people and philosophical puzzles about what is and is not 'translatable'. No one of these concerns is new. (See, for example, the concern with 'translation' in 'Scripture, Consensus and Community' in Chapter Thirteen.) But they are brought together here in ways that combine practical theological concern and the technicalities of semiotics (the study of signs). Reading this essay requires discerning the connection between Lindbeck's practical theological point and the 'untranslatability'.

One way to do this is to notice that the central theological point is that the Church 'is called to serve other religions for the sake of the neighbor, for the sake of humanity, for the sake of God's promise to Abraham that through his seed all nations will be blessed' – a theology of service that extends back to the earliest essay in this volume (Chapter Six). But, if the gospel's uniqueness is this practice of 'servanthood', why does Lindbeck take the reader on what he calls an 'idiosyncratic' journey through Israel's election and untranslatability to arrive at this point? There are at least three reasons readers need to keep in mind in order to follow this essay from its claims about untranslatability through Israel's election to the gospel's unique servanthood.

First, Lindbeck presumes readers who know that we live in a world plagued by the combativeness and violence of competing, comprehensive ways of life and thought: 'Comprehensive' here means two things. A comprehensive way of life and thought (a) embraces all life and thought

* George A Lindbeck, 'The Gospel's Uniqueness: Election and Untranslatability', *Modern Theology* **13** (1997), pp. 423–50.

and signs (which are studied by the 'semiotics' Lindbeck mentions) (b) while being itself unembraceable. For example, Christians are called (b) to be disciples of Christ not simply at one or two times and places of their lives but throughout those lives (comprehensively) and (b) to follow no false gods, christs or competing ways of life and thought. Lindbeck's description here of 'classic hermeneutics' (roughly, as we saw in Chapter Thirteen, the traditional practices it takes to interpret Scripture) is a description of the way Christian life and thought is thus doubly comprehensive.

However, at this stage of his argument Lindbeck is trying to offer what he calls a 'formal' definition of untranslatability. Although the example I just gave was of Christian life and thought, the two components of comprehensiveness apply to many other ways of life and thought – Jewish and Muslim, Marxist and American. Generalizing this formal description, we could also say that a 'comprehensive' way of life and thought is one that (a) 'translates' every conceivable human reality (b) while being 'untranslatable' into any other conceivable human reality. This 'double claim of comprehensiveness' – (a) and (b) – is what Lindbeck means by 'untranslatability' in the title of this essay. (Note that he means something quite different by 'translation' from the English to the Chinese language.) There are many contenders for untranslatability, although by definition only one can ultimately be successful.

Second, given this understanding of untranslatability, Lindbeck argues that existing Christian strategies for negotiating 'the untranslatable' (concern about the salvation of other religions and dialogue) have yielded decreasing returns. For example, traditional Christian concern about the salvation of non-Christians at its best (see Chapter Six), important as it is for Christian missionary activity, presumes salvation by Christ and asks *how* this can be. But salvation by Christ is precisely the point disputed by other contenders for untranslatability. The more liberal strategy of 'dialogue', even and particularly at its best, does not help comprehensive ways of life and thought deal with precisely those points in which they find themselves untranslatable in relation to each other.

But there is a third reason Lindbeck takes the indirect, idiosyncratic route to theological servanthood, and it has to do with what Lindbeck calls more 'material' concerns. The Church called to such servanthood by the unique and untranslatable gospel is marred by 'supersessionism' with regard to the election of Israel. 'Supersessionism' is differently defined nowadays, and there are clearly different kinds of it. But in this essay 'supersessionism' means the presumption or claim that Christianity *replaces* the Jewish people as God's elect people. Lindbeck argues that the Church does not 'replace' Israel but 'extends' Israel from a Jewish community to a community of Jews and Gentiles.

These three reasons form the background for Lindbeck's constructive thesis. He argues that the Church extends rather than replaces (a) God's gratuitous and irrevocable choice of Israel, (b) Israel's witness to the world of redemption and (c) our doxological response of love of God for God's own sake. Readers should keep their eyes out for how, in each of these cases, Lindbeck shows how Israel can contribute to a renewed Christian theology of servanthood – for example by combining loyalty to the Church and self-criticism, exclusivity and humility. He concludes with some suggestions on how Christians can extend this to the nations, praying for our contemporary Babylons. And he promises to return to the issues of servanthood and violence in part two, which is not yet published.

This essay is an enlarged version of the first of two lectures on 'The Uniqueness of the Gospel in the Context of Religious Pluralism'.[1] Instead of limiting myself to cultural-linguistic preliminaries, as I have in previous treatments of interreligious relations, I here go beyond prolegomena to an attempt at theological construction.[2] The excuse for doing so is that not much theological attention has been given to religions as community-forming semiotic systems nor, related to this, to their uniqueness as formally untranslatable and as materially consisting of the unsubstitutable memories and narratives which shape community identities. More specifically, it has thus been little stressed in modern times that the story of Israel as the uniquely Chosen People functioned in the premodern anti-Marcionite ecclesial mainstream as an integral part of the gospel. Jesus' uniqueness was inseparable from that of Israel's Messiah, and Christians thought of themselves as the continuation of the elect community and were deeply influenced both positively and negatively in their relation to non-biblical religions by the Old Testament's communal memories and narratives. Whether and how Israel as type and example can or should similarly guide Christians in the contemporary context is the topic of both this and the second paper which originally accompanied it.

This first paper deals with 'whether' and the second paper with 'how' this guidance remains a possibility. The 'whether' depends, I shall suggest, on retrieving the classic Christian hermeneutics for which, despite its supersessionism, Israel's story was ingredient in the gospel. Only if this precritical interpretation of Scripture can be postcritically appropriated in a non-supersessionist form will it be useful in contemporary pluralistic settings.

The second and unpublished paper turns, then, to how Israel's example might be helpful, and takes the risk of proposing servanthood as a currently useful model for Christian interreligious relations. The Church is called to serve other religions for the sake of the neighbor, for the sake of humanity, for the sake of God's promise to Abraham that through his seed all nations will be blessed.

The outrageous inferences which can be drawn from this conclusion perhaps need to be blocked now at the outset. It is not Muslims, Hindus, Buddhists and, most emphatically of all, not Jews who are in this perspective called to servanthood. Christians got the idea of a servant people from the Jews *via* Jesus, but that forbids rather than authorizes them to apply it to others rather than only to their own communities. Nor is the serving role everywhere and always the primary one for the Church in reference to other religions. It could be complicity in genocide to propose it in our time, for example to southern Sudanese Christians. Not that God might not be calling them – not to mention their north Sudanese Muslim persecutors – to serve through suffering, but that is for them to decide. This particular summons to service as a communal vocation is aimed at the historically mainline churches, the ecclesial bearers of the great tradition. It assumes, as we shall see, a particular way of viewing the contemporary situation which makes their help to other religions in the mode of servanthood important in promoting the common good. That, at any rate, is the argument of the second paper.

In this first lecture, I begin with some reasons for the idiosyncratic approach I have adopted, and then deal with semiotic comprehensiveness as the source of the formal uniqueness understood as untranslatability which is common to all world religions, with the hermeneutical strategies which differentiate and intensify this common uniqueness, with the nature and possible retrieval of Israel's exemplary role, and with the material uniqueness of Israel and the Church as God's elect or chosen people(s).

Why Idiosyncrasy?

One abnormality of this approach is that it brackets the animating interests of most discussions of interreligious topics. Dialogue between religions, for example, is neglected even when proposing strategies for dealing with pluralism in the second lecture. The fundamental break with convention, however, is the by-passing of soteriological concerns. There is nothing in what follows about the salvation of individuals, i.e. nothing about whether Socrates, Confucius or, for that matter, Adolf Hitler get to heaven. One could be a universalist like Origen, an anti-universalist like Jonathan Edwards or a quasi-universalist like Barth, von Balthasar or Rahner, and either agree or disagree with much of the argument in these papers. Not that individuals and their salvation are unimportant. It is simply that the uniqueness of the gospel in relation to pluralism as we shall discuss it concerns the untranslatability of the message and the uniqueness of the elect community, not individual salvation.

Similarly we shall say little about the closely related though not identical issue of religions as bearers of salvation. The currently most common taxonomy for classifying views on this problem, you recall, is the tripartite division into exclusivist, inclusivist and pluralist positions.[3] Exclusivists affirm the soteriological uniqueness of some one religion by denying saving efficacy to all others, while inclusivists also affirm uniqueness but in a weaker sense by granting the presence of saving grace in other religions but limiting its fullness to only one. Pluralists deny soteriological uniqueness completely because there is for them no one religion which is ascertainably superior in salvific power to all others. Once again, however, there is no logically compelling connection – though there may be variable, non-logical elective affinities – between uniqueness understood soteriologically and as untranslatability. Some exclusivists will agree and some disagree with the theses I shall propose, and the same holds, though with modifications, for inclusivists and pluralists. Soteriology is not excluded by the approach we are pursuing, but it is also not necessarily included.

This bracketing of the normal concerns has practical advantages. There are reasons for thinking that the context which favored soteriological and dialogical foci in discussions of interreligious relations is disappearing. That context is the aftermath of the age of western hegemony, an aftermath which is not yet truly postcolonial but is instead neocolonial. In this period, the West continues to set the agenda by the reactions it provokes even if not by its intentions or direct influence. The fixation on salvation, it appears, is a religious instance of this reactive tendency. Concern for saving souls in anything like the usual Christian sense is not found or is not central in most or perhaps all non-Christian or non-biblical religions,[4] yet these have been forced to take it seriously in opposition to the intentional or unintentional proselytizing associated with western missionary expansion.

This non-Christian anxiety in combination with Christian feelings of guilt, so it can be argued, supply the underlying motivation for dialogue. The conversation had been fueled by hope that the understandings of salvation which legitimate proselytism will be replaced by benign ones compatible with amicable relations between religions.[5] This is an agenda which is of interest to non-Christians to the extent they felt threatened by Christianity, but not otherwise.

If so, the dialogue becomes very different when the concerns of non-Christian religions are no longer skewed by Christian hegemony. These religions will then shape the agenda not reactively but actively in terms of their own native interests. They have for the most part not conceived their mission as universalistically as Christians, and even if they have, as in the case of Islam, salvation in the Christian sense is not the issue. In the absence of any single unifying theme such as salvation, multi-lateral interreligious discourse is likely to wane in favor of bilateral varieties. In summary, the current major options in regard to uniqueness whether pluralist, inclusivist or exclusivist are irrelevant to the actual relations of religions except in situations where fear and guilt regarding Christian proselytism are salient. That is a contextual reason for attempting a different, non-soteriological approach.

Other reasons have to do with the exhaustion of the research program and with the anomalies it has developed. The soteriological lode has been thoroughly mined, and only low-grade ore remains. The options earlier mentioned have all been well worked out and over. First, pluralism such as John Hick's holds that Jesus is the sole Savior for Christians no more and no less than is Buddha, Moses or Mohammed for the adherents of each respective religion. Each may be experientially or subjectively the unique mediator of transcendence for some believers (which description, not surprisingly, is christologically biased despite attempts to make it religiously neutral and universally usable).[6] Second, inclusivists such as Rahner straddle the fence (at least from non-Christian perspectives) by holding that the *gratia Christi* is savingly at work in other religions unbeknownst to their adherents.[7] The third and exclusivist family of positions covers a wide range. On one extreme are those who hold that non-biblical religions may be humanly admirable, capable of teaching much of value to Christians, instrumental in carrying out God's purposes, and yet not saving. They say, to give a Barthian gloss to this position, that those who never become gospel believers may nevertheless enter the life of the world to come *solo Christo* in ways which have no intrinsic relationship to either religiousness or non-religiousness. It is God who decides who will belong to his elect communities of public witness, and proselytism is beside the point. At the opposite side of the exclusivist option are unreconstructed proselytizers for whom snatching heathen souls from the burning is the all-absorbing goal of relations to non-Christians (as well as to most Christians). This last group, needless to say, does not participate in the dialogue. The result is an unresolved anomaly. Those whose misdeeds the dialogue is intended to correct are the ones with whom the dialoguers are least in communication. The soteriological approach has done much to combat proselytism, quiet fears and assuage guilt feelings, but the harvest is over, the situation has changed, and internal contradictions are developing. New directions are needed.

The direction represented by starting with uniqueness as a question of translation, not salvation, has the advantage of adaptability to postcolonial pluralism and, related to this, of concerning itself with each religion on its own terms. The impoverished abstractions of a purportedly universal though residually Christian idiom are replaced by the rich particularities of native tongues. The contrast is not altogether dissimilar to that between general linguistics and comparative literature.

As this similitude suggests, however, not all the advantages are on one side. The gravest objection to the approach we are adopting is that it makes interreligious dialogue more difficult. Conversation between religions is pluralized or balkanized when they are seen as mutually untranslatable. Not only do they no longer share a common theme such as salvation, but the shared universe of discourse forged to discuss that theme disintegrates. There are ways of getting around this obstacle such as bilingualism (to borrow a suggestion from Alasdair MacIntyre to which we shall return), but genuine bilingualism (not to mention mastery of many religious languages) is so rare and difficult as to leave basically intact the barrier to extramural communication posed by untranslatability in religious matters. Those for whom conversation is the key to solving interreligious problems are likely to be disappointed.

Intramural discourse on interreligious problems could, in contrast, flourish. Clarity grows and honesty increases when each religion considers its relation to others in terms of its emic categories, its native tongue, instead of contorting and distorting its heritage to fit the constraints of a purportedly universalizable etic idiom of salvation. Yet on the other side of the ledger, what is good by internal standards is not necessarily so by external ones. Renewing the grammatical and rhetorical riches pruned away in deference to alien sensibilities increases the power of the message for linguistic insiders, but if there are outsiders for whom the message is evil, the gospel of Satan not God, such improvement spells disaster. Whether the greater intrareligious authenticity, faithfulness and honesty made possible by seeing uniqueness as untranslatability compensates for the increased potential for interreligious combativeness and violence is a central concern of the second lecture.

In the meantime, we need to remember that contexts are not under our control and we may have to make the best of a bad situation. As current East Asian challenges to the discourse of the international human rights illustrate, the universal languages (or 'Esperantos' as some have called them) in which Enlightenment modernity seeks to deal with the common problems of the global village are not likely long to survive the western cultural hegemony under which they developed. Whatever our theory, the problems posed by barriers to translation may come in practice to dominate interreligious relations. This is the practical case for risking idiosyncrasy; as pluralism increases, what is now marginal may shortly become central.

Yet the timeliness of an approach is not by itself sufficient reason for adopting it. What one day looks like the wave of the future may on the next prove to be a receding tide as the *deutsche Christen* tragically exemplify. Thus even if postmodern pluralism is on its way to global triumph, this does not justify abandoning the Enlightenment search for a common concern, whether salvation or something else, to facilitate interreligious communication. Better arguments than relevance to current trends are needed to warrant the risk of increased balkanization. Before proceeding with these better arguments, however, a word about their general character is in order.

They are internal rather than external to religious traditions; without them, some religions would unravel. In the historic Christian mainstream, the strongest of these internal considerations have been biblical. The Bible, to be sure, says nothing explicitly about whether its message or that of any other religion can be translated. Implicit answers to this question are embedded, however, in classic interpretive practices. These practices, in the first place, involve the claim that the biblical message or gospel[8] when rightly used constitutes a discourse disclosing the meaning of everything humanly conceivable with unique and thus necessarily untranslatable depth and fullness. Other religions or non-religions may claim similar comprehensiveness entailing, whether or not this is recognized, similar untranslatability, but it is logically impossible for more than one of these claims to be true, and it is possible that none are. Christians hope and trust, needless to say, that it is the biblical claim which holds.

Second, the particular localized constellations of interpretive strategies characteristic of different religions (and of traditions within religions) when dealing with their scriptures may also be unlike any others. In contrast to the hermeneutical uniqueness implied by comprehensiveness, however, this text-specific variety is contingent. Biblical and non-biblical religions construe their respective scriptures in formally similar as well as dissimilar ways, but though the particular mix is likely to be different in each case, this uniqueness seems to be the product of historical accident rather than structural necessity. Yet this does not diminish its importance for our purposes. Despite its regional and contingent character, the classic Christian hermeneutics supplies the indispensable forms articulating Israel's material uniqueness as example for the Church in a religiously pluralistic world. We shall now turn to these topics: comprehensiveness (entailing uniqueness and untranslatability), classic hermeneutics and Israel's example.

The All-interpreting as Uninterpretable

Three preliminary comments are in order. First, in reference to philosophical issues, I shall assume that the kinds of untranslatability of which we shall shortly see examples are not ruled out by Donald Davidson's now classic argument[9] to the effect that the very notion of incommensurable or untranslatable conceptual frameworks or languages is incoherent because, as he points out, some common measure or idiom, some ability to translate, is necessary in order to recognize instances of untranslatability or incommensurability. My use of the term does not refer to the strong sense of untranslatability Davidson has in mind, but to what Charles Peirce would perhaps call a 'vague' sign determinable only by its context and use. Alasdair MacIntyre has suggested[10] that what is untranslatable in a language or tradition of inquiry is recognizable even without a common communicative system to the degree interpreters acquire competence in the alien tongue. Those for whom that tongue is 'a second first language' can recognize and flag what is untranslatable in it without falling into the contradiction of supposing (or allowing others to suppose) that they have thereby provided a translation. This seems to me a satisfactory end-run around Davidson's problem, but even if it is not, there may be other ways of meeting the difficulty.

A second introductory remark is that it is conceptual or categorical translation that we shall be speaking of, not translation from the original Greek or Hebrew of the Bible into other natural languages. One of the major differences between Judaism and Christianity, on the one hand, and Islam, on the other, is that linguistic translations have been important for adherents of the two biblical religions ever since the Septuagint, whereas the Koran in Arabic is mandatory for religiously serious Muslims. In Islam, in other words, translation is doubly impossible, whereas we are assuming that natural languages have the grammatical flexibility and lexical potential to develop into adequate vehicles for biblical meanings, and are asking whether the conceptual and categorical idioms associated with non-biblical comprehensive outlooks have similar capacities.

The third remark is that this is not an empirical but rather a dogmatic issue. Scholarly research can never settle the question of whether there are non-biblical languages which can adequately accommodate all that can be said in the biblical one or vice versa. Claims about these matters are embedded in the practices and may be articulated in the formal doctrines of religious communities, but these claims have for the purposes of research the character of hypotheses which can be empirically more or less plausible, but can never be decisively refuted or confirmed until the eschaton.

In the hope that examples will be clearer than abstractions, let us look at the double claim which entails untranslatability as this occurs in the biblical case. It is classically affirmed, first, that every humanly conceivable reality can be translated (or redescribed) in the biblical universe of discourse with a gain rather than a loss of truth or significance whereas, second, nothing can be translated out of this idiom into some supposedly independent communicative system without perversion, diminution or incoherence of meaning. Calvin spoke of seeing the world fully and clearly only when looking through the spectacles of Scripture, and Aquinas affirms that all entities and truths of whatever nature are *revelabilia*, that is, capable of entering into the sphere of revelation, of being seen in relation to God as known in and through the scriptural witness. Karl Barth makes very much the same claim (though in a conceptuality which seems to me less adequate) regarding the all-inclusive or all-absorbing character of 'The Strange New World' of the Bible.[11] In short, the Bible as interpreted within the Christian mainstream purports to provide a totally comprehensive framework, a universal perspective, within which everything can be properly construed and outside of which nothing can be equally well understood. This double claim of comprehensiveness constitutes the general form of untranslatability.

An over-simple analogy or two may be helpful. Any number can be translated from the Roman into the Arabic system of numeral signs without loss and, in a sense, with gain of meaning because of increased economy of form, and efficiency and multiplicity of uses. Conversely, however, there is one notion which is fundamental to the Arabic system which cannot be translated into the Latin one, viz. zero. There is no sign for zero in Roman numerals. Because of this additional sign, any school child in our day is capable of arithmetical calculations, that is, can make numbers mean and do things, which were beyond the capacity of even the greatest classical mathematicians. In this illustration, the biblical analogues to the powerful zero would, I suppose, be the Tetragrammation and the Trinity signifying the God whose identity is unknown except through his scripturally witnessed dealings with the world. It is this sign which makes the Bible in some of its interpretations fund a universe of discourse embracing others without itself being embraced.

A very different set of contrasts between more and less comprehensive idioms is suggested by comparing literary and botanical interpretations of, let us say, William Blake's poem 'O rose, thou art sick!/The invisible worm,/ That flies in the night,/In the howling storm,/Has found out thy bed/Of crimson joy;/And his dark secret love/Does thy life destroy.' The botanist who thinks she has found rose bushes and hitherto unseen and tempest-loving nocturnal insects similar or identical to the ones she supposes Blake was referring to would, we would say, be making a category mistake, and we would be appalled at the way she would butcher the poem in the course of making it, she imagines, more veridical. This is similar, so the theological interpreter could say, to what happens when one translates the Bible into an alien conceptuality. The difference between the two cases is that because all reality is assimilated, is redescribable, in the biblical idiom, there is no third language (comparable, for example, to the ordinary English of this discussion) in which the category mistake can be identified and the errors of translation rectified. Everything is clarified when looked at through biblical lenses (to which, needless to say, ordinary English would be only a very partial analogue), and is distorted without these lenses. This double claim of comprehensiveness, to repeat, is the general form of biblical and ultimately gospel untranslatability.

What, then, of other religions? There can be any number of claimants to the kind of untranslatability implied by comprehensiveness, but the prize winner stands alone. The notion of a truly comprehensive outlook defines a class of, at most, a single member, a form which can be instantiated but once. Thus of all the religious and professedly non-religious *Weltanschauungen* which aspire to embrace without being embraced, only one, if that, can be ultimately successful.

From the perspective of an anti-religious secularism for which human reason is supreme, this analysis makes interreligious relations into a Darwinian free-for-all, a continuation on the sacral level of nature red in tooth and claw; but from the biblical perspective, such secularism is no less idolatrous than the worst of the religions it seeks to relativize for the sake of peace. It narcissistically worships its own notion of reason rather than at the altar of the one true God. No reconciliation is possible between the secular and biblical outlooks thus understood, and to the degree they claim universality, they are, like other religious and philosophical world views, both untranslatable and competitive. A detached observer would say, as Metternich did of France and Austria, that it is not their differences but what they have in common which makes them fight: they both want Tuscany. In emic terms, however, it is the differences which count: rationality against superstition in the one case, and God against idols in the other.

Before getting into such material oppositions between interpretive outlooks, however, more needs to be said about their formal differences. We turn, then, from what they share, their common drive towards hermeneutical hegemony, to the varied means they use in its pursuit.

Classic Hermeneutics

Religions employ a variety of interpretive strategies in their attempts to make originally limited or localized outlooks all-encompassing. In so far as they are formal, these strategies can be used in the service of different religious or non-religious outlooks, but they tend to be put together in hermeneutical schemae or packages which are specific to particular traditions. I shall first sketch the classic biblical hermeneutics before comparing it to those of other aspirants to universality.

The classic biblical hermeneutics as I shall describe it was implicit from the beginning in all mainstream premodern traditions of interpretation. Its main features were articulated already by Irenaeus, but are present in Christian readings of the Old Testament before there was a New Testament, and are in part derivative from the techniques of scriptural interpretation embedded in the Tanakh as these are described by Jewish biblical scholars such as Michael Fishbane.[12] Furthermore, this classic pattern did not disappear with the modern age, even though it did lose scholarly and theological standing and was abandoned by both liberals on the left and fundamentalists on the right. Liturgies retain the pattern, and homiletics continues to be influenced by it. In the United States, if I may judge by the example of some of the students I have had, it remains particularly powerful in black churches.

The principal formal characteristics of this hermeneutics for our purposes are four in number.[13] First, canonical interpretation: a collection of highly diverse literature was read as a single work. Second, interpretation was guided by what can perhaps best be likened to rules of grammar. As in the case of grammar, these rules were embedded in the speech and practices of the community quite apart from conscious knowledge of their existence, but were at times articulated, most extensively by Christians, in church doctrine and theological reflection. (Jews, in contrast, more often explicated the grammar of the faith in halachic and haggadic commentary.) Of special importance for unifying the canon were the grammatical habits of attributing all its writings to a single source (in the biblical case, a divine author or authorizer), a central subject matter (Christ for Christians and the Torah for Jews), and a dominant purpose (the formation and guidance towards the messianic age of covenanted peoples).

A third major feature of this hermeneutics was the place it gave to narrative in its construal of the biblical outlook. The framework consisted of a transhistorical metanarrative stretching from the beginning of time to its end, telling of events and realities remote from ordinary experience (and in that sense, moderns say, partly mythical). This metanarrative supplied the cosmic setting for the realistic narratives in which the central realities, the events decisive for the community, were recounted (viz. the stories of God's dealings with his world through Israel and, for Christians, also and climatically through Jesus). Fourth – and here the difference between classic and modern (including both fundamentalist and historical-critical) interpretations becomes most salient – the narrative structure is enfleshed by figuration (or, to speak with medieval elaborateness, by typology, tropology and anagogy). In such figural interpretation, analogy and metaphor function both to unify and extend the plain sense (i.e. the sense which is obvious to a given community of readers, and which is therefore itself historically variable rather than an unchanging 'literal' meaning ingredient in the text).[14]

In conjunction with the other features we have mentioned, figuration turns the Bible into a cross-referencing, interglossing semiotic system which can be used even now, some would claim, to assimilate by redescription all the worlds and world views which human beings construct in the course of history. Such grammatical features as the four principle ones just enumerated can remain unchanged even while the lexicon expands indefinitely. As in the case of natural languages, the competent speakers of the biblical tongue generate a potentially limitless number of sentences with unprecedented or novel meanings to fit the innumerable and unpredictable contingencies of life in space and time. Inexhaustible semantic novelty is compatible with syntactic continuity.

This classic hermeneutics is not formally unique: analogies to each of the major features we have mentioned can be found in other hermeneutical schemes in which canons function to help construct communities (or cultures, civilizations or, in ideological employment, political states or parties) with cosmic legitimation. Confucianism, Hinduism and Buddhism, for example, as well as the western philosophical tradition, having diversified canons which are read as having some sort of unity deriving from a common source (e.g. philosophical reason or Buddhist enlightenment), subject matter and aim. The framing of every comprehensive outlook, furthermore, is arguably a narrative one even when time is cyclical and the story is that of eternal return. In addition, narratives of a more realistic kind are important in any *Weltanschauung* which seeks to encompass rather than replace the world of ordinary experience. Finally, figuration cannot be escaped when using a particular text to interpret other realities. Much as Jews and Christians read the universe through their scriptural canons, so the Greeks saw themselves through Homeric eyes (sometimes in astonishing detail and with world-transforming import if Robin Lane Fox is to be trusted on Alexander the Great).[15] Similarly, mechanistic materialists of a now defunct kind interpreted all reality through the lens of Newton's physics. In short, to repeat, classic biblical hermeneutics is not formally unique.

Yet, like the other hermeneutical enterprises we have mentioned, it is so shaped by the material with which it deals, the particularities of the texts which for it are sacred, that its similarities to others are superficial. These similarities are family resemblances with little explanatory power. They cannot be developed into a general hermeneutics with regional applications. Indeed, no such general hermeneutics is useful, and the contemporary tendency to move from theories of interpretation to the reading of specific texts, at least religious ones, is misguided. The methods devised to redescribe the Pythagorean theorem as a poem or Blake's verse about a sick rose as a botanical diagnosis must be unprecedented in order to fit the peculiar subject matters. They are underivable from poetic and botanical interpretation in other contexts though the outcomes must be enough like poetry and botany respectively to be classifiable in those rather than some other genre. Similarly, the interpretive procedures which turn the Koran, Pali canon and Confucian classics into sacred texts have little in common except the outcomes. In all three instances, the texts in question have functioned, as we have said, to construct communities (or civilizations, cultures and, in their ideological misuse, political states and parties) with claims to cosmic or comprehensive legitimacy.

The same two points hold *mutatis mutandis* for the classic biblical hermeneutics. In its case also the text became religious (cultural-linguistically speaking) by being employed to build community within a wholly comprehensive setting. Also its methods were so molded by the particular texts it used that they have only surface resemblances to other hermeneutical approaches. The Bible is thus its own interpreter, not as bare text, but in its classic construal. Although it was the Reformers who first formulated this dictum in opposition to late medieval claims to the contrary, it was implicit in catholic practice from patristic times. The heretics erred, so it was regularly argued, not because they failed to submit to ecclesiastical authority, but because they ignored the *scopus* of scripture as the communally edifying and canonically unified word from God. The contention was in effect that words of God are audible in classic scriptural reading which cannot be heard through any other method or from any other source. Thus it seems that the biblical good news or gospel is in some respects unique and untranslatable not only because of its sharable claim to universality, but also because of its peculiarities. It needs to be interpreted in its own classic terms and not by general methods external to it if we are to understand the meaning it has, not only in the past, but in the present and future.

What then is the formal role of Israel in the classic hermeneutics? Can and should its function as example for the Church be retrieved? These are the general questions we shall deal with in the next section before turning in the final section of this paper to the material guidance the example of Israel provides.

Israel as Example and the Hermeneutics of Retrieval

The Bible of the Jews, usually in its Septuagint version, was, we recall, the whole of the Bible for the writers, the so-called apostolic authors, of what later was canonized as the New Testament. These authors, to be sure, interpreted this Bible in the light of what we now pallidly call the Christ event. They were the first to begin the process of expropriating the Tanakh and turning it formally though not materially into a different book, the Old Testament (which, to betray my prejudices, is the only honest name for this collection of writings in their Christian usage). The interpretive flow, however, was as much or more from the Old to the New as the reverse. Because it was for the first generations of Christians the only written word of God, it was the privileged source of the terms, concepts, images and models which they used in understanding Jesus and the Jesus movement to which they belonged. Nor should the influence of contemporary Judaism be forgotten. Except in those cases where their new faith gave them reason to think the contrary, they assumed that the Old Testament was what was believed and practised in the Judaism of their own day in which all of them at first had been reared. The interpretive practices they developed are what we earlier described as classic biblical hermeneutics. All the formal features we noted were present from the first generation as can be seen already in St Paul, the earliest of the apostolic authors.

Given these habits of reading and Israel's role as source (in the sense of second cause) and subject matter of the Old Testament, it was inevitable that the early Christians interpreted Jesus, their own communities and their relations to non-biblical peoples in Israel-like ways. The articulation of the grammar of this relationship in reference to Christ was that Israel, the Messianic people, is the type of which Jesus, the Messiah, is the antitype, the fulfillment. In post-biblical generations, the Church also was increasingly said to be the antitype or fulfillment of Israel, not as identical to Christ, but as replacing Israel in the status of the Messianic people. The Jews became simply pre-Messianic. This supersessionism, however, is a distortion of the grammar of the relationship in some New Testament writers, most notably Paul. If one reads the Bible as a canonical unity and takes the strand represented by Paul as hermeneutically central, then, as will later be explained more fully, the grammar of the Israel/Church relation is better articulated as that of prototype to ectype.[16]

That Christians thought of the Church as in some sense Israel is a commonplace, but it has generally been supposed that the resemblance, whatever it is, breaks down in relation to the Gentiles. It was said that the synagogue unlike the Church had no universalist aspirations and did not seek to win the heathen, but it is now general knowledge that this is too simple. Jews also were into the business of converting pagans, and some did this with an eagerness which some Christians found unseemly. Why else would the words of Jesus criticizing Pharisees for their proselytizing zeal (Matt. 23.15) have been preserved? The main difference on this point was that the Jews required more of converts from paganism than did at least the Pauline Christians who omitted circumcision. When it came to overall stringency, however, the non-Gnostic Christians whether Jew or Gentile were intensely Jewish. Martyrdom in order not to dishonor the Name was mandatory for them also.

The reason Israel was exemplary in this and other compelling ways was that Christians identified themselves as the same people of God of which the Old Testament speaks with matter-of-fact literalism or realism. Their churches simply were Israel – Israel in the New Age, to be sure, and Israel as including the uncircumcised who believed in the Jewish Messiah, but nonetheless Israel. This conviction is reflected in the New Testament. The ecclesiology of the Apostolic writings is, one might say, Israel-ology. Everything that their Scripture, viz. the Old Testament, says about Israel can apply also to the Church except what is implicitly or explicitly excluded. Thus the ecclesiological silences of the New Testament, which are many, can be rightly filled with Old Testament material. The relevance of the example of Israel from this early Christian perspective extends far beyond what is recorded *expressis verbis* in the Gospels and Epistles. In reference to Christians in religiously pluralistic situations, any or all the diverse relations of Israel to other peoples could serve in analogous circumstances as negative or positive precedents. To be sure, as later patristic authors emphasized when discussing what was already for them the primitive science of Genesis and – much more difficult in their eyes – the 'immoralities' of the patriarchs, God accommodates his word to particular times, places and persons; some of his past instructions will never again have renewed application now that the Messianic era has begun *in nuce* in Jesus. Yet even the objectionable deeds and happenings in Israel of old 'were written down for our instruction, upon whom the end of the ages has come' (1 Cor. 10.11) precisely because the commonwealth of Israel, now messianically expanded to include Gentiles (Eph. 3.11–22), remains one and the same people of God.

Much of this early understanding of the Church endured despite later supersessionist modifications according to which the Church replaces rather than expands Israel and is thus properly called 'New Israel' – a term not found in the New Testament. Up through the Reformation, the Church was Israel and Israel was 'the church in the Old Testament' (as Calvin put it) for most Christians in ways which were operationally significant and not simply verbally ornamental. In two respects, however, the change from

Church as expansion to Church as replacement of Israel was crucially significant. First, this change relegates unbelieving Jewry to the status of a rejected rather than elected people.

Second, it makes the Church (along with Christ) the antitype, the fulfillment, of Israel, rather than its ectype. If so, it is chiefly what is good about Israel of old, not what is bad, which is prototypical of the Church. The stories of unfaithfulness and the thunderings of the prophets were read as directed first against Jews, second against heretics and third against unrighteousness in professedly Christian societies. The real Church, however that was defined, could not be culpable of wickedness comparable to that of Israel before Christ, nor of Jewry *post Christum*. This supersessionist distortion left the classic hermeneutics formally intact, but deprived it of critical leverage against Christian triumphalism of every kind, but especially against anti-Judaism.

Not all supersessionism, however, has been classic in character. One can think of Christianity as replacing Israel, not by fulfilling it and thereby in a sense continuing it, but by rejecting it as that which is bad or inferior. Here supersession ceases to be a supplanting or taking the place of another in a birthright as Jacob did to Esau, and becomes instead a matter of temporal succession in which a better religion follows a worse one with which it has no necessary connections. The most extreme version of this position was that of Marcion (though anticipations are to be found, e.g. in the Epistle of Barnabas), for whom Israel had never been elect and was the creature of Satan, not God. Ever since the 16th century, quasi-Marcionite views have become pervasive, not necessarily in Christology or the doctrine of God, but in ecclesiology. The Church did not start in Old Testament days with Israel or Abraham or as Augustine put it, Abel, but with Jesus Christ when he founded it, as Matt. 16.18 suggests on Peter (as some Roman Catholic apologists said) or on the faith Peter confessed (as Protestants replied with, by the way, the weight of the pre-Reformation exegetical tradition on their side) or at Pentecost (as especially some spiritualists emphasized though with considerable mainstream support). Sometimes this detachment of the Church from Israel was accompanied, especially in liberalism, by a corresponding separation of Christianity as a whole from Judaism; they are simply two different religions with historical but no theologically significant connections. The Old Testament ceases to be authoritative for Christians and is regarded as an exclusively Jewish text.

Some of these religious dualists (or pluralists, as the case may be) regard Judaism as an inferior religion and are thus implicitly or explicitly anti-Jewish and quasi-Marcionite; it is not unfair, I think, to cite both Schleiermacher and Harnack as examples. Others, paradoxically, are motivated by philosemitism or, at least, anti-antisemitism. Because supersessionism denies the continuing legitimacy of Judaism after Christ, it is for them the root of Christian anti-Judaism which, in turn, is ultimately the cause of the Holocaust. Their motive for denying that Christianity fulfills and thus replaces Judaism is to protect Jews against Christian aggrandizement, while Harnack's similar denials arose from the desire to purge Christianity of Judaizing corruptions (which for him were particularly strong in Roman Catholicism).[17] Anti-supersessionism, in short, can be either pro- or anti-Jewish.

In our day, however, it is only its pro-Jewish face that is publicly displayed. It is out of concern for Jewish safety and guilt for Christian crimes that Christians, so the argument goes, must stop believing that Jesus is the Jewish Messiah. This belief, it is claimed, is the taproot of the Christian triumphalism and contempt for others which has inflicted untold suffering on humankind, but especially on Jews. That Nazis and the contemporary Christian militia also want a *Judenfrei* Jesus is forgotten.

Just because some anti-supersessionists are evil does not mean, however, that supersessionism is good. The enormity of the wickedness it has occasioned or caused make it indefensible; and if the classic hermeneutics and its Israel-like ecclesiology – the Church as Israel and Israel as example – are inherently supersessionist, one must rejoice at their massive weakening across the theological spectrum from right to left in recent centuries. Their retrieval would be unthinkable.

What, however, if the Israel-like Church in its original version does not replace but rather expands Israel to embrace Gentile believers? One advantage from the perspective of continuity with the historic tradition is that the classic Christological claims are on this view undiminished. Israel's story and Jesus the Messiah continue to be related as type to antitype, promise to fulfillment, shadow to reality. It will be recalled that in ecclesiology in contrast to Christology, however, Israel and the Church are, in this original version, prototype and ectype, not, as they have been through most of later Christian history, type and antitype. The terms are archaic, but not the contemporary significance: the Church of believers in Christ has never been scripturally or normatively the fulfillment of Israel. It was not so even in its beginnings, and much less now when, in addition to a fragmentation worse than that of Judaism, the Church has become simply Gentile rather than the assembly of Jew and Gentile. The light of the Messianic dawn which, Christians believe, shines more brightly in the Church than in Israel before, or unbelieving Israel after Christ, also makes the Christian potential for unfaithfulness greater. The Church is not less under God's judgment, and no less in need of the example of Israel both before and after Christ than, let us say, the diaspora of Ezekiel's day was in need of the Exodus prototype. Something like this is a plausible understanding of the biblical witness regarding the relation of Israel and the Church when it is read classically as a canonical whole from the vantage point of the New Testament and, in the New Testament, from the vantage point of Paul.

Elements of this understanding of biblical ecclesiology as both Israel-like and non-supersessionist are seeping gradually here and there into contemporary scholarship, but it remains alien to most theologians as well as to the overwhelming majority of ordinary Christians from the fundamentalist right to the liberal left. Even though it can claim to be consistent with historical-critical method (for it does not contradict and in part depends on what appear to be as good reconstructions as we have of how Scripture was construed in its original settings), it is notoriously absent from much of the purportedly most radical contemporary biblical scholarship.[18] The Jesus Seminar, for example, sometimes seems as dogmatic in its banishing of Jewishness from Jesus as were the *deutsche Christen*, even if for opposite reasons. Scholars at the other extreme who in their capacity as historians insist on the full Jewishness of Jesus and his disciples even after he had become for them the resurrected Messiah who will come again are likely also, however, to be resistant to Israel as example and the hermeneutics on which it depends. Even if early Christians thought of the Church and practised interpretation as we have described, this by itself is no reason for imitating them.

Mere imitation, however, is not what is being suggested. The retrieval of premodern hermeneutics is critical rather than uncritical, and that makes a difference. Classic interpretation retains the primacy because it is the source of the constructive proposals for what the text means now in our time and place, but the bases of these proposals must now undergo the corrective scrutiny of historical criticism. When these bases are removed by such criticism, the proposal loses its scriptural authority.[19]

This combination of modern and premodern approaches, it may be worth noting, is possible only from the premodern side. Classic hermeneutics is able to absorb historical criticism, but not vice versa. To start with the latter and supplement it with a garnishing of the former (as some critics seem to me wrongly to suppose my colleague, Brevard Childs, is doing) is to invite disaster. This is because modern biblical scholarship cannot transgress its confinement to a limited swath of reality without violating its *raison d'etre*. The classic hermeneutics, in contrast, is intrinsically unrestricted. Its task, as we have observed, is to interpret all reality religiously by capturing the universe in the embrace of biblical language. Modern methods of interpretation are part of the booty and are to be used like other treasures of God's good creation to glorify him and bring all thoughts into captivity to Christ.

The contributions of these interpretive methods are secondary, but they are also in their proper place indispensable to the health of the historic tradition at this stage of history. Not the least of the corrective accomplishments of historical criticism from the perspective of this essay is that it releases classic hermeneutics from the thrall of supersessionism and makes the example of Israel once again available to the Church. In the background, moreover, are other achievements without which retrieval would be impossible. Historical criticism when rightly used is the main bulwark against the ravages of fundamentalism, on the one hand, and the allegorizing individualism of pietistic and existentialist reading, on the other. It is from critical history that we know that the literalism of the first is a modern invention and the individualistic inwardness of the second is, despite Bultmann, remote from the Bible. Without the use of historical-critical tools, there could be no retrieval of classic hermeneutics.

Yet, to return to the obvious, critical history is constructively helpless. In the absence of any functional equivalents to the classic canonical, grammatical (or doctrinal), narrational and figural interpretive strategies which we earlier sketched, it possesses no means of its own to move from what texts meant in the past to what they can and should mean now for believers. It is thus incapable of providing communally persuasive guidance in the present for Christian faith and life, and the hermeneutical supplements devised to repair its failures (most brilliantly, perhaps, by Bultmann) are also unsuccessful. Non-fundamentalist mainstream churches are now reaping the bitter fruits of this interpretive paralysis. Thus, to summarize, it seems that contemporary Christian communities are likely to remain adrift apart from the retrieval of premodern scriptural interpretation including the prototypical role that this gives to Israel, and it also seems that historical criticism is a necessary (though not sufficient) condition for this retrieval providing its focus is corrective and it is not made into a launching pad for tradition-independent speculations.

In view of the immensity of the psychosocial obstacles to the hermeneutical retrieval of Israel as example, however, it needs to be observed in conclusion that the intellectual barriers appear to be weakening. This weakening is in part exemplified by the increased appreciation of classic biblical interpretation among contemporary literary theorists and critics, but I am told by some of those who are better informed than I am about such matters that philosophical and other developments should also be mentioned. Literary theory together with philosophy have thus produced a more positive attitude towards premodern hermeneutics in some segments of the intellectual *avant garde* than at any time since Spinoza's presumed demolition of tradition in the *Tractatus Politicus*. It is becoming possible even for thinkers in tune with the *Zeitgeist* to see that there is nothing in the basic features of premodern hermeneutics which prevents critical retrieval.

The first step towards retrieval is to reject the biblical scholars' version of the philosophical category mistake of evidentialism, i.e. the proviso that traditional readings must be supported by historical-critical evidence in order to be accepted. On the contrary, it is wrong for those seeking to work within a tradition to reject its beliefs and interpretations simply because there is no critically acceptable evidence for them. To follow this rule consistently could not help but produce paralysis if for no other reason than that everything we do, say and think is dependent on inherited background convictions of unknown or unknowable evidential grounding. On the other hand, it is equally important to take seriously evidence *against* a traditional interpretation. One must weigh the critique and examine the challenged interpretation to see how important it is for the web of belief. When the role of the challenged interpretation is not crucial and especially, as in the case of supersessionism, if it can be shown to conflict with centrally important strands within the tradition, then historical criticism wins. As has already been said, it has a veto power rather than a positive role in the grounding and development of faith.

The second step towards retrieval is one which we have also already discussed. It is the insight that the literary techniques of premodern interpretation in conjunction with their contemporary refurbishings are needed for constructive work. Various modes of figuration in particular make it possible to advance discussable rather than arbitrary proposals as to what ancient texts could mean here and now for communities which want to take them as authoritative.

Contemporary discussions of evidentialism provide philosophical warrants for the hermeneutical mind-set I have just described, but so also does the Anselmic theological approach to faith seeking understanding shared by the Reformers, Karl Barth, von Balthasar and, I would argue, also Thomas Aquinas. Nevertheless, this mind-set remains deeply problematic. Professedly postmodern ideologies have not freed themselves from evidentialism; they continue to assume that it is intellectually immoral to believe without what modernity has defined as evidence. From Nietzsche on, what they have chiefly done is simply draw skeptical conclusions from thoroughly modern premises. No wonder, then, that the postcritical retrieval of premodern hermeneutics on which the present argument depends is likely to create cognitive dissonance.

This dissonance will increase for some as we turn now from formal considerations to what is materially unique about Israel as prototype of the Church.

Election

We have already noted that material uniqueness in the classical biblical context centers on election. The background for this is an understanding of the universe as permeated with what scientists call singularities – once-for-all events – except that, in contrast to the methodological atheism of science, one and the same cause is assigned to all singularities, viz. the wholly free will of God. Among the world religions, only the three western mono-theisms, Judaism, Christianity and Islam, have this conviction. It applies first to creation itself. The universe exists only because God freely chose to create it out of sheer good pleasure for no humanly knowable reason whatsoever (and certainly not because of anything we would recognize as a need nor because the divine well-being is thereby enhanced). The catena of choices by which the world's redemption is accomplished is similarly unique, a series of unconditional singularities. God was under no necessity to call Abraham, choose Israel, bestow the Torah, send his Son, the Jewish Messiah, that the world might live, open the ranks of the chosen people to the uncircumcised nor, finally, to promise in and through all these acts to establish his reign at the end of time. These events are interlocking and interdefining so that the full significance of election becomes more and more apparent as one considers them together. The choice of Israel is primary, that of Jesus is for Christians climactic, and that of the Gentile church derivative. (It is derivative for non-supersessionists because it is a matter of being added to Israel through Jesus.)

Yet while it is true that one cannot fully understand election on this view without reference to Jesus and the Church, the Old Testament accounts of Israel are basic. They, more than the New Testament, tell what it means to be God's chosen people; and what they predicate of Israel, it will be recalled, also applies to the Church unless there are biblical indications to the contrary. In this section, we shall look at this Old Testament data on election under the three headings of, first, God's graciousness, second, his purposes and Israel's uniqueness and, third, the response he wants from his elect people. Some implications of these three points for the service of other religions will be mentioned in passing, and a final sub-section will point forward to that call for servanthood which issues from the present essay.

Grace Alone

The *sola gratia*, the unconditionality of grace, is seen most clearly in God's choice of Israel. It has two aspects: first, there was no reason for the choice and, second, it is irrevocable. God is faithful; he cannot break his promises; he must fulfill his oath. Thus, as various New Testament writings repeatedly say, it was necessary that the Messiah come and suffer and die. The necessity in question, as Aquinas among others points out, does not diminish God's utter freedom in sending the Son precisely because it is dependent on prior, on Old Testament, gratuity. Fully unconditional grace is not only uncaused: it is irrevocable.

Christians have recognized this in reference to the promises to Abraham and the coming of Jesus (Paul on this point is almost tediously insistent), but not in reference to Israel or the Church. Some consideration of the biblical evidence is called for.

One *locus classicus* for the initial unconditionality of election is Deut. 7.6–8. I quote two verses from a Jewish translation:[20]'For you are a people consecrated to the Lord your God: of all the peoples on earth the Lord your God chose you to be his treasured people. It is not because you are the most numerous of peoples that the Lord set his heart on you and chose you – indeed, you are the smallest of peoples.' This emphasis on the insignificance of Israel should not be interpreted, as some contemporary Christians are inclined to do, as pointing to a reason for God's choice. God did not choose Abraham because of his virtue, on that Christians and Jews can agree, but also he did not choose him because he was poor, wretched or an outcast, for he was none of these things. When we look at Abraham's call, in which Israel's foundational election takes place, we discover, as one Jewish author observes, that there is here 'no clue as to why God elects Abraham and his progeny or as to why Abraham obeys the call. Unlike Noah who is elected to save humankind and his family and self from the flood . . . and who obviously responds to God's call because of the biological drive of self-preservation, there is no reason given here either for God's choice or Abraham's positive response to it. Any righteousness attributed to Abraham is seen as subsequent not prior to God's election of him'[21](cf. Gen. 26.5 and Neh. 9.7–8).

This subsequent righteousness does, to be sure, make him lovable. As Aquinas put it in unwitting agreement with this rabbinic opinion, God's love causes lovableness rather than is caused by it. Moreover, this lovableness is communal, not simply individual. It passes on to Abraham's descendants, and it is in part because of the goodness of the select few that God remains faithful to faithless Israel. The survival of the people in the desert depended on God's love for Moses who pleaded on more than one occasion that he be destroyed rather than they.

Because of this pleading, Christians have seen in Moses a type of Christ and have tropologically applied this typology to individual believers. They survive God's wrath because Christ pleads for them, and because other believers, members of his body, pray for them. Christians have been oddly remiss, however, in not extending this figuration communally from Israel to the Church. Why should not Christians say somewhat as do the Jews that God loves the Church, not because of its merits and not in an exclusionary fashion because of Christ, but also because of the ancestors in the faith from Abraham, Sarah, Moses and David, to Teresa of Avila, Kagawa, Martin Luther King and John XXIII? If this were to become a widespread conviction, the Church's *de iure* lovableness might become increasingly *de facto*.

This priority of God's decree over human action brings us to the second aspect of the unconditionality of God's grace. Even when Israel (and the Church as part of Israel) is *de facto* desperately unfaithful and unlovable, election is not revoked. Looked at in canonical context, God's call and covenant remain unconditional for Israel no matter what its behavior. The rabbinic tradition at least in part agrees with this, but Paul goes further. According to Rom. 11.29ff., the continuation of God's promised is not ruptured even by Israel's rejection of the Messiah. Hosea and Ezekiel in some way surpass even Paul. They are the most vivid of all with their pictures of the adulterous spouse. In whoring after false gods, so Ezekiel in particular affirms, Israel becomes worse than the heathen nations – *corruptio optimi pessima est*, as the pagan poet puts it – but God does not abrogate his covenant.

There is New Testament support in both the Pauline epistles and the letters to the seven churches in Revelation for the ecclesial use of this irrevocability of Israel's election, yet Christians have ignored this. Having denied by their supersessionism that Israel remains God's beloved despite its unfaithfulness, they could not claim the irrevocability of God's promises on the Church's behalf. Christians have either assumed with the Catholics that the Church does not sin in itself but only its members or, with the Protestants, that it ceases to be the true Church when it does. Both positions, it can be argued, are triumphalistic. They make impossible that combination of unbreakable communal loyalty despite unflinching recognition of unbearable communal sins characteristic of Jesus and the prophets. Such an ecclesiological *simul justus et peccator* has never been part of the Christian mainstream. The Reformers who predicted the *simul* of individuals did not apply it to what they regarded as adulterous churches such as that of Rome (at least the Reformed did not, and the Lutherans were ambivalent).

In any case, an Israel-like self-critical recognition of the possibilities of corruption and unfaithfulness of the community in which one deeply and unshakably participates is self-evidently of both intrareligious and interreligious significance. It helps account for that sense of common peoplehood which Jews, even secularized Jews, have retained through the vicissitudes of history, but which Christians have largely lost – and often, it seems, congratulate themselves on losing. This sense of peoplehood makes a difference both extramurally in relation to other religions, but even more intra-murally. The potential for communal self-criticism embedded in election when this is undergirded by the *sola gratia* is perhaps unparalleled. It implies that Jews and Christians can be maximally critical of their own communities without disloyalty, as is abundantly illustrated by their own Scriptures. Perhaps this is not only a biblical possibility – Socrates comes to mind – but it is at present more salient in Judaism and Christianity than anywhere else. It could be of service to other religions if the biblical example of joining criticism and loyalty could provoke them to emulation. We shall have more to say of this in the next lecture.

God's Purpose and Uniqueness of Witness

Though God is utterly free in choosing this people rather than that, his election *sola gratia* does have a purpose. The Genesis text (12.1–4) says that he wished to make of Abraham 'a great nation' and a 'blessing'. 'All the families of the earth will bless themselves by you.' Isaiah goes on to say that Israel shall be 'a light to the nations' (42.6); the New Testament applies this verse to Jesus; and Jesus, in turn, tells his followers they are 'the light of the world' (Matt. 5.14) or, in the words of Ephesians, 'light in the Lord' (5.8). God's aims are multifaceted, but at least one aim in choosing Israel, Jesus and Church is the redemption of the world.

The role of the Messiah, to be sure, is different from that of the elect peoples. He is redemption itself, while they are witnesses. The New Testament version of this point is that Christ alone is the true light 'that enlightens every one coming into the world' (Jn 1.9), but this leaves open the question of whether that light is pointed to only by Israel and the Church. Are there perhaps other religious or non-religious communities claiming comprehensive views which also mediate knowledge of the ultimate nature and meaning of the universe? Can, in other words, the truth about 'the one thing needful' be uttered in languages other than that of Zion? If not, then God has elected only Israel and the Church to be witnesses to his redemptive purposes. Untranslatability in the biblical context entails the uniqueness of their communal witness to salvation.

It will be recalled that this is not a question about individual salvation. Those who developed the later rabbinic views on the Noahide covenant and the possibilities of life in the world to come for righteous Gentiles also believed that only Israel is the elect witness to the one true God. Nor are we here concerned with the issue of whether non-biblical religions may be vehicles of salvation for their adherents. God can use any means he wishes to save whomever he chooses, but that does not mean non-biblical religions become witnesses. It could be that God employs them to promote his saving purposes despite rather than because of their self-descriptions or self-understanding. Even though they are not headed for what Christians call the New Jerusalem, they may nevertheless stop at way-stations which, unbeknownst to themselves, bring their passengers closer. Finally, the problem is not whether biblical religions can learn more even about salvation from others. Perhaps Buddhists, Muslims, Freud and Marx can teach Christians and Jews much of salvific value just as geocentricists can instruct heliocentricists about the world in which we live even while being wrong in their overall interpretations of the data. In short, to be unique witnesses to salvation is quite different from being the unique means or vehicle. Witnessing to salvation is a matter of pointing all things to the true God who, in view of what we have called untranslatability, can be rightly identified only in the unique language of the elect peoples.

The interreligious importance of this shift from soteriology to untranslatability or, in this context, from means to witness of salvation, is that it is a move from triumphalism to modesty which nevertheless remains faithful to the Bible. If it is true, as we can plausibly postulate, even if not prove, that all religions of world importance affirm a comprehensiveness which implies untranslatability, then the biblical affirmation of uniqueness is no longer uniquely offensive. When uniqueness is thought of in terms of means of salvation, as Christians (but not Jews) have usually done, it becomes difficult to avoid unbiblically arrogant claims for the Church and, at the same time, retain the exclusivist biblical understanding of election. Insofar as the appeal of pluralism and to a lesser degree inclusivism is owing to their opposition to arrogance, they are biblically justifiable, but this appeal is purchased, it seems, at the cost of incoherence: the basic grammar of election, which is central to biblical faith, is shattered.

That the Bible on the whole is exclusivist in regard to communal witness even if not individual salvation scarcely needs proof; even so, it is well to remind ourselves of some of the evidence. There is not the slightest suggestion in the Old Testament that any nation beside Israel is especially beloved of God as means of blessing to all peoples. In the New Testament, John reports Jesus as saying to the Samaritan woman at Jacob's well, 'Salvation is of the Jews', and Paul, echoing Isaiah and the Psalms, declares that every knee will bow to the Messiah, to Jesus, before God becomes all in all (conflating 1 Cor. 15.26ff. and Phil. 2.10). Gentile nations and their rulers may have their salvific roles (Cyrus, remember, is called 'Messiah'), but only in relation to the chosen peoples. Amos 9.7, to be sure, hints that God may call other nations (and, by canonical extrapolation, other religions) to tasks independent of the elect people, but though I have argued elsewhere that this hint is grammatically important and theologically extensible, it does not warrant pluralism. The roles to which heathen nations may be elected, so it seems, are either not blessings in the strong biblical sense or else they are not for all, not universal. The communities which God uses in public history as witnesses are in their self-understanding in the Abrahamic line. In short, Scripture read classically by Christians agrees with rabbinic Judaism in not ascribing the possibility of a universal redemptive role to any communal traditions except those of biblical faith. (What this implies for relations with Islam with its emphasis on Abraham, I should perhaps add, is beyond my competence to discuss. The question requires much more knowledge than I have.)

Response

Let us assume in agreement with rabbinic and Christian scriptural interpretation that the basic response which God desires from those whom he elects, and ultimately from all, is praise, doxology, joy in God and God's creation. From this it follows that the fundamental witness of the elect peoples to the coming Kingdom is in being communities which whole-heartedly laud and bless the Holy Name. This centrality of doxology is a major theme in two major theologians of this century, Karl Barth and, even more, Hans Urs von Balthasar, but it has been more consistently maintained down through the centuries by Jews than by Christians. The rabbis frequently urge, for example, that the primary response God wants is not gratitude: it is self-centered to respond to God only because of the good he has done us. To be sure, Scripture tells us that we love God because he first loved us, but this love is climatically, as Bernard of Clairvaux so tirelessly stressed, love of God for his own sake, and the expression of that is praise. Obedience, that is, Torah-observance, is itself also doxological according to this rabbinic interpretive tradition. Those who learn rightly to observe the precepts and commandments (non-reductively summed up in love of God and neighbor) find these intrinsically satisfying, intrinsically enjoyable. It is through their performance that the presence of God is experienced. They are not an instrumental means to some extrinsic good such as the accumulation of merit, the cultivation of virtue or the benefit of neighbors. They are their own reward and for that reason meritorious, virtue-producing, and neighbor-benefiting. Doxologically-minded Christians, needles to say, agree. God's self-communication occurs in and through the Church's liturgical, communal and diakonal practices as these are done for their own sake in praise of God not for some extrinsic good. Faithful witness is doxology and vice versa.

In this communal doxological perspective, the relation between praise of God in the community's life and worship and the service of outsiders might be compared to that between faith and works in Reformation theology: the second is a necessary but, in one sense, accidental by-product of the former. The parallelism is not perfect, but there is an analogy. Torah-observance on the account I have just given includes instructions in the story, ritual and the doxological use of the law, i.e. the following of the law as a means of grace. This corresponds to the right preaching of the word, the proper administration of the sacraments and the doxological, that is, the third use of the law. When all three are present, then praise will flourish, and from that praise will flow the words and deeds which make the faithful community a light and witness to the Gentiles.

How that witness functions, however, depends on the circumstances. It is under God's guidance, but it is beyond the Church's or any human control. Indeed, it is beyond human perception except, perhaps, in retrospect. Faithful witness will sometimes attract converts, but in other situations it will repel them, and exactly the same can be said about unfaithfulness. Some of the most laudable aspects of Christian missions in modern times have been related to imperialism and colonialism; David Livingston's struggle against the slave trade is an example. Rice Christians have sometimes become martyrs for the faith, and not only virtue but also whoredom can attract converts. Communities of biblical faith may on occasion awaken envy, but this envy may lead either to imitation, which may be helpful or harmful to the imitators, or to persecution, which may be in various degrees justified or unjustified. Finally, the apostolic injunction, for which rabbinic parallels are easy to find, that God's chosen people should live at peace with all insofar as this is possible, may prove on occasion unfeasible. Israel has taken up arms at various times for causes which have been both just and unjust, and so have parties and countries which regarded themselves as bearing witness to the cause of Christ. It seems that no general answer can be given to the question of how the chosen peoples are or should be a light for communities of other faiths.

Yet there are two guidelines of action that are everywhere applicable which need to be mentioned before we turn to some introductory remarks on servanthood as a conclusion of this present essay. First, communal faithfulness is fundamental. It is not only individuals but communities, Israel and the Church, which are enjoined not to bring shame on God's holy name. Faithful witness takes precedence over what the wider society thinks is its welfare and, indeed, over one's own community's welfare as judged by these same alien standards. Faithfulness *in extremis* leads to martyrdom, as we have already noted. One proof-text for this is Jesus' statement that he came to bring, not peace, but a sword.

Faithfulness, however, is not foolhardiness. It must be exercised with prudence: wise as serpents and harmless as doves. This brings us to the second guideline, the test in terms of which prudence is to be exercised. It may sound repellently ethnocentric, but the survival and welfare of the chosen people is a criterion for distinguishing between the prudent and imprudent. That special concern for one's own group should be part of one's social and political responsibilities has become foreign to many Christians, but it remains familiar to Jews. Especially since the Holocaust, they have had to relearn that insuring communal survival may sometimes take precedence over other duties. It would be a crime, so Emil Fackenhiem says, to hand Hitler a posthumous victory.

Christians thought similarly about themselves in premodern times. Because they saw themselves as in some sense Israel, they took for granted that they should pray for the peace of the Church even more fervently than for the nations, and that the peace of the nations was for the sake of the peace of the Church. Christians who were poor or persecuted were of more concern than other needy ones; and one rejoiced more when Christians did what was right, and mourned more when they did what was wrong than in the case of others. Because it is the community in its corporate existence which is chosen by God to witness to the world, members have responsibilities for each other and for their own people as a whole which do not extend to society at large or to other groups. Premodern supersessionist Christians in some ways spiritualized the notion of the Church as Israel, but much of its sense of concrete peoplehood remained.

Servanthood

It is in the context of this sense of chosen peoplehood with its concern for earthly as well as spiritual common welfare that the Church – the 'elect lady', as II John calls her – needs to understand her serving role in our religiously pluralistic world. Her motives are not disinterested; she serves others in part for her own sake. But because it is as an earthly people that God chooses her, this prudence on her own behalf is God-approved. Jeremiah tells the exiled Jews to seek the welfare of that most unlikely of cities, Babylon, because that is where they dwell. They should pray the Lord on its behalf 'for in its prosperity you shall prosper' (29.7). And so also, as it happens, will Babylon's gods. They also will be served by what benefits Babylon. Society and religion cannot be separated.

That inseparability has in some respects endured throughout the vast changes of the last 2,600 years. Despite modern secularization theorists from Weber on, there is a growing suspicion that morality disintegrates and social viability weakens in the absence of culturally powerful, meaning-conferring and community-sustaining comprehensive outlooks. Without such outlooks, whether biblical or non-biblical, the prospects for communal and personal flourishing both inside and outside the churches become dimmer and dimmer.

If so, Christians cannot be indifferent to the welfare of other faiths. Furthermore, they have special potentialities and therefore special responsibilities to help them. With the exception of Judaism, Christianity has had vastly more varied experiences than any other world religion with attempts to sustain canopies of cosmic meaning in societies ranging from the primitive to the hyper-modern. Christianity has had a major impact on other religions and their societies even where ecclesial presence has been small. The churches have provided both negative and positive examples to Hindus, Buddhists and Muslims, not to mention others. Their service has often been that of the blind leading (and provoking) the blind, but the effects of their unwitting servanthood have been volcanic. It is too early to assess whether the good outweighs the bad, but the outcome of the past will largely depend on how Christians act in the future.

How they can and should function is the topic of a paper yet to be published, but enough has been said, I hope, to indicate why the theme is servanthood. Seeking and praying for the welfare of the earthly cities in which Christians live cannot be separated from concern for the religions without which these societies could not in many cases survive. It is on how these religions sustain these societies that the worldwide diaspora of peoples of biblical faith is increasingly dependent for the peace without which they cannot freely and communally glorify and witness to the Name which is above every name. Thus helping other religions is imperative. The service of God and neighbor in this case intersects with communal self-interest.

The investigation of what this servanthood concretely signifies in the classic and yet postcritical approach we are proposing naturally focuses on the exemplary role for the Church of Israel's story, not only in its Old Testament rendition, but also in its postbiblical Jewish continuation. This is not the place to expound the details, but it is perhaps well, in conclusion, to insist on modest expectations. Because of the pervasiveness on both right and left of Christendom's supersessionist heritage, the next phase of this discussion is likely to be unpersuasive or disconcerting both to conservatives and liberals. The case for serious attention to the Israel-like aspect of the Church may be compelling, but it is not likely to appeal to most Christians as long as present polarizations continue.

Notes and Further Reading

Introduction: Radical Traditions: Evangelical, Catholic and Postliberal

1. See Lindbeck's review of Jenson's *Unbaptized God. The Basic Flaw in Ecumenical theology* (Minneapolis: Fortress, 1992) in *Pro Ecclesia* III (1994), p. 235.

2. 'A Panel Discussion. Lindbeck, Hunsinger, McGrath, and Fackre', *The Nature of Confession. Evangelicals and Postliberals in Conversation*, (eds), Timothy R Phillips and Dennis L Okholm, Downers Grove: InterVarsity Press, 1996, p. 247. The best place to start to find Lindbeck's Lutheran theology is probably the ecumenical documents that Lindbeck has signed – for example, those collected in *Growth in Agreement. Reports and Agreed Statements of Ecumenical Conversations on a World Level*, (eds), Harding Meyer and Lukas Vischer, New York/Ramsey: Paulist Press and Geneva: World Council of Churches, 1984, pp. 167–275; for a list of dialogues in which Lindbeck has participated, often as co-chair, see the bibliographies cited in note 18 below. For other samples of his Lutheran theology, see 'The Confessions as Ideology and Witness in the History of Lutheranism', *Lutheran World* 7 (1960/61), pp. 388–401; 'The Lutheran Doctrine of the Ministry: Catholic and Reformed', *Theological Studies* 30 (1969), pp. 588–612; 'The Augsburg Confession in the Light of Contemporary Catholic–Lutheran Dialogue', (with Vilmos Vajta), in *The Role of the Augsburg Confession: Catholic and Lutheran Views*, Philadelphia: Fortress, 1980, pp. 81–95; 'Lutheran Churches', *Ministry in America*, (eds), David S Schuller, Merton P Strommen, Milo L Brekke, New York: Harper & Row, 1980, pp. 414–45; 'Ebeling: Climax of a Great Tradition', *The Journal of Religion* 61 (1981), pp. 309–14; 'Lutheranism. I. A Lutheran Perspective', in, *Dictionary of Fundamental Theology*, (eds), René Latourelle and Rino Fisichella, New York: Crossroad, 1994, pp. 609–12.

3. 'A Panel Discussion. Lindbeck, Hunsinger, McGrath, and Fackre', *The Nature of Confession. Evangelicals and Postliberals in Conversation*, (eds), Timothy R Phillips and Dennis L Okholm, Downers Grove: InterVarsity Press, 1996, p. 246. He also says that the postliberal research agenda is 'more likely to be carried on by evangelicals than anyone else' (p. 253). This ambivalence arises out of Lindbeck's narrative of the rise of evangelicalism from the Reformed tradition in Chapter Four of this collection.

4. *The Book of Concord* is the 1580 collection of the basic creeds and confessions of the Evangelical Lutheran Church. See *The Book of Concord. The Confessions of the Evangelical Lutheran Church*, (ed.), Robert Kolb, Wengert (trans.) and James Schaffer, Philadelphia: Fortress Press, 2001.

5. 'The Meaning of Satis Est, or ... Tilting in the Ecumenical Wars', *Lutheran Forum* 26 (1992), pp. 19–27. See also 'Ecumenical Directions and Confessional Construals', *Dialog* 30 (1991), pp. 118–23; 'The Church Faithful and Apostate', *Lutheran Forum* 28 (1994), pp. 12–19 along with the further reading suggested in the introductions to Chapters Three and Four below.

6. On conflicts with and about Christian ecumenism, see 'Ecumenism and World Mission', *Lutheran World* 17 (1970), pp. 69–77; 'Doctrinal Standards, theological theories and practical aspects of the ministry in the Lutheran Churches', *Evangelium-Welt-Kirche*, (ed.), Harding Meyer, Frankfurt am Main: Verlag Otto Lembeck/Josef Knecht, 1975; 'Two Kinds of Ecumenism: Unitive and Interdenominational', *Gregorianum* 70 (1989), pp. 647–60; 'Non-theological Factors and Structures of Unity', *Einheit der Kirche. Neue Entwicklungen und Perspektiven*, (eds), Günther Gassmann and Peder Nørgaard-Højen, Frankfurt am Main: Verlag Otto Lembeck, 1988; 'Ecumenical Theology', *The Modern Theologians*, (ed.), David Ford, 1st edn, Oxford: Blackwell, 1989, pp. 255–73; 'Ecumenical Imperatives for the 21st Century', *Currents in Theology and Mission* 20 (1993), pp. 360–6.

7. 'A Great Scotist Study' (review of Etienne Gilson's *Jean Duns Scot*), *Review of Metaphysics* 7 (1954), pp. 422–35; 'Participation and Existence in the Interpretation of St Thomas Aquinas', *Franciscan Studies* 17 (1957), pp. 1–22, 107–25; 'Thomism', *Handbook of Christian Theology*, (eds) Marvin Halverson and Arthur A Cophen, New York: Meridian, 1958, pp. 361–3; 'The A Priori in St Thomas's Theory of Knowledge', *The Heritage of Christian Thought*, (eds), Robert E Cushman and Egil Grislis, New York: Harper, 1965, pp. 41–63; 'Medieval Theology', *The Encyclopedia of the Lutheran Church*, Minneapolis: Augsburg, 1965, volume 2, pp. 1510–16; 'Discovering Thomas', *Una Sancta* 24 (1967), pp. 45–52; 44–8; 67–75; 25 (1968), pp. 66–73; 'Response to Bruce Marshall', *The Thomist* 53 (1989), pp. 403–6 ('. . . my cultural-linguistic account of religious belief is in part a clumsy rendition in modern philosophical and sociological idioms of what Aquinas often said more fully and more precisely long ago').

8. George A Lindbeck, *The Future of Roman Catholic Theology*, London: SPCK and Philadelphia: Fortress, 1970, pp. 1–3; 41 (note 23).

9. 'A Panel Discussion. Lindbeck, Hunsinger, McGrath, and Fackre', *The Nature of Confession. Evangelicals and Postliberals in Conversation* (see note 2 above), p. 246. Lindbeck also here says that Hans Frei is 'the decisive figure in this particular research program ... by a very large margin' (p. 247). The best introduction to postliberal theology is William Placher, 'Postliberal Theology' in *The Modern Theologians*, (ed.), David Ford, 2nd edn, Oxford: Basil Blackwell, 1997.

10. For reviews of *The Nature of Doctrine* in English and German, see Hütter's and Müller's list in *Christliche Lehre als Grammatik des Glaubens. Religion und Theologie in postliberalen Zeitalter*, trans. Markus Müller; introduction Hans G Ulrich and Reinhard Hütter, Gütersloh: Kaiser, 1994, pp. 206–7. In English I would note especially the review symposia in *The Thomist* 49 (1985), pp. 392–472 and *Modern Theology* 4 (1988) as well as the essays in Bruce Marshall, (ed.), *Theology and Dialogue. Essays in Conversation with George Lindbeck*, Notre Dame: University of Notre Dame Press, 1990, and Phillips and Okholm, (eds), *The Nature of Confession* (see note 2 above).

11. George A Lindbeck, 'Vorwort zu der deutschen Ausgabe', *Christliche Lehre als Grammatik des Glaubens*, pp. 16–22.

12. 'Vorwort zu der deutschen Ausgabe', *Christliche Lehre als Grammatik des Glaubens*, pp. 21–2.

13. See, for example, the authors in *Understanding the Rabbinic Mind. Essays on the Hermeneutic of Max Kadushin*, (ed.), Peter Ochs (Atlanta: Scholars Press, 1990); Peter Ochs, 'A Rabbinic Pragmatism', *Theology and Dialogue. Essays in Conversation with George Lindbeck* (Notre Dame: University of Notre Dame Press, 1990), pp. 213–48; the authors in *Reasoning after Revelation. Dialogues in Postmodern Jewish Philosophy*, (eds), Steven Kepnes, Peter Ochs and Robert Gibbs (Boulder: Westview Press, 1998).

14. For critics from the Barth-strand of the Reformed tradition, see George Hunsinger, 'Truth as Self-Involving. Barth and Lindbeck on the Cognitive and Performative Aspects of Truth in Theological Disclose', *Journal of the American Academy of Religion* 61 (1993), pp. 41–56 and Bruce McCormack, 'Beyond Nonfoundational and Postmodern Readings of Barth: Critically Realistic Dialectical Theology', *Zeitschrift für dialektische Theologie* 13 (1997), pp. 67–95. From other strands of the Reformed tradition, see Brevard S Childs, 'The Canonical Approach and the "New Yale Theology"', *The New Testament as Canon. An Introduction*, Philadelphia: Fortress Press, 1984, pp. 541–6; Amy Plantinga Pauw, 'The Word is Near You. A Feminist Conversation with Lindbeck', *Theology Today* 50 (1993), pp. 45–55; Phillips and Olkham, (eds), *The Nature of Confession* (see note 2).

15. See Lindbeck's review of Jenson's *Unbaptized God. The Basic Flaw in Ecumenical Theology* (Minneapolis: Fortress, 1992) in *Pro Ecclesia* III (1994), pp. 232–8 as well as Robert W Jenson, *Systematic Theology*, volume 1, *The Triune God*, New York: Oxford University Press, 1997, pp. 6, 17, 18, 19 and volume 2, *The Works of God*, New York: Oxford University Press, 1999, pp. 238, 239, 294; Reinhard Hütter, *Suffering Divine Things. Theology as Church Practice*, Grand Rapids: Eerdmans, 2000, especially pp. 40–69; Bruce Marshall, 'Aquinas the Postliberal Theologian', *The Thomist* 53 (1989), pp. 353–406; 'Thomas, Thomisms, and Truth', *The Thomist* 56 (1992), pp. 499–524; *Trinity and Truth*, Cambridge: Cambridge University Press, 2000. See also Marshall's essay on Lindbeck in *A Handbook of Contemporary Christian Theologians*, (eds), D Musser and J Price, Nashville: Abingdon, 1996, pp. 271–7 and Michael Root's 'Truth, Relativism, and Postliberal Theology', *Dialog* 25 (1986), pp. 175–80.

16. John Milbank, *Theology and Social Theory. Beyond Secular Reason*, Oxford: Blackwell, 1990, pp. 382–8. For a critical response to Milbank, see Rusty Reno, 'The Radical Orthodoxy Project', *First Things*, February, 2000, pp. 37–44. For a different Catholic reading of the postliberal research agenda, see James J Buckley, 'Postliberal Theology: A Catholic Reading', *Introduction to Christian Theology*, (ed.), Roger A Badham, Louisville: Westminster John Knox, 1998, pp. 89–102.

17. Gordan Kaufman's review is in *Theology Today* 42 (1985), pp. 240–41; David Tracy, 'Lindbeck's New Program for Theology: A Reflection', *The Thomist* 49 (1985), pp. 460–72. See also James Gustafson, 'The Sectarian Temptation. Reflections on Theology, the Church, and the University', *Proceedings of the Catholic Theological Society of America* 40 (1985), pp. 83–94; Sheila Davaney, *Pragmatic Historicism*, Albany, New York: State University of New York Press, 2000.

18. See Bruce D Marshall, (ed.), *Theology and Dialogue*, pp. 283–98; and George A Lindbeck, *Christliche Lehre als Grammatik des Glaubens*, pp. 199–207 (bibliography by Müller and Hütter); Andreas Eckerstorfer, *Kirche in Postmodernen Welt: Der Beitrag George Lindbecks zu Einen neuen Verhältnisbestimmung*, Innsbruck: Tyrolia Verlag, 2001.

19. I chose the articles and wrote this introduction after consulting with a few students of Lindbeck's writings: Frederick Bauerschmidt, Steve Fowl, George Hunsinger, Reinhard Hutter, Bruce Marshall, William Placher, Eugene Rogers, Michael Root, Arthur Sutherland and David Yeago. All thought that some of the essays included on my original list (most included in this final volume) were exactly right. None thought that all of them were – and most had plausible alternative selections. Several made detailed comments that I have incorporated into this introduction or into the introductions to the essays, including Peter Ochs and Stanley Hauerwas. Minor changes have been made to the essays and endnotes to create consistency of style and appearance across the volume, and some brief annotations to the text have been added in the endnotes.

Chapter One: Community and Confession: An Israel-like View of the Church

Further Reading in Lindbeck

For an earlier autobiographical piece, see the interview in Patrick Granfield, *Theologians at Work*, New York: Macmillan, 1967, pp. 151–64.

Chapter Two: Reminiscences of Vatican II

1. For Vatican II's sixteen major documents, see Norman P Tanner, SJ, (ed.), *Decrees of the Ecumenical Councils*, London: Sheed & Ward and Washington, DC: Georgetown University Press, 1990, Volume II (Trent to Vatican II), pp. 817–1135; the classic commentary, written during and immediately after the Council, is Herbert Vorgrimler, (ed.), *Commentary on the Documents of Vatican II*, various trans, New York: Herder and Herder, 1967.

Further Reading in Lindbeck

'Roman Catholicism on the Eve of the Council', in *The Papal Council and the Gospel*, (ed.), Kristen E Skydsgaard, Minneapolis: Augsburg, 1961, pp. 61–92; 'Preface', 'Pope John's Council: First Session', 'Paul VI Becomes Pope: Second Session' (with Warren Quanbeck) and 'Church and World: Schema 13', in *Dialogue on the Way: Protestants Report from Rome on the Vatican Council*, (ed.), George A Lindbeck, Minneapolis: Augsburg, 1965, pp. v–ix, 18–71, 231–52; George A Lindbeck, *The Future of Roman Catholic Theology*, London: SPCK and Philadelphia: Fortress, 1970; 'Vatican II and Protestant Self-Understanding', in *Vatican II. Open Questions and New Horizons*, (ed.), Gerald M Fagin, Wilmington: Michael Glazier, 1984, pp. 58–74.

Chapter Three: Martin Luther and the Rabbinic Mind

1. See the essay on Kadushin by Peter Ochs and Theodore Steinberg in *American National Biography*, (eds) John A Garraty and Mark C Carnes, New York: Oxford University Press, 1999. Kadushin's major book is currently being edited by Jacob

Neusner and published by Global Publications (Bingham, New York). For Jewish responses to Lindbeck's dialogue with Jewish thinkers, see the introduction to this volume (note 13).

2. G Wigador, 'The Reaction of Jews to Luther', *Immanuel* 20 (Spring, 1986), pp. 101–3. Hayim-Hillel Ben-Sasson. 'The Reformation in Contemporary Jewish Eyes', *Proceedings of the Israel Academy of Science and Humanities* IV: 12 (1971), pp. 239–336 is a major study of this subject.

3. Specifically, in *The Rabbinic Mind* (henceforth *R M*) and the *Weimar Ausgabe*.

4. Luther's fellow magisterial Reformers – those, like John Calvin, who led the conservative mainline Reformation (Reformed, Anglican and Lutheran) in contrast to the anabaptists, enthusiasts and Socinians on the left – may have shared this characteristic with him. Whether they did so more or less than Brother Martin is, however, too large a theme to broach in this study.

5. For example, *R M* 33.

6. The standard English edition is that of T G Tappert (Philadelphia: Muhlenberg – later Fortress – Press, 1959, and repeatedly reprinted). My citations are occasionally modified or supplemented by reference to the original German and Latin (both from Luther's hand) which, though consistent with each other, are not always identical. The standard critical edition of the originals is in the *Bekenntnisschriften evangelisch-lutherischen Kirche*, (ed.) H Lietzmann *et al.*, Goettingen: Vandenhoeck & Ruprecht, 1952. These catechisms were more 'rabbinic' in the sense of being more concerned with practice rather than with the exposition of theological ideas, than was the Jewish catechetical literature which developed under Enlightenment influence. See n. 7, below.

7. For the prevalence of these charges, see August Hasler, *Luther in der Katholischen Dogmatik*, Munich: Max Hubner Verlag, 1968, pp. 58–98.

8. Peter von der Osten-Sacken, *Katechismus und Siddur*, Veroeffentlichungen aus dem Institut Kirche und Judentum vol. 15, Munich: Chr. Kaiser Verlag (1984), 14. The traditional ordering of topics may, as a matter of fact, be influenced by Jewish catechisms for gentile proselytes in the first centuries of the CE; and, interestingly enough, the Jewish ones which appeared from 1587 until well into the 19th century were indirectly influenced by Luther's. *Ibid.*, 99 ff: cf. JJ Petuchowski, 'Manuals and Catechisms of the Jewish Religion in the Early Period of the Enlightenment'. A Altmann, (ed.), *Studies in Nineteenth-Century Jewish Intellectual History*, Cambridge, M A: Harvard University Press, 1964), pp. 47–64. I have borrowed this and other references and ideas from Osten-Sacken sometimes, I fear, without acknowledgement, but it should be emphasized more than Osten-Sacken does, that Luther's influence on the Jewish catechisms mediated *via* Roman Catholic and, later, Enlightenment models which were less 'rabbinic' than Luther's.

9. *R M* 6, 12, 31 f., 280 ff., etc. As I read Kadushin, any systematic ordering by formal logical principles (as opposed to informal, 'grammatical' and rhetorical ones) is in his vocabulary 'philosophical' even when the contents of the teaching are supposed to be derived entirely from revelation rather than reason. If so, the search for an unchanging system of doctrine in the Bible (exemplified most clearly by the later Calvinism of, for example, the Westminster Confession of 1647, but from which Lutheran Orthodoxy and modern Protestant fundamentalism are not exempt) is 'philosophical'. For my understanding of Kadushin on philosophy, as for much

else, I am indebted to conversations with Peter Ochs and to his published and unpublished writings. He should not, however, be blamed for my applying Kadushin's notion of 'organic' interrelatedness to Luther's *topoi*.

10. Luther's 'organicist' tendencies may be more indicative of Christianity's Jewish roots rather than of Luther's 'rabbinic' mind. As befits a conservative reformer, Luther was here continuing the Catholic heritage as was his wont unless it conflicted with what he understood to be the clear word of scripture. Many scholars, not least Lutheran ones, tend to belittle this conservatism. They stress what was original in Luther's thought, and interpret this as opposed to his 'medievalism'. If he had been farther removed from the middle ages, as were later Protestants, he would have written differently, as did the authors of, for example, the Heidelberg (1563) and Westminster (1647) Catechisms. It is on the basis of such speculations that Luther's traditionalism, Catholicism, and, in the present instance, Jewishness, are often dismissed. Yet in the present instance, this cannot be done. When one turns to what is original in the catechesis, the impression of Jewishness is in some respects heightened.

11. *WA TR* (i.e. Table Talk) 5,581 f., cited by Albrecht Peters, 'Die Theologie der Katechismen Luthers anhand der Zuordnung ihrer Hauptstuecke'. *Luther-jahrbuch* 43 (1976), pp. 34f.

12. *BC* 344f. and 411–20. The trinitarian rationale for the divisions is the only one Luther mentions in the catechisms, but the narrative rationale is the operative one. In explaining the Second Article on Jesus Christ, for example, he includes the whole post-creation sweep of history before Christ, beginning with the Fall (*BC* 414), even though this is not explicitly mentioned in the Creed (which moves directly from the First Article, quoted in full in the footnote below, to a synopsis of the story of Jesus).

13. For example, the First Article, the summary of the first chapters of Genesis, reads simply 'I believe in God, the Father almighty, maker of heaven and earth' (*BC* 411).

14. *BC* 414f.

15. A scholar's popularized, delightful and widely used collection of Luther's 'haggadic midrash' is Roland Bainton's *The Martin Luther Christmas Book*, Philadelphia: Fortress Press, 1952, which deals with the birth narratives, now supplemented by the same editor-translator's *The Martin Luther Easter Story*, Philadelphia: Fortress Press, 1983, which covers the Holy Week cycle of texts. Luther's biblical commentaries are not less haggadic than his sermons, but as these were chiefly delivered as part of his academic responsibilities as an Old Testament Professor, they deal chiefly with the Tanakh; given the general tendency of Christians to neglect this part of their canon, these sermons have not been excerpted for mass circulation. Luther's Genesis Lectures of 1535–45 are a particularly rich source. See *WA* Vols. 42 ff., and *Luther's Works* (henceforth *L W*), Philadelphia: Fortress Press, various dates, Vols. 1 ff.

Luther knew snippets of medieval rabbinic exegesis at second hand, chiefly through Nicolas of Lyra, and, while he often disagreed with it on theological grounds, he preferred it to the allegorizing of his Christian predecessors. It should be observed, however, that Luther focussed on the stories of individuals – the patriarchs and matriarchs, and, in other places, Moses, Ruth, David, *et al.* He neglected narratives which deal primarily with the calling and forming of Israel as a people. For example, he never mentioned Exodus in the catechisms, and rarely elsewhere, despite its importance in the traditional cycle of liturgical readings with which Luther grew up and which he retained. Part of the explanation for this neglect is that he preferred 'haggadic midrash' to the kind of typological interpretation which had given the Exodus, for example, the importance it had in the early church as a prefigurement of resurrection with Christ through baptism. The stories which interested Luther, in contrast, were those he could expand into *exempla* for the lives of saints (that is, 'sinners justified by faith') in all times and places. Like the rabbis as described by Kadushin (*RM* 102 ff.), he had no use for philosophical allegorizing, and this deprived him of a device for giving Christian significance to texts which have to do with Israel as a people. There are, however, non-allegorical ways for Christians to utilize the communal narratives. For example, Calvin, who belonged basically in Luther's exegetical camp, gave great theological prominence to the people of Israel as type and *exemplum* of the Church. A comprehensive study (which, however, does not single out the issues here discussed) is Heinrich Bornkamm, *Luther and the Old Testament*, Philadelphia: Fortress Press, 1969.

16. *BC* 342, 365ff.

17. *RM* 132.

18. *RM* 258.

19. *Sifre* to Deut. 11.22, end; cited in *RM* 142.

20. *BC* 414.

21. *BC* 419.

22. Who, because of the epistemological priority of narrative, really are distinct.

23. Kierkegaard's objections to Hegel's philosophical interpretations of trinitarian and incarnational themes are structurally similar.

24. *RM* 340ff.

25. *RM* 341, 365ff.

26. A function compatible with a wide variety of interpretations of the nature of these truth claims.

27. *RM* 297 ff.

28. Kadushin does not discuss the logical differences of different types of dogma; *mattan torah*, for example, is formally unfalsifiable just as is the principle 'everything has a cause': it warrants certain types of inquiry rather than being itself subject to testing. The claim that the Exodus actually happened, in contrast, is theoretically, even if not practically falsifiable: it is conceivable that it is not even legend or saga, but sheer invention. The resurrection of the dead, in turn, is verifiable or falsifiable in a logically different way, i.e. under conditions which are beyond present conceivability. Kadushin is right in thinking that none of these distinctions are intrareligiously important (though they may be for external or apologetic purposes, and to this degree projects such as that of Maimonides are more legitimate than Kadushin thinks), but it is crucial, at least in biblical religions, that believers have what a Whiteheadean might call a 'propositional feeling' or attitude toward the 'mighty acts of God' dogmatically identified as crucial, and it is not clear that Kadushin recognizes this. Without such an attitude, true worship or what Kadushin speaks of as 'normal mysticism' would be impossible. For further discussion of doctrines as primarily 'rules' which nevertheless allows for their propositional functions, see my *The Nature of Doctrine*, Philadelphia: Westminster, 1984.

29. The pre-Reformation tradition generally took Paul's 'freedom from the law' to mean from the 'ceremonial' law, not from the decalogue or from New Testament precepts. Furthermore, it held that the scriptural laws which remain in force are less and less oppressive as a person grows in love and thus obeys more and more willingly and cheerfully. Other Reformers, such as Calvin, resembled the older tradition on this second point more than Luther did, and spoke of a 'third use' of the law which applies to those justified by faith and which is guiding rather than coercive and accusatory. Luther disagreed with Calvin by not speaking of a *tertius usus legis*. See n. 26, *infra*.

30. The term 'bilocated', needless to say, is not found in Luther, but this is the image suggested by the synthesis of his varied pictorial and conceptual descriptions in Wilfred Joest, *Ontologie der Person bei Luther* (Goettingen: Vandenhoeck & Rupprecht, 1967). The concept which Luther sometimes employed to explicate the metaphors is that of the 'conscience' as the faculty of self-evaluation through which God's double judgment – justified in Christ, yet sinner – is mediated. To accept God's judgment, as is done in faith, is to have a twofold self-image (as a modern might put it) and a twofold self. A dissertation in progress at the University of Chicago by Randall Zachman deals with these themes at length.

31. A brilliant overview of the influence of Augustine's and Luther's interpretations of Paul is Krister Stendahl's 'The Apostle Paul and the Introspective Conscience of the West', *Harvard Theological Review* 56 (1963), pp. 199–215, and frequently reprinted. The essay retains its suggestive value despite the need for correction in details.

32. cf. Nietzsche and, in a different vein, Ingmar Bergman.

33. *BC* 365–411.

34. *BC* 342–4, 349–56.

35. The predominance of *halakhic*-like interpretation in the Catechisms is increased when one considers that the sections on the Lord's Prayer, baptism, and eucharist are, despite the material differences, formally comparable to the rabbis' halakhic regulations of worship. It should also be noted that these sections were for Luther a kind of Christian commentary on Sabbath observance. He interpreted the third commandment (in his numbering) as a particular expression of the general principle that worship should be regular (indeed daily) and that one day of the week (whether the seventh or first apparently makes no difference) should be set aside for assembling the larger community. While such generalizing interpretive strategies were not unique to Luther, he was more cavalier about the specifics of the scriptural precepts than most Christians (who at least felt the need, for example, to argue the case for changing the Sabbath from Saturday to Sunday, etc.). In this respect, Luther was less rather than more rabbinic than the tradition.

36. *BC* 342f.

37. *BC* 361.

38. *BC* 419.

39. Luther took the need for this outward proclamation more seriously than did most members of the natural law tradition.

40. *BC* 407.

41. *BC* 411.

42. *BC* 407.

43. *WA* 42, 80; *LW* 105.

44. *BC* 408.

45. Including, most emphatically, the earthly blessings attached to what, in his numbering, was the fourth commandment: 'Honor thy father and thy mother' (*BC* 383 ff.).

46. *BC* 408; cf. 407.

47. *BC* 411.

48. The reference was to the past and specifically, according to the editor, to Matt. 23.5 (which actually, however, has to do with 'scribes and Pharisees'). Contemporary Jews were mentioned several times in passing, but simply as instances of unbelievers, along with Turks, false Christians, hypocrites and heathen (e.g. *BC* 419). Invective, such as it is (and there is relatively little in the Large Catechism and none at all in the Small), was reserved for papists.

49. *BC* 410; cf. 360.

50. *BC* 352.

51. *BC* 411. I have here used the Latin and thus depart slightly from the English translation, which at this point follows the German.

52. *BC* 366 f.

53. *BC* 411.

54. Yet, in the Catechisms, Luther avoided the full technical theological formulation which recurs constantly in the controversial writings: 'Justification by faith alone without the works of the law'. Nor did he cite Rom. 3:28, from which the theological formulation is taken, with the exception of the one word 'alone'. (The biblical verse and the theological formulation were not to be sure, neatly separated in Luther's mind. He felt free to insert the word 'alone' into his German Bible translation in order better to render the full force of what he believed Paul had in mind. Cf. n. 29 *infra*.)

55. Thus it is possible for the threat of God's wrath against those who abandon faith to be good news, gospel. Luther said that God has not only 'promised to hear and be gracious to all unworthy men ... but most strongly commanded us to pray, trust, and receive [the Gospel] on pain of his eternal displeasure and wrath ... Thus must we drive out the devil's suggestion' that God will not be merciful. 'Treatise on Good Works', *LW* 44, 62.) I am indebted to David Yeago, PhD candidate at Yale, for reminding me of this text as well as for a number of other suggestions.

56. For example, *WE* 4.

57. *RM* 18–21.

58. In the Catechisms, he never called them 'laws', even though, insofar as rewards and punishments are attached to them, they also function as such in a secondary sense. In other writings, where these functions were in question, he did not hesitate to describe the Ten Commandments as God's fearsome law.

59. *BC* 339.

60. *BC* 375.

61. Albrecht Peters has called this a *usus puerilis praeceptorum et ceremoniarum* ('a use for children of precepts and rituals'), because Luther speaks of it chiefly in connection with the education of children (*Gesetz u. Evangelium*, Gütersloh, 1981, p. 40). This *usus*, however, is simply coextensive with the commandments in their function as *doctrina* or instruction, and thus applies to everyone whether young or

old, justified or unjustified. It is quite different from the civil use of the law, for that is a matter of enforcing norms by rewards and punishments. Instruction, in contrast, has to do with training in skills to be voluntarily exercised. As a moment's reflection on the difference between 'driving instructions' and 'traffic laws' makes clear, instruction may be legally required without ceasing to be instruction. Thus it is quite possible to require everyone in the church or in a country to learn the Catechism without thereby turning its commands into laws, as the papists do, for example, with communion and confession (*BC* 341, 454, 457).

Luther's major objection to medieval canon law was that, even when it legislated practices of which he approved, it enforced them by religious sanctions and, for certain infractions, by civil ones as well. In contrast, he argued that religious communal discipline should be promoted by 'socialization into commands' rather than by the earthly or heavenly punishments and rewards by which laws are enforced. While Luther's principle may have helped prepare for religious liberty, it did not require it: following catechetical instructions, such as church attendance, could not be compelled, but learning the Catechism could be required under penalty of expulsion for those who refused, for example papists and Jews (cf. *BC* 339). Luther's notion of an instructional use of commandments differed from the Calvinists' 'the third use of the law', because the latter functioned instructionally only for true Christians, with justifying faith. At this point, the Luther of the Catechisms seems in theory closer to the rabbis: whole societies could in some measure be instructed in the commandments. In practice, however, the Calvinists went further than the Lutherans – and not only in New England – to train entire populations in biblical injunctions: blue laws were chiefly a Reformed rather than Lutheran phenomenon. Perhaps the Calvinists would have been less grimly legalistic (and more rabbinic?) if they had thought in terms of Luther's instructional commandments rather than the three uses of the law.

62. *BC* 67. It is important to note that, on this account, the problem of sin is not that human beings are unable to merit salvation, but that they desire to do so: to desire reward is to make good deeds unrewardable. Luther did not use the language of 'total corruption' or 'bondage of the will' in the Catechisms, but was concerned to make the point that good works, however great, are in violation of the first commandment if done instrumentally for the sake of extrinsic goods. Because the commandments provide instruction in the 'natural law' inscribed in the heart – 'orders of creation', as Lutherans prefer to say – deontology coincides with an ethics of virtue.

Luther's insistence that thankfulness to God is the source of all good is similar to the rabbinic emphasis on thankfulness. 'The rabbis and the people they taught were always eager to find fresh manifestations of God's love and God's justice' (*WE* 73). 'A man is duty bound to give thanks for the evil just as he gives thanks for the good . . . Whatever be the measure He metes out to thee, be thou exceedingly thankful to him' (Mishnah quoted in *WE* 67). Thus, when Luther excluded merit and affirmed salvation by grace and faith alone, he generalized a doxological principle that he shared with the rabbis. In polemical contexts, however, he generally gave an anthropological grounding to *sola gratia* and *sola fide* by arguing from human sinfulness, the bondage of the will and the terrified conscience. The result was an unrabbinically dark picture of fallen human nature, uncharacteristic of the Catechisms.

The question of whether theological polemics or catechesis better represents Luther's fundamental outlook largely turns on whether one thinks of him as starting anthropologically with sin or theocentrically with the first commandment. The case for the latter is that it more economically asserts Luther's major concern: to give all credit to God, none to oneself. It excludes *ab initio* the possibility that, if human beings were better or sinless, they would be able to merit salvation. When one starts with human sinfulness, however, this possibility is left open and must be disposed of in a second and quite distinct argument.

63. The contrast here is between what Luther denounced as the 'theology of glory' with its impressively other-worldly spirituality and the 'theology of the cross', which frees human beings for the seemingly commonplace tasks God ordains. Kierkegaard's praise of the 'knight of faith' and Bonhoeffer's of 'religionless Christianity' are structurally similar, except that, in these instances, the cross frees human beings for the modern this-worldliness of ethically responsible secular existence rather than that of a distinctive communal tradition molded by the catechetical instructions.

For Luther, to oppose theologies of glory was also to reject 'other-worldly' mysticism in favor of the proper personal religion, which is faith in God *pro me* and *pro nobis*. Kadushin similarly opposed esoteric merkabah mysticism (see, for example, *RM* 260 f. and *WE* 178 ff.), in favor of 'normal mysticism', which was analogous, although not identical, to Luther's 'faith'. In an unpublished paper, Kristen Lindbeck has asked if normal and esoteric mysticism may not often have a more symbiotic relationship in Judaism than Kadushin allows. A comparable question may be asked regarding the relation between faith and mystical or pietistic spirituality in Christianity. Contrary to many Lutherans, and perhaps Luther himself, it seems that mystical and pietistic experientialism can support, rather than compete with, faithful, this-worldly observance of God's commands.

64. Paul's statement was part of his argument that full Torah observance should not be required of gentile Christians; but while he may well have believed that Jewish Christians should remain observant, he held that they also are not justified by this anymore than are gentiles who 'do by nature the things of the law' (Rom. 2.14). Faith in the God known in Christ was also for Jewish Christians the sole condition for justification, for otherwise there would not be that equality, despite different degrees of Torah observance, which was necessary for the unity and harmony of the Church. Thus Luther's universalizing and radicalizing of justification by faith was a continuation of what was already in Paul an 'emphatic trend' (to borrow a term from Kadushin).

65. Which, in the case of the papacy, he thought was only theoretical and not practically possible.

66. *BC* 416.

67. *BC* 440.

68. W Beinert, *Martin Luther und die Juden. Ein Quellenbach*, Frankfurt, Evangelisches Verlagswerk, 1982. Ibid. *Die Juden und Martin Luther – Martin Luther und die Juden: Geschichte, Wirkungsgeschichte, Heransforderung*, New Kirchen-Vluyn, 1985. In a study sponsored by the Anti-Defamation League, Johannes Wallmann has shown that Luther's anti-Jewish diatribes were scarcely ever cited until they were resurrected by the Nazis. Reprinted in *Lutheran Quarterly*.

69. See my 'The Story-Shaped Church'. *Scriptural Authority and Narrative*

Interpretation, (ed.) G Green, Philadelphia: Fortress Press, 1987, pp. 161–78. In a fashion consistent with Luther's haggadic understanding of dogma, I discuss how ecclesiastical supersessionism might be avoided without denying the historic Christian claims that Jesus is the Messiah for Jews as well as gentiles. The reader should be warned that in that discussion, as in the present one, the focus is on intra-Christian problems, not Jewish–Christian relations.

70. David Ruderman, Gene Outka and Peter Ochs read an earlier draft of this essay and made suggestions, all of which would have improved it, and some of which I have followed. I am greatly indebted to them.

Further Reading in Lindbeck

'Erikson's *Young Man Luther*: A Historical and Theological Reappraisal', *Soundings* 56 (1973), pp. 210–27; 'Luther on Law in Ecumenical Context', *Dialog* 22 (1983), pp. 270–4; 'Modernity and Luther's Understanding of the *Freedom of the Christian*', in *Martin Luther and the Modern Mind*, (ed.) Manfred Hoffman, *Toronto Studies in Theology* 22, Toronto and New York: Edwin Mellen Press, 1985, pp. 1–22.

Chapter Four: Article IV and Lutheran/Roman Catholic Dialogue: The Limits of Diversity in the Understanding of Justification

1. See *The Book of Concord. The Confessions of the Evangelical Lutheran Church*, (trans. and ed.) Theodore G Tappert, Philadelphia: Fortress Press, 1959, pp. 30, 107–68.

2. See *Joint Declaration on the Doctrine of Justification*, Grand Rapids: William B Eerdmans, 2000. For a symposium at the contentious moment when it seemed that the Lutheran World Federation had accepted and the Vatican rejected the Joint Declaration, see *Pro Ecclesia* VII (Fall, 1998).

3. The fullest case for the compatibility of contemporary interpretations of classic positions is that developed in the monumental work of Otto Hermann Pesch, *Theologie der Rechtfertigung bei Martin Luther und Thomas von Aquin*, Mainz: Matthias Grünewald Verlag, 1967. Vinzenz Pfnür has powerfully argued that the classic positions were compatible even in the 16th century context in his *Einig in der Rechtfertigungslehre? Die Rechtfertigungslehre der Confessio Augustana (1930) und die Stellungnahme der katholischen Kontroverstheologie zwischen 1530 und 1535*, Wiesbaden: F. Steiner, 1970. Much the same conclusion is reached by the recent joint Lutheran/Roman Catholic commentary, *Confessio Augustana: Bekenntnis des einen Glaubens*, (eds) H Meyer and H Schütte, Paderborn and Frankfurt am Main: Verlag Bmifacius-Druckerei, 1980, esp. pp. 106–39.

4. A good illustration of this attitude is the essay by Robert Jenson in *The Role of the Augsburg Confession: Catholic and Lutheran Views*, (ed.), JA Burgess, Philadelphia: Fortress, 1980, pp. 151–66.

5. Chicago: University of Chicago Press, 1948, pp. 193–4.

6. Formulations such as this are, to be sure, oversimplifications as Paul Tillich recognizes in, *inter alia*, his more complex discussion of the relations of Augustine and Luther in *Systematic Theology*, Vol. 3, Chicago: University of Chicago Press, 1963, pp. 226–7.

7. *The Book of Concord*, (ed.), TG Tappert, Philadelphia: Muhlenberg, 1959, p. 161. Melanchthon simply quotes 'God crowns his gifts to us', whereas the full citation from Augustine's *On Grace and Free Will*, chap. 15 is 'If, then, your good merits are God's gifts, God does not crown your merits as your merits, but as his own gifts.'

8. A recent presentation of this general view of the relation between Augustine's *sola gratia* and Luther's *sola fide* is James F McCue, '*Simul justus et peccator* in Augustine, Aquinas, and Luther: Toward Putting the Debate in Context', *Journal of the American Academy of Religion*, XLVIII (1980) pp. 81–96.

9. *Lutheranism: The Theological Movement and its Confessional Writings*, Philadelphia: Fortress, e.g., p. 42.

10. *Enchiridion Symbolorum* (eds H Dentinger and Schönmetzer, 33rd edn), 1548.

11. For Ebeling, see *Dogmatik des christlichen Glaubens*, Vol. 1. Tübingen, 1979, pp. 186, 222, 232, 348, 351–5. For Jenson, see *Lutheranism*, pp. 64–8, 103–9.

12. *Luther und Thomas im Gespräch*, Heidelberg: Kerle, 1961.

13. Pesch, *Theologie der Rechtfertigung*, pp. 935–48.

14. *Rechtfertigung in neuzeitlichen Lebenzusammenhang*, 1974, p. 120.

15. *Ibid.*, pp. 116 ff.

16. Tappert, *The Book of Concord*, pp. 293–4.

Further Reading in Lindbeck

'A New Roman Catholic View of Justification', *Ecumenical Review* 11 (1959), pp. 334–40; 'A Question of Compatibility: A Lutheran Reflects on Trent', *Justification by Faith. Lutherans and Catholics in Dialogue*, volume 7, (eds), H George Anderson, *et al.*, Minneapolis: Augsburg, 1985, pp. 230–40; as well as the ecumenical documents that Lindbeck has signed, including those collected in *Growth in Agreement Reports and Agreed Statements of Ecumenical conversations on a World Level*, (eds), Harding Meyer and Lukas Vischer, New York/Ramsey: Paulist Press and Geneva: World Council of Churches, 1984, pp. 167–275 and *Justification by Faith. Lutherans and Catholics in Dialogue VII*, (eds), H George Anderson, T Austin Murphy and Joseph A Burgess, Minneapolis: Augsburg, 1985, pp. 13–74.

Chapter Five: The Reformation Heritage and Christian Unity

1. Evangelical Alliance.

2. A Lutheran Reformed agreement. See William G Rusch and Daniel Fr Martensen, (eds), *The Leuenberg Agreement and Lutheran Reformed Relationships*, Minneapolis: Augsburg, 1989.

3. *Baptism, Eucharist and Ministry*. Faith and Order Paper No. 111, Geneva: World Council of Churches, 1982. A document (approved in Lima, Peru) developed by many Christian Churches (Orthodox, Catholic, Protestant and others), summarizing their 'convergence' on baptism, Eucharist and ministry.

4. See, for example, BA Gerrish, *Grace and Reason; a study in the theology of Luther*, Oxford: Clarendon Press, 1962; *Continuing the Reformation: essays on modern religious thought*, Chicago: University of Chicago Press, 1993.

5.The 'Calvinistic' claim that the Son exists 'beyond or outside' (*extra*) his humanity, in contrast to the Lutheran claim that the Son exists only 'within' (*intra*) that humanity. These two slogans summarize controversies over a range of issues involving the identity of Jesus Christ and his presence, especially in the Eucharist.

6. not able to hold the infinite

7. 'High sacramental realists' might be described as those who confess that Jesus Christ is really present in the eating and drinking of the eucharistic bread and wine, where 'really' here means neither merely spiritually nor physically but 'sacramentally'. But there are (as Lindbeck goes on to point out) 'high' and 'low' versions of 'sacramentalism'. More practically, 'high sacramental realists' might be described as those who practise the Eucharist regularly (e.g. every Sunday), although Disciples of Christ practise Eucharist regularly with a 'low' or non-sacramental theology of their practice.

8. A time 'when a clear-cut confession of faith is demanded', which tolerates no compromise on the gospel (Formula of Concord X [*Book of Concord*, p. 493]).

9. Consultation on Church Unity Consensus (1985) in *Growing Consensus. Church Dialogues in the United States, 1962–1991*, (eds), Joseph A Burgess and Jeffrey Gros, FSC, New York/Mahwah: Paulist Press, 1995, pp. 11–67.

10. The Barmen Declaration (1934) was a common Reformed and Lutheran confession of faith in the face of the rise of Hitler's Third Reich and German Christianity. See John H Leith, (ed.), *Creeds of the Churches*, 3rd edn, Atlanta: John Knox Press, 1982, pp. 517–22.

Further Reading in Lindbeck

'Barth and Textuality', *Theology Today* 43 (1986), pp. 361–76 [A critical appreciation of the premier 20th century Reformed theologian]; 'A Panel Discussion. Lindbeck, Hunsinger, McGrath and Fackre', *The Nature of Confession, Evangelicals and Postliberals in Conversation*, (eds), Timothy R Phillips and Dennis L Okholm, Downers Grove: InterVarsity Press, 1996, pp. 246–53 [similarities and differences between Lindbeck's theology and North American evangelicalism].

Chapter Six: Unbelievers and the 'Sola Christi'

1. This article is a revised and condensed version of portions of an essay, ' "Fides ex auditu" und die Erlösung der Nicht-Christen. Wie denken der Katholizismus und der Protestantismus darüber?' published in *Das Evangelium und die Zweideutigkeit der Kirche*, (ed.), V Vajta, Göttingen: Vanderhoeck and Ruprecht, 1973, pp. 122–45. Much fuller references to the literature are given there.

2. 'Existentiale Interpretation und Anonyme Christlichkeit', *Zeit und Geschichte: Festschrift für R. Bultmann*, (ed.), E Dinkler, Tübingen: Mohr, 1964, p. 375.

3. *Theological Investigations* trans. Karl H-Frugen, vol V (Baltimore: Helicon Press, 1966), pp. 355–6.

4. Denzinger-Schönmetzer, *Enchiridion Symbolorum*, 32nd edn, Freiburg: Herder, 1963, p. 781.

5. See K Rahner, *Schriften zur Theologie* **VIII**, Einsiedeln: Benziger, 1967, pp. 187–212.

6. For references and a critical Lutheran discussion of Barth and others on this point, see U Kuhn, 'Christentum ausserhalb der Kirche', *Erneuerung der eine Kirche:*

Festschrift für H. Bornkamm, Göttingen: Vanderhoeck and Ruprecht, 1966, pp. 290–97.

7. The fullest documentation in English is in K Riesenhuber, 'The Anonymous Christian according to Karl Rahner', in A Roper, *The Anonymous Christian* trans. J Donces, New York: Sheed and Ward, 1996, pp. 145–79.

8. See U Kuhn, *Christentum ausserhalb der Kirche*, for a discussion of this point.

9. See his 'Erwägung zu einer Theologie der Religionsgeschichte', *Grundfragen Systematischer Theologie*, Göttingen: Vanderhoeck and Ruprecht, 1967, pp. 252–95.

10. For references, see P Althaus. *Die Letzten Dinge*, 9th edn, Gütersloh: Gütersloher Verlagshans/Gerd Mohr, 1964, p. 188, n. 2.

11. U Kuhn, *Christentum ausserhalb der Kirche*, pp. 296–7, gives illustrative citations.

12. *Christian Revelation and World Religions*, London: Burns and Oates, 1967, p. 10.

13. For a full discussion of the cases of both Troeltsch and Niebuhr, see SM Johnson, *H. Richard Niebuhr and the 'Essence' and 'Finality' of Christianity*, Yale University, unpublished PhD dissertation, 1973.

14. WJ Dalton, *Christ's Proclamation to the Spirits*, Rome: Pontifical Biblical Institute, 1965, pp. 22–3; Bo Reicke, *The Disobedient Spirits and Christian Baptism*, Copenhagen: E. Munksgaard, 1946, pp. 47–9.

15. *On the Theology of Death*, New York: Herder, 1961.

16. *Theological Investigations* V, Baltimore: Helicon Press, 1966, p. 7.

17. WA 4, 147, 23ff. (Schol. to Ps. 101.3), cited by S Ozment, *Homo Spiritualis*, Leiden: EJ Brill, 1969, p. 121.

18. V Preller, *Divine Science and the Science of God*, Princeton: Princeton University Press, 1967.

19. *Theological Investigations* IV, Baltimore: Helicon Press, 1966, pp. 323–46.

20. P Berger and T Luckmann, *The Social Construction of Reality*, New York, 1966.

21. See esp. the articles, with extensive bibliographies, on religion by C Geertz and R Bellah, *International Encyclopedia of the Social Sciences* XIII (New York: Macmillan, 1966, pp. 396–414.

22. This is well illustrated by SA Erickson's comparison of Heidegger and Wittgenstein in *Language and Being: An Analytic Phenomenology*, New Haven: Yale University Press, 1970.

23. W Sellars, *Science, Perception and Reality*, New York: Humanities Press, 1963, p. 6.

24. P Holmer, 'Language and Theology', *Harvard Theological Review* LVIII (1965) pp. 241–61.

25. *The Christian of the Future*, New York: Herder and Herder, 1967, p. 85.

Further Reading in Lindbeck

The first note in the article says that this work is a condensing of a longer essay, which is now available in a more convenient form than that shown in that note: '*Fides ex auditu* and the Salvation of Non-Christians. Contemporary Catholic and Protestant positions', in *The Gospel and the Ambiguity of the Church*, (ed.), V Vajta, Philadelphia: Fortress, 1974, pp. 92–123. See also *The Nature of Doctrine*, pp. 55–63.

Chapter Seven: Ecumenism and the Future of Belief

1. *The Future of Roman Catholic Theology*, London: SPCK, 1970, p. 9. Lindbeck cites the most crucial literature at the time on eschatology throughout this book. See the introduction of this volume for an explanation of the phrase 'realistically future eschatology'.

Further Reading in Lindbeck

'The New Vision of the world and the Ecumenical Revolution', *Religious Education* 62 (1967), pp. 83–90; *The Future of Roman Catholic Theology*, Philadelphia: Fortress Press and London: SPCK, 1970; 'The Sectarian Future of the Church', in *The God Experience*, (ed.), JP Whalen, SJ, New York: Newman, 1971, pp. 226–43.

Chapter Eight: Hesychastic Prayer and the Christianizing of Platonism: Some Protestant Reflections

1. The term 'affective' mysticism is borrowed from Edward Cuthbert Butler, *Western Mysticism: The Teachings of SS Augustine, Gregory and Bernard on Contemplation and the Contemplative Life*, New York: Dutton, 1923.

2. Per Olaf Sjogren, *The Jesus Prayer*, London: SPCK, 1975.

3. Mircea Eliade, *Yoga: essai sur les origines de la mystique indienne*, Paris: Geuthner, 1936, pp. 86–8; *Techniques de Yoga*, Paris: Gallimard, 1948, pp. 253–4. For a comparison of the Muslim *dhikr* and both yoga and hesychasm, see L Gaudet, 'Un problème de mystique comparée', *Revue thomiste* 52–3 (1952–3). Endre von Ivánka, *Plato Christianus*, Einsiedeln: Johannes Verlag, 1964, pp. 148ff., provides one of the few discussions (albeit far too brief) of the relation of yoga and hesychasm by a theologian rather than a comparative religionist. FC Happold. *Mysticism*, Harmondsworth: Penguin, 1971, pp. 127 and 221, refers to the Jesus Prayer as a mantra.

4. *Byzance et le christianisme*, Paris: Presses Universitaires de France, 1964. Cf. John Meyendorff, *Byzantine Hesychasm*, London: Variorum Reprints, 1974, esp. Article VIII, 'Society and Culture in the Fourteenth Century: Religious Problems'. This is a reprint from the *XIVe Congres international des études byzantines*, Rapports I, Bucharest 6–12 septembre 1971, pp. 51–65.

5. von Ivánka, *Plato Christianus*, pp. 389–445, esp, the first pages.

6. Esp. his 'Le thème du "retour en soi" dans la doctrine palamite du XIVe siècle', *Byzantine Hesychasm* reprinted from *Revue de l'Histoire des Religions* 145 (1954), pp. 188–206.

7. Irénée Hausherr, *Hésychasme et Prière*, Orientalia Christiana Analecta, 1966, esp. pp. 50–63, 129–54; and *Noms du Christ et Voies d'Oraison*, Rome: Pontificio Istituto Orientale, 1960.

8. Quoted by Sjogren, *The Jesus Prayer*, pp. 14–15.

9. Quoted by Timothy Ware, *The Orthodox Church*, Baltimore: Penguin, 1963, p. 314.

10. The original of this citation is in I Hausherr, 'La méthode d'oraison hésych-

aste', *Orientalia Christiana* 9 (1927), pp. 159, 164–5. A French translation is in J Meyendorff, 'Le thème du"retour en soi"', *Byzantine Hesychasm*, p. 192, and an English translation (which I have partly followed, although with emendations) is in George Màloney, *Russian Hesychasm*, The Hague: Mouton, 1973, p. 271.

11. Suzanne Langer, *Philosophy in a New Key*, Cambridge, MA: Harvard University, 1942.

12. Erik Erikson. 'Ontogeny of Ritualization', *Philosophical Transactions of the Royal Society of London*, 1966.

13. For the notion of a 'condensed symbol', see Mary Douglas' treatment of the Eucharist in her book *Natural Symbols*, New York: Random House, 1973, p. 69.

14. Esp. *Noms du Christ*.

Chapter Nine: Infallibility

1. *Decrees of the Ecumenical Councils*, volume two, *Trent to Vatican II*, (ed.), Norman E Tanner, SJ, London: Sheed & Ward and Washington DC: Georgetown University Press, 1990, pp. 811–16.

2. Dogmatic Constitution on the Church, *Decrees of the Ecumenical Councils*, volume two, pp. 849–900. Chapter III on the hierarchical constitution of the Church (as vigorous an affirmation of papal primacy and infallibility as Vatican I) must be read in the light of Chapter II (on the Church as people of God) and Chapter I (on the Church as the 'mystery' or sacrament of God). This amalgamation of old and new can, of course, be variously interpreted.

3. K Rahner has probably done more than anyone else to popularize this theme. See esp. his *Christian of the Future*, New York: Herder, 1967, pp. 77–101.

4. Christianness, modernity, unity.

5. 'The Pope, as we all know, is undoubtedly the greatest obstacle in the path of ecumenism.' H Küng, Y Congar, D O'Hanlon (eds), *Council Speeches of Vatican II*, New York: Paulist Press, 1964, p. 20.

6. See the introduction to this volume.

7. See esp. *Paul Tillich, The Protestant Era*, abridged edn, Chicago: University of Chicago Press, 1957, pp. 94–112, 222–33.

8. This is documented at length in J Pelikan, *Obedient Rebels; Catholic Substance and Protestant Principle in Luther's Reformation*, New York: Harper, 1964.

9. The best survey of the evidence on this point in English is in H. Küng, *Structures of the Church*, New York: Nelson, 1964, pp. 106–48.

10. See esp. *Unitatis Redintegratio*, nos. 14–24, esp. no. 17 in WM Abbot, (ed.), *The Documents of Vatican II*, New York: Guild America Association, 1966, pp. 357–66, esp. p. 360.

11. This treatment of the relation of identity, community and tradition is largely, though indirectly, dependent on the work of Erik Erikson. See esp. his *Young Man Luther*, New York: Norton, 1958.

12. Aquinas specifically says that for Aristotle when writing *On Interpretation* – that is, as a logician – analogical names, including the names of God, are equivocal. STI, 13, a. 10 *sed contra* & ad. 4.

13. See B Lonergan, *Doctrinal Pluralism*, Milwaukee: Marquette University Press, 1971, pp. 56–7 where he speaks of 32 differentiations of consciousness which

must be multiplied by two because of the distinction between the 'converted' and 'unconverted' consciousness.

14. This point was made in Bishop Gasser's official commentary on the Vatican I definition of infallibility. See Mansi, *Collectio Conciliorum*, 52: 1214.

15. *Verbum Dei*, no. 11 (Abbott, *The Documents of Vatican II*, p. 119) speaks of Scripture as *sine errore*, but not in such a way as to exclude errors in matters which 'do not pertain to salvation'. See the discussion in H Vorgrimler, (ed.), *Commentary on the Documents of Vatican II*, New York: Herder, 1967; 3, 199–246.

16. Hans Küng, *Infallible? An Inquiry*, New York: Doubleday, 1971, p. 175; cf. p. 181 for a fuller formulation.

17. Luther speaks at times of the universal Church as infallible or unable to err, e.g. *Werke*, Weimarer Ausgabe (henceforth *WA*) 1883ff., 51, 510f., 512f., 518. Cf. P Althaus, *The Theology of Martin Luther*, Philadelphia: Fortress, 1966, p. 360.

18. Hans Küng, *Infallible?*, p. 183.

19. For the case in favor of infallible propositions, see G Lindbeck, *The Infallibility Debate*, (ed.), J Kirvan, New York: Paulist Press, 1971, pp. 107–52, esp. pp. 108–21.

20. In teaching (ed.).

21. *WA* 26, 155, 167, 168; 27, 52. Cf. 'Die Kindertaufe bei Luther', *Lutherische Monatshefte*, 1 (1962), pp. 67–73.

22. See n. 8.

23. Scripture alone.

24. Luther did not start by questioning the authority of councils, and was only reluctantly driven in the Leipzig Disputation of 1519 to admit that the Council of Constance (1414–18) had erred in some of its condemnations of John Huss. *WA* 2, 279ff.

25. Cf. R Baumer, 'Luthers Ansichten über die Irrtumsfähigheit des Konzils', *M. Schmaus zum 70, Geburtstag*, (eds), L Scheffczyk *et al.*, Munich: Schöningh, 1967, pp. 987–1003 and J Koopmans, *Das altkirchliche Dogma in der Reformation*, Munich: Kaiser, 1955, esp. pp. 14–48.

26. The Protestant conditions for a council which they would accept are in *Corpus Reformatorum* (Halle/Saale, 1834–66), 2, 962.

27. For example, J Chrysostomus, 'Das ökomenische Konzil u. die Orthodoxie', *Una Sancta*, 14 (1959), 177–86. There are exceptions, as Küng points out in *Infallible?*, p. 201.

28. Küng, *Infallible?*, pp. 202–4.

29. Otto Semmelroth, *Zum Problem Unfelhlbarkeit. Quaestiones Disputatae 54*, Freiburg: Herder, 1971, pp. 204–6.

30. The eternal Pastor, Jesus: the first words of Vatican I's Constitution on the Church, the last chapter of which defined papal infallibility.

31. Denzinger-Schönmetzer (DS), 3050–75. For the following interpretation of Vatican I, see Walter Kasper, 'Primat u. Episkopat nach dem Vatikanum I', *Theologische Quartalschrift*, 142 (1962), pp. 47–83.

32. Infallible definitions are infallible of themselves, not from the consent of the church (ed.).

33. Literally, from the chair; figuratively, when exercising the office of shepherd and teacher of all Christians.

34. The possibility of a heretical pope was widely admitted, not only before

Vatican I, but even by conservative canonists afterwards, e.g. FX Wernz and P Vidal, *Jus Canonicum II. De Personis*, 3rd edn, Rome: Gregorianum, 1943, pp. 513–21.

35. For example H Küng, *Structures of the Church*, pp. 257–68.

36. Even a conservative Catholic historian such as H Jedin admits this, e.g. his *Kleine Konziliengeschichte*, Freiburg: Herder, 1961, p. 10.

37. Of the faith, essential to the faith (ed.).

38. R McBrien, in J Kirvan (ed.) *The Infallibility Debate*, pp. 49–51.

39. For a recent statement of Orthodox problems with the papacy, see Kéramé, 'Basis for the Reunion of Christians', *Journal of Ecumenical Studies*, 8 (1971), pp. 792–814.

40. N Chomsky comments on the contrast between 'surface' and 'deep' structures or grammars and how little we know of the latter in e.g. his *Language and Mind*, New York: Harcourt, Brace & World, 1968, pp. 4, 14ff.

41. L Wittgenstein's concept of what he calls 'depth-grammar' is markedly different from Chomsky's, but he is in agreement that it does not correspond to the articulated rules of our 'surface-grammars' (which include formal logic, etc.). Cf. e.g. his *Philosophical Investigations*, Oxford: Blackwell, 1958, no. 664.

42. The sociology of knowledge here referred to is well represented by, among others, Peter Berger, *The Sacred Canopy*, New York: Doubleday, 1967.

43. See Edmund Schlink, 'The Structure of Dogmatic Statements', in *The Coming Christ and the Coming Church*, Philadelphia: Fortress, 1967, pp. 16–84.

44. Esp. in John Courtney Murray, 'Leo XIII: Two Concepts of Government', *Theological Studies* 14 (1953), pp. 551–67; 15 (1954), pp. 1–33.

45. This literature is surveyed in JT Ford 'Infallibility – from Vatican I to the Present', *Journal of Ecumenical Studies* 8 (1971), pp. 768–91.

46. While the early Protestants were generally convinced of the impossibility of papal reform, some of them nevertheless agreed with Melanchthon that if the Pope 'would allow the Gospel, we, too, may concede to him that superiority over the bishops which he possesses by human right, making this concession for the sake of peace and general unity among the Christians who are now under him and may be in the future'. TG Tappert, (ed.), *The Book of Concord*, Philadelphia: Muhlenberg, 1959, pp. 316–17.

47. *L'Osservatore Romano* is a newspaper owned by the Holy See and published in Vatican City.

48. Abbott, *The Documents of Vatican II* pp. 14–56.

49. Bringing the Church up to date.

50. Küng, *Infallible?*, p. 152.

51. Walter Kasper, 'Zur Diskussion um das Problem der Unfehlbarkeit', *Stimmen der Zeit* 188 (1971), pp. 363–76.

52. Hans Küng, 'The Historical Contingency of Conciliar Decrees', *Journal of Ecumenical Studies* 1 (1964), p. 111.

53. Karl Rahner, 'Replik', *Stimmen der Zeit* 187 (1971), pp. 145–60.

54. For example, McBrien, in J Kirvan (ed.), *The Infallibility Debate*, pp. 42–3.

55. What I have called the 'historian's awareness' corresponds to Lonergan's 'scholarly consciousness'. *Doctrinal Pluralism*, pp. 19ff.

56. For the present state of the historical discussion, see Paul de Vooght, *Papal Ministry in the Church. Concilium* 64, (ed.), Hans Küng, New York: Herder & Herder, 1971, pp. 148–57.

57. Francis Oakly, *Council over Pope?*, New York: Herder & Herder, 1969.

58. Brian Tierney, 'Origins of Papal Infallibility', *Journal of Ecumenical Studies* 8 (1971), pp. 841–64. This is excerpted from Tierney's forthcoming book of the same title to be published shortly by EJ Brill of Leiden.

59. Küng, *Infallible?*, p. 105.

60. RM Brown and Gustave Weigel, *American Dialogue*, New York: Doubleday, 1960, p. 55.

61. Brown and Weigel, *American Dialogue*, p. 55.

62. The norm norming but not normed (ed.).

63. Küng in *Infallible?*, p. 220, speaks simply of 'Scripture's unique precedence in the faith of Christians'.

64. Relevant to this are Rahner's many writings on 'anonymous Christianity', 'transcendental' and 'categorical' revelation and the development of dogma.

65. J Kirvan (ed.), *Infallibility Debate*, pp. 1–33 and pp. 35–65, respectively.

66. *Infallibility Debate*, p. 21.

67. *Infallibility Debate*, p. 17.

68. *Infallibility Debate*, p. 16.

69. *Infallibility Debate*, pp. 29–30.

70. Hans Küng, 'Im Interesse der Sache', *Stimmen der Zeit* 187 (1971), esp. pp. 105–22.

71. Baum, in J Kirvan (ed.), *Infallibility Debate*, pp. 13–16.

72. Kasper, 'Primat u. Episkopat nach dem Vatikanum I', *Theologische Quartalschrift*, p. 373.

73. *De servo arbitrio*, WA 18, 603.

74. From JJ Hughes' translation in *Theological Studies* 32, (1971), 205.

75. Kasper, 'Primat u. Episkopat nach dëm Vatikanum I', *Theologische Quartalschriff*, p. 366.

76. For a fuller discussion of this procedure, see my article, 'Reform and Infallibility', *Cross Currents* 11 (1961), pp. 345–56.

77. Thomas Kuhn, *The Structure of Scientific Revolutions*, 2nd edn, Chicago: University of Chicago Press, 1970.

78. Karl Rahner, *Theological Investigations*, 6, Baltimore: Helicon, 1970, p. 308.

79. Kasper, 'Primat u. Episkopat nach dem Vatikanum I', *Theologische Quartalschrift* p. 373.

80. Karl Rahner, *Stimmen der Zeit* 187 (1971), p. 153.

81. See n. 42.

Further Reading in Lindbeck

'Reform and Infallibility', *Cross Currents* 11 (1961), pp. 345–56; 'The Infallibility Debate', in *The Infallibility Debate*, (ed.), John J Kirvan, New York: Paulist Press, 1971, pp. 35–65; 'Papacy and *Ius Divinum*: A Lutheran View', in *Papal Primacy and the Universal Church. Lutherans and Catholics in Dialogue* V, (ed.), Paul C Empie and T Austin Murphy, Minneapolis: Augsburg, 1974, pp. 193–208; 'Lutherans and the Papacy', *Journal of Ecumenical Studies* 13 (1976), pp. 358–68; 'Problems on the Road to Unity: Infallibility', *Unitatis Redintegratio 1964–1974*, (eds), Gerard Békés and Vilmos Vajta, *Studia Anselmiana* 71, Frankfurt: Verlag

Otto Lembeck; Verlag Josef Knecht; Rome: Editrice Anselmiana, 1977, pp. 98–109; 'The Reformation and the Infallibility Debate', in *Teaching Authority and Infallibility in the Church. Lutherans and Catholics in Dialogue* VI, (eds), Paul C Empie, T Austin Murphy and Joseph A Burgess, Minneapolis: Augsburg, 1980, pp. 101–19.

Chapter Ten: The Church

1. Charles Gore, (ed.), *Lux Mundi, A Series of Studies in the Religion of the Incarnation*, 12th edn, New York: Thomas Whittaker, 1890 (Original Preface, 1889), p. xli.

2. HF Hamilton, *People of God: An Inquiry Into Christian Origins*, London: Oxford University Press, 1912.

3. For the pre-Vatican II literature, see the incomparably thorough survey by Ulrich Valeske, *Votum Ecclesiae*, Munich: Claudius Verlag, 1962.

4. These three descriptions of the Church are simply juxtaposed in the first three chapters of *Lumen gentium*, the Dogmatic Constitution on the Church. For further discussion and references to the literature, see George Lindbeck, *Future of Roman Catholic Theology*, Philadelphia: Fortress Press, 1970, pp. 32–3; and H Rikhof, *The Concept of the Church*, London: Sheed & Ward, 1981. For many of those in English-speaking countries who began their theological careers in the 1950s, including myself, Bishop JEL Newbigin's *Household of God*, London: SCM Press, 1953, has been influential. Under the rubric 'Congregation of the Faithful', it integrates the 'people of God' motif with 'Body of Christ', and 'Community of the Holy Spirit' into a trinitarian pattern which could provide a wider framework for the present sketch.

5. This does not mean that a sacramental understanding of the Church is necessarily unevangelical, but rather that it is often regarded as such. See, e.g. a comment such as that of FW Katzenbach: 'Im Gegensatz zu Lindbeck . . . halte ich die ekklesiologische Verwendung des Begriffs "Ursakrament" für gefährlich.' In *Oecumenica: Jahrbuch für ökumenische Forschung 1967.* (ed.) FW Katzenbach and V Vajta, Gütersloh: Gerd Mohn, 1967, p. 222, fn. 40.

6. See, e.g. Karl Rahner, 'Current Problems in Christology', in *Theological Investigations*, Baltimore: Helicon Press, 1961, 1:150 and throughout.

7. A somewhat fuller version of much of the material in the next two sections is to be found in George Lindbeck. 'The Story-Shaped Church: Critical Exegesis and Theological Interpretation', in *Scriptural Authority and Narrative Interpretation*, (ed.), G Green, Philadelphia: Fortress Press, 1987, pp. 161–78.

8. My understanding of this circle as it affects theology is heavily dependent on David Kelsey, *The Uses of Scripture in Recent Theology*, Philadelphia: Fortress Press, 1975.

9. Krister Stendahl's summary of the philological and etymological evidence in *Die Religion in Geschichte und Gegenwart*, 3rd edn, 3:1297–1304, is both precise and concise.

10. I am chiefly indebted to Hans Frei for my understanding of narrative and its place in Scripture. See Hans Frei, *Eclipse of Biblical Narrative*, New Haven: Yale University Press, 1974; and, most recently, his 'The "Literal Reading" of Biblical Narrative in Christian Tradition: Does It Stretch or Will It Break?' in *The Bible and*

the Narrative Tradition, (ed.), Frank McConnell, New York and Oxford: Oxford University Press, 1986, pp. 33–77. For further details on my indebtedness to Frei, see George Lindbeck, *The Nature of Doctrine*, Philadelphia: Westminster Press, 1984, pp. 13–24.

11. It is noteworthy that the Second Vatican Council is ambiguous on whether the Church as well as Christ is the antitype 'mystically prefigured' by Israel (in the Declaration on Non-Christian Religions, no. 4). It is therefore wrong to attribute to it an unequivocal continuation of the older view as seems to be done by B Klappert, *Israel und die Kirche*, Munich: Christian Kaiser Verlag, 1980, p. 19, with whom in most other respects I am in agreement.

12. Krister Stendahl, *Paul Among Jews and Gentiles*, Philadelphia: Fortress Press, 1976, p. 37.

13. I have dealt somewhat more fully with the topics of the last two paragraphs in the essay cited in n. 7 above.

14. The key contrast here is between denotation and connotation. But, on JL Austin's distinction between the 'performance of an act *of* saying something' (a locutionary act) and the 'performance of an act *in* saying something' (an illocutionary act), see *How to Do Things with Words*, New York: Oxford University Press, 1962, p. 99.

15. Karl Barth, despite his popularization of the nature of the Church as event, is in large part an exception to this generalization. The story-shaped people of God embracing both Christians and Jews is usually referentially primary in the later volumes of the *Church Dogmatics*. It is well to observe in this connection, however, that the popularity of the designation 'people of God' in recent ecclesiology (manifesting itself not least in the second chapter of the Vatican II's Constitution on the Church) does not necessarily indicate a return either to narrative or denotative concreteness. Often 'people of God' is treated as an attributive rather than a denotative term. Thus, for example, Paul Minear discusses it as an 'image' of the Church logically comparable to others such as 'body' or 'bride' (*Images of the Church in the New Testament*, Philadelphia: Westminster Press, 1960, pp. 66–104). In such an approach, 'people of God' becomes competitive with other attributions, and warnings against overemphasis may seem appropriate (as in fact happens in Raymond Brown, *The Churches the Apostles Left Behind*, New York: Paulist/Newman Press, 1984, pp. 60 and 83). One author who in practice recognizes that 'people of God' in the Bible, like 'America' in ordinary usage, is usually a denotative term, and that, when employed this way, it makes no more sense to inveigh against overuse than in the case of 'America' or 'church' when those are the referents of discourse, is Nils A Dahl, *Das Volk Gottes*, 2nd edn, Darmstadt: Wissenschaftliche Buchgesellschaft, 1962.

16. All the bodies that profess the Lordship of the Christ Jesus witnessed to by the canonical Scriptures in ways that purport to be consistent with membership in, e.g. the World Council of Churches would qualify as 'empirical churches' for the purpose of this essay. As we shall see, some bodies that are not in fact acceptable for World Council membership, such as those which approve apartheid, are nevertheless 'empirical churches' on this reckoning because of what they as communities 'profess' or 'purport' to affirm. Greater precision than this, while important in some contexts, does not seem to be necessary for the following discussion.

17. Salvation and damnation in the ultimate sense depend on decision for or against the Messiah, for or against the kingdom, and as this is for the most part possible only for those who hear the message within the context of communities that look for or know the Messiah, it is there that both salvation and damnation are chiefly present. Because Christian antisemitism has made the message inaudible within the synagogue, this double presence, as was earlier suggested, now applies chiefly to the Church. For a further discussion of this thesis, see Lindbeck. *The Nature of Doctrine* pp. 55–63.

18. This outlook can be used to support rather than undermine the increasing contemporary concern in all churches about 'indiscriminate' baptism. When the psychosocial dimension is lacking in an initiatory rite, it turns in effect into play-acting and therefore lacks the traditional condition for validity that a right intention, 'the intention to do what the Church does', be present, not only in the celebrant but also the other principals. It was because of this condition that pagans, because they presumptively did not intend to rear their children as Christians, could not have them baptized. It is no doubt right to trust God to supply for deficiencies of intention and therefore not 'rebaptize' in doubtful cases, but this does not excuse that acquiescence to the profaning of sacred things which has become increasingly rampant as de-Christianization has emptied baptism of psychosocial content. That content remained powerful under Christendom: baptism was not play-acting. It made one a Christian, and being Christian, however distorted in understanding and practice, was fundamental to personal and communal identity, i.e. to peoplehood.

19. In modern pluralistic societies it is admittedly difficult to draw the boundaries between 'cultural-linguistic groupings'. Many individuals are socially alienated or unlocated in such a way that they do not belong to any 'people' (*ethne*, *laos* or *genos*) in the classical and biblical senses of these terms. Even in the case of highly assimilated Jews, not to mention secularized Christians, it is often difficult to say whether or not they belong to the Jewish people in the biblical and classical 'cultural-linguistic' sense. Perhaps 'no people' (1 Pet. 2.10) is a way to classify deracinated modern masses of whatever provenance. For a discussion of religions as cultural-linguistic systems (and therefore, by implication, of their adherents as constituting 'peoples'), see Lindbeck, *The Nature of Doctrine*, pp. 30–45.

20. These remarks apply chiefly to diaspora situations such as those of the first centuries and, increasingly, the present. Where the socioreligious identity of those 'evangelized' is already Christian, an emphasis on bringing as many people as possible into the churches can be construed as a call to the unfaithful to become faithful. From this perspective, the basic purpose of much Protestant revivalism since the days of Edwards and Wesley is unimpeachable, however questionable some of the techniques. Yet another set of problems is posed by mass conversions such as those which occurred after Constantine, among the northern barbarians, and on some modern mission fields (the Khazar would be a medieval Jewish parallel). When, as in such cases, one socioreligious identity collapses and multitudes seek for a new one, the Church cannot deny entry. It should no doubt seek to insist on a prolonged and exacting catechumenate as did Ambrose, Chrysostom and Cyril of Jerusalem in the face of the masses seeking baptism after the Empire became officially Christian. Yet such devices have repeatedly failed, and whole societies have become nominally Christian, with the result that membership becomes easy, almost automatic and

276 Notes to pages 159–60

totally comprehensive. The justification has been that there is no salvation outside the Church (which does not necessarily mean that it is easy within it) or, more evangelically expressed, saving faith comes only through the gospel message, and this message is unlikely to be heard outside communities of faith. Whatever the merits of such reasoning when Christendom is intact, it invites disaster when Christendom fades. The churches now increasingly consist of people who have been culturally and linguistically de-Christianized and yet retain a residual attachment to the ancestral faith. Return to stricter standards of membership seems imperative if distinctively Christian identity is to be maintained, but this means abandoning the notion that it is the Church's business to entice as many as possible by catering to whatever is currently popular whether on the conservative right or the progressive left.

21. One necessary though not sufficient condition for the liberating developments within western history has been the persistent effort of the Church to be the Church: to break the power of tribal traditionalism so that Christian serfs could marry freely and choose church vocations; to preserve the freedom of the Church over against secular authority; to order church life democratically (as in the case of the Reformed tradition); to abolish slaveholding among adherents (as in the case of those Quakers and Moravians with whom, in effect, abolition started). The stubborn deviancy of Judaism has exerted a structurally similar liberating influence. Like all worldly liberations, those stemming (in part) from the communities of biblical faith have not been unambiguously good. This becomes particularly evident when one thinks of modern science, of laissez-faire capitalism, and of secularized messianism, not least in its Marxist form. (Freudianism should perhaps be added to the list given the crucial role of Freud's Jewishness in his theory-building according to some recent studies.) None of these liberating dynamisms would have been possible, so historians plausibly surmise, in a culture uninfluenced by biblical faith. Yet these have contributed to many of the horrors as well as glories of our contemporary world. The chosen people and its Messiah have indeed brought release to the captives (Isa. 61.1; Luke 4.18), but this release has also been not peace but a sword (Matt. 10.34). Such world-transforming consequences can be seen in the biblical perspective as the use God makes in both mercy and judgment of the witness of his people; but it is the witness, not the transformation of the world, which is their mission. It is this which they are consciously to pursue. The consequences are unknown and unknowable byproducts which must be left in the hands of God.

22. The Reformers shared the early Catholic consensus that the ministry of word and sacrament is divinely instituted, and they also understood ordination as sacramental, i.e. as a rite whereby God in response to the prayers and actions of the community empowers for service. Their objections to calling ordination a sacrament were directed against late medieval views that it conferred a special personal sanctity and made priests members of a privileged caste rather than servants of the gospel. (See George Lindbeck, 'Karl Rahner and a Protestant View of the Sacramentality of the Ministry', in Proceedings of the Catholic Theological Society of America 21 (1967), pp. 267–88). In any case, the medieval distortions and the later Protestant disregard of the early Catholic consensus are now being overcome among both Roman Catholics (Vatican II) and non-Catholics. In church-oriented ecumenical circles, even if not on popular and ecclesiastical levels, the understanding of the

ordained ministry articulated in the Faith and Order Lima document, *Baptism, Eucharist and Ministry*, is now widespread. Further, it has been generally agreed both in the 16th century and in the contemporary ecumenical movement that the wider unity of the Church should be given synodal and conciliar expression. It is the question of whether it should also be papally and/or episcopally structured which has been the divisive issue.

23. This point that one and the same institutional structure may be both of divine and of human right played an important role in the Lutheran and Roman Catholic discussions of the papacy, and seems to be widely accepted. For contributions to those discussions, see George Lindbeck, 'Papacy and *"jus divinum"* ', in *Papal Primacy and the Universal Church*, (ed.), PC Empie and others, Minneapolis: Augsburg Publishing House, 1974, pp. 193–207, and C Peter. 'Dimensions of *jus divinum* in Roman Catholic Theology', in *Theological Studies* 34 (1973), pp. 227–50.

24. This is not simply a 'natural law' argument to the effect that health in ecclesiastical as in legal systems depends on respect for precedent. As the Gospels make clear, and as increased historical knowledge of his milieu confirms, Jesus was much more traditionally Jewish than Christians have generally supposed. It was what he did and what was done to him, especially the crucifixion and the resurrection, not his teachings per se, which were the novelty. The new is enduringly significant to the extent that it renews and transforms the past rather than destroys it, but the avoidance of destructive loss in the face of apocalyptic newness requires profound respect for tradition (which, needless to say, must be sharply differentiated from unwillingness to change). This is one reason Paul the traditionalist has in the long run been much more powerfully innovative than the gnostic antitraditionalists.

25. A time 'when a clear-cut confession of faith is demanded' which tolerates no compromise on the gospel (Formula of Concord X [*Book of Concord*, p. 493]).

26. This pattern of argument had its origins in the Lutheran Reformation of the 16th century, but, with the disappearance of belief that there is a single biblical pattern of church organization, it is now widespread also among other Protestants. It can be used against dogmatic anti-episcopalianism as well as against dogmatic pro-episcopalianism (as happens, e.g. in the Lutheran churches of Sweden and Finland, where the retention of the historic succession in the face of free-church absolutism becomes, in effect, *status confessionis*).

27. I take this comparably decisive period to be, not that of Jamnia, but that of the formation of Ezra's pentateuchal Torah during the exile (as James A Sanders in effect argues in his *Torah and Canon*, Philadelphia: Fortress Press, 1972).

28. I abstract from the question of infallibility which concerns the nature of doctrine more than it does that of organizational structures, and needs to be considered in reference to the Bible and the Church as a whole as well as councils and popes. See Lindbeck, *The Nature of Doctrine*, pp. 98–104.

29. This is essentially the position taken by the Lutheran participants in the official American dialogue with Roman Catholics reported in Empie, *Papal Primacy and the Universal Church*. Papal primacy is acceptable but not the claim to irreversibility.

30. The question of irreversibility, it should be noted, is that of continuity, not of permanence of structural forms. Location in Rome is not essential (there was, after all, the Avignon interlude); and, as Karl Rahner speculatively suggested (in an

interview which has not been published in the *Theological Investigations*), the papal function could be exercised by, e.g. a committee of three whose jurisdictional powers might be no greater than that of the secretary of a Quaker meeting or the Stated Clerk of a Presbyterian General Assembly (the examples are my own). What is essential, however, is that such transformations take place by papal self-limitation, not by imposition from, e.g. a council or by revolution. It is the continuity of the institution which is said to be guaranteed, and therefore also the irreversibility (= infallibility) of the corresponding dogmatic development. Even if the Pope never again spoke *ex cathedra* or exercised 'immediate and universal' jurisdiction in the sense of Vatican I, the possibility of doing so under appropriate circumstances (if or when these should ever recur) would remain.

31. See George Lindbeck, 'The Reformation and the Infallibility Debate', in *Teaching Authority and Infallibility in the Church*, (ed.), PC Empie and others, Minneapolis: Augsburg Publishing House, 1978, pp. 101–19, 312–16, esp. Thesis 5, 315–16, for a fuller discussion of the potentially marginal character of disagreements over the irreversible (i.e. 'irreformable' or 'infallible') character of at least some dogmatic decisions and, by extension, of the structural developments to which they refer.

32. Decentralization of the type envisioned here would make possible great variations in Jewish–Christian relations (which, as Karl Barth among others has noted, may well be crucial to the future of the Church), in ecumenical developments, and in canon law between different localities and regions. Christians in one area might be in a position to move much faster on some matters than those in other areas, and this would, of course, be reflected in the candidates they proposed to lead them (for initiation of episcopal candidacies would be a local matter as in the early church). If the proposed candidates in a given region were consistently in favor of, e.g. communion with the local Anglicans and/or the ordination of women, and these candidates were acceptable to neighboring churches, Rome would have difficulty in persistently refusing its consent. If it were to do so, to mention one difficulty, some sees might be left vacant indefinitely. The papal role in such a situation could be to mediate between regions of the Church that disagreed on these issues so that different local practices could develop without schism. Nothing similar to this, needless to say, is likely to occur in the next generation or two apart from world-historical or ecclesiastical events of the magnitude of World War II or Vatican II. But, on the other hand, there is no reason to suppose that the possibilities of upheaval and change in the next half century will be any less than in the last 50 years.

33. While the Augustana has come to be regarded as Lutheran property, it was in its origins more nearly a pan-Reformation manifesto than were any of the other 16th-century confessions. See Brian Gerrish, 'Strasbourg Revisited: The Augsburg Confession in Reformed Perspective', in *The Augsburg Confession in Ecumenical Perspective*, (ed.), H Meyer, Geneva: Lutheran World Federation, 1981, pp. 129–61.

34. This was written together with Heinrich Fries, *Unity of the Churches: An Actual Possibility*, Philadelphia and New York: Fortress Press and Paulist/Newman, 1983. The most recent report from the international Lutheran and Roman Catholic dialogue, *Facing Unity*, Geneva: Lutheran World Federation, 1984, proposes a model of the unity Christians seek which corresponds more closely to the one outlined here.

Further Reading

Lindbeck explores these issues further in 'The Constitution on the Church: A Protestant Point of View', in *Vatican II. An Interfaith Appraisal*, (ed.), John H Miller, Notre Dame: University of Notre Dame Press, 1966, pp. 219–30; 'There is No Protestant Church', *Una Sancta* 23 (1996), pp. 91–100; *The Future of Roman Catholic Theology*, Philadelphia: Fortress Press and London: SPCK, 1970, especially chapter 2; 'The Sectarian Future of the Church', in *The God Experience*, (ed.), JP Whalen, SJ, New York: Newman, 1971, pp. 226–43; 'The Story-shaped Church: Critical Exegesis and Theological Interpretation', in *Scriptural Authority and Narrative Interpretation*, (ed.), Garrett Green, Philadelphia: Fortress, 1987, pp. 161–78; 'The Eucharist tastes bitter in the Divided Church', *Spectrum* 19, Yale Divinity School (1999) including the essay on 'Scripture, Consensus, and Community' in Chapter 13 of this volume.

Chapter Eleven: Toward a Postliberal Theology

1. The type of theology I have in mind could also be called 'postmodern', 'postrevisionist' or 'post-neo-orthodox', but 'postliberal' seems best because what I have in mind postdates the experiential-expressive approach which is the mark of liberal method. This technical use of the word is much broader than the ordinary one: methodological liberals may be conservative or traditionalist in theology and reactionary in social or political matters (as the reference, on p. 185 of this chapter, to the pro-Nazi *Deutsche Christen* is meant to indicate).

2. Clifford Geertz, *The Interpretation of Cultures*, New York: Basic Books, 1973, pp. 3–30. The quotations that follow in this paragraph are taken in order from pp. 17, 21, 13, 10 and 26.

3. EE Evans-Pritchard, *Nuer Religion*, Oxford: Oxford University Press, 1956 p. 84. This 'notorious ethnographic example' is cited by TMS Evans, 'On the Social Anthropology of Religions', *Journal of Religion* 62/4 (1982), p. 376.

4. Unlike David Tracy, *The Analogical Imagination*, New York: Crossroad Publishing Co., 1981, I am using 'classic' to refer to texts that are culturally established for whatever reason. Tracy's model, in contrast to mine, is experiential-expressive. For him classics are 'certain expressions of the human spirit [which] so disclose a compelling truth about our lives that we cannot deny them some kind of normative status' (p. 108).

5. This and the following descriptions of intratextuality were composed without conscious reference to deconstructionism, but, given the current prominence of this form of literary theory, some tentative comments on similarities and dissimilarities may be desirable in order to avoid misunderstandings. First, intratextualism, like deconstructionism, does not share the traditional literary emphasis on a text as that which is to be interpreted, whether (as in the now-old 'New Criticism') as a self-contained aesthetic object or 'verbal icon' or as mimetic or as expressive or as pragmatic. (For the meaning of these terms, see Meyer H Abrams, *The Mirror and the Lamp: Romantic Theory and the Critical Tradition*, Oxford: Oxford University Press, 1953; cited by MA Tolbert, *Religious Study Review* 8/1 (1982), p. 2.) Instead, intratextualism treats texts – to use a phrase applied to languages in earlier chapters

– as 'mediums of interpretation', and thus shares the deconstructionist emphasis on texts as constituting the (or a) world within which everything is or can be construed. Related to this, in the second place, is a common concern (as will later become apparent) with what Christopher Norris, speaking of Paul de Man, calls 'the play of figural language', 'the grammar of tropes', and 'the rhetoric of textual performance', (Christopher Norris, *Deconstruction: Theory and Practise*, London and New York: Methuen & Co., 1982, pp. 106, 108.) In the third place, however, the great difference is that for the deconstructionists there is no single privileged idiom, text or text-constituted world. Their approach is *inter*textual rather than intratextual – that is, they treat all writings as a single whole: all texts are, so to speak, mutually interpreting. One result is that what in the past would have been thought of as allegorizing is for them an acceptable mode of interpretation. In an intratextual religious or theological reading, in contrast, there is (as this chapter later notes at length) a privileged interpretive direction from whatever counts as holy writ to everything else. Other differences as well as similarities are discussed by Shira Wolosky in a treatment of Derrida's relation to Talmudic modes of interpretation ('Derrida, Jabes, Levinas: Sign Theory as Ethical Discourse', *Journal of Jewish Literary History* 2/3 [1982], pp. 283–301). It should incidentally be noted, however, that Derrida's understanding of Christian interpretive method as presented in this article is quite different from the typological approach, which I shall argue was historically dominant. It may be that Derrida's view of what is characteristically Christian in these matters has been influenced by the experiential-expressive hermeneutics of Paul Ricoeur, whose student he once was.

6. Thomas Aquinas, *ST* I.1.10.

7. For the structure, though not all the details, of my understanding of typological interpretation, see Hans Frei, *The Eclipse of Biblical Narrative*, New Haven: Yale University Press, 1974, esp. pp. 1–39.

8. Charles Wood, *The Formation of Christian Understanding*, New Haven: Westminster Press, 1981, pp. 42, 101, and throughout.

9. See my review of Gerhard Ebeling's *Dogmatik des Christlichen Glaubens*, in *Journal of Religion* 61 (1981), pp. 309–14.

10. Hans Frei, *The Eclipse of Biblical Narrative*, pp. 39ff.

11. For the general way of looking at the problem of scriptural interpretation presented in this paragraph, though not for all the details, I am indebted to David Kelsey, *The Uses of Scripture in Recent Theology*, Philadelphia: Fortress Press, 1975.

12. This way of putting the matter is dependent on Hans Frei, *The Identity of Jesus Christ*, Philadelphia: Fortress Press, 1975.

13. In addition to Hans Küng's *On Being a Christian*, trans. Edward Quinn, New York: Doubleday & Co., 1976, see his 'Toward a New Consensus in Catholic (and Ecumenical) Theology', in Leonard Swidler, (ed.), *Consensus in Theology?* Philadelphia: Westminster Press, 1980, pp. 1–17.

14. This is the focus of attack in Hick (ed.), *The Myth of God Incarnate*, Philadelphia: Westminster Press, 1977.

15. Edward Schillebeeckx, *Jesus: An Experiment in Christology*, trans. Hubert Hoskins, New York: Seabury Press, 1979.

16. David Tracy, *Blessed Rage for Order*, New York: Seabury Press, 1975.

17. Karl Barth's way of doing this is described and critically but sympathetically assessed in David Ford, *Barth and God's Story*, Frankfurt: Peter Lang, 1981. See

also D Ford, 'Narrative in Theology', *British Journal of Religious Education* 4/3 (1982), pp. 115–19.

18. David Kelsey, *The Uses of Scripture in Recent Theology*, p. 48.

19. David Kelsey, *The Uses of Scripture in Recent Theology*, p. 48.

20. Richard Rorty partly illustrates this possibility of doing philosophy intratextually, but the inevitable vagueness of his canon of philosophical texts makes him verge on a philosophical version of deconstructionism. See his *Consequences of Pragmatism*, University of Minnesota Press, 1982, esp. essays 6 (on Derrida), 8, and 12, and the Introduction.

21. Gerhard von Rad, *Old Testament Theology*, trans. DMG Stalker, 2 vols., San Francisco: Harper & Row, 1962, 1965.

22. See Chapter 1, n. 30.

23. For example, the pioneering work *Toward the Year 2000*, (ed.), Daniel Bell, Boston: Beacon Press, 1969, now seems extraordinarily dated.

24. My own two minor exercises in this genre are basic to the following paragraphs. See 'Ecumenism and the Future of Belief', *Una Sancta* 25 (1968), pp. 3–17 [Chapter 7 in this volume] and 'The Sectarian Future of the Church', in Joseph P Whelan, (ed.), *The God Experience*, Westminster: Newman Press, 1971.

25. Northrop Frye, *The Great Code: The Bible and Literature*, Harcourt Brace Jovanovich, 1982.

26. For the argument of this paragraph, see George Lindbeck, '*Theologische Methode und Wissenschaftstheorie*', *Theologische Revue* 74 (1978), pp. 267–80. This article has not been published in English.

27. What I have in mind here might be called 'assimilation by interpretation' and is to be distinguished from what Cardinal Newman, using the same name, listed as the third mark of authentic doctrinal development. The analogies he used were organic, not interpretive: for example, a plant assimilates foreign material from its environment. (John Henry Newman, *An Essay on the Development of Christian Doctrine*, New York: Doubleday & Co., Image Books, 1960, pp. 189–92, 338–60.)

28. Basil Mitchell, *The Justification of Religious Belief*, London: Macmillan & Co., 1973.

29. Brian Gerrish, *Grace and Reason: A Study in the Theology of Luther*, Oxford: Oxford University Press, 1962, esp. pp. 168–71; Philip Watson, *Let God Be God! An Interpretation of the Theology of Martin Luther*, Philadelphia: Muhlenberg Press, 1947, pp. 73ff.

30. Thomas Aquinas, *ST* I.1.8, ad 2.

31. Thomas Aquinas, II–II.2.10.

32. Cf. n. 26, above.

33. Paul Tillich, *Systematic Theology*, vol. 2, Chicago: University of Chicago Press, 1957, pp. 154–8, esp. p. 157. Tillich says that the 'picture of Jesus of Nazareth becomes indissolubly united with the reality of the New Being', but does not in this place affirm the converse relation. For a fuller discussion of Tillich's view of the finality of Christ, see George Lindbeck, 'An Assessment Re-assessed: Paul Tillich on the Reformation', *Journal of Religion*, 63 (1983), pp. 376–93, esp. p. 391f.

34. Such attitudes are also widespread in Europe, where church attendance is much smaller than in the United States. See H Hild (ed.), *Wie stabil ist die Kirche? Bestand und Erneuerung: Ergebnisse einer Meinungsbefragung*, Gelnhausen: Burckhardthaus-Verlag, 1974. See also Gerhard Szczesny, 'Warum ich als Nichtchrist

Weihnachten feiere', in H Nitschke (ed.), *Was fällt ihnen zu Weihnachten ein?*, Gütersloh: Gütersloher Verlagshaus Gerd Mohn, 1978, pp. 50ff.

35. Cf. Kelsey, *The Uses of Scripture in Recent Theology*, pp. 39–50 and throughout also Ford, *Barth and God's Story*; but I have learned to think about Barth in this way above all from conversations with Hans Frei.

Further Reading in Lindbeck

'Creeds and Confessions', in *The New Encyclopedia Britannica*, 15th edn, Chicago: Encyclopedia Britannica Inc., 1998, volume 26, pp. 785–88; 'The Church's Mission to a Postmodern Culture', in *Postmodern Theology, Christian Faith in a Pluralist World*, (ed.), Frederick B Burnham, New York: Harper & Row, 1989, pp. 37–55.

Chapter Twelve: Foreword to the German Edition of The Nature of Doctrine

1. References to the sources mentioned in this paragraph are found at the appropriate place in the body of the book.

2. These words are quoted from David Tracy, 'Lindbeck's New Program for Theology', *The Thomist* 49 (1985), pp. 460–72 (465). Tracy, it should be noted, does not claim that my views are self-contradictory, but rather that their true character is disguised by avant garde rhetoric. Another commentator on the relation of my work to Barth reaches the conclusion that I am best interpreted as a crypto-Thomist (George Hunsinger, 'Truth as Self-Involving', *Journal of the American Academy of Religion* 61 (1993), pp. 41–56). My own view, as the reader of what follows will discover, is that there are ways of understanding all three of these theologians which are harmonizable with pretheological postliberalism. In the more properly theological or dogmatic teaching and writing which I have done over the years, the basically Lutheran character of my ecumenically 'evangelical-catholic' outlook is, I would hope, unmistakable.

3. See Reinhard Hütter's account of these two writers in 'Ethik in Traditionen', *Verkundigung und Forschung* 35 (1990), pp. 61–84.

Chapter Thirteen: Scripture, Consensus and Community

1. As was pointed out by Cardinal Ratzinger and others in the discussion of this paper, pre-Reformation allegorizing did not always have the features to which the Reformers objected. In any case, the distinction between typology and allegory which I make in this sentence requires clarifications which are beyond the scope of this paper.

2. The work of my colleague, Hans Frei, especially his *Eclipse of Biblical Narrative* New Haven: Yale University Press, 1974, has been decisive for my own thinking on these matters, but I also owe much to two other colleagues, David Kelsey and Brevard Childs, and to those, beginning with Henri de Lubac and Jean Daniélou, who have contributed to a better understanding of the functions of typology in patristic and medieval exegesis. As this is not, in its present form, a scholarly paper, but a reflection from a Reformation perspective on the role of the Bible and its interpretation in the life of the Church, I have felt free to refrain from extensive footnoting. Fuller documentation of the sources of my thinking on these issues is to be found in my book, *The Nature of Doctrine*, Philadelphia: Westminster, 1984

and most of the undocumented sources are, I hope, familar enough to need no explicit acknowledgment.

3. See especially the work of Professor Frei mentioned in note 2. He, more than any other theological commentator on these developments of whom I know, has been aware of the extensive discussions of both the logical and literary features of narrative which have developed especially since Erich Auerbach's *Mimesis: The Representation of Reality in Western Literature*, Princeton, 1953 but unlike most other theologically interested commentators (of whom Paul Ricoeur might serve as an example), he has resisted the tendency to develop a general hermeneutical theory of narrative (sometimes even an anthropology) which is then applied to the Bible. Each text should be interpreted in its own terms: the Bible has its own hermeneutics. This conviction underlies the present essay and is well illustrated by Frei's recent essay, 'The "Literal Reading" of Biblical Narrative in the Christian Tradition', in *The Bible and the Narrative Tradition*, (ed.), F McConnell, Oxford, 1986.

4. Jeffrey Stout, *The Flight from Authority*, Princeton, 1983.

5. On the nature of the intertwining, see Hans Frei's essay cited above at the end of note 3.

6. I here follow the general view that although Vatican II did not explicitly reject a two-source interpretation of Trent's statements on Scripture and tradition, it nevertheless favors a one-source construal.

7. Ronald Thiemann, 'Radiance and Obscurity in Biblical Narrative', in *Scriptural Authority and Narrative Interpretation*, (ed.), G Green, Philadelphia: Fortress, 1987, pp. 21–41.

8. In its Anglo-American forms, this recognition of radical historicity is not necessarily associated with skepticism, relativism or irrationalism. The truth available to human beings in this life is 'justified belief', and the fact that the canons of justification vary does not make the search for truth and the use of the best available canons any less imperative. The kind of Aristotelianism and Thomism represented by such authors as Alasdair MacIntyre, Victor Preller, David Burrell and Fergus Kerr is compatible with this position, and its relation to Thomas Aquinas in particular is discussed by Bruce Marshall in *The Thomist* [see the editor's introduction, note 15, p. 255 above]. The argument, much oversimplified, is that while Aquinas was wholly non-relativistic about truth (God knows things as they actually are), he is not so about knowledge (creaturely knowledge is in accord with ('the mode of the receiver'), and therefore has room for a recognition of historicity which is neither skeptical nor irrationalist. Needless to say, the present argument is also compatible with other philosophical positions.

9. It may be helpful to offer some clarifications in order to avoid confusion between this use of 'textuality' and Jacques Derrida's deconstructionism. Derrida, despite his exaggerations, is not wholly wrong in claiming that writing is prior to speaking and polysemy to univocity. It is not the text, but only the 'present' word, the word as used in a situationally specific speech act, which has a single, fixed meaning. Derrida's theological error is to suppose that Christians have historically understood the logos, the Word incarnate, in terms of the ontotheology against which he polemicizes. Jesus Christ has never been treated in practice (whatever may have been true of doctrine or theology) as similar to a speech act with a single unchanging meaning, but is now, as the ascended Lord, just as much a living person as in his days on earth. His present meaning – what he says

to believers through Scripture, worship, etc. – continues to be 'new every morning'.

A further point is that the emphasis on textuality involves an endless and an undecidable play of signification only when one refuses (as do the deconstructionists) to give privileged status to a given text and given hermeneutic. This refusal, however, is arbitrary. It is as if one were to deny the legitimacy of taking as primary the geometric meaning of Euclid's *Elements* just because this book can also be viewed as intertextually related to the whole of literature, and can be read with an indefinite number of purposes and meanings, including self-subversive ones. Apart from such deconstructive narrowness, however, the emphasis on textuality vividly makes the point that a textbound faith, far from being rigidified, is open to hearing God speak in many ways through Scripture.

In summary, premodern Bible reading shares with deconstructionism the refusal to make primary such derivatives from the text as doctrines (understood, e.g. as universal propositional truths about reality), historical reconstructions or existential descriptions of the human condition (each of which, if thought to catch the deeper meaning of the text, involves a kind of 'ontotheology'). It also shares with deconstructionism the emphasis on close reading and multiple meanings. The difference is that there was, for premodern Jews and Christians, unlike modern deconstructionists, a privileged text and privileged mode of interpretation. Thus within the indicated limitations, modern literary approaches with their emphasis on textuality increase the possibility of a retrieval of the classic hermeneutics.

10. When whales and bats are redescribed as mammals they come to be understood as quite different from fish or birds, and yet they remain thoroughly distinct from each other and from other mammals. Similarly, the worlds of early, medieval, Reformation or contemporary Christians remain quite different from each other when biblically redescribed. 'Absorbing contemporary reality into the scriptural text', to repeat an earlier phrase, is logically the reverse of translating the scriptural message into contemporary thought forms, but it need not be an archaizing project.

Barth and von Balthasar, however, differ in their redescriptions in that the latter is more positive than Barth about the contributions to the faith of 'Christianized' worldviews or philosophies (e.g. Platonism). He seems to me, however, to be equally insistent (e.g. against Rahner), on the fundamental 'untranslatability' of the biblical message. The present argument is compatible on these points with both Barth and von Balthasar, though, where they differ, it perhaps tilts toward von Balthasar.

11. I have commented briefly on some of the strengths and weaknesses of Barth's exegesis in 'Barth and Textuality', *Theology Today* 43 (1986), pp. 361–76.

12. As I come to the end of this chapter I am finding myself acutely aware that it is a counter-instance of what it recommends: it does not refer the reader to the biblical text. It is too long as it is, and I have tried, not altogether successfully, to omit scriptural citations. Yet if the form were to fit the message, it should be rewritten, in premodern fashion as a commentary on such interglossing passages as Deut. 6.4–9; 2 Tim. 3.15–17 and Luke 2.45–7. Historical criticism would help in ascertaining the views to which these passages were opposed (both originally and canonically), and typology would provide the warrant for finding analogies (and therefore guidance) in later church history and the present. Augustine's precepts for applicative interpretation, especially the rule of charity, would have to be observed, as also the self-critical force of the *simul justus et peccator*. The resulting essay would be longer, but also more interesting. It would be genuinely theological, a

first-order attempt to get guidance from Scripture, instead of a second-order account of the need and possibility of doing so. Yet everything in the present essay could also find a place in the rewritten one.

Further Reading

'The Problem of Doctrinal Development and Contemporary Protestant Theology', in *Man as Man and Believer*, (eds), Edward Schillebeeckx and Boniface Willems, *Concilium* 21, New York: Paulist Press, 1967, pp. 133–49; 'The Bible as Realistic Narrative', in *Consensus in Theology? A Dialogue with Hans Küng and Edward Schillebeeckx* (ed.), Leonard Swidler, Philadelphia: Westminster, 1980, pp. 81–5; 'The Story-Shaped Church: Critical Exegesis and Theological Interpretation', in *Scriptural Authority and Narrative Interpretation*, (ed.), Garrett Green, Philadelphia: Fortress, 1987, pp. 161–78; 'Atonement and the Hermeneutics of Intratextual Social Embodiment', in *The Nature of Confession. Evangelicals and Postliberals in Conversation*, (eds), Timothy R Phillips and Dennis L Okholm, Downers Grove: InterVarsity Press, 1996, pp. 221–40.

Chapter Fourteen: The Gospel's Uniqueness: Election and Untranslatability

1. Delivered at a conference of the Australian/New Zealand Association of Theological Studies in Canberra, 24–8 September, 1995.

2. The cultural-linguistic perspective on religions in terms of which I have previously discussed their uniqueness and pluralism is not to be confused with a theology of religions. While compatible with at least some religious outlooks (including Christian ones) its origins are in the social sciences and in philosophy. See *The Nature of Doctrine: Religion and Theology in a Postliberal Age*, Philadelphia: Westminster; 1984, esp. Chap. 3, pp. 46–72.

3. One comprehensive classification of the literature of this topic in terms of this tripartite taxonomy is Alan Race, *Christians and Religious Pluralism: Patterns in Christian Theology*, Maryknoll: Orbis Books, 1986

4. For books criticizing descriptions of religions as having a common aim or goal (whether this be called 'salvation' or something else), see Paul J Griffiths, *An Apology for Apologetics: A Study in the Interreligious Dialogue*, Maryknoll: Orbis, 1991; JA Dinoia, *The Diversity of Religions: A Christian Perspective*, Washington DC: Catholic University of America, 1992; S Mark Heim, *Salvations: Truth and Difference*, Maryknoll: Orbis, 1995.

5. The removal of proselytism, it should be added, does not guarantee good relations nor, on the other hand, is openness to receiving converts from other religions always incompatible with friendliness. If one draws a distinction, as is often done, between 'proselytism' and 'evangelism', the former but not the latter is unacceptable. Proselytism but not evangelism (which would include much of what is called missionary work) involves the use of unacceptable means such as bribery, misrepresentations and psychological pressures or physical or legal coercion to gain adherents.

6. John Hick, *An Interpretation of Religion*, New Haven: Yale University Press, 1989.

7. The early essay, 'Christianity and Non-Christian Religions', *Theological*

Investigations, Vol. 5, London: Darton, Longman & Todd, 1966, remains Karl Rahner's basic exposition of his position.

8. 'Gospel' is here used in what the Lutheran Confessions call the 'broad' rather than 'narrow' sense. The former encompasses the whole of God's biblical word in its informing and condemning and not only its consoling functions.

9. In 'The Very Idea of a Conceptual Scheme', republished in his *Inquiries into Truth and Interpretation*, Oxford: Clarendon, 1985, pp. 37–54.

10. In *Whose Justice? Which Rationality?*, Notre Dame: Notre Dame University Press, 1988, pp. 370–88.

11. This parallelism between Aquinas and Barth has recently been argued at length by Eugene Rogers, *Thomas Aquinas and Karl Barth: Sacred Doctrine and the Natural Knowledge of God*, Notre Dame: Notre Dame University Press, 1996.

12. *Biblical Interpretation in Ancient Israel*, Oxford: Clarendon Press, 1985.

13. Hans Frei, Brevard Childs, Moshe Greenberg and Erich Auerbach have been most often in my mind as I have read and pondered 'classic hermeneutics' over the decades, but outside of my obvious dependence on Frei and Auerbach in regard to the nature and role of biblical narrative, I would be hard put to identify what I owe to each.

14. For this characterization of the literal sense I am particularly indebted to Kathryn Tanner, 'Theology and the Plain Sense', in Garrett Green (ed). *Scriptural Authority and Narrative Interpretation*, Philadelphia: Fortress Press, 1987 and for theological and historical backing, to Hans Frei's earlier essay, 'The "Literal Reading" of Biblical Narrative', republished in *Theology and Narrative Selected Essays* (eds), G Hunsinger and W Placher, New York: Oxford University Press, 1993.

15. See his biography, *Alexander the Great*, London: Penguin, 1986.

16. Israel understood as prototype functions as both positive and negative example to that which resembles it, viz. the Church as ectype. The prototype/ectype relation leaves open questions of superiority and inferiority. If some creature were to be designated as prototypically mammalian, for example, it might well be regarded as superior to some mammals in some respects, and inferior to others.

17. I have analyzed Harnack's attitude on these matters in a hitherto unpublished paper.

18. As Paula Fredericksen points out in, 'What You See is What You Get', *Theology Today* 52 (1995), pp. 75–97.

19. It must be added, however, that the scholarly removal of scriptural support from traditional teachings does not by itself settle the issue of whether or not they are consistent with Scripture. Contemporary interconfessional dialogues have made this abundantly clear. Ecumenically minded and historically critical Roman Catholics and Protestants come generally to agree that there is no direct biblical evidence one way or another by which controversies over Mary and the papal office, for example, could be settled, and their disagreement then centers on whether Church and tradition suffice to dogmatize about such scripturally open questions. Supersessionism, however, is not a scripturally open topic in the same way as are these teachings. The problem is not that the Bible is silent, but that it says too many different things. It seems blatantly to contradict itself. These apparent contradictions are irresolvable for single-minded historical-critics, whereas classicists both must and can resolve them by their commitment to a theologically and figurally unified

canonical reading centering on Jesus Christ as realistically depicted in the Gospel narratives. This classic approach, however, does not by itself suffice to determine which side should be accorded hermeneutical primacy, and gentile bias has regularly tipped the balance in the supersessionist direction. This bias can be corrected, however, by historical-critical awareness of the profound Jewishness of the New Testaments seeming suprsessionism, and once this happens, the anti-supersessionist case becomes compelling on classic hermeneutical grounds (indeed, so compelling that even without benefit of historical criticism it has prompted sporadic gentile philosemitism throughout Christian history)

20. *Tanakh: A New Translation*, Philadelphia: Jewish Publication Society, 1985.

21. David Novak, *The Election of Israel*, Cambridge and New York: Cambridge University Press, 1995, p. 115.

Further Reading

Lindbeck explores these issues further in 'The Jews, Renewal and Ecumenism', *Journal of Ecumenical Studies* 2 (1965), pp. 471–3; 'Jewish–Christian Dialogue', *Journal of Ecumenical Studies* 3 (1966), pp. 146–7; 'Christians between Arabs and Jews', *Worldview* 22/9 (1979), pp. 25–6, 35–9; 'Response to Michael Wyschogrod's "Letter to a Friend" ', *Modern Theology* 11 (1995), pp. 205–10; 'Postmodern Hermeneutics and Jewish–Christian Dialogue: A Case Study' and 'What of the Future? A Christian Response', in *Christianity in Jewish Terms*, (eds), Tikva Frymer-Kensky, David Novak, Peter Ochs, David Fox Sandmel and Michael A Signer, Boulder: Westview Press, 2000, pp. 106–13 and 357–66; in *Who do you say that I Am? Perspectives at the End of the Millennium*, University of Notre Dame Press, forthcoming. See also Chapter One of this volume.

Modern names index

Subject index

adiaphoras 160
aggadah see narrative
aggiornamento 132, 271n. 49
Alexander the Great 235
allegorization 280n. 5
Ambrose of Milan, St 275n. 20
American/British relations, parallels to
   Reformed/Lutheran relations 54–5
amidah 22, 24
anonymous Christians, salvation 77, 80–7
anthropology, theology 46–7
anti-papalism, and papalism 131, 132–41
anti-Semitism, in the Church 153
apartheid, Lutheran attitudes to 51
applicability
   and theology 170–2, 172–3
   relationship with theology and
      futurology 184–8
Aristotelianism, Christianization 211
Aristotle xiv, 34, 46, 135, 210, 211, 269n.
   12
Athanasius 148
Augsberg Confession, acceptance and
   interpretation 52
Augustine of Hippo, St xi, xvi, 194
   and predestination 211
   and supersessionism 239
   and the use of allegory 178
   and the use of the Bible 212, 220, 284n.
      12
   and transubstantiation 65
   doctrine of salvation 33, 38, 41, 44, 48, 60
   extratextuality and the Bible 177
   on grace 265n. 7
   sensus fidelium 201
authority
   and literary texts 218–20
   and social conditioning 217–18
   loss among the churches 214–17

Baptism 22, 24, 158
   in a dechristianized society 275n. 18
   infant baptism, Luther's teaching as
      against the Anabaptists 127
Baptism, Eucharist and Ministry (Lima
   Report) 56, 74, 75, 162, 221, 265n.
   2, 277n. 22
Barmen Declaration 266n. 9
Barnabas, Epistle 239
believers, deification through union with
   Jesus Christ 115–16, 117
Bernard of Clairvaux, St 72, 107, 206, 249
Bible
   and historicity 182
   common ignorance about 203
   role within a sectarian Church in a
      secularized society 101
   translatability 231–2
Bible reading
   and Church authority 214–17, 219–20
   and modernity 208–17
   and the *sensus fidelium* 204–17, 220–2
   in the premodern period
      and deconstructionism 284n. 9
      and the development of the Church
         204–8
   twentieth century 211–17
biblical canon
   and intratextual theologies 181–2
   development 204–5
biblical criticism, bishops' attitudes
   towards at Vatican II 16
biblical hermeneutics 234–6
   and Israel's role 237–43
   consensus-and-community-building
      potential 202–3
bishops, at Vatican II 11–12, 15–17
Blake, William 232, 236
Bogomils 112–13